Human Resource Development in the Public Sector

D0060818

Across the world, countries are attempting to develop their health and social care policies and practices to address the global challenge of increasing demand and pressurized supply created by ageing populations, emerging technologies and finite financial and human resources. This book presents examples of attempts to develop HRD practices in health and social care contexts in Ireland, the Netherlands, Romania, Russia, the UK and the USA, providing a comprehensive survey of human resource development research and practice in public and voluntary health and social care organizations around the world.

The chapters in this collection are grounded in the evidence-based research of HRD and draw on a number of different research approaches from large-scale surveys to in-depth interviews, involving action research, ethnography and empowerment evaluation, and employing critical incident technique and statistical, discourse and grounded analyses. The book explores workplace learning, management development, evaluation of learning and development and wider organizational issues including organizational learning, culture and values, and organizational commitment.

This volume disseminates the results of a wide range of HRD research and practice, and will provide a valuable resource for HRD practitioners and managers to help them understand and enhance their roles in developing the workforce.

Sally Sambrook is Director of Postgraduate Studies (Business Studies) and former Programme Leader for the MSc in Health and Social Care Leadership at the University of Wales, Bangor. She is Associate Editor of HRDI and an active member of the University Forum for HRD. **Jim Stewart** is Professor of Human Resource Development at Nottingham Business School, Nottingham Trent University, and Chair of the University Forum for HRD. His previous book *HRD in Small Organisations*, is also available from Routledge.

Routledge studies in human resource development
Edited by Monica Lee
Lancaster University, UK

HRD theory is changing rapidly. Recent advances in theory and practice, how we conceive of organizations and of the world of knowledge, have led to the need to reinterpret the field. This series aims to reflect and foster the development of HRD as an emergent discipline.

Encompassing a range of different international, organizational, methodological and theoretical perspectives, the series promotes theoretical controversy and reflective practice.

Human Resource Development in the Public Sector

The case of health and social care

Edited by Sally Sambrook and Jim Stewart

 Routledge
Taylor & Francis Group

LONDON AND NEW YORK

First published 2007
by Routledge
2 Park Square, Milton Park, Abingdon, Oxon, OX14 4RN

Simultaneously published in the USA and Canada
by Routledge
270 Madison Ave, New York NY 10016

Routledge is an imprint of the Taylor & Francis Group, an informa business

Transferred to Digital Printing 2008

© 2007 Editorial matter and selection, Sally Sambrook and Jim
Stewart; individual chapters, the contributors

Typeset in Garamond by Wearset Ltd, Boldon, Tyne and Wear

British Library Cataloguing in Publication Data
A catalogue record for this book is available from the British Library

Library of Congress Cataloging in Publication Data
A catalog record for this book has been requested

ISBN10: 0-415-39410-4 (hbk)
ISBN10: 0-415-48806-0 (pbk)
ISBN10: 0-203-96831-X (ebk)

ISBN13: 978-0-415-39410-9 (hbk)
ISBN13: 978-0-415-48806-8 (pbk)
ISBN13: 978-0-203-96831-4 (ebk)

Dedication

This book is dedicated to the memory of Alan Moon, Executive Secretary Emeritus of the University Forum for HRD. The subject of HRD would not be as strong as it is in the UK and the European mainland were it not for the hard work, dedication and considerable skill and charm that Alan brought to his roles in the former Institute of Training and Development and the UFHRD. The editors of this book and many of the contributors benefited professionally and personally from knowing Alan and we as editors are proud and pleased to pay tribute to his contribution to HRD through this dedication and the content of the book.

Contents

Figures

Tables

Contributors

Kenneth R. Bartlett, PhD is associate professor of human resource development within the Department of Work, Community, and Family Education at the University of Minnesota. His PhD in Human Resource Education is from the University of Illinois at Urbana-Champaign. Originally from New Zealand, he has focused his research interests on the process and outcomes of human resource development with a strong interest in organizational commitment, and HRD in the public sector. Other research interests are related to international HRD, HRD evaluation, as well as career and technical education.

Professor Rona S. Beattie is currently Head of the Division of Human Resource Management and Development at Caledonian Business School, Glasgow Caledonian University. She is a Chartered Fellow of the CIPD. Her research and teaching interests include line managers as developers, mentoring, human resource management (HRM) in the public and voluntary sectors. She has published in edited collections, reports and in HRM, HRD and public management journals including *Employee Relations*, *Public Management Review*, *Regional Studies*, *International Journal of Training* and *Development and Management Learning*.

Marjolein G.M.C. Berings is a PhD-student in the Department of Human Resource Studies at Tilburg University, The Netherlands. Her main interests are in learning processes at work. She focuses on on-the-job learning styles and strategies. She studies how employees' self-awareness of these issues contributes to workplace learning and mainly concentrates this research on the nursing profession.

Dr Nadine Bristow DBA, MSc, BSc(Hons)Psych, DipPsych, DTM, CPP, FCIPD, FInstLM, MBPS, MIHM, developed Acorn Training and Consultancy Services – a practice providing human resource development and consultancy support services to a national portfolio of NHS Trusts, the Department of Health and a variety of diverse voluntary/private sector organizations. Nadine specializes in action learning facilitation and executive coaching. In addition to consultancy practice, Nadine is currently a Business

Governor of a major college of further education, an independent member of Merseyside Police Authority Misconduct Panel, an independent assessor of the General Medical Services contract in primary care, a visiting fellow at Manchester Metropolitan University Business School and a Member of Birmingham Employment Tribunal. Prior to consultancy, Nadine worked as a senior manager/deputy director within the NHS specializing in management development, human resource management and development, and then more latterly organizational development. She was awarded a Doctorate in Business Administration late in 2001 for her research concerning the evaluation of action learning as a tool for developing and evaluating clinical leadership within the NHS.

Dr Nicholas Clarke MSc MSc (Econ) CQSW MIPD is a lecturer in Organisational Behaviour and HRM at the University of Southampton School of Management. He gained his PhD in Psychology from the University of Exeter in 2000 examining the impact of in-service training within social services. His main areas of research are in workplace learning and organization development within health and social care contexts and he has published numerous journal articles in the areas of training effectiveness and workplace learning. Prior to working in academia, Nicholas occupied roles within both health and social care settings as a senior manager and practitioner, as well as a management consultant both in the UK and Australia. He is currently working on research examining the effectiveness of new OD interventions to improve collaboration in health-social care networks, and a range of projects relating to workplace learning.

David Cooper is Deputy Director of Human Resources in an NHS Acute Hospital Trust. He has responsibility for leading both the HR Operational and Learning and Development teams, and is heavily engaged currently in managing the largest programme of change to employment terms, conditions and pay in the history of the NHS. Immediately prior to joining the healthcare sector he worked for a number of years as the HR Director of an SME in the IT sector. Before that he spent over 20 years in Further Education, first as a lecturer, then as a senior manager, and subsequently as a senior executive with responsibility for initiating, developing and running the HR function of a newly incorporated FE College.

Thomas N. Garavan is senior lecturer in the Department of Personnel and Employment Relations, University of Limerick. He is considered the leading academic and researcher in the field of training and development in Ireland. He is author of more than 60 academic articles, editor of the *Journal of European Industrial Training* for the past seven years, and associate editor of *Human Resource Development International* for the past three years. He is also a member of the Academy of Human Resource Development. He is co-author of the leading academic text *Training and Development in Ireland*, which is widely used by students in Irish universities.

Dr John P.T.M. Gelissen is Assistant Professor of Research Methodology at Tilburg University, The Netherlands. His dissertation, 'Worlds of welfare, worlds of consent: public opinion on the welfare state' (2001), dealt with the explanation of inter- and intra-country differences in public support for welfare state arrangements. Currently, his main research interests are comparative public opinion research and qualitative and quantitative research methods.

Kate Gilbert spent the early part of her career in the public and voluntary sectors, as a manager, trainer and consultant in the fields of family education and education for people with disabilities. For some years she managed an adult education centre for people with severe learning disabilities, and developed a commitment to 'joined up thinking' and integrated services. Joining the University of Wolverhampton in 1991 as a lecturer in public sector management, she soon became involved in project work in the Former Soviet Union and spent much of the 1990s working in several regions in Russia. Kate completed a doctorate at UMIST in 2000, the theme of which was the adaptation of Western consultants working in management development projects in Russia. She worked in Italy for three years, and in 2004 returned to the UK as Head of Department of Human Resources, again in the University of Wolverhampton Business School.

Claire Gubbins is a lecturer in the Department of Management and Marketing, University College Cork. She specializes in the areas of human resource management, management and organizational development and change. Previous to this she lectured in the Department of Personnel and Employment Relations, University of Limerick. She completed her doctoral research at the University of Limerick focusing on the social capital, careers and job performance of human resource development (HRD) professionals. She received the Government of Ireland Research Scholarship for this research awarded by the Irish Research Council for the Humanities and Social Sciences. She has a number of journal articles, book chapters and conference presentations in the areas of HRD, HRM, organizational behaviour and social capital. Her other research interests include knowledge management, trust and social capital, management development and HRM in the public sector.

Kathy D. Hall, PT, EdD, is an Assistant Professor in the Physical Therapy Program in the College of Health Sciences, Midwestern University, Downers Grove, Illinois, USA. Her recent research involves identifying characteristics of lifelong learning of physical therapists, exploring methods by which physical therapists choose to pursue their professional development, and examining factors that might influence those choices. At Midwestern University she chairs the education committee that determines the curriculum and educational policy for initial professional education in the physical therapy program. Dr Hall has conducted continuing professional education courses for members of multiple health professions.

Bob Hamlin is Emeritus Professor of Human Resource Development at the University of Wolverhampton in the UK, and a Fellow of the Chartered Institute of Personnel and Development. Professor Hamlin has published principally in the field of human resource development and organizational development. His current research interests include managerial and leadership effectiveness, management behavioural competencies, management culture change, and managerial coaching behaviour. He is actively engaged in collaborative practice-grounded partnership-research with a number of UK private and public sector organizations, including NHS Hospital Trusts, and is also active as a management training and development consultant. Professor Hamlin is Honorary Treasurer of the UK-based University Forum for Human Resource Development.

Carole Hogan is founder and Managing Director of Carole Hogan Associates. She has more than 25 years experience in consulting and researching. Her particular areas of expertise are; management development centres – programme design, delivery and evaluation; leadership development; developing coaching and mentoring relationships; competency analysis and development; training and learning programme design, delivery and evaluation; organizational learning; interpersonal skills and performance management. Carole is currently also a doctoral candidate focusing on the area of learning. Her main research interests include: psychology of learning, learning organizations; mentoring and coaching; learning styles, learning strategies and methods; training design and management development processes. She is co-author of *Making Training and Development Work, A Best Practice Guide*.

Jane Keep is a senior visiting Fellow at HSMC, University of Birmingham and a freelancing OD practitioner on the processes of strategic change. She has studied, researched, taught and practised HR and OD for over 15 years at a senior level in the NHS and wider public sector and, more recently, the voluntary sector (having worked in the public sector for 26 years). Her work emphasizes organizational development, change and strategic human resources in the context of change in complex local systems, HR, values-based working and complex learning methodologies as well as participatory cultures. Jane has worked at a senior level within the NHS, including at national policy level, and is highly experienced in working with individuals and groups, with Chief Executives, Boards, as well as multidisciplinary NHS professionals. She has also undertaken a number of research and action research projects, and written key HR papers, and other evaluation papers for the NHS. She has worked briefly overseas in Hong Kong, Africa and Europe, and has worked extensively on leadership and OD in Eire. She has prepared evidence on Parliamentary Health Select Committees and worked with trade unions, think tanks, and media on HR and organizational change. She has an

MPhil in Critical Management (Lancs) and an MSc in SHRD. She has a number of related publications.

Brigid Milner, BA, MBS, Chartered FCIPD, is a lecturer in Strategic Human Resource Management in the Department of Management and Organisation at Waterford Institute of Technology (WIT), Ireland. She is a board member of the Centre for Management Research in Healthcare and Health Economics. Brigid is currently undertaking her Doctorial Thesis investigating quality accreditation system implementation, focusing on the process of accreditation as a means of improving quality in healthcare. Her research interests include: strategic human resource management, public sector human resource management and team-based quality management in healthcare.

Dr Rob F. Poell is Associate Professor of HRD in the Department of Human Resource Studies at Tilburg University, The Netherlands. His research interests focus on workplace learning and the organizing strategies used by employees, managers and HRD practitioners. Rob publishes regularly in *Management Learning*, *Human Resource Development Quarterly*, *Human Resource Development International*, *Adult Education Quarterly*, *Applied Psychology International Review*, and other scientific journals.

Laura Purcell, BBS, Graduate CIPD, has just completed her masters by research at Waterford Institute of Technology, Ireland. She is a member of the Centre for Management Research in Healthcare and Health Economics. Laura investigated several issues across a number of acute-care sites surrounding the development of management competencies for clinical nurse managers, the presence of a learning transfer climate and the extent to which management development activity can contribute to organizational culture change. Her research interests include: Management Development, Public Sector Human Resource Management and Learning Transfer.

Clair Roberts was born on the Isle of Anglesey and has lived in North Wales for most of her life. She is in the process of completing her doctoral thesis at the School for Business at the University of Wales, Bangor. Since embarking on her PhD, Clair has won the Lloyd-Jones Award twice for her research into Corporate Entrepreneurship and her business consultancy services to local SMEs. Clair's research interests span organizational behaviour, HRM and corporate strategy, most particularly organizational learning, corporate entrepreneurship and organizational change. Clair also works as Marketing and Administration Manager for a new Management Development centre project that is being set up in conjunction with the Business School.

Alice J. Salzman, PT, EdD, is Assistant Professor and Co-Director of Clinical Education in the Department of Physical Therapy and Human Movement Sciences in the Feinberg School of Medicine, Northwestern University, Chicago, Illinois, USA. Her research interests focus on the professional development of physical therapy clinicians and academicians. In addition to clinical education, her physical therapy teaching interests include psychosocial issues for physical therapists and professional role development. She has presented continuing education for physical therapists on topics related to clinical education. As a Credentialed Trainer for the American Physical Therapy Association Clinical Instructor Education and Credentialing Program, she prepares physical therapy clinicians to become effective clinical educators. Through participation in Health Volunteers Overseas, she has presented continuing education for physical therapy clinical educators in developing countries.

Dr Sally Sambrook studied and worked at Nottingham Business School for eight years, and retains her links there as a Visiting Research Fellow in HRD, working closely with Professor Jim Stewart and supervising and assessing DBA students. Sally joined the University of Wales, Bangor (UWB) in 1999, and after several years as Lecturer in Human Resource Management (HRM), joined the Faculty of Health, where as Programme Leader she developed the MSc in Health and Social Care Leadership. Sally led several MSc modules, including Research Methods, Managing and Developing People, Organizational Behaviour and Leadership, and was recently awarded a Teaching Fellowship for excellence in teaching. Sally has now returned to Bangor Business School as Senior Lecturer and Director of Postgraduate Studies (Business Studies). With her nursing background and involvement in training other nurses, Sally's research interests include studying human resource development (HRD) within the health service. In addition, Sally researches the changing role of HRD professionals, managers and learners, explores the factors influencing learning in work and has recently become interested in a critical approach to the study of HRD. Sally has published numerous journal articles, edited texts and book chapters on HRD and was awarded Outstanding Paper, by the Emerald Literati Club in 2005. She is also Associate Editor of Human Resource Development International.

Anne Squire is currently a Senior Lecturer, Teaching Fellow, and Director of the MSc Programmes at the School of Nursing, Midwifery and Health Studies, University of Wales, Bangor. Anne has extensive experience as both a Health Practitioner and as Educationalist preparing health and social care professionals and others for practice. Her recent work has included the development of MSc in Public Health and Health Promotion, MSc in Nursing Science and MSc in Health Science courses. Her recent research includes projects in community care and the health promotion empowerment of older people in the UK and Romania. Anne acts as a consultant/trainer for the British Association for Services to the Elderly and was a consultant/trainer for HelpAge International from 1990–2002. She runs many workshops for older people, carers and professionals. Anne has been working in Romania since 1992 up to the current time with HelpAge International working with older people, carers, lay people and professionals initiating community education empowerment programmes for health promotion with older people. She has served on numerous national advisory bodies in the UK, Welsh Assembly Government and Romania, concerning health promotion, public health, older people, national occupational standards in health promotion and public health. Anne is the sole author of *Health and Well Being for Older People: Foundation for Practice* (2002) published by Balliere Tindall. She has also authored many articles and book chapters.

Jim Stewart is Professor of Human Resource Development and has worked at Nottingham Business School since January 1992, previously as both Senior Lecturer and Reader in HRD. He provides academic leadership in HRD, which includes developing learning and teaching, research activities and publications, and supervising doctoral candidates. Jim launched and led the School's MSc in Human Resource Development from 1993 to 1998. In 1998 he launched the Doctorate in Business Administration as Acting Course Leader and he is currently Joint Course Leader with Professor Colin Fisher. The Nottingham Business School DBA is now one of the most successful in the UK. Jim's main research interest is the meaning and practice of HRD, with a particular interest in the connections between HRD and lifelong learning. An additional but related focus is learning and teaching in business and management undergraduate programmes. He is author of *Managing Change through Training and Development* (1996) and *Employee Development Practice* (1999) and co-editor of *Understanding HRD: a Research-based Approach* (2002), *HRD in Small Organisations* (2003) and *New Frontiers in HRD* (2004) the latter two being the outputs of an ESRC Seminar grant for which Jim was joint award holder. He has also published many articles in academic and professional journals as well as numerous conference papers. Jim's research activities are supported by his membership of the University Forum for HRD, for which is also the Chair. As well as being a member of the editorial boards of a number of academic journals, including UK Editor for *HRDI* and Reviews Editor for *IJTD*, Jim is very active at a national level with the CIPD.

Ferd J. Van der Krogt is Associate Professor of Human Resource Development in the Department of Education, Radboud University Nijmegen, The Netherlands. He is very interested in research and theory about organizing learning in organizations and the strategies of workers.

Margaret Woodlock is the HR Manager and member of the senior management team within the Dublin Dental School and Hospital, Dublin, Ireland. She holds a Masters Degree from Keele University in Industrial Relations and a Diploma in Personnel Management from the National College of Ireland. Margaret has 19 years' experience working as a HR professional within both the private and public sector. She previously worked for such organizations as Motorola and Organon Ireland, which is part of the AKZO Nobel group.

Acknowledgements

Sally and Jim would like to thank all the authors for their valued contributions and assistance during the editorial process, without which this book would not have been possible.

They would also like to extend their thanks to the publishers, and particularly Monica Lee, Series Editor, for being so positive about such an innovative text, and Katherine Carpenter and Terry Clague who provided invaluable guidance during the whole process.

As usual, Jim would like to thank his wife Pat and son Paul for their continuing support.

Sally would personally like to thank Nyree Hulme for her exceptional professionalism and editorial skills in preparing the manuscript for publication. Without her, you would not be reading this. In addition, sincere thanks are extended to Ruhi Behi, Head of School, and Professor Jane Noyes, both at the School of Nursing, Midwifery & Health Studies at the University of Wales, Bangor, for their support. Finally, Sally wishes to thank Sam for his eternal patience and love during yet another writing project.

Part I

HRD and organizational issues

1 HRD in health and social care

Sally Sambrook and Jim Stewart

Background

This book focuses on human resource development (HRD) in the changing, and complex, context of health and social care. As an emerging field, there have been a number of HRD texts published since the mid 1990s. In the UK, the first was by Stewart and McGoldrick (1996), which was an attempt to start defining the field and which included a variety of contributions about a range of HRD interventions and issues. It was followed by Hargreaves and Jarvis (1998), which drew upon the adult education agenda, and by Wilson (1999), which provided a new perspective upon employee development. Walton (1999) then attempted to differentiate HRD and strategic HRD from the earlier work on employee development. However, all these works are essentially textbooks and are not research based, although in some cases they are research informed.

To date there have been very few books that are grounded in evidence-based research in the field of HRD. Only Lee *et al.* (1996), McGoldrick *et al.* (2001) and Woodall *et al.* (2004) have made an explicit attempt to do so. However, in the former case, the agenda was tightly located, focusing as it did on developing HRD in the post-command economies shortly after the 'velvet revolution' in East-Central Europe. In contrast, the book by McGoldrick *et al.* (2001) takes a significant focus upon the research process and research design, rather than reporting or disseminating primary research findings. Similarly, in the USA, Swanson and Holton (1997) focused on how to do HRD research, rather than provide research-based HRD. In addition, each of the books identified so far have taken a generic approach to HRD, with many focusing mainly on HRD practices in large, private organizations. However, it can be argued that HRD practices vary substantially in different contexts, for example, in large and small organizations, and in private and public sectors. Small steps towards analysing HRD in more specific contexts have been taken by Tjepkema *et al.* (2002) examining HRD in European learning organizations and Stewart and Beaver (2004) with their edited text *HRD in Small Organizations*. However, no text yet has examined HRD in the health and social care context.

Looking at health services alone, this is a large and important sector of national economies, yet there is little theoretical or empirical material concerning the difficult processes of learning and development in health care organizations. Managing learning and development in the health service is a complex process (Burchill and Casey 1996: 124). A review of the literature reveals how each specific professional area is managing training, education and development, for example management development for clinicians (Dopson 1996; Ashburner 1996), and continuing professional development for doctors, nurses and allied health professionals, together with organization development (Stewart 1993) and management development (Thompson 1994). The responsibility for coordinating this rests with specialist HRD practitioners. There is, however, very little literature that examines this intricate role. In their informative text, Leopold *et al.* (1996) explore the relationship and tensions between management and professionalism in the health service, and examine the role of human resource managers. However, there is no mention of the role of human resource *development* specialists – whose role is to manage and coordinate the development of professionals and managers, amongst others – nor the training and development function. Burchill and Casey propose 'to examine issues associated with overall staff development within the context of a NHS trust,' (Burchill and Casey 1996: 120) in their chapter entitled 'Human Resource Development,' but then proceed to describe what is generally labelled 'training and development,' and make no reference to HRD. In addition, they state that, 'Training and development are, of course, a part of human resource planning' (Burchill and Casey 1996: 124).

Turning to social services, few texts have been found that assist HRD professionals develop social care workers, and these appear outdated. Examples include Allan *et al.*'s (1992) 'Promoting Women: Managing Development and Training for Women in Social Service Departments' and Brown *et al.*'s (1997) 'How to Evaluate Your Training Activity' and the Social Services Inspectorate (1994) report on 'Users' View on Training for the Community.'

We have noted specific changes within the NHS and social services framework, creating the need to understand better the organization and delivery of learning and development activities. However, there are also pressures to provide integrated health and social care services, thus expanding the scope of the emerging challenges facing HRD practitioners in this context. In response, we believe that this is the first text to examine HRD across the merging health and social care contexts.

Purpose and context

This book arises out of the need for a text to bring together HRD in the complex context of health and social care organizations. The book contains chapters based on recent or current research and practice, and has an intended international readership of students, academics, researchers, HRD practitioners, managers and policy makers interested in human resource development in this context.

Across Europe and the world, countries are attempting to develop their health and social policies and practices to address the global challenge of increasing demand and pressurized supply, created by ageing populations, emerging technologies and finite resources (financial and human). This text provides examples of attempts to develop HRD practices in health and social care contexts within Ireland, The Netherlands, Romania, Russia, the UK and the USA. Thus, the book is international in both scope and appeal.

Part of the focus of the book will be on HRD within health and social care organizations in the United Kingdom, and it provides illuminative insight and case material into the core issues that impact upon HRD in this context globally. Health and social care organizations are large and important sectors of the British and global economy, yet there is little collated research associated with how employees are developed in this specific context. The British National Health Service (NHS) provides an interesting case study in which to investigate human resource development. With the NHS Plan, a national HR strategy and the establishment of the National Health Service University (NHSU) – although this has recently been re-organized and re-branded – there seems to be considerable HRD activity, but little published research in the form of a comprehensive text to assist decision-making and inform stakeholders of current HRD practice. Stakeholders include national and UK governments with their political agenda; professional bodies, such as nurses, therapists and doctors with their clinical agenda; various levels of managers with their managerial agenda; and, not least, HR practitioners with their own professional agenda. These stakeholders have varying needs of HRD and practice and talk of HRD in varying ways. For example, Department of Health documents refer to workforce development and lifelong learning; professional bodies prefer to use the terms 'continuing medical education,' or 'continuing professional development.'

There are many diverse influences on the NHS (Glover and Leopold 1996), and recently there have been many changes within, and specific to, the NHS. Major changes include the creation of the *internal market*, with new roles as *purchasers* and *providers* of health care, the creation of *Trust status* for hospitals, giving greater freedoms associated with the managing and financing of health care provision, and, more recently, the concept of Foundation hospitals, a new status afforded to high performing organizations. With these, there is the possibility of greater freedoms within the sphere of employment management, and developing employees. Training, education and development is a particularly heterogeneous area within the health service. There are a range of health professions – covering medicine (physicians, surgeons, general practitioners), nursing (including midwifery and health visiting), and professions allied to medicine, often referred to as PAMs and more recently allied health professions (therapists, technicians) –

in which training, education and development occurs at specific stages –
pre-registration, post-registration and continuing, and can be compulsory or
elective. Traditionally, responsibility for such development has been at the
national level, with the government deciding how much can be spent on the
health service, and professional bodies translating policy priorities and
funding constraints into training, education and development requirements.
These are based on forecasted 'manpower' plans and take into account 'lead
times' – how long it takes to train these professionals. Another important
group is support staff, including care assistants, porters, administrators, and
unqualified technicians, who all require some degree of training and development, at least initially, if not on a continuing basis. A further group is
managers, including clinicians (nurses, PAMs and doctors) as well as business managers. New freedoms and responsibilities for the financing and
managing of health care provision have enabled changes in job design, such
as multi-skilling, team working and greater autonomy. These changes can
create training, education and development needs.

In the social care context, with similar HRD complexities, there is an
increasing emphasis on developing social care as a profession to achieve
quality and help integrate care across professional boundaries. Two new
bodies have been formed that will regulate training, services and staff: the
General Social Care Council (GCSS) and the Training Organization for the
Personal Social Services (TOPPS 2002).

Health and social care are becoming increasingly integrated with the
delivery of 'seamless' services. This new text offers an empirical contribution
to our understanding of HRD in this specific context and a theoretical contribution to HRD in general. There is evidence of the growing need for
resources to support HRD professionals in this specialist context with the
recent launch of the journal *Learning in Health and Social Care* edited by Professor Michael Eraut and published by Blackwell Science Ltd.

Aims

This book provides a comprehensive and up-to-date overview of human
resource development research and practice in public and voluntary health
and social care organizations across the world. The overall aims are to disseminate the results of a wide range of HRD research and practice, and to
provide a resource to inform teaching, learning and professional practice.
The book is eclectic, providing examples of a number of different research
approaches from large-scale surveys to in-depth interviews, involving action
research, ethnography and empowerment evaluation, and employing critical
incident technique and statistical, discourse and grounded analyses.

The specific aims are as follows.

• To explore and assess the various and varying terms and meanings associated with 'human resource development,' in the health and social care

context, such as workforce development, lifelong learning, continuing professional development, and organizational learning;

- To describe and analyse the current context of research and practice;
- To evaluate a range of current approaches;
- To provide a range of examples of research and practice to inform and support the teaching of HRD as a subject within health and social care management and leadership programmes, and provide examples from this specific context that may be included in more general HRD programmes;
- To provide a resource to academics and students researching HRD practice
- To provide insights and glimpses of good practice for HRD practitioners.

Structure

We have divided the book up into four parts: HRD and Organizational Issues; Management Development; HRD and Workplace Learning: and Evaluating Learning. Many of the chapters present new work that either challenges many of the established assumptions underlying the field of HRD, or adds new empirical insights into the complex context of health and social care.

In this opening chapter, we establish the scope of the field of HRD and its emergence in the health and social care context. We draw attention to the limitations of the current theoretical basis of the field of HRD in this context and outline the challenges presented in the subsequent chapters. These are clustered around four themes.

The first part considers links between HRD and wider organizational issues, including discourses, cultures, values, organizational learning and organizational commitment. This sets the broad organizational context for the following sections.

In Chapter 2, Sally Sambrook discusses the multiple discourses of HRD. Her chapter highlights the complexity of HRD within the NHS, identifies the range of stakeholders involved in learning and development, and explores multiple discourses associated with the diverse range of stakeholders. The chapter draws upon recent research exploring discourses of HRD with various developers in the context of NHS Trust hospitals using qualitative case study research, involving semi-structured interviews with more than 20 nurses, trainers, business managers and allied health professionals. Discourse analysis has been employed to explore and make sense of the diversity of discourses. The chapter ends by questioning the need for shared meaning amongst the various professionals involved.

Chapter 3 examines the notion of creating awareness of the value of HRD in the context of Dublin Dental Hospital, in Ireland. Thomas Garavan and colleagues report the main findings of a survey of attitudes to HRD conducted within an Irish health care organization. The promotion of human resource development as an organizational practice and as a core value is a continuous challenge for training and development professionals. Although HRD might be better understood in the more industrial or manufacturing type organization, it is less well understood in the health sector in Ireland. In addition to quantitative survey data, the authors also report qualitative data (analysed from a discourse perspective), which highlight the attitudes and perceptions of key internal stakeholders and their motivation to participate in training and development. The case study particularly focuses on the barriers to HRD found in the organization and the role of situational factors in explaining the quality and quantity of training and development activities. The chapter concludes with a discussion of the study findings for the creation of a learning culture, the enhancement of learner motivation and the role of line managers and supervisors as enablers of HRD in organizations. The chapter specifically considers the feasibility of a business partner model of HRD within health care organizations.

In Chapter 4, Clair Roberts and Sally Sambrook offer a preliminary exploration into the context and processes of organizational learning and corporate entrepreneurship within Welsh NHS Trust hospitals. They critique and then synthesize the two separate literatures on organizational learning (OL) and corporate entrepreneurship (CE) literature, and consider their relevance to, and application within, the NHS. The chapter then proceeds to explore the complex relationship between learning, creativity, innovation and change and identifies examples of OL, innovation and creativity in the NHS and implications for HRD. The chapter includes empirical material from two Welsh Trust hospitals and demonstrates how organizational learning and corporate entrepreneurship are intricately related and symbiotically enacted in the NHS. It is proposed that evidence of innovative practices within health care organizations may be usefully transferred to other sectors to further enhance creativity and change.

In the final chapter in this part, Kenneth Bartlett reviews HRD and organizational commitment in health and social care. Recent reforms within the health and social care systems of many nations have resulted in an increased emphasis on the recruitment, training, development and retention of qualified and quality human resources, issues linked to organizational commitment. It is argued that HRD assumes greater importance during times of restructuring and reform, and as health and social care organizations become more complex, the need for HRD is increasingly recognized. Organizational commitment is both an outcome of HRD but also influences training and development activities. This chapter defines organizational commitment, and summarizes current research from various international health and social care contexts, including the USA, New Zealand and Malaysia. This unique meta-analysis of current research will provide a range of examples of practices to assist health and social care managers and HRD practitioners foster organization commitment in their employees.

A key element of HRD is management development. Part II focuses on management development in the health and social care context. Here, we turn our attention to notions of 'becoming' a manager, managers as role models, models of management development and the impact of management development in the UK and Ireland.

Nadine Bristow opens this part and explores becoming a manager in the NHS. Her chapter explores the social constructions employed as managers use language, talk and discourse to construct their sense of self. She focuses on the issues surrounding 'becoming a manager' in the health care context, the different learning styles of managers and their impact, and the discourses used to describe their development. She draws upon ethnographic research, including observations and semi-structured interviews, with a range of managers across the NHS.

In Chapter 7, Rona Beattie explores environmental, organizational and individual influences on line managers' roles as facilitators of learning in social care voluntary organizations. This chapter explores the influence environmental and organizational variables have on developmental relationships and line managers' attitudes and behaviour within the Scottish voluntary social care context. The theoretical element focuses on adult learning, organizational learning, and voluntary sector management theory. The chapter draws upon research conducted in the empirical context of two large voluntary social care organizations, analysing managers as developers. Case study research, including document analysis and semi-structured interviews ($n = 60$), is analysed using grounded theory. The findings are synthesized and presented in a developmental manager model.

In Chapter 8, Bob Hamlin and David Cooper provide insights into managerial and leadership effectiveness in the British health service; provide evidence of best practice; and demonstrate the universality of managerial and leadership effectiveness within the UK public sector. Highlighting the lack of both British and American empirical research, this chapter critically reviews literature from the UK public sector, in general, and the NHS in particular, addressing complaints associated with contingency approaches. The authors draw on current research within two NHS Trust hospitals, and using the Critical Incident Technique, a Behavioural Item Questionnaire is developed, which is then employed to conduct comparative analyses (a) between the two case studies and (b) with the NHS New Transformational Leadership Questionnaire. The chapter concludes with the presentation of a generic model of managerial (leadership) effectiveness.

In the final chapter in this part, Laura Purcell and Brigid Milner explore management development in the Irish health service. They identify the impact of management development activities on the quality of work life within nursing, focusing on competencies, and transfer of training. Recent case study research within an Irish acute health care hospital involved the development of an internal questionnaire, administered to more than 20 clinical nurse managers at the three levels, C1, C2 and C3. Findings indicate a gap in nurse management development, and the need to equate the various dimensions of competence with the realities of the workplace.

Another important aspect of HRD within health and social care organizations is professional development, particularly through workplace learning. Part III focuses on HRD and workplace learning, exploring this in the United Kingdom, the Netherlands and the US.

In Chapter 10, Rob Poell and Ferd van der Krogt study how HRD practitioners create tailored learning in the Dutch health care sector. They provide a critical overview of the educational and organizational literature on workplace learning and introduce the concept of customization strategies. These can involve one of two approaches – tailoring training programmes (focusing on HRD activities); and connecting learning programmes to everyday learning (work-related activities). The chapter draws on current action research, with seven HRD practitioners engaged in 13 learning programmes. Findings suggest that HRD practitioners use few customization strategies and pay little attention to individual learning paths.

Staying with the Dutch health care sector, in Chapter 11, Marjolein Berings and colleagues investigate what and how do nurses learn on the job. They explore the relationship between the content and process of learning, provide a critique of on-the-job learning and learning styles and relate this to the complex context of post-registration nurse development. The chapter draws upon current empirical research conducted with nurses in different wards of a Dutch academic hospital. Twenty nurses were observed and interviewed, and findings analysed using grounded theory. The authors identify six main categories of content; and six main categories of process and then relate these to the identified nurse learning styles.

In Chapter 12, Nicholas Clarke focuses on workplace learning in UK hospices. He investigates the extent to which hospices utilize different sources of workplace learning; how they assess workplace learning; and identifies organizational factors supporting workplace learning. The author provides a critique of workplace learning, situated learning, informal learning, and communities of practice. Current empirical research within the context of hospices includes a questionnaire survey of 120 hospices across the UK, followed up by workshops with staff involved in HRD. The chapter identifies sources of, and the extent to which HRD practitioners use, workplace learning.

In the last chapter in this part, Alice Salzman and Kathy Hall consider the continuing professional development of Physical Therapists in the USA. They describe a conceptual framework for the Continuing Professional Development/Education (CPD/E) of Physical Therapists (PTs), focusing on allied health professionals within the American health care sector. The authors critically explore how PT lifelong learners are defined; how PTs are prepared during their professional education to be lifelong learners; what PTs identify as significant development experiences; and how HRD and CPD/E work together. The chapter draws upon recent research in the form of a national survey of academic and clinical PTs regarding the knowledge, skills, and attitudes required of PTs; followed by interviews with clinical educators. Findings suggest that effective CPD/HRD requires a partnership between individuals, the employer, the professional body and Higher Education.

The final part, evaluating learning and training, turns our attention to the critical evaluation of HRD practices and interventions across a range of British, European and international health and social care organizations.

In Chapter 14, Nicholas Clarke considers the limitations of in-service training in Social Services. He explores the impact of a training programme designed to improve the needs assessment skills of care managers in the UK social services context. The chapter critically examines factors influencing the transfer of training, including supervision and social support. Empirical research conducted in the social care sector to evaluate in-service training involved a repeated measures, pre/post test experimental design, using a case vignette to assess needs assessment knowledge and skills before, soon after and then three months after the two-day training programme. In addition, qualitative self-report data were used. Findings suggest that the programme failed to change behaviour, and recommendations are made to consider using work-based learning methods.

In Chapter 15, Anne Squire evaluates health education and training in Romania. She provides a unique insight into the issues associated with delivering health promotion training in an international context. The chapter critically examines theories of health promotion and cultural issues, and draws upon ongoing research in this Eastern European country. The chapter describes empowerment evaluative research conducted in Romania from 1992–2002, which includes programmes of education and training for older people and professional and voluntary carers, with the aim of enabling people to develop their own solutions to their own problems. The input of the education programmes aimed to provide people with the necessary tools of analysis that were relevant to their circumstances, which was important in a country such as Romania, where the political, social, and health situation was changing rapidly. The training programmes were participative with the central value being that all the work was a commitment to empowerment using the Freire (1972, 1974) philosophy that we all have things to learn from each other. A variety of data collection methods were used that were decided by the participants and the researchers using an empowerment research method. The approach used was quite new to all the participants, who at first wanted to be told what to do by the so-called 'UK experts'! The benefits of the empowerment approach for the situation in Romania were realized because all the participants were involved in the training programmes and the evaluation. This widespread ownership of the project, its implementation, findings and solutions promoted unanticipated changes. Although, at first, the participants found it difficult to be fully involved in the planning and interpretation of the programmes, later in the project they took part in and commented on the research methodology quite freely and critically discussed how appropriate it was to them as Romanians. The chapter explores the many difficulties encountered, but reports how – slowly – the value of international partnership was acknowledged.

Similarly, in Chapter 16, Kate Gilbert explores HRD in the context of Russian social care work. This chapter provides a further international dimension to the consideration of HRD in health and social care settings, by presenting a study of the development of professionalism within social care in Siberia, in the Russian Federation. In the Soviet Union, the profession of social worker did not exist, to a great extent because the social problems giving rise to ill-health, poverty and fractured lives were not acknowledged. Vulnerable members of society were pathologized as individuals and their needs excessively medicalized. The years of 'glasnost,' the opening up of information, and the subsequent political and economic collapse of the command economy swept away the existing system of social care and simultaneously exposed the true extent of dependency within the vast population. Social care workers themselves have been drawn from the large population of engineers, scientists and soldiers who found themselves cast out of their lifelong professions by the economic collapse. In order to survive, let alone to meet the challenge of burgeoning need, institutions and professions within the care arena have had to transform themselves and wrestle with the new realities, within a context of environmental change that has no parallel in the UK or anywhere else in the Western world. This chapter aims to shed light on the development of the new profession of social care worker, and the social work manager, through a study of an HRD intervention involving Action Learning Sets as the key approach. It is believed to be the first time that the concept of Action Learning, as propounded by Reg Revans, has been introduced to Russia. Neither the technique itself, nor the experiential learning theory that is its basis, were familiar to the participants. In order to make sense in Russian, the Action Learning Sets were dubbed 'Self-training groups' by the participants. The chapter addresses questions such as: To what extent is Action Learning transferable across national and professional/sectoral cultures? What impact did this HRD intervention have on the participants' practice, and on their view of themselves as professionals within the context of an emerging profession? What lessons might be drawn from this experiment for further HRD interventions within the Russian social care context, and elsewhere?

In the final chapter in this part, Jane Keep investigates the impact of integrating learning methodologies in a large scale, collaborative, systems-based learning network in the NHS. She asks, 'How can HRD practitioners combine learning methods to produce an effective national HRD programme?' There is a critical evaluation of theories of combined learning, systems thinking, action learning/research, knowledge management, and reflective practice. The chapter synthesizes and evaluates a range of initiatives within the UK NHS, such as NHS Beacons. Adopting an action research/learning and reflective practice approach, the author describes the development of an evolving learning network, which has been independently evaluated. Findings suggest that using a combination of learning methodologies is powerful, and changed local practice. However, the chapter also highlights the risks and consequences of such an approach.

Chapter 18 presents our conclusions. In this concluding chapter, we pull together threads from the preceding chapters, analysing similarities and differences and potential reasons for these, and identifying common emerging themes and contradictions etc. Some of the key trends emerging within health and social care organizations are:

- the attempt to improve managerial effectiveness through rethinking management development;
- the need to re-think workplace learning to ensure it is tailored to meet needs and is assessed appropriately;
- the significant use of action research and learning in the UK and across Europe and the USA to enhance HRD practices, particularly in emerging health and social care professions;
- and the need to critically evaluate HRD interventions in this complex European and global context.

To conclude, this book focuses on a large number of distinct case studies and offers a variety of methodological approaches that capture the diversity of research and practice in health and social care across the globe. We hope that this book will provide a deeper insight of contemporary HRD research and practice in this complex and dynamic context.

References

Allan, M., Bhavnani, R. and French, K. (1992) *Promoting Women: Managing Development and Training for Women in Social Services Departments*, London: HMSO.

Ashburner, L. (1996) 'The role of clinicians in the management of the NHS,' in J. Leopold, I. Glover and M. Hughes (eds) *Beyond Reason: The National Health Service and the Limits of Management*, Stirling Management Series, Aldershot: Avebury, pp. 3–14.

Brown, K., Holloway, I. and Wheeler, S. (1997) *How to Evaluate Your Training Activity*, Bournemouth: National Association of Training Officers in Personal Social Services.

Burchill, F. and Casey, A. (1996) *Human Resource Management: The NHS A Case Study*, MacMillan Press.

Dopson, S. (1996) 'Doctors in management: a challenge to established debates,' in J. Leopold *et al.* (eds) *Beyond Reason: The National Health Service and the Limits of Management*, Stirling Management Series, Aldershot: Avebury, pp. 173–188.

Freire, P. (1972) *Pedagogy of the Oppressed*, Harmondsworth: Penguin.

Freire, P. (1974) *Education and the Practice of Freedom*, London: Writers and Readers Publishing Co-operative (originally published in Portuguese 1967).

Glover, I. and Leopold, J. (1996) 'The future: realism and diversity,' in J. Leopold, I. Glover and M. Hughes (eds) *Beyond Reason: The National Health Service and the Limits of Management*, Stirling Management Series, Aldershot: Avebury.

Hargreaves, P. and Jarvis, P. (1998) *Human Resource Development Handbook*, London: Kogan Page.

Lee, M., Letiche, H., Crawshaw, R. and Thomas, M. (1996) Management education in the New Europe, London: Routledge.

Leopold, J., Glover, I. and Hughes, M. (eds) (1996) *Beyond Reason: The National Health Service and the Limits of Management*, Stirling Management Series, Aldershot: Avebury.

McGoldrick, J., Stewart, J. and Watson, S. (eds) (2001) *Understanding HRD: A Research Based Approach*, London: Routledge.

Social Service Inspectorate (1994) *Users' Views on Training for Community Care*, London: Social Services Inspectorate.

Stewart, J. (1993) *Organization Development: History, Perspectives and Relevance to NHS Organizations*, Bristol: NHSTD.

Stewart, J. and Beaver, G. (eds) (2004) *HRD in Small Organizations: Research and Practice*, HRD Research Monograph Series, London: Routledge.

Stewart, J. and McGoldrick, J. (1996) *Human Resource Development: Perspectives, Strategies and Practice*, London: Financial Times, Pitman Publishing.

Swanson, R.A. and Holton, E.F. III (1997) *Human Resource Development Research Handbook*, San Francisco, CA: Berrett-Koehler.

Thompson, D. (1994) *Developing Managers for the new NHS*, Harlow: Longman.

TOPPS (2002) *The National Occupational Standards for Social Work*, London: Training Organisation for the Personal Social Services.

Tjepkema, S., Stewart, J., Sambrook, S., Horst, H., Mulder, M. and Scheerens, J. (eds) (2002) *Towards Learning Organizations in Europe: Challenges for HRD Professionals*, HRD Research Monograph Series, London: Routledge.

Walton, J. (1999) *Strategic Human Resource Development*, London: Financial Times Prentice Hall.

Wilson, J.P. (1999) *Human Resource Development: Learning and Training for Individuals and Organizations*, London: Kogan Page.

Woodall, J., Lee, M. and Stewart, J. (2004) *New Frontiers in Human Resource Development*, HRD Research Monograph Series, London: Routledge.

2 Discourses of HRD in the NHS

Sally Sambrook

Introduction

This chapter attempts to highlight the complexity of HRD within the NHS, identify the range of stakeholders involved in learning and development, and explore multiple discourses associated with the diverse range of stakeholders. The chapter draws upon recent research exploring discourses of HRD with various developers in the context of NHS Trust hospitals. Qualitative case study research involved semi-structured interviews with more than 20 nurses, trainers, business managers and allied health professionals. Discourse analysis has been employed to explore and make sense of the diversity of discourses. The chapter ends by highlighting the diverse discourses of HRD and the close association between these and (professional) identities.

Aims and objectives

As identified in the opening chapter, the British National Health Service (NHS) provides an interesting case study in which to investigate stakeholder perspectives (Garavan 1995a, b, c) and multiple discourses of human resource development (HRD). I suggest these stakeholders – doctors, nurses, managers, the government etc – have varying needs of HRD and talk of HRD in varying ways (Sambrook 2000, 2001, 2006). Department of Health documents refer to workforce development and lifelong learning; professional bodies prefer to use the terms continuing medical education, or continuing professional development. This range of stakeholders and discourses might suggest some potential difficulties in talking about and understanding HRD. Without shared meanings, agreeing HRD agendas within the NHS might be problematic. The overall aim of this chapter is to offer an empirical contribution to our understanding of HRD in this specific context and a theoretical contribution to HRD in general.

To achieve this, my first objective is to provide a brief discussion of researching discourses of HRD, after which I review HRD within the NHS, and identify the key stakeholders. Second, following a brief methodological discussion, I present my research findings, the evidence of the multiple discourses of HRD, and highlight the problematic nature of mixed messages for stakeholders in HRD. Finally, I offer some conclusions and suggestions to help stakeholders develop a shared understanding of HRD. Whilst plurality, diversity and complexity are features of a post-modern organizational context, it is argued that some attempt to find common understandings and shared meanings of the processes and practices associated with (what has become defined in academic literature as) HRD is necessary to meet the needs of the various stakeholders. If we can't agree on the talk, how can we take action to ensure learning and development – however defined or labelled – is encouraged, facilitated, supported and celebrated so we can help individuals and organizations develop.

The theoretical context: researching discourses of HRD

HRD can be conceptualized as a discursive and social construction (Sambrook 1998, 2000, 2001; Sambrook and Stewart 1998). Social phenomena, such as HRD, are created through language, symbols and words, of which discourses are a part. The term 'discourse' can be used in (at least) two ways: as a verb – to talk about, and as a noun – to describe a particular way of talking about something expressed through one's choice of discursive resources (words). As a noun, a discourse is more than an item of vocabulary – it is a rational and legitimate way of talking about and engaging in practices. Meanings are derived from social interactions, and are created through developing shared understandings. Meanings can be learned, for example, by using and sharing new language. The 'new' language of HRD incorporates discursive resources from the notions of culture, strategy and economics, for example. Some argue (Moorby 1996) that if training and development specialists use language recognized and legitimized by business managers, rather than their own functional jargon, managers might understand and listen. It is important to research how HRD is accomplished through the use of particular language, how different discourses are employed by organizational actors, and how HRD is talked about in this discursive diversity.

A discursive construction can be defined as a bundle of discursive resources, or a linguistic repertoire (Potter and Wetherell 1987). These repertoires contribute to the overall social construction of reality (Berger and Luckman 1967), in that we use them to frame an aspect of social life in a particular way, highlighting certain characteristics and playing down others. Discursive constructions are all around us, such as 'managing diversity' and 'new Labour,' and in the NHS there has been a discursive shift from 'competition' to 'collaboration' and from 'patients' to 'clients.' These are all new ways of framing existing or emerging theories and social phenomena, which are interpreted and talked about in new ways. As a discursive construction, HRD is a particular way of framing changes in training and development through choosing a particular bundle of discursive resources, such as 'mandatory training' or 'personal development,' 'training officers' or 'learning facilitators.'

A wider interest in discourse has now emerged in the field of HRD. As in the fields of management and human resource management previously, we are now debating the use of the 'label' HRD and its associated discourses. We are considering whether this is the most appropriate way to describe our professional activities, and whether this 'new' label describes distinctly new approaches to, and practices within, learning and development or is simply used as a marketing tool, to re-package our products and services, and extend our lifecycle. However, there is some concern about whether we should be spending (wasting) time arguing over labels (Holton 2002; Ruona 2002; Walton 2002). Many resist and resent the inclusion of 'human resources' in a description of their occupational role, preferring instead 'people' as the focus of their professional learning and development activities. Or, in the NHS, the preferred label appears to be 'workforce.'

So, how do NHS stakeholders talk about HRD, and is this influenced by, for example, a 'traditional' business or nursing professional background? I suggest (Sambrook 2006) that how we talk about the practices associated with developing people not only attempts to describe and influence how we think and go about HRD, but is also associated with our sense of personal and professional identity (Watson 2003). This also influences how HRD is perceived by other organizational and societal stakeholders. So, it is important to explore and clarify discursive resources (labels, or jargon – whatever we choose to call these) used by HRD stakeholders to help us understand how the learning and development activities we practice, teach and research are talked about, and thus understood by our partners/stakeholders.

This chapter explores discourses of HRD in one particular context, the British National Health Service (NHS).

The empirical context: The emergence of 'HR' in the NHS

The NHS provides an interesting case study in which to explore the complexities, changes and challenges of HRD. Some might argue the NHS is a critical, if not chronic, case in terms of the need to establish effective workplace learning. Driven by social, economic and political imperatives, the NHS is experiencing significant ongoing redevelopment, redesign and restructuring as manifest in key strategies such as the NHS Plan, Agenda for Change, and the Modernization Programme, with their associated discourse of change and improvement. These have a substantial bearing on human resourcing, and particularly HRD. Various initiatives have emerged, such as the national HR strategy (HR in the NHS Plan, DoH 2002), the NHS University (NHSU), Individual Learning Accounts (ILAs), and lifelong learning (Working Together, Learning Together, DoH 2001). However, little research has explored the diverse and dynamic roles of those practitioners tasked with developing health care workers, and the tensions between the needs and aspirations of the various stakeholders, and particularly the tensions between meeting service and individual needs.

When examining the development of HRD in the NHS, it is useful first to consider the emergence of HRM in the British health service. Bryson *et al.* (1996) report the language of HRM started to be used in the national health service in the 1980s. With the new freedoms granted with 'Trust' status in the 1990s, hospitals were able to consider more flexible approaches to people management. However, HRM activities were diverse and lacked strategic direction. It was not until 2002 that the NHS had a national HR strategy (DoH 2002) and became a formal element of the NHS Plan (DoH 2000, 2003). People management within the NHS has recently been thrust into a strategic position to help bring about the modernization of the service envisaged by the current Labour government, where 'Workforce underpins the modernization agenda' (DoH 2002: 4). This new emphasis on HR, and its impact on organizational performance, is accompanied by research. 'Human Resources with attitude' is the phrase used by Professor David Ulrich to describe a function with the confidence to insist on people-based solutions to NHS problems (cited in DoH 2002: 8). Professor James Buchan, a member of the National Workforce Taskforce, reviewed US Magnet hospitals and HRM in healthcare for the Department of Health and concluded that, 'the message from the key research on Human Resources management and organizational performance is that the evidence base, although relatively "young" and limited, does provide general support that good practice Human Resources management ... can make a positive difference to the performance of the organization' (DoH 2002). Good HR practices lead to better outcomes, clinically and for staff (DoH 2002: 39). In addition, an Aston University study (West *et al.* 2002) linked appraisal and small-team working with a reduction in post-operative death rates. Whilst there is a growing focus on HR(M) research, there is little in relation to HRD.

HRD in the NHS

Managing learning and development in the health service is a complex process (Burchill and Casey 1996: 124). A review of the literature reveals how each specific professional area is managing training, education and development, for example management development for clinicians (Dopson 1996; Ashburner 1996), and continuing professional development for doctors, nurses and PAMs, together with organization development (Stewart 1993) and management development (Thompson 1994). The responsibility for coordinating this rests with HR practitioners, yet very little literature examines this complex role.

Leopold *et al.* (1996) explore the relationship and tensions between management and professionalism in the health service, and examine the role of human resource managers. However, there is no mention of the role of human resource development specialists – whose role is to manage and coordinate the development of professionals and managers, amongst others – nor the training and development function. Dowding and Barr (2002) employ the term HRM, yet their discourse does not include HRD, but training, developing and 'nurturing.' Burchill and Casey propose 'to examine issues associated with overall staff development within the context of a NHS trust,' (Burchill and Casey 1996: 120) in their chapter entitled 'Human Resource Development,' but then proceed to describe what is generally labelled 'training and development,' and make no reference to HRD. In addition, they state that, 'Training and development are, of course, a part of human resource planning' (Burchill and Casey 1996: 124). They argue that training and development 'have to be linked clearly to the trust business plan and strategy and . . . meet statutory and professional body requirements . . . They have to take account, also, of individual needs . . . The objective of training and development is to improve overall and individual performance' (Burchill and Casey 1996: 124). Later they state that, 'The role of the human resource professional is to coordinate all the information and fit it to the business plan' (Burchill and Casey 1996: 125).

HRD in the NHS comprises various and varied elements including professional development, management development, leadership development and other forms of work-related learning. Although HRD is not explicitly mentioned, *learning* is considered central to modernizing the NHS. A key role of managers is to provide opportunities for learning, and perhaps help create organizational learning. However, as Nutley and Davies (2001) note, whilst continuing professional development (CPD) has an important role to play in improving learning, there is also a need to pay more attention to collective (organizational) learning. Managers are an important stakeholder in HRD, both in terms of their role in facilitating the development of their colleagues and in their own development. However, management development in the NHS appears to occur in professional silos. As Winyard (2003) notes, the introduction of general management in 1984 created fault-lines between doctors and managers, highlighting the incompatibility of managerially determined targets with the essence of professional practice, and led to the development of a management agenda disconnected from healthcare. Perhaps multi-professional management development could clarify the roles and contributions of clinical and managerial staff and help restore a sense of shared purpose in the running of the NHS. However, as I argue later, developing health professionals (particularly nurses, who are predominantly female) into managers is fraught with issues of identity. Hewison and Griffiths (2004) argue that leadership development is central to the modernization agenda, as indicated in key policy documents, and a range of leadership development programmes (including nursing) have been developed to meet this need. However, they also argue that leadership is only one of the changes required to improve health care, and too much emphasis on this

without an equal concern for transforming NHS work organizations themselves could result in leadership joining the list of management 'fads' that
have characterized health care in recent years.

One possible fad is the 'evidence-based' approach to almost everything in
the NHS. Evidence-based practice is deemed central to the 'modernization'
of health care in current UK policy, drawing on the rise of evidence-based
medicine and, more recently, evidence-based (nursing) practice, and now
emerging with evidence-based management in health care. Greener (2004)
identifies some of the pressures on senior health managers in the NHS and
suggests how 'knowledge' and 'knowing' might be brought together in the
NHS to move it more towards an evidence-based approach to management.
Hamlin (2002, 2005) also supports the development of evidence-based management. His research within a UK NHS Trust Hospital identified criteria
of managerial effectiveness at the middle and front-line levels of management, which, when compared against those from a similar study in a non-
NHS organization, suggest the notion of the 'universally effective manager.'
However, Hewison (2004) also examines evidence-based management in the
NHS and doubts whether it is possible, suggesting an alternative approach
based on the notion of 'craft.' This, perhaps, takes into account the contingencies of diverse managerial contexts where contested terrains require constant negotiation and re-construction of the managerial role.

Having briefly explored HRD in the NHS context, I now turn to the
empirical research.

Exploring discourses of HRD in the NHS – the original research

To explore discourses of HRD, empirical research, in the form of ethnographic case studies, was conducted in two NHS Trust hospitals in the East
Midlands (Trent Region) during 1997–98. The findings have been published elsewhere (Sambrook 1998, 2000, 2001). However, the main contribution of the study was the development of a typology of HRD discourses –
that is, the identification of three 'typical' ways of thinking and talking
about learning and development activities within Trust hospitals, which I
called Tell, Sell and Gel. Utilizing the concept of discursive action, I constructed a model of ideal types based on academic and practitioner accounts.
It suggests three ideal types – or approaches to 'development.' Not one of
these exists in 'reality,' nor in a pure form. The model provides a framework
for simplifying the multiple and complex realities, highlighting key aspects
as a means of enabling individuals to analyse and compare their own practices, and consider possible alternatives, but is not intended to be prescriptive. Associated with each ideal type is a discourse. The use of a particular
discourse by an individual might reveal which ideal type is being used to
influence their actions. Whilst the discourses of Tell, Sell and Gel may
compete, I would suggest that elements of each may be necessary, so the dis-

cursive action of HRD practitioners could perhaps include instruction, promotion and consultancy. However, there is a danger with competing discourses of mixed messages and meanings (Watson 1994).

Having identified these three ideal types and discourses associated with learning and development, it is important to remember that these emerged out of the various factors influencing HRD and the NHS at that time. However, it could be argued that much has changed in the health service, and wider environment, since the original research was conducted, not least the process of devolution and, with it, the delegation of powers to the National Assembly for Wales (and the Welsh Assembly Government) and the creation of NHS Wales. Thus, a key aim of the current research project has been to extend the empirical base of the earlier research by investigating HRD in other Trust hospitals within the context of the British National Health Service, and particularly within Wales.

Stakeholders in, and discourses of, HRD

Given the complexity of HRD within the NHS, and following the problematic issues of trying to 'define' HRD (Lee 2001; McLean 1998; McGoldrick *et al.* 2001, 2002; Swanson 1999), it might be more useful to identify specific aspects of HRD that we can research. In earlier research (Sambrook 1998), I focused on four key aspects: strategy, structure, stakeholders and services/products of HRD, exploring the purpose of HRD (the why), where 'it' is located, who is involved and how it is accomplished. These various aspects can influence how HRD is articulated and enacted, thus shaping multiple and possibly competing discourses of HRD. Here, I focus on who is involved (trainers, management developers, managers, NVQ coordinators etc). Focusing on the human dimension of HRD, a stakeholder model identifies all those involved in developing health care workers. However, all four aspects are interrelated. For example, the structural dimension reveals how HRD is separated into discrete silos within the distinct health professions and non-health areas such as clerical and managerial. Therefore, where HRD is located and how it is structured within a multidisciplinary NHS hospital can influence who is involved, and how, whether they are located within the HR or Nursing directorates, within the main hospital, or out in the community. Physical location and professional affiliation shape the identities of those involved in learning and development, and identities influence discourse (Watson 2003).

We have already noted that there are various stakeholders in HRD. Garavan suggests that, 'the evolution of a strategic HRD concept has also highlighted the need for the application of a stakeholder theory to HRD within organizations,' (Garavan 1995c: 11). He then explains that, 'within the context of strategic HRD, a stakeholder is anyone whose actions can affect the management of strategic HRD activities within the organization,' (Garavan 1995c: 11). Lee (1998: 533) argues that there is, 'a wide range of understandings of HRD . . . a range of different providers, (and) a range of different stakeholders and needs.'

Drawing upon research literature and empirical data, a potential functional stakeholder model for HRD within a hospital is shown in Figure 2.1.

The model identifies those parties having a stake, or interest, in HRD activities within a Trust hospital. Some of these are in competition: for example, is professional development provided by internal staff or externally through a university's School of Nursing or Medical School? External providers, such as FE colleges, can provide valuable funding through NVQs, but do they understand the organization's culture and service needs, and how can quality be assured? Also there are tensions, such as does HRD meet organization/service needs or personal/professional needs, or is it possible to meet both? Within the medical profession, there are 'staff' (non-training) and 'training' grades (for those pursing a career at consultant level), and 'protected time' – much coveted by other health professionals – for 'continuing medical education' (CME). Much learning and development within the NHS focuses on professionals, although there are many non-professionals. Trade unions have an important role in promoting lifelong learning, for example, through Unison's Return to Learn programme and their advocacy of learning through union learning representatives, which created the momentum for the NHSU for *all* staff.

In addition, we could add the wider range of stakeholders, the government, economy, public and media, for example, which each influence, or are influenced by, the health service. The government has introduced new terms into the discourse, such as 'workforce' development, Individual Learning Accounts, and Performance Review. It has also changed the organization of the NHS again by creating Foundation Hospitals, with 'new' freedoms to manage, and – to address the complex and diverse pay scales associated with different professions, roles and levels – established new generic pay grades through the Agenda for Change structure.

It is argued that the diverse range of stakeholders identified above leads to multiple discourses of what – so far in this chapter – has been generically labelled HRD. But we now have, for example, workforce development, professional nurse development, medical education, NVQs and management development, each with their distinct discourses. However, to be able holistically to manage the development of health care workers within the NHS requires stakeholders to be able to talk to one another, but this might be impeded by the use of different discourses. This chapter focuses on the discourses (accounts) of several key stakeholders in one Welsh Trust hospital.

Methodology

The original research explored HRD in two Trust hospitals in England. I identified two Trust hospitals that provided distinctly similar, yet also contrasting, case studies, or potential 'models' of HRD. To extend the empirical

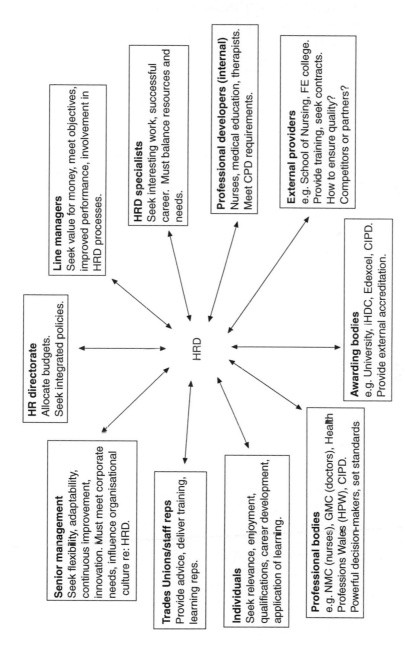

HR directorate
Allocate budgets.
Seek integrated policies.

Line managers
Seek value for money, meet objectives, improved performance, involvement in HRD processes.

HRD specialists
Seek interesting work, successful career. Must balance resources and needs.

Professional developers (internal)
Nurses, medical education, therapists. Meet CPD requirements.

External providers
e.g. School of Nursing, FE college. Provide training, seek contracts. How to ensure quality? Competitors or partners?

Senior management
Seek flexibility, adaptability, continuous improvement, innovation. Must meet corporate needs, influence organisational culture re: HRD.

Trades Unions/staff reps
Provide advice, deliver training, learning reps.

Individuals
Seek relevance, enjoyment, qualifications, career development, application of learning.

Professional bodies
e.g. NMC (nurses), GMC (doctors), Health Professions Wales (HPW), CIPD. Powerful decision-makers, set standards

Awarding bodies
e.g. University, IHDC, Edexcel, CIPD. Provide external accreditation.

HRD

Figure 2.1 Stakeholder analysis: needs and influences.

data, I approached another two Trust hospitals, in Wales, having moved there myself. They are similar in that both provide acute and community services and serve similar localities. They are different in terms of size, structure of the HR function and training and development provision. To protect their identity, I call the two NHS Trusts the District and the Regional.

The intention was to replicate the original ethnographic research. However, although much documentary material was gathered, it was not possible to conduct participant observations. Consequently, primary research data were collected from in-depth interviews with more than 25 participants (stakeholders) involved in HRD, including Directors of HR, Training Managers, Nurse Developers, Medical Educators, Directorate General Managers (DGMs), Nurse Managers, Business Managers and other Allied Health Professionals, with 11 practitioners from the District and 14 from the Regional. In this chapter, I present findings from the District.

Semi-structured interviews were conducted during 2001–02, and these lasted from half an hour to two hours. This generosity of time, given their heavy workloads, suggested some practitioners assigned significant importance to, and demonstrated particular interest in, their development roles. As with the original research, the research questions deliberately used the terms 'learning and development' and 'training and development' rather than 'HRD' to try to ensure that participants used their own language and were not unduly influenced by the researcher's language. Each interview was tape-recorded, transcribed and analysed using discourse analysis. This involved seeking similarities and differences between cases and stakeholders, and was followed by a comparative analysis with the discourses of HRD emerging from the original research.

This chapter can present only some of the findings and will focus on a range of participants in one hospital to illustrate some of the distinct discourses associated with different stakeholders. Having identified the range of potential stakeholders in HRD, I shall present findings from various participants. These include: the Training and Development Manager, an NVQ Coordinator/Facilitator (professional nurse developer), and three senior managers – Directorate General Managers (DGMs) with different professional backgrounds. These participants are selected for the similar and novel discursive resources they employed on the key themes of HRD structure, doing HRD, managers and management development, and HRD as learning. Table 2.1 provides brief biographical details of the participants.

Some findings

I present my findings focusing on the key themes of HRD structure, doing HRD, HRD as learning and, finally, nurse managers and management development.

Table 2.1 Brief biographical details of the participants

The District

Role and background

A1 – Training Manager
A3 – DGM Community/Head of Nursing, nursing background
A4 – DGM Acute (Medicine), graduate general management trainee
A7 – DGM Acute (Surgery), nursing background
A9 – NVQ Coordinator, nursing background

HRD structure

It was interesting that both of the Welsh Trust hospitals had Directors of Human Resources and Human Resources Directorates, as did the original two Trusts, but there was no mention of HRD and specialists were called Training Managers.

When asked about their role and what they were called, the Training Manager at the District commented:

> It's a bit too groovy that terminology [internal consultant] for us you know. It's a huge role, if it's OD today, if it's stand-up customer care training tomorrow, that's what we do. We're not precious about anything ... We don't call ourselves OD consultants, we don't call ourselves internal consultants. We're quite happy being called training ... [HRD?] No, we don't get hung up on that sort of thing, really we don't.

In the original research the two Trusts had different HRD structures: one had integrated all its learning and development into an Organizational and Professional Development Unit under the HR Director. The other retained the common structure with medical education and professional nurse development within their professional areas, and 'general' training and development etc within the HR directorate. At the District, the Training Manager explained

> We're in between the two, an evolutionary stage ... I don't think you will find a typical model in the Welsh Trusts, I think you'll find they're more varied. I say this because I'm on an all Wales Group and I know that they're approached very differently ... You asked me how these are integrated: we are like most other people, having the training and development department, which is my department, which is a HR function, and then of course, there's nurse education, and we have a School of Nursing on site, and then of course there's Post Graduate Medical Education ... and health and safety, then there's the CPR trainer,

there's lots of people delivering training in the Trust ... and we appointed a new DNS (Director of Nursing Services) and her remit was to have an Education Committee and that has brought together all the elements.

It is interesting that it is the DNS (a nurse) who has the important role of bringing together the diverse aspects of HRD. The *Training* Department at the District isn't very large to serve 4500 staff, comprising the Training Manager (who reports to the HR Director) and her Deputy (the two management trainers), three NVQ facilitators and admin staff.

Still thinking about structure, when asked about reconfiguration, the Training Manager had initially thought,

> Oh gosh, we'll have to go out into the community hospitals and clinics and deliver training. You know we can't expect them to come to the centre, but actually that didn't emerge and people prefer to come and be in a multi-disciplinary group ... and it gets them away from the workplace and they can concentrate on their learning ... with the exception of a few things that you might do like ... bullying and harassment awareness, appraisal awareness, you might take out on a roadshow.

So, there is an element of the Sell discourse – going to the customer, rather than the customer coming to the centre. It is interesting that the Training Manager uses the term 'centre,' because the training function is located away from the main hospital, where senior management and HR are located. In addition, as we hear later, other participants talk about the training department as *not* being central, which is perceived as being symbolic. In addition, the amount of space allocated to training might be symbolic.

> Most of what we do we actually now deliver in two training rooms that we've managed to secure on the top floor of this building so people actually come here, and it is rather nice because it breaks down some of the barriers between what were different Trusts.

The building is at one of the other community (peripheral) hospitals. However, professional nurse development and medical education are both located in the main acute hospital.

This structural tension was articulated by the District NVQ Coordinator, a nurse, who had been in post just over a year. The role involves facilitating and *managing* the NVQ process. The key theme from her interview was how professional nurse development 'fits' in an HR directorate. The NVQ Coordinator explained the training function was split across

> two sites. They're in [training department in a community hospital] and we're here, and it makes sense for us to be here because, you know, most

of my work ... I look after the main hospital site ... It is on base, so people can come and see me, pop in. A lot of work is done on the corridors, you bump into people, you know, just general networking, so it wouldn't make sense for us to be in [training department].

This replicates findings from other nurse developers in the original research. Referring to a former colleague, 'when she took over the post, she was in [training department] and felt quite isolated and disjointed from us, because we are our own little team.' The location of NVQ training in the general training department, within the HR Directorate, is problematic.

> We're nurses in a non-nursing directorate, which is really quite hard actually, hard for me professionally. I've got nobody to talk to and for some bizarre reason we seem to communicate on very different levels ... They don't seem to know where I'm coming from quite often, when I talk about professional development I'm talking about, you know, my professional development as a nurse ... There seems to be a bit of a wall there ... I find it quite difficult in that I've never had anyone to talk to.

The professional distance between the nursing NVQ staff and the other training staff appears exacerbated by the physical distance between the main hospital and the training department. I asked about the relationship with the training department, 'I don't identify with the training side at all.' I wondered about team meetings. 'We have team meetings ... twice a month ... they're a waste of time ... they talk a lot about HR stuff ... And I don't feel it's my, I'm not interested in Human Resource strategy ... I just wish we weren't in a management directorate ... we need to be in a nursing quality directorate. It's all about nursing quality.' The NVQ Coordinator continues, 'I think it would be nice, my little directorate' and laughs. But the serious point is made that 'I don't think we see each other's roles very well.' I wondered if it would help if they were based at the same site: 'Oh no, God. Oh God no.' The previous manager had been located in the training department 'and she nearly had a nervous breakdown over there. It was dreadful being there, dreadful, isolated.' It was better being in the main hospital because 'there is professional support from being within the hospital, just by, you know, chatting to other nurses and bumping into people.' This emerged as a crucial issue in the original research. 'I feel very isolated, very stand alone, very exposed.'

This highlights the difficulties of locating an element of professional nurse development within an HR Directorate.

However, these difficulties are not necessarily experienced out in the field. The DGM for Medicine, a non-health professional, is new to the post, although has worked for the Trust in a management role before. Unlike many DGMs, she has no health professional background. 'I joined the health service as a general management trainee, graduate trainee ... No, no, I am one of the, there's five general managers in this Trust and I'm the only one who's not a nurse . . . so I'm the oddball!' When I asked the District DGM, Medicine ask about training and development, she replied,

> There is a training and development department . . . and they do seem to get involved in a lot of training, particularly management type training, management type development . . . Our [training] department's in [place]. It's actually not in the same area as HR . . . I probably think of it as different, only because it's physically separate . . . I don't think we should be off the main site . . . I mean it's not exactly the hub . . . I don't know that it was deliberate but it is symbolic, isn't it.

This DGM suggests that the training department should be located centrally, along with HR, and explains further. 'But then you've also got the School of Nursing, you see the training department doesn't do the clinical stuff, it's the School of Nursing which is on this site and it does all clinical, so training is very split up.' I asked if this caused problems. 'No, because we're very clear about, School of Nursing deals with nursing issues, junior doctors and medical staff go through the respective colleges, post-grad education, there's a lot of medical staff. The training department's for like admin and clerical, management, I think people are quite clear about it.'

Activities associated with learning and development in the health service are very diverse and seldom labelled HRD. The Directorate General Manager (DGM) for Community Services at the District, is a nurse who manages the service and is also Head of Nursing there, and manages both professional nurse development and other forms of HRD.

> Well, in this Trust we have our own, we use the term training and development . . . We have our own department, and we have two aspects of training and development. We have organizational managerial training and development, we also have professional training and development, and, for our purposes, we more or less use the training and development department for managerial and organizational development. All our professional developmental needs are done elsewhere, but it's all still part of the *package* . . .

This recognizes HRD is split between managerial/organizational, the responsibility of the training department and professional development, done elsewhere. As in many Trusts, which have accommodation problems, in this Trust, the Training and Development department was located 'off-site' which was considered 'not deliberate, but symbolic.'

The DGM for Medicine continues 'T&D is fragmented, not high enough profile.' A colleague also states that 'the main problem is that it's offsite' (interviewee A7). However, some don't think of T&D as separate. 'I don't see them as two separate things it's just that we organize them as two separate things, because our training department doesn't concern itself with continuing professional development' (A3). Given the physical separation of HRD, and the large geographical area of community directorates, the DGM explains,

> ...I have seven community hospitals, and community nursing ... I've got a lot of staff, and I can't pull them all off the street at the same time, or pull them all off the ward at the same time to attend training. The training department are good, they will actually come out to different areas.
>
> (A3)

Doing HRD

At the District there were three strands to the 'training and development function': management development, national vocational qualifications (NVQs) and corporate things like communication skills.

> We identified certain skill areas that we decided that all managers should have, such as recruitment, appraisal, performance management etc ... We intended to roll that out as a policy to say all managers must go through this training ... but we found that even before we rolled it out we were being overwhelmed.
>
> (A1)

This might suggest a Tell approach, deciding what skills managers should have, but lack of capacity has prevented this being accomplished. Lack of capacity emerges as an important theme, and, linked with the lack of centrality and physical space, might suggest the general training function is a low priority, or, conversely, that there is so much demand for this that existing resources cannot meet.

An interesting element of the District Training Manager's discourse related to the relationship with, and expectations of, directorate managers.

> What I expect managers to do for me every year ... is to draw up a Directorate training plan, based on the business plan, based on the appraisals etc, to cost and prioritize it and to give me an overview of the benefits of training that they did last year, an evaluation exercise ... managers are really expected to do that.

This also, again, suggests a 'business' dimension, either to relate better to business managers or to indicate the Training Manager's own construction of HRD drawing upon managerial discursive resources. However, there were references to a more learning orientation, but the 'business case' dominated. Focusing on the limited resources, the District Training Manager continues,

> Our priority, you can't meet them all (organizational and personal), the resources are so limited, I mean we would love to be, you know, the sort

of learning organization that says that any learning is of value, you know, and it's absolutely great, of course it is, but not when people are so pressed that they can't be released for training, not when you haven't got enough capacity in the training department to deliver, you've got to target it on service needs and organizational needs, you have to do that.

I asked about the HR Strategy in NHS Plan.

We haven't felt too stressed by it because people are already doing it, we do have performance review already ... there are things in there like Individual Learning Accounts, but we haven't grappled with all that ... we don't feel there's any huge gap, the problem is the sheer volume ... and trying to think creatively how you can deliver that without compromising quality is the challenge for us.

Again, there is reference to the sheer volume. Drawing on a more 'business' discourse, and linking this with discourses of mandatory/elective training familiar in the health context, the Training Manager commented that there is,

So much demand, so very different sorts of training, and like every other Trust it runs lean with not an awful lot of spare. We're pulling people out for all sorts of different things. And so the view has been taken now that we would identify certain categories of training as mandatory ... and of course, there's been a long debate about what fits into mandatory and what fits into development. And there's a paper just going to the Board ... that says unless you have completed *x*, *y*, *z* which is mandatory for your staff group then you will not have permission to do any other form of training, which will actually target resources where they're needed most.

This suggests a Tell approach, rather than Sell or Gel, but this may be the only possible response given the limited resources and legal requirements.

In general, in the District, the HRD team were considered proactive in organizational and managerial development; 'they tell you what courses are available,' and 'sell' their wares through flyers, lists, road shows, and respond by tailoring courses. Also, there appears to be support by senior management.

The District DGM, Community Services comments, 'I think this Trust has a very positive attitude towards uh, learning, which comes from the top [the Chief Executive?] Yes, and the Board. We have on our Board [a Professor] who ... champions the cause of training ... also there is, I think there's just an acceptance that you can't, you can't move forward unless you're training, and unless you're willing to learn.' The discourse here focuses on *training*. The DGM continues, 'you have a good training department who get out there and *tell* people what's what, you know, they *tell* people what courses are running.' This may suggest a Tell approach, but the verb appears to be used to promote (sell) HRD. The downside is the small size of the department and lack of capacity. Releasing staff from the service is also problematic, as 'everybody's absolutely swamped with work.' Yet, perhaps a true focus on learning – rather than training – might be less problematic.

The reference to 'package' earlier also suggests a sell approach to HRD, which is confirmed by the DGM Community Services.

> I meet fairly regularly with the training and development people and if I find that there is a training need within my directorate then I ring them up and I ask them, can you meet this training need, they'll either say yes or no. If they say no, it's usually from a capacity point of view, that they can't actually fit it in. If they can, they will *tailor make* a course or a day, a training day, that meets that need.

This might refer to my Sell ideal type of HRD, and reiterates the District Training Manager's comment about lack of capacity. I asked the DGM what type of things.

> Well I've asked them if they would take some work for us with senior managers along investigation techniques and discipline. From a capacity point of view they were not able to do that, but because they weren't able to do it they've actually picked it up and they've taken it and said, look, they've gone to the Trust, and said look, this is a training need that's been identified in more than one directorate so we need to do it.

This further supports the Sell approach, responding to demand. I asked about the two separate aspects, but was told, 'I don't necessarily see them as two separate things it's just that we organize them as two separate things because our training department doesn't concern itself with continuing professional development.'

I asked where training and development activities took place. The District DGM, Community Services replied, 'I have seven community hospitals, and community nursing . . . I've got a lot of staff, and I can't pull them all off the street at the same time, or pull them all off the ward at the same time to attend training. The training department are good, they will actually come out to different areas.' Again, this suggests a sell approach, where the trainers will go to the client.

The District DGM Community Services noted that HRD is devolved. She explained, 'we have our own training strategy as a directorate,' which included professional nurse development and management development, and this is reviewed every 12–18 months

> because things change . . . Well there's all sorts of things that change within the NHS, there's the structural, organizational requirements, which are constantly changing, and also the legal requirements.

The discourse now focuses on constant change and the need to meet legal requirements. There is a devolved training budget but this is 'not huge' and this is used 'for any training that we buy in; anything that we have from the training department is free, but we have to pay expenses obviously.' Again, there is negotiation (gel) with staff in terms of funding learning for organizational, professional and/or personal needs (fees, study leave etc). At first, it seems that learning/training is about going on courses.

Time (to go on courses) is repeatedly identified as the biggest issue. However, there is other in-house training and learning, including using link nurses to update specialist information and ward meetings. When asked about nurses' perceptions of training, one DGM explains 'they would talk about the requirements for continuing professional development,' but not necessarily going on courses. So, other forms of learning were also recognized, but to meet professional requirements. Often, it isn't lack of budget that inhibits learning and development but service pressures. 'The big tensions are resources, there's very little elasticity left . . . having quite a lot of money but no time to spend it . . . the different things that compete, the service is under so much pressure' (A7).

The theme about 'protected time' emerges, and is closely associated with the different 'rules' for professional development between doctors and nurses.

> It's not got a high enough profile I suppose . . . The demands of the service come first and . . . training and development take time and they need to invest time in supporting people through training and development, be it going on a course, be it secondment, be it shadowing, be it whatever. . . . There's an issue about protected time, junior doctors by and large get the protected time because of the law and because of the regulations that they're working out of. Medical staff have formally protected time for teaching, education, training. If you're a nurse working on a ward that's permanently hammered, if you're a ward sister, the ward is permanently hammered. Their difficulty is ensuring they can release staff.
>
> (A4)

A further tension is the notion of 'equitability,' where some staff appear to engage in more formal activities than others, suggesting HRD is 'disproportionate.'

In terms of resources, one DGM, like all the others, is responsible for planning training to meet service needs, and recognizes the competition between professions for scarce resources and the need to 'sell' their patch.

> I think what the whole Health Service has got itself into is we have become increasingly specialized, both doctors and nurses . . . and also if you have that specialization, you know, the demand for resources increases because they want, everybody wants the best for their patch and that's just difficult.
>
> (A4)

One possible way of addressing these issues is to consider HRD as learning, rather than training.

HRD and learning

In my original research, I noted the shift towards learning. One of the (few) references to a learning discourse related to an annual Welsh conference. The District Training Manager explained:

> The HR Director for NHS Wales had been talking to a group and saying 'well in health services we need to learn to work differently, change things, their thinking of work patterns,' so from that we took the strand of learning to learn differently . . . so it's going to take people out of their comfort zone I think a bit, which we're hoping will have a like catalystic effect and so it's kind of called 'creating a future' . . . there's going to be some sort of NLP stuff . . . doing things like drumming and juggling and goodness knows what else, so it's very, very different . . . we're trying to open the thinking.

Linked to this is a shift away from thinking about learning as 'going on courses' although the Training Manager appears to be mixing discourses (Tell, Sell and Gel). 'Part of the guidance booklet that goes with our appraisal system talks about *learning* can happen in a number of ways and that you could use shadowing, mentoring, secondments, these sorts of *training*, to *support* learning.' Having 'a sense they were just thinking, "oh well, I've got to do CPD, I've got to do a course,"' the District Training Manager conducted a mini survey within the Trust and found that,

> people are actually doing a variety of things . . . the people who are really good at that are people like the therapists . . . and the nurses are quite good at secondments . . . there has been a shift.

In addition,

> there is a positive *learning* culture . . . really and truly, you can palpably feel it as you go around the Trust . . . because the School of Nursing is onsite . . . there's a post-doc medical centre . . . I haven't any responsibility for that . . . [and] I suppose it's probably the calibre of the business managers that we have. They're excellent, so they're very pro-*training*.

This suggests a discursive (or conceptual) tension between the terms learning and training. As the DGM, Medicine notes, 'I mean as individuals I think we are conditioned to a certain extent to say training and development is going on a course, reading a book or sitting an exam, we're not conditioned to think training and development means any kind of opportunity which encourages you to learn something new.'

Many of the DGMs talk about informal opportunities for learning. Given the pressures staff and the service are under, this might be one way of overcoming some of the barriers associated with going on courses, discussed earlier. 'My personal philosophy is providing opportunities for staff where they feel valued, learning doesn't have to necessarily take place in a classroom, identifying one new thing or doing one new thing each day is active learning, it's not just putting a list of courses up' (A7). He continues, 'there are lots of ways to learn, it's not just sitting in front of somebody who chalks and talks.' This suggests a shift to the Gel approach.

Nurse managers and management development

In the original research, as here, there was evidence of duplication of learning activities, particularly around management development. 'Some things can overlap sometimes in so far as post basic education for nurses will cover some aspects of management and we deliver management.'

Talking about these two aspects of HRD, the District DGM Community Services explains,

> I'm head of nursing as well so obviously as far as the professional side of it is concerned then my role is to make sure that everybody has sufficient training to do the job. And the same with managerially as well, you can't put people, nurses particularly, into a management job just because they're good nurses...

On the issue of nurses becoming managers, one DGM explains,

> a lot of our ward sisters are having to take on extra management duties, and to do that we've made some very subtle changes. We've actually changed the title to ward manager from ward sister, and we've ... given them the opportunity to act up as the hospital manager, or to attend meetings, to do shadowing, sending some of them on a ... management course ...
>
> (A3)

This suggests that being a nurse with good clinical skills and expertise does not necessarily equip you to become a good manager. There is also reference to professional identity (Traynor 1999), 'because you're a nurse first and, before you become a manager you're a nurse.' (A3) In addition, there is recognition that development does not necessarily have to be formal, but can include other informal forms of learning.

Talking of HRD amongst health professionals, one DGM who does not have a health professional background explains, 'I think one of the problems with the Health Service is that we all go down the professional route for training ... There's a lot of emphasis on clinicians now, we're on about management and opportunities for that, it doesn't work the other way round. But there's so many professional groups to understand that it's probably impossible' (A4). Yet, interestingly, in terms of management development she wondered why managers don't 'sit and think ... audit ... don't take me the wrong way, managers are scrutinized, (unlike doctors).' This DGM is concerned that managers do not get the same development opportunities, whereas clinical staff, 'you must do continuing professional development.' She explains further. 'There's an emphasis on everybody to do CPD isn't there. ... Continuous Professional Development, which a lot of people still see as going off on a course, and that's not necessarily the best way to learn is it. Things like secondment, special projects, things like that I would say, just my view.' This is the DGM who earlier mentioned being 'conditioned' to think of training and development as going on a course, reading a book or sitting an exam. This reinforces the earlier views on learning, and Nutley and Davies' (2001) concerns regarding the focus on CPD.

Some interpretations, conclusions and critical analysis

Given the constraints of the chapter's length, I have only been able to share the accounts of selected stakeholders in HRD in one Welsh NHS Trust hospital. Having identified the range of discursive resources employed by these stakeholders in HRD, it is interesting to examine who uses these and how these might shape or be shaped by their professional identities. A particularly interesting dimension is the transition from *being* a nurse to *becoming* a manager (Watson and Harris 1999) and the ways in which different individuals cope, as articulated in their language use. This chapter highlights some of the discursive struggles to maintain one's professional (nursing) identity when promoted to managerial positions (Watson 1994, 2003). For example, a discursive resource used by many participants, and interesting given the context, was the notion of 'looking after.' This particular discourse emerged in my interview with the District NVQ Coordinator. 'I look after the main hospital site ... she looked after the community.' This was an important theme and could be related to her professional identity and role as a (caring) nurse. On the issue of the difficult transition from nursing to management (Allen and Hughes 2002), one of the DGMs (A3) argues that 'you can't put people, nurses particularly, into a management job just because they're good nurses,' whilst another (B7) comments that 'there's a stereotype of nurses, if you're a nurse you're not very good at business, which I don't believe.' Both of these are nurses themselves and appear to have made that transition with little difficulty, and have adopted the new managerial discourse without such apparent difficulty of changed identity.

Various discursive resources have been identified, illustrating the diversity of talk about HRD within the NHS. As one DGM commented, 'I think we're using the same words but it means something completely different' (B5). Not one participant used the term HRD – it was always 'training and development' or 'professional development' or 'managerial and organizational development' and sometimes 'learning.' Nor was there much use of the government's preferred term 'workforce development.' Whilst it was recognized by our senior managers that their roles included a responsibility for HRD – through managing training budgets, approving study leave and providing learning opportunities – there were mixed feelings about the training and development function within their Trust. Yet, this is a difficult role in the NHS where HRD is separated into 'professional' and 'other': 'nursing gets the big money' or 'the emphasis is always on clinicians' while training and development is 'only' about managerial and organizational development. Yet, there is some evidence of 'agreed talk' about how learning and development – however defined or labelled – is structured, managed, encouraged and facilitated to help individuals and the organization/service develop. Understanding this can help inform and enhance HRD practice in this complex, dynamic context, and this chapter makes a small contribution, providing further evidence of the multiple ways in which HRD is articulated and accomplished by a range of stakeholders.

Finally, I acknowledge there are some limitations with the study. First, I have only presented findings from one Trust. However, the discourses of training, learning, caring and competition are evident in the second Trust, too. Second, I have focused only on a Welsh Trust. Yet, my findings do indeed confirm those gathered earlier in the two English Trusts. Further research is needed to explore discourses of HRD further afield, perhaps through international comparative analyses.

Key learning points

- There is evidence to support the *Tell, Sell, Gel* typology of HRD in the NHS (Sambrook 1998).
- Discursive resources employed by stakeholders in HRD might shape or be shaped by their professional identities.
- A particularly interesting dimension is the transition from *being* a nurse to *becoming* a manager (Watson and Harris 1999) and the ways in which different individuals cope, as articulated in their language use.
- Key themes have emerged focusing on the complex and fragmented structure of HRD in this context. The fragmentation arises out of the diversity of professional and non-professional health care workers and their diverse HRD needs.
- Attempts have been made to integrate the different elements of HRD, but this is constrained by strong and separate professional bodies and resisted by personal professional identities.
- Further tensions arise between meeting service and/or individual needs, and where individual needs can be both personal and professional.

- Much HRD is geared to meeting legal and CPD (professional) requirements.
- In attempting to meet CPD needs, there is a shift away from 'going on courses' and a move towards other forms of 'learning.'

Acknowledgement

I would like to thank the University Forum for HRD, who funded the project to extend the original doctoral research.

References

Allen, D. and Hughes, D. (2002) *Nursing and the Division of Labour*, Basingstoke: Palgrave Macmillan.
Ashburner, L. (1996) 'The role of clinicians in the management of the NHS,' in J. Leopold, I. Glover and M. Hughes M (eds) *Beyond Reason: The National Health Service and the Limits of Management*, Stirling Management Series, Aldershot: Avebury, pp. 3–14.
Berger, P.L. and Luckmann, T. (1967) *The Social Construction of Reality*, Harmondsworth: Penguin.
Bryson, C., Jackson, M. and Leopold, J. (1996) 'Human resource managers as professionals in managing change in NHS trusts,' in J. Leopold, I. Glover and M. Hughes (eds) *Beyond Reason: The National Health Service and the Limits of Management*, Stirling Management Series, Aldershot: Avebury, pp. 37–57.
Burchill, F. and Casey, A. (1996) *Human Resource Management: The NHS A Case Study*, MacMillan Press.
DoH (2000) *The NHS Plan: A Plan for Investment, A Plan for Reform*, London: Department of Health.
DoH (2001) *Working Together, Learning Together*, London: Department of Health.
DoH (2002) *HR in the NHS Plan*, London: Department of Health
DoH (2003) *Delivering the HR in the NHS Plan*, London: Department of Health.
Dopson, S. (1996) 'Doctors in management: a challenge to established debates,' in J. Leopold, I. Glover and M. Hughes (eds) *Beyond Reason: The National Health Service and the Limits of Management*, Stirling Management Series, Aldershot: Avebury, pp. 173–188.
Dowding, L. and Barr, J. (2002) *Managing in Health Care*, Harlow: Pearson Education.
Garavan, T. (1995a) 'HRD Stakeholders: their philosophies, values, expectations and evaluation criteria,' in *Journal of European Industrial Training* 19(10): 17–30.
Garavan, T. (1995b) 'Stakeholder analysis: the implications for the management of HRD,' in *Journal of European Industrial Training* 19(10): 45–46.
Garavan, T. (1995c) 'Stakeholders and strategic human resource development,' in *Journal of European Industrial Training* 19(10): 11–16.
Greener, I. (2004) 'Talking to health managers about change: heroes, villains and simplification,' *Journal of Health, Organisation and Management* 18(5): 321–335.
Hamlin, B. (2002) In support of evidence-based management and research-informed HRD through HRD professional partnerships: an empirical and comparative study, *Human Resource Development International* 5(4): 467–491.

Hamlin, B. (2005) 'Towards universalistic models of managerial leader effectiveness: a comparative study of recent British and American derived models of leadership,' *Human Resource Development International* 8(1): 5–25.

Hewison, A. (2004) 'Evidence-based management in the NHS: is it possible?' *Journal of Health, Organisation and Management* 18(5): 336–348.

Hewison, A. and Griffiths, M. (2004) 'Leadership development in health care: a word of caution,' *Journal of Health, Organisation and Management* 18(6): 464–473.

Holton, E.F. III (2002) 'Defining HRD: too much of a good thing?' *Human Resource Development Review* 1(3): 275–276.

Lee, M.M. (1998) *Human Resource Development in the United Kingdom: A Partial Exposition.* Proceedings of the AHRD Conference, pp. 528–535.

Lee, M.M. (2001) 'A refusal to define HRD,' *Human Resource Development International* 4(3): 327–341.

Leopold, J., Glover, I. and Hughes, M. (eds) (1996) *Beyond Reason: The National Health Service and the Limits of Management*, Stirling Management Series, Aldershot: Avebury.

McGoldrick, J., Stewart, J. and Watson, S. (2001) 'Theorizing human resource development' *Human Resource Development International* 4(3): 343–356.

McGoldrick, J., Stewart, J. and Watson, S. (2002) 'Researching human resource development,' in J. McGoldrick, J. Stewart and S. Watson (eds) *Understanding Human Resource Development: A Research-based Approach*, London: Routledge, pp. 1–17.

McLean, G. (1998) 'HRD: a three-legged stool, an octopus, or a centipede,' *Human Resource Development International* 1(4): 375–377.

Moorby, E. (1996) *How to Succeed in Employee Development Maidenhead*, McGraw-Hill.

Nutley, S.M. and Davies, H.T.O (2001) 'Developing organizational learning in the NHS,' *Medical Education* 35(1): 35–42.

Potter, J. and Wetherell, M. (1987) *Discourse and Social Psychology: Beyond Attitudes and Behaviour*, London: Sage.

Ruona, W. (2002) 'Town forum,' Proceedings of the annual AHRD conference, Hawaii, Feb–March.

Sambrook, S. (1998) 'Models and concepts of human resource development: academic and practitioner perspectives,' PhD Thesis, Nottingham Business School, Nottingham.

Sambrook, S. (2000) 'Talking of HRD,' *Human Resource Development International* 3(2): 159–178.

Sambrook, S. (2001) 'HRD as an emergent and negotiated evolution: an ethnographic case study in the British National Health Service,' *Human Resource Development Quarterly* 12(2): 169–193.

Sambrook, S. (2006) 'Management Development in the NHS: nurses and managers, discourses and identities,' *Journal of European Industrial Training*, 30(1): 48–64.

Sambrook, S. and Stewart, J. (1998) 'HRD as a discursive construction,' Professors Forum, IFTDO World Conference, Trinity College, Dublin.

Stewart, J. (1993) *Organisation Development: History, Perspectives and Relevance to NHS Organisations*, Bristol: NHSTD.

Swanson, R. (1999) 'HRD theory, real or imagined?' in *Human Resource Development International* 2(1): 2–5.

Thompson, D. (1994) *Developing Managers for the new NIIS*, Harlow: Longman.

Traynor, M. (1999) *Managerialism and Nursing: Beyond Oppression and Profession*, London: Routledge.

Walton, J. (2002) 'Town forum,' Proceedings of the annual AHRD conference, Hawaii, Feb–March.

Watson, T.J. (1994) *In Search of Management Culture, Chaos and Control in Managerial Work*, London: Routledge.

Watson, T.J. (2003) *Sociology, Work and Industry*, 4th edn, London: Routledge.

Watson, T.J. and Harris, P. (1999) *The Emergent Manager*, London: Sage.

West, M.A., Borrill, C., Dawson, J., Scully, J., Carter, M., Anelay, S., Patterson, M. and Waring, J. (2002) *International Journal of Human Resource Management* 13(8): 1299–1310.

Winyard, G. (2003) 'Doctors, managers and politicians,' *Clinical Medicine, Journal of the Royal College of Physicians* 3(5): 465–469.

3 Transitioning to a strategically aligned HRD function

The case of a health services organization

Thomas N. Garavan, Claire Gubbins, Carole Hogan and Margaret Woodlock

Introduction

Human resource development (HRD) as an activity has become more pervasive in organizations. It is increasingly used as a strategy to achieve competitive advantage (Tjepkema *et al.* 2002). HRD is more likely to be utilized in multinational organizations, however there is evidence that it is now more frequently used in public sector organizations (Deloitte 2004). HRD departments vary considerably in how they are structured. They vary in terms of the level of centralization, the types of activities they perform, the extent of networking and whether they are strategic or more operational in focus. A significant number of medium to large sized organizations typically have centralized training and development functions (Garavan and Heraty 2001), which are increasingly referred to as human resource development functions (Garavan and Carbery 2003). There is also considerable debate concerning the extent to which the HRD function must, or should, be strategic in outlook. Some training and development functions adopt a primary provider model (Blanchard and Thacker 2004). In this scenario, each element of the training and development process is handled by specialists. This model is typically found in a stable environment and it usually requires a large centralized training staff. A provider model tends primarily to be adopted by larger organizations (Lee 1988; Gerber 1987). An alternative model involves the training function acting as a manager or intermediary. The role of the function is to select and manage training suppliers. This strategy is typically adopted by organizations whose training needs are likely to vary considerably over a short period of time (Carnevale 1990; Rossett 1996). Other organizations are likely to use a more mixed strategy (Blanchard and Thacker 2004). In a mixed strategy, decision-making is centralized for some training activities and decentralized for others. Some organizations conduct on-going training needs internally and contract to external providers for all new training. The mixed strategy allows the organization to be adaptable to the changing environment and it puts the

HRD function in a more flexible position to respond. It is possible to argue that the language of strategic HRD, as well as its intentions, is very much focused on enhancing organizational capability through the enhancement of individual competencies. There is less emphasis on a learning discourse. This is perhaps one of the more unsatisfactory elements of the strategic HRD paradigm.

A central argument and tenet running through the choice of training and development strategy is the concern to ensure the strategic alignment of HRD. Strategic alignment emphasizes horizontal and vertical dimensions. Horizontal strategic alignment focuses on the interrelationships between HRD professionals and HRD stakeholders including employees, line managers, top managers, relevant training providers and HRD activities. Strategic alignment also emphasizes the link between HRD activities and strategic organizational goals and objectives (Wognum and Mulder 1999). Commentators (Barney 1991; McIntyre 2004) highlight three strategic roles for HRD; HRD involvement in shaping the organization's competitive position; the use of HRD strategies to support the competitive strategy of the organization; and the development and implementation of its own strategy.

It should be pointed out that scholars are still searching for an integrated theory of strategic human resource development. It is generally defined as a planned pattern of human resource capabilities and functional level HRD activities intended to enable the organization to achieve its goals. We adopt a more configurational perspective of HRD in this chapter. We argue that HRD practices should seek both horizontal and vertical integration. This suggests that certain bundles of HRD practices are appropriate because they fit together to support particular employee behaviours and competencies. These behaviours and competencies are appropriate given the particular organization's context.

The adoption of strategic models of HRD has become a relevant issue for public sector organizations in Ireland. The Irish public sector has experienced significant wide-ranging changes in recent years, in particular the introduction of more business-focused and customer-led approaches to how they operate (Lawler and Hearn 1995; Mavin and Bryans 2000; Williams *et al.* 2003). There is increasing demand for improved quality and efficiency of services and differing customer demands. These changes are coupled with strict financial controls and increased accountability. Public sector organizations are now increasingly concerned with ensuring that their employees have the competencies and skills to be effective in this changing context. The increasing business and customer focus has brought with it the recognition that organizations should invest in training and developing their people (Finn 1997; Deloitte 2004). Training and development is increasingly used to cope with the many transitions that public sector organizations are likely to experience. There is positive evidence in the Irish context that public sector employees consider training and development to be important. They also perceive training and development as one of the most accepted techniques for addressing and coping with the pressures for change, both currently and in the future (Williams *et al.* 2003; Deloitte 2004).

The roles of HRD professionals in organizations have been understood in a multiplicity of ways. Those most frequently highlighted in the literature include transition from operational to strategic, qualitative to quantitative, policing to partnering, short-term to long-term, administrative to consultative and functionally orientated to business orientated (Ulrich 1997; Swanson 1994). HRD professionals are expected to create value and deliver results (Rummler and Brache 1992). They are increasingly focusing on defining the deliverables of HRD (Ulrich 1997; Lynton and Pareek 2000) and are expected to perform a business partner role. This brings the strategic alignment issue increasingly into focus.

The aims of this chapter are as follows.

- To emphasize some of the characteristics and debates that are associated with strategic HRD.
- To document and explain initiatives taken by a health services organization to implement a strategic HRD model.
- To outline and explain the contributions of various stakeholders to the implementation of a strategic HRD model.
- To explain how various stakeholders perceived their respective roles and practices in respect of the delivery of HRD.
- To examine how stakeholders perceived the HRD model, in terms of the extent of their participation in, and perceptions of, value and quality of training and development activities.

The chapter reports on a study that was conducted in a health services organization. This organization took a particular initiative to enhance its approach to the training and development of employees. Dublin Dental School and Hospital (DDS&H) was seeking to respond to a Government-published report; the Action Plan for People Management (Department of Health and Children 2002), which set out recommendations to develop human resource management practices in the health sector. Under the Action Plan, the organization aimed to move its HRD function to a more strategic position and use it as a vehicle for change management; ultimately focused on facilitating the provision of a better service to customers. The organization was concerned that the HRD function contributed to the development of a learning environment and that the function be perceived as more productive, learner-oriented and strategically integrated. The HRD manager was concerned with creating ownership of training and development across the organization. The organization has begun this journey and perceives that over an 18-month period it has made significant progress.

The chapter is structured in the following way. We first consider and review the literature on strategic HRD and discuss characteristics of a strategically aligned training and development function. We then describe the data collection and analysis process followed by a discussion of our results. The final sections of this chapter focus on identifying the implications of our findings for both theory and practice.

Theoretical context

Characteristics of strategically aligned HRD

An examination of the relevant literatures (Holton and Baldwin 2003; Gilley and Gilley Maycunich 2003) illuminated five characteristics of strategic HRD alignment that are relevant. Participation, involvement and support of key stakeholders in HRD; information in the form of key insights into HRD learning needs; formalization, which refers to the nature of consultation and information gathering processes used by the HRD department; HRD goals and objectives which focus on the choices that are made, the content of HRD programmes and activities and the target groups that are addressed; and the learning culture and climate that exists within the organization.

Participation, involvement and support

Participation, involvement and support are considered three important and related components of effective strategic alignment. Participation can be defined as active involvement of stakeholders in decision-making concerning HRD. Support is defined as the level of support available to employees before attending training and development activities and post training in terms of applying skills and knowledge learned in training on the job. Three key internal stakeholders are likely to have involvement in HRD decision making; employees, line managers and top managers. External training providers may also have an involvement, however, we will only focus here on internal stakeholders.

EMPLOYEES

Employee involvement and participation in the training and development process is increasingly highlighted (Blyton and Turnbull 1998; Garavan and Heraty 2001; Marchington and Wilkinson 2002). There is evidence that management generally favour a unitary approach. It is usual for management to decide if and how employees are involved and they are disposed towards participation and involvement in day-to-day operational issues. This area provides less significant scope for employees in terms of decision-making input. Blyton and Turnbull (1998) advocate that employee involvement is predicated on maintenance and control over the training and development agenda.

There is evidence that non-traditional learners are less likely to have any involvement in decision making concerning HRD (Maguire and Harrocks

1995; Forrester *et al.* 1995). However, employees are likely to benefit more than others from some form of participation in decisions concerning HRD (Holton and Baldwin 2003). That is, it is likely to enhance self-esteem to participate in subsequent learning events. Garavan and Carbery (2003) found that confident learners (such as those who are better educated) are more likely to participate in training opportunities. This study found that particular barriers inhibited participation and involvement. These included poor self-confidence, lack of motivation, a perceived lack of management and peer support and work restrictions. Employee involvement and participation is therefore likely to form a continuum signifying different levels of employee involvement in HRD decision-making. At one end of the continuum the employee has no involvement and at the other end there is employee control of the HRD agenda. It is likely that the situation in a particular organization will fluctuate depending on the issues and the urgency of the decision. Marchington and Wilkinson (2002) have argued that employee involvement in HRD decision-making may be beneficial because it can help employees understand what the organization is trying to do and, in turn, have an impact on post-training performance. There is clear evidence that employee involvement in the HRD process is crucial to gaining commitment to learning and the development of skills (Garavan and Carbery 2003).

Support is an important concept in the context of HRD. Broad and Newstrom (1992) have argued that the majority of training investments do not produce full and sustained transfer of new knowledge. Brinkerhoff (1997) summarized studies, which demonstrated that as little as 8 to 12 per cent of what trainees learn is translated into improved job performance. Lack of support is manifest in a number of ways including hostile co-workers, resistant subordinates, uninterested supervisors and an inappropriate learning culture. Several commentators (Jones 1995; Bates 2003; Naquin and Baldwin 2003) argue that the employee's immediate supervisor is the most proximate in terms of influencing the learner's behaviour. Brinkerhoff (1997) highlights that the unsupportive supervisor ignores, dis-encourages skill use or punishes employees who are not going to use the skills they have learned. The unsupportive employee will continue to repeat old behaviours with the result that managers and employers will come to view training as a waste of time. Naquin and Baldwin (2003) emphasize the importance of management and the trainee's immediate supervisor in providing pre-programme support and thus facilitating post-programme transfer of learning. Cohen (1990) found that trainees who entered training expecting some kind of supervisory follow-up reported stronger intentions to transfer what was learned.

LINE MANAGERS

The emergent concept of strategic partner (Schuler 1992; Barney and Wright 1998) contends that HRD departments should help line managers resolve business issues and align HRD activities with the achievement of organizational goals. Strategically focused HRD functions rely on the commitment and involvement of line managers. Lee and Chee (1996) found that amongst the characteristics of organizations at the top end of the HRD maturity scale, HRD was perceived as supporting business strategy and HRD specialists and line managers worked in partnership with each other. Line managers are recognized as being in the best position 'to take an active role in developing people, whose performance they are expected to manage' (Garavan and Carberry 2003) and 'play a key role' in assisting the transfer of new skills (Donovan 2000). Hyman and Cunningham (1998) argued that line managers tend to be task oriented which diverts their attention away from HRD issues due predominately to production priorities.

Line managers are crucial stakeholders whose role in HRD is often under-developed for a variety of reasons including attitudinal, structural and cultural. The literature highlights a range of challenges inherent in line manager involvement in HRD. Maxwell and Watson (2004), for example, divide these into conceptual and practical challenges. Particular conceptual challenges highlighted include; line manager commitment to HRD, line manager understanding of HRD issues and trust between line managers and HRD professionals. An additional conceptual challenge focuses on the power and contradictions inherent in the role. Sloman (2003) acknowledges that many managers appear to be under-trained and often not motivated to develop employees. Renwick and MacNeil (2002) argued that line managers may not be sufficiently committed to properly carry out HRD activities. De Jong *et al.* (1999) likewise question the commitment of line managers to HRD. Thornhill and Saunders (1998) argued that the rejection by line managers of HRD responsibilities is likely to impact negatively on the status of the HRD function and the perception of HRD amongst employees.

The line manager role is a complicated one in terms of HRD responsibility because of the inherent power issues. The line manager role in the HRD literature tends to be described in a variable context and primarily determined by the level and degree of HRD responsibility that is devolved to them. Brewster and Larsen (2000) argue that the power relationship between line managers and top management is indicated by the degree to which line managers are delegated full responsibility for HRD and HRM activities. Yip *et al.* (2001) suggest that hierarchical rank may not be as significant for the line manager as their ability to integrate strategic and operational level information. They are in close proximity to daily operations, their team and customers. They have the opportunity to get a detailed knowledge of operational realities and this enables certain decisions to be made. The line manager is required to balance a range of structural and political interests without having sufficient power and authority to influence top management. They are required to balance their own interests with those of top management. This line or middle manager role is complex. Renwick (2003) points out that it consists of a balancing of political and workload pressures which often militate against being able to prioritize people management and HRD issues sufficiently.

A number of practical challenges are also present. Specific challenges include; line managers' abilities to carry out HRD activities; line manager training in HRD philosophy and values; and perceptions of organizational support for HRD. These are important elements of successful devolvement of HRD and participation in HRD decision-making. Numerous commentators have highlighted that a lack of training in HRD may reduce its priority for line managers (Brewster and Soderstrom 1994; de Jong *et al.* 1999). The perception that there is support for HRD at the level of the organization is important to line manager acceptance of HRD. Particular perceptions of support that are conducive to line managers thinking positively about HRD include the perception that senior managers and directors believe in HRD and that HRD is an investment rather than a cost.

TOP MANAGEMENT

There is support for the proposition that top management support and involvement in HRD is one of the key characteristics of a strategically aligned HRD function. This support is likely to advance the status of HRD and ensure that it makes a significant contribution to the organization's strategic plans (Brinkerhoff and Gill 1994). Fricker (1994) for example highlights that 'chairmen and chief executives need to recognize the value of learning as the primary force to facilitate and achieve change in their organization.' He also argues that senior executives have a key role in ensuring that line managers share their commitment to HRD. The top management's leadership role requires them to match their espoused support with consistent demonstrable commitment (Baldwin and Magjuka 1991). This may take a number of forms such as; making their commitment visible; ensuring that chief executives take an active role in the delivery of HRD and maintaining a strong financial commitment to HRD. Dyer and Holder (1988), in the context of HRD, pointed out that the 'most powerful of the counteracting forces probably is top management.' Many commentators have cited the importance of direct access to top management through a formal reporting relationship. Budhwar (2000) argues that without top management support, human resource activities will fail to be part of the early stage of the strategic decision-making process.

Top management support, participation and involvement is frequently missing (Carnevale 1990; Guest *et al.* 2001). There is likely to be espoused support but this is less frequently followed up by demonstrable actions (Holton and Baldwin 2003). Specific indicators of this lack of commitment include the way that the training and development function is expendable and that training and development budgets are among the first to be cut (Zimsky and Iannozzi 1996); the tendency to view the training component in isolation or as peripheral instead of being visible and central; the positioning of training and development in the organization chart and the relationship of HRD with the HRM function. Senior managers frequently espouse the view that training is a nice-to-have reward for well-behaved employees. Therefore, senior management may relegate it to a narrowly defined support role.

The level of top management support and involvement has important implications for the political role taken by the HRD specialist. Some commentators have argued that the uptake of HRD involves a battle with internal organizational power structures and the adoption of a more political approach on the part of HRD professionals.

Information

Information in the context of a strategically aligned HRD function refers to the extent to which it has systems and processes in place to identify and gain insight into the issues that have a HRD solution. The literature highlights that data from various organizational levels are needed to decide which HRD goals and objectives should be given priority in order to align HRD activities with other organizational goals.

The generation of this information may be secured through a number of processes including training audits (Clardy 2004), proactive and reactive training needs analyses and training evaluation processes. Gilley *et al.* (2002) point out that one of the best ways to develop a strategic partnership approach is to identify and audit HRD activities. They view the audit as a beneficial way of identifying the values and benefits of HRD interventions and to determine if HRD activities are of value to stakeholders in meeting their goals.

Training needs analyses are central to the effective generation of data and information. They have value in determining which problems can be solved through HRD. Several HRD theories highlight that the competencies that employees possess, need to be managed and controlled (Fomburn *et al.* 1984). It follows, therefore, that the development of employees should be consistent with the general requirements imposed by the organization. Huselid (1995) highlights that the effectiveness of the organization depends on the extent to which human resource strategies and business strategies fit together. Tannenbaum and Yukl (1992) argue that any strategic change in direction, adjustment of policy or procedures or change in structures and work systems must be assessed for its effects in terms of learning needs. It is also important that when selecting HRD strategies, conformity with company strategy and culture must be considered. The analysis of training and development needs helps to provide this necessary information. Rossett (1999) highlights that many HRD professionals fail to see needs analyses as an important activity. They are often likely to see it was a waste of time, energy and effort. Line managers and senior management often hold this view. Numerous commentators have highlighted the need to gain support for needs analyses (Rossett 1992; Rummler and Brache 1995). This is done to gain support through the identification of internal sponsors and advocates. HRD professionals need to acknowledge that information comes from a variety of sources including internal sources, such as top management, direct supervisors, employees, position description, and external sources such as other similar organizations.

Various commentators criticize the lack of meaningful evaluation of training activities (Warr *et al.* 1999; Blanchard *et al.* 2000; Brinkerhoff 2005). Kirkpatrick (1994) highlights that many HRD specialists will think about doing more but will not do so for several reasons; thorough evaluation is not considered important or urgent; they lack the skills to perform it and there is no pressure from senior management to perform it. Moller and Mallin (1996) found that lack of time is an important reason for not conducting evaluations. The lack of effective evaluation means that there is insufficient information to use for revising programmes and selling HRD to stakeholders.

Formalization (consultation and communication)

Consultation and communication are essential elements of strategically aligned HRD. These elements refer to the approach that HRD specialists use to interact with key stakeholders. Central to the development and implementation of a partnership model is the need to develop collaborative relationships. A number of commentators (Gilley and Eggland 1992; Block 1999) have highlighted that HRD professionals need to recognize that clients bring considerable experience and are a valuable resource to be acknowledged and tapped. This may be difficult for some HRD professionals to implement. This may arise due to power politics. Evidence suggests that knowledge is used at the individual level for both control and defence (Brown and Woodland 1999) and that if individuals perceive that power comes from the knowledge they possess, it is more likely they will be less consultative and hoard knowledge.

It is also likely that key internal stakeholders may resist consultation and joint ownership. Line managers may resist consultation initiatives and fail to see the benefits. There may be a perception that HRD professionals do not understand the real business of the organization and only serve to create a distraction rather than add value. It is also possible that the HRD professional may consider that line managers may not have the skills to provide valuable information and suggestions (Torrington and Hall 1998). Mulder (1992) has reported that using managers as trainers, for example, is not without problems. Thijssen (1997) also supported the criticism of the manager as trainer as they have little time for these activities, are not trained for the role and are not paid for the task.

Garavan and Carberry (2003) indicate that HRD professionals are more prone to utilizing a single sovereign model of operation rather than a more networked model. There is, however, evidence that the more effective practitioners are more likely to network and form alliances with key internal stakeholders (Tjepkema *et al.* 2000; Poell *et al.* 2003). Trust also appears to be an important issue (Gilley and Gilley Maycunich 2003). A lack of trust will likely inhibit consultation possibilities and prevent a successful relationship emerging.

Learning culture and climate

Organizational culture and climate influences the acceptability of HRD and its ultimate effectiveness (Bates *et al.* 1997). Olsen (1998), for example, highlights that the existence of a positive culture will positively impact the transfer of learning. Rao (1999) highlights that specific elements of a learning culture include a proactive orientation, trust, authenticity, openness, risk taking and self-awareness. Bates (2001) defines a continuous learning culture as a reflection of an organization's belief system that regards learning as a key responsibility of all employees. It also incorporates values, which support learning and its use. The general proposition holds that where positive values in respect of learning are widely shared throughout the organization they have the potential to influence participation in training and perceptions that HRD can add value. Gilley and Maycunich Gilley (2003) are strong advocates of a learning culture. They argue that such cultures are the result of a collaborative effort between all stakeholders in the organization. They identify a number of benefits that may be derived from having such a culture including greater employee commitment, high performance, enhanced organizational capability and developmental readiness.

HRD goals, objectives and strategies

The menu of HRD goals, objectives and strategies is considerable. HRD goals and objectives vary considerably in their reach and focus. Some interventions focus on skills, others on attitude change, some are directed towards individuals and others towards groups. The reasons for participating in HRD programmes will vary considerably. Wognum (1995) and Rossett (1987), for example, suggest five major reasons for HRD. The reasons can focus on the improvement of work performance, the improvement of certain work practices and change and renewal in the organization. Wognum and Mulder (1999) found that the main emphasis for HRD was for change and renewing purposes, while improvement-related programmes came a close second.

The literature on the strategic integration of HRD highlights that it is first of all necessary for the organization to recognize the need to strategically align HRD. This requires a number of specific organizational responses. These may take the form of HRD representation at senior levels in the organization, the formalization of HRD policies and selection of appropriate strategies, the development of systems for information collection and consultation with stakeholders. It will also involve an increase in line managers' HRD responsibilities and very clearly articulated HRD goals and objectives. These are important factors but of themselves insufficient. It also requires a commitment by the HRD professional to be strategic in outlook to understand the key business issues and values and to possess effective business acumen including, where possible, line management experience. In addition, top management commitment to HRD and the development of a culture and climate appropriate to HRD are also necessary.

Empirical context

Research site and participants

The context of the study of Dublin Dental School and Hospital (DDS&H) is described in Table 3.1. The participants in the study were employees of DDS&H. Each employee received a questionnaire and invitation to participate in an interview with a member of the research team.

A total of 114 questionnaires were returned and used for analyses. This represents a response rate to the questionnaires of 36.1 per cent. Over 37 per cent of the respondents were management level, representing senior management, consultants and academics (18.9 per cent) and line managers and team leaders (18.9 per cent). Over 62 per cent of the respondents were non-management. Non-management categories included technical, operational and nursing staff (41.4 per cent) and administrative staff (20.7 per cent).

Forty employees agreed to participate in an interview with one of the research team. Over 62 per cent of these interview respondents were non-management, consisting of technical, operational and nursing staff (47.5 per cent) and administrative staff (12.5 per cent). Over 37 per cent of the interview respondents were at management level; senior managers, consultants and academics (27.5 per cent) and line managers and team leaders (10 per cent).

Table 3.1 Context of study

The Dublin Dental School and Hospital is an organization that is associated with Trinity College Dublin and the Eastern Regional Health Authority. The main function of the school and hospital is to educate and train in all dental disciplines, to provide dental care to the public and to produce research in dentistry. The School and Hospital employs 315 people. Traditionally, DDS&H utilized an ad hoc, reactive training and development model. In the past year, action has been taken by the HR department to introduce a more proactive, learning-orientated and strategically integrated model. The current philosophy is aimed at creating ownership for training and development across the organization and empowering employees through such training and development.

Method

We used a questionnaire to gather employee perceptions of various aspects of the HRD function. The questionnaire included items developed by Holder Kunder (1998) to measure perceptions of strategic integration, effectiveness and value of the HRD function, and support and involvement of management for HRD. A factor analysis conducted on all the items revealed a different factor structure from those utilized by Holder Kunder (1998). The scales utilized in this study included the following:

- *Strategic Integration, Involvement and Support of Management.* This 12-item scale focused on how respondents perceived that the HRD system was strategically integrated, encouraged involvement and had support from management. The reliability coefficient alpha in this study was 0.95.
- *Effectiveness of Systems for Evaluation and Learning Transfer.* This seven-item scale measured respondents' perceptions of the effectiveness of evaluation and the learning transfer processes. The reliability coefficient alpha of this scale for this study was 0.91.
- *Perceived Value of the HRD Function.* This five-item scale measured respondents' perceptions of the value of the HRD system. The reliability coefficient alpha for this scale in this study was 0.89.
- We also asked respondents to indicate the extent of their participation in various types of training and development activities and their perceptions of the quality of these activities.

Semi-structured interviews were utilized to gather opinions concerning the quality of training, relevance to the job, opportunities for learning transfer and factors that facilitated and hindered learning transfer. We also asked questions on the involvement of line management, top management and employees in the training and development system. These interviews ranged in duration from 20 to 45 minutes. These interviews were recorded when permission was given, otherwise detailed notes were taken.

Fieldwork

The fieldwork was conducted over a one-month period. Before conducting the study, the HR manager informed all department managers about the study and requested that they both inform and encourage staff to participate. It was important to gain the commitment of managers to the study because the nature of the work of some staff in the organization required that they secured rostered time-off to participate in the interviews and complete the questionnaires. Following these communications, the HR manager then sent an email to all employees to inform and invite them to participate in the study. However, number of nursing staff did not have access to email. The HR staff collaborated with the library to organize computer access. A paper-based option was also available to employees if they preferred. The HR staff held a promotion day to encourage staff to come to the library and participate in the study. All participants who volunteered their names on the questionnaire were entered into a draw for a prize. The research team sent a total of three reminder emails to employees of DDS&H to encourage them to complete their questionnaires or to participate. An online questionnaire tool (www.surveymonkey.com) was utilized to administer the questionnaire and collect the data.

The study findings

Perceptions of strategic alignment, involvement and support of management

Table 3.2 presents a summary of perceptions of strategic alignment, involvement and support of management. Responses were given on five-point Likert scale, where 1 represented strong disagreement and 5 represented strong agreement. Respondents perceived that there was support from top management for HRD. The analysis does however reveal that while top management value and support HRD, the structures and processes currently in place do not reflect a strategically integrated HRD function. The perceptions of managers are similar to those for non-management. Managers do not perceive that current structures are appropriate or reflect a strategically integrated HRD system. Managers do however perceive that they should be involved in and support HRD processes and activities.

Examination of the qualitative data reveals a similar set of concerns and perceptions to those revealed by the quantitative data.

Perceptions of involvement and support

Respondents generally perceived that management were broadly supportive of their partaking in training and development activities.

> Management are very proactive and positive about training and development, particularly HR. There seems to be a very positive attitude to developing people in the organization over the last 2 years.
>
> (Administrator)

> [The manager] that I answer to is totally supportive and would be very proactive in encouraging myself and the girls.
>
> (Nurse)

> There is a good level of management 'buy-in' to training.
>
> (Manager)

Evidence of supportive management behaviour could be detected from how

Table 3.2 Perceptions of strategic alignment, involvement and support of management

Scale items	All levels (n = 114)		Management only (n = 33)		Non-management only (n = 43)	
	Mean	S.D.	Mean	S.D.	Mean	S.D.
Top managers see T&D as an important way of helping the department achieve its mission	3.87	1.019	4.00	1.104	3.78	0.960
Top managers show commitment to T&D by spending time promoting and delivering it	3.55	1.131	3.73	1.073	3.47	1.126
Top managers strongly support the development of new skills and knowledge among all levels of employees	3.81	1.179	4.02	1.093	3.72	1.183
Even during budget cuts your top managers do all they can to maintain T&D opportunities for their employees	3.67	1.120	3.88	1.131	3.52	0.097
The kinds of T&D activities that are encouraged relate to what top managers are trying to accomplish for your department	3.61	1.145	3.64	1.224	3.59	1.102
Top managers help their employees meet personal T&D goals and needs	3.36	1.128	3.64	1.100	3.18	1.117
Top managers are closely involved in determining the department's T&D goals and activities	3.48	1.115	3.67	1.162	3.36	1.074
The department provides a program of T&D activities that meet the needs of employees	3.24	1.156	3.49	1.121	3.09	1.160
Structured learning activities are built into the job so that employees are constantly learning	3.06	1.225	3.33	1.183	2.88	1.228
Department managers personally provide T&D for their employees	3.33	1.106	3.66	0.998	3.11	1.127
The department offers a broad selection of courses and other T&D activities	3.04	1.117	3.17	1.175	2.96	1.081
In general, the department supports me in my efforts to continuously improve my knowledge and skills	3.63	0.969	3.77	0.770	3.54	1.070
Overall scale	3.45	0.899	3.66	1.095	3.35	1.111

some managers organized or ran specific training initiatives as per the department needs, followed up with trainees' post training, made attempts to facilitate learning transfer, allocated time for training initiatives and adapted the training initiatives provided by HR to suit the department's needs.

> The team leader runs an induction programme and my manager runs relevant technical programmes for the team.
>
> (Technician)

> I allocate 1 hour a week to each team member for e-learning. Training is fantastic but I think everybody has to make it their own and that is where some departments are going wrong. They are getting feedback and instructions from HR but I think you have to take ownership of it in your own department and adapt it to suit your department.
>
> (Manager)

> I did the PDP[1] course . . . and there is a follow-up with the lab manager in the next 2 weeks.
>
> (Team Leader)

> I ran my own mini team exercise in my department for an hour.
>
> (Manager)

Evidence of lack of support

Respondents' accounts also revealed some variation in the *degree* of support provided by management. There was evidence that some managers, while verbally supportive were less *actively* supportive. These accounts illustrate how respondents were able to differentiate the existence of support and the degree of support. For example some managers were reported as being supportive but did not get involved, did not initiate the drive for training and development, did not focus on the training needs of the individual and were supportive only as a matter of process.

> [Some levels of management] are cooperative but won't get involved.
>
> (Officer)

> My boss is very easy going. If you make suggestions [for training] to him, he doesn't knock them on the head. You may have to tell him twice about it and he will say no problem.
>
> (Officer)

> I will get a lot of support from my manager but I will have to drive it. I need support to come from the top down in case I don't see some areas [for development].
>
> (Manager)

Probably, he [manager] had a laugh and said 'you know you better do the PDP training.

(Officer)

There were specific examples of this lack of management support and involvement. For example respondents mentioned lack of follow up and assistance in transferring learning.

My manager has never said 'I will do your PDP with you.' We had a team meeting once and mentioned PDP and I felt that the consultant hadn't bought into it.

(Manager)

[If there was] follow up. If we did sit down or someone made us . . . and discuss your ideas and come up with solutions . . . they would feel more connected, feel not as isolated.
  (Officer on motivating those near retirement to get more involved in training initiatives)

I was having my PDP with my manager and she was taking all the notes and she was supposed to send me all the notes. After three weeks I am still waiting for my SMART goals . . . I am very unhappy about the meeting . . . I had the feeling she wasn't following through on what she was saying.

(Officer)

We also found strong evidence to indicate that although management were involved and supported training and development activities, they were sometimes ineffective in doing so. For example, respondents' accounts illustrated evidence of ineffective selection for training.

They [managers] need to focus on the person and the job they are doing rather than throw them out [throw employees onto programmes]. It should be discussed more, a more collaborative decision regarding what I do and don't attend.

(Officer)

My manager picks which ones I should go on when she could be missing out on ones I think I need myself, I should be able to choose courses.

(Officer)

I can't follow through on some of the courses because of my job [courses not applicable to job].

(Officer)

I attended [the course] because I was told to by my manager.

(Technician −2 and Officer −2)

Respondents' accounts also highlighted that ineffective selection for training could also be attributed to the system used by HR to get employees to attend training.

I have seen on a quarterly basis the list of training courses they ran by email. One of the concerns I have is that sometimes once the email goes out, there seems to be a rush to fill places and you are told we [HR][2] want 2 people from your team . . . when I started this role I put people on a course that looking back now wasn't the right thing to do . . . after the person attended the course we found out that she should have attended another course first.

(Manager)

It should be made clear [which programmes trainees need to do first]. They [HR] should have a sequence or plan in place and let us know.

(Manager)

These findings help explain the low mean rating reported for the items assessing the selection of courses offered by the respondents' departments. That is, trainees may perceive that there is a poor selection of training offered by the department partly because they are attending training initiatives that do not meet their needs.

Perceptions of support for different organizational levels

Interestingly, a number of accounts suggested that there were differing perceptions regarding what levels or type of staff the training focused on and consequently who was supported. For example, respondents did not regard temporary staff as needing training, some respondents emphasized the need to focus the training more towards the production laboratories and the nurses, some considered training to be available to all and some considered the training to be more focused towards younger people and administrative and secretarial staff.

I have not implemented the skills [from the PDP training for managers] yet as I have not had the opportunity. Some staff on maternity leave and others are temporary. I don't see the need to implement here [with temporary staff].

(Manager)

DDSH continuously invest in their people, particularly their young people.

(Administrator)

Training was always there for consultants and clinical staff but now its for all.

(Officer)

The organization is very committed to training and development particularly for the administrative and secretarial staff.

(Consultant)

The teaching labs get financial support for whatever they want and that is discrimination for us at the production lab as there is never enough funding going to us. They believe we will learn as we go. (Technician)

The nursing group needs more support and encouragement.

(Consultant)

Possible explanations for perceived levels of support

A number of respondent accounts illuminated a number of possible explanations for the current perceived level of management support and involvement. The reasons cited, which may help explain perceptions of lesser levels of support, included scheduling difficulties due to the nature of work in the hospital, concerns regarding losing the value of training when employees leave the organization, lack of time, union issues, management feeling threatened and difficulties in finding ways to continuously develop their staff.

She [manager] would be quite interested in having us all trained but it doesn't work that way. We would be the busiest part of the hospital so if one of us is missing, the others have to carry the extra weight, and so she can't say that every Wednesday you can go on a course.

(Officer)

I lost a good secretary because she was not supported to undertake a degree course. She left the organization and is now doing it at night. At the same time another person had been funded to do a computer course and then left the organization.

(Consultant)

With team building it was suggested we send all our team. But who was going to run the department? It's not feasible.

(Manager)

My manager hasn't carried out a PDP with me as union issues need to be resolved before this can happen.

(Nurse)

The other reasons cited which may help explain the existence of support from some managers included the PDP initiative.

> Managers are very supportive and very anxious that we do it [training]. It's the Personal Development Planning thing.
>
> (Officer)

Provision for on-the-job learning and pre-programme support

We did not find qualitative evidence to explain the low mean rating allocated to the provision for structured learning activities built into the job. A large number of respondents, however, reported that they commenced their role without any training. If they required any help, training in the form of 'sitting-by-nellie' was provided.

> When I came in I was trained in my job by the person who was leaving but only for 3 days before she left, but I needed 3 weeks. When I started I was given a tour of the building ... there are 3 departments here and I am still blurry on what they do and I work with them. Somebody coming in not knowing dental terminology, they should be informed.
>
> (Officer)

One administrator commented on the on-the-job training provided at DDS&H. However she seemed unsure as to what the definition of on-the-job training was; she incorporated induction programmes and manuals in her definition.

> DDS&H has an educational and development ethos and uses this in respect to on-the-job training in that induction programmes and manuals are in existence for clerical and clinical staff in my area. We are strong on coaching and one-to-one development.

It is therefore important to add that the incidences of on-the-job training are, by their very nature, inherently difficult to measure and even more so in an organization where the concepts of training, development and learning are still being introduced.

In relation to selection for training and pre-programme support, analysis of the interviews reveals that the majority of respondents were selected to attend training programmes based on management or HR selection without consulting the respondent or self-selection by respondents on the basis that they felt that the training could help them with their job. A number of respondents indicated that the extent to which they were involved in the decisions regarding attending programmes improved post PDP programme; that is, a respondent's selection for training was based on a developmental discussion with their managers. Thus, little or no evidence of pre-programme support was found. Two respondents suggested such support as a recommendation for improving the current system.

> Staff need to be consulted about their needs, the objectives and benefits should be outlined.
>
> (Manager)

> We should be given a bit more notice and information about the content and the source of the training programmes.
>
> (Administrator)

An additional issue worth noting is that the majority of respondents stated that their manager was their key point of contact and source of information on all matters related to training and development. This illuminates the need to focus on the extent of management involvement and support in both operational and strategic training and development activities.

Perceptions of strategic integration

There was some evidence to indicate that management recognized the need to have a strategically integrated training and development system based on organizational and departmental objectives and training needs.

> Training and development is vital for the organization's success.
>
> (Team Leader)

> Training and development needs to be set into context and signposted at every stage.
>
> (Manager)

> Staff need to be consulted about their needs.
>
> (Manager)

> Any training and development needs to constantly focus on organizational objectives.
>
> (Consultant)

Information on the effectiveness of systems for evaluation and learning transfer

Table 3.3 provides a summary of respondent perceptions in respect of the gathering of information on training and development. The item with the highest mean was concerned with level one evaluation; employees' satisfaction with training and development activities. Conversely, the lowest means were recorded for items focused on measuring the degree to which DDS&H

Table 3.3 Perceptions of the effectiveness of systems for evaluation and learning transfer

Scale items	All levels (n = 114)		Management only (n = 33)		Non-management only (n = 41)	
	Mean	S.D.	Mean	S.D.	Mean	S.D.
Employees are held accountable for using what they've learned in their T&D activities back on the job	3.32	1.056	3.11	1.051	3.45	1.048
Managers are held accountable for following up and encouraging their employees to apply what they've learned through training back on the job	3.28	1.161	3.29	1.315	3.27	1.060
After employees receive T&D, they are asked to provide feedback on their satisfaction with the course	3.57	1.009	3.57	1.092	3.56	0.964
After employees receive T&D they are asked to provide feedback on how much they have learned	3.20	1.013	3.12	1.122	3.25	0.950
After employees receive T&D they are asked to provide feedback on what material they put into practice in their job	3.11	0.994	2.94	1.179	3.22	0.854
Employees are asked to provide feedback on the effectiveness of the T&D, which their managers received	2.94	1.095	2.97	1.185	2.92	1.045
Managers are asked to provide feedback on the effectiveness of the T&D, which their employees received	3.03	1.143	3.09	1.269	2.98	1.037
Overall scale	3.18	0.882	3.15	1.173	3.23	0.994

has evaluation systems in place aimed at recording other people's perceptions of a trainee's change in performance post-training. The qualitative comments are illuminative in terms of understanding these ratings.

Facilitators and evidence of learning transfer

The facilitators cited included follow-up discussions with the manager, provision for role plays and feedback during the programme, assistance provided by manager to put learning into action, follow-up action plans, manager-requested feedback on what took place in the course and how it could be used in the job and manager-adapted training programmes to suit the specific department. Of those respondents who had positive perceptions of the structures in place for learning transfer, it is interesting to note that in one department both the manager's perceptions and her subordinates' perceptions of the structures to encourage learning transfer were positive. These particular respondents' accounts are reported here along with some specific examples of incidences of learning transfer.

> Training is fantastic but I think that everybody has to make it their own ... You have to take ownership of your department and adapt it [training and development activities provided by the HR department] to suit your department. It's worked in my department and I've gotten brilliant results from it.
>
> (Manager)

> At the Tuesday morning meetings we are asked to give feedback on courses and we write up a report so others can read on what we've done.
>
> (Nurse)

> Employee X would always have been very volatile as in very unhelpful and saying [to a customer] she maybe wouldn't have such a thing [that customer requested]. But now [post training on customer care] she is saying well hang on now, we don't have any at the moment but I will go down to stores and see what happened and what the problem is and I will get back to you. They [the customer] go away a little happier.
>
> (Manager)

A number of other respondents provided examples of specific incidences where they, their subordinates or their managers used their learning from a course on the job, thus providing evidence of learning transfer.

> They [managers] went through the PDP training. It's better now than the 8 month review we did when I was working as an officer.
>
> (Senior Nurse)

Now [post training on team building] I will cover other areas ... Say I was finished my work I would go over and help them [others in team], even though it has nothing to do with what I am doing but I can slot into any place ... before the course I might be saying I couldn't cover such an area. The course helped me [on] how to deal with it better. It changed my attitude.

(Officer on team building course)

Interestingly, a large number of the accounts suggest that the extent of management involvement and support is the distinguishing factor between those respondents who had positive perceptions of the effectiveness of current learning transfer and those who had less positive perceptions. Thus, it would appear that trainees rely strongly on their managers to help them transfer their learning.

Barriers to learning transfer

Specific barriers to learning transfer cited included lack of time to implement learning, difficulties putting theory in to practice, lack of follow up from the manager, lack of follow up on training by trainers, lack of scope in job to use knowledge and skills, lack of management willingness to change practices, training programme not specifically designed for DDS&H context and difficulty introducing concepts still unfamiliar to other staff.

I didn't get a chance to implement the problem solving course [material].

(Technician)

About three months ago I attended a programme on feedback and mentorship for students but there has been no follow through on this.

(Consultant)

The training was fine apart from the problem of too much theory and it is difficult to put into practice. The problem is getting follow through from this.

(Administrator)

A lot of it is organizational behaviour based. The theory and examples are based on the more private industry and not within the remit of the public sector because we are very different. I felt that in training it was hard to bring it back to your domain.

(Manager)

I'm facing a wall. I don't deal with the public anymore ... I can't put the things [from the customer care programme] into practice like if I was at the front desk.

(Officer)

Systems for evaluation of training and development

Despite the fact that the item on level one evaluation received the highest mean rating of all items in this particular scale, it was still only 'average.' Two possible reasons may help explain this rating. The first is the fact that level one evaluation is a relatively new introduction in DDS&H and so a number of respondents may base their ratings on training and development activities conducted prior to the introduction of the level one evaluation system. Second, a respondent's comment indicated what he considered to be a fault in the feedback system used.

> I suppose a feedback system [for giving opinions on the training etc]. They already have that but they ask questions they want to hear rather than leaving a blank space to fill in e.g. what do you think of the trainer?
>
> (Assistant)

One respondent's comment alluded to the fact that her manager conducted a somewhat basic level two and three evaluation. However, there was no evidence to indicate that any formal systems for levels two to five evaluation exist in DDS&H. The lowest means were recorded for items focused on measuring the degree to which DDS&H has evaluation systems in place aimed at recording other people's perceptions of a trainee's change in performance post-training. Although there were no formal systems in place at DDS&H for this form of evaluation, the interviews revealed a few incidences where staff and management were observing others' performance post-training. This suggested a foundation for the development of more formal systems.

> I feel my staff work more efficiently as a team now [post team building programme].
>
> (Manager)

> Employee X . . . [post training on customer care] . . . is troubleshooting a lot more now.
>
> (Manager)

Table 3.4 Number of training activities undertaken and perceptions of quality of training undertaken

Type of training	Participation in		Quality of	
	Mean	S.D.	Mean	S.D.
Voluntary	1.96	1.629	3.61	0.997
Mandatory	2.04	1.734	3.36	0.903
On-the-Job	1.87	2.024	3.50	0.990

> Every time I've been on a course, [my manager] asks me, what was covered and how can you use what you learnt in your job. She has been very supportive.
>
> (Nurse)

Management also recognized the lack of and consequent need for other levels of evaluation.

> In relation to the benefit/value of training, it is currently very difficult to assess. It needs to be benchmarked so that the organization can gauge the return financially and on other levels, e.g. level of staff motivation, decreased absenteeism etc.
>
> (Manager)

> They need to look into [further] evaluation of training.
>
> (Manager)

> Value for money is crucial . . . Transparency should provide information on 'here's who applied for training and here's how the money was spent.'

Participation in learning and quality of learning

Respondents were asked to indicate how many voluntary, mandatory and on-the-job training activities they had undertaken in the past year. Table 3.4 shows the mean participation rates in each category of training. Although the participation rates appear low, they compare favourably with the participation rates reported in a benchmark study of training and development in Ireland (Garavan and Carbery 2003). The benchmark study reported participation rates to be 1.42 and 1.92 in voluntary and mandatory training activities respectively. A participation rate of 2.01 was reported in the benchmark study for on-the-job training, which is higher than that reported for DDS&H.

We also assessed the quality of training and development at DDS&H at three levels; voluntarily attended training, mandatory training and on-the-job training. It is pertinent to look at the quality ratings of programmes undertaken as these perceptions may influence perceptions of overall value. Table 3.4 displays the quality ratings for each of the three categories of training and development. All of the quality ratings are above the mid-point of the quality scale and again compared favourably with the benchmark study (Garavan and Carbery 2003). The benchmark study reported quality ratings of 3.15, 3.16 and 3.14 for voluntary, mandatory and on-the-job training activities respectively.

Respondents were asked to comment on specific learning interventions they had undertaken and how valuable they found them. These accounts provide insights into how they attributed their quality ratings and their perceptions of the value of these programmes.

The positive accounts indicate that respondents considered the training they had undertaken to be valuable, worthwhile and of benefit to both the organization and their job performance. They cited that training was valuable in terms of motivating staff and improving employee performance, ability, knowledge and confidence to do their jobs and work on their own initiative.

> I did the PDP training . . . I found it very good and it's an excellent way of motivating new staff and motivating older members of the team.
>
> (Manager)

> It was good. It gave me more confidence to deal with students and dentists.
>
> (Nurse)

> A lot of stuff I knew but it was good to have it reinforced.
>
> (Officer)

> It was very useful and practical. It helps me to analyze problems better and explore options and solutions rather than being overwhelmed by the problem.
>
> (Nurse)

> I'm able to deal with customers and problems more myself now rather than phoning someone for help.
>
> (Officer)

One respondent emphasized on-the-job training as more beneficial than formal training.

> I enjoyed the training courses . . . I don't think it [training function and training programmes] do a great deal. I think it comes from hands-on experience. It's [training] a reminder of what I am doing and helps me broaden my horizons.
>
> (Officer)

Conversely, another respondent suggested that the current systems in place for on-the-job training needed to be improved.

> It [introduction to DDS&H] needs a structure. When I came in I was trained in my job by the person who was leaving but only for 3 days before she left, but I needed 3 weeks.
>
> (Officer)

The lack of perceived relevance of training activities was an important issue in terms of how respondents perceived the quality of training.

Table 3.5 Perceptions of value of HRD

Scale items	All levels (n = 114)		Management only (n = 33)		Non-management only (n = 52)	
	Mean	S.D.	Mean	S.D.	Mean	S.D.
T&D activities provide learning that is practical for use on the job	3.79	0.846	3.56	0.998	3.95	0.699
T&D gives employees an opportunity to learn the skills and behaviours that will help them to get rewarded and promoted	3.52	1.017	3.36	1.099	3.61	0.959
The T&D activities supported by the department are worth the time and money spent on them	3.78	0.929	3.83	0.985	3.75	0.899
The T&D activities supported by the organization are worth the time and money spent on them	3.70	0.937	3.76	0.969	3.67	0.924
The time I spend on T&D is time well spent	4.03	0.785	4.00	0.939	4.05	0.678
Overall scale	3.76	0.748	3.70	0.998	3.81	0.832

It [customer service training] wasn't related to the hospital. Didn't take anything from it.

(Manager)

That was grand enough. . . . I'd say it was more relevant to a hospital than a dental hospital for some reason.

(Officer)

Training initiatives received positive appraisals where they: were perceived to be relevant to trainees needs, utilized relevant examples, were relevant and useful to the role of the trainee, utilized appropriate learning strategies and methods, facilitated learning transfer and utilized a good trainer.

There was a role play, dealing with a difficult situation and then we got feedback on how well we did and didn't do . . .

(Senior Nurse)

It [team building programme] was a reminder to be there for other people. . . . I found the trainer very good.

(Officer)

It [problem solving course] was very useful and practical. It helps me analyse problems better . . .

(Nurse)

Value of HRD to the organization

The average perceived value of the training and development system was 3.76. The highest mean item rating was attributed to the item on 'the time and money spent on training and development is well spent' and the lowest mean item rating was that on training and development enables employees to develop skills and knowledge that will help them to get rewarded and promoted. Table 3.5 presents the results on perceptions of value.

Management perceptions of the value of HRD

With respect to perceptions of how valuable management considered training and development, we found that the perceptions were positive. Management recognized how training and development benefits the organization and recognized the value of training and development to the organization and their respective departments.

They [management] know that training and development is vital to holding onto people.

(Administrator)

The PDP training will pay off in the long run because of the positive motivational spin offs.

(Team Leader)

The organization gets a good return on its investment in training. There is a direct return when people are still with us because they are more effective in their jobs. In addition those who left the organization were also useful in that they provide a secondary return by providing contacts and we can call in a favour from them.

(Consultant)

Non-management perceptions of value

A number of non-management respondents emphasized the generic value of training and development. Those cited included organization success and development, better customer service and staff that work harder and progress quicker.

Training is very important because my last job was dead end and offered no hope for advancement. If people feel that the organization is interested in its workers then people will work harder and progress more.

(Technician)

It's well worth the investment because you need to invest in your people to develop the organization.

(Administrator)

Very [important]. If your staff are well trained you are getting a better service.

(Nurse)

Other non-management respondents commented on the value of training and development for DDS&H and its employees specifically. These accounts also highlighted that training provided in DDS&H was perceived to be valuable for organization success, achieving objectives, employee performance and improving employee retention.

Training and development is integral to helping me to achieve my objectives.

(Administrator)

While none of the respondents suggested that training was of no value, some of the accounts helped explain why a number of respondents regarded some training to be less valuable. For example, certain types of training were perceived to be less valuable than others. These included training on 'people skills' and training without certification from a recognized institute.

I think others in my area feel like, sure, we know these people skills already, we would be a little cynical.

(Officer)

I think a lot of that [people management] comes naturally. Yes it would be nice to get some training in them [staff management, interpersonal skills, organizational skills] but I wouldn't jump on it and go seeking them.

(Officer)

I'm a firm believer that training without certification is useless because I can have 60 students in for a lecture and I can give them their training, they can sit down the back and be asleep all day and they've still done it whereas if they have to study for a semester and get certified then they actually learn . . . I also know a course given . . . where they made their own certificates to give people and that's no good either, it has to go through the rules [professional body].

(Technician)

Possible explanations for perceptions of value

Accounts given in relation to specific courses respondents had undertaken at DDS&H provided further insights. Ineffective selection for training resulted in the programmes undertaken being perceived as less valuable. Also, lack of follow-up by managers or HR resulted in training being perceived as a waste of time. Lack of information, training not specifically designed for DDS&H, and lack of evaluation were also highlighted as concerns, which may lead to training and development at DDS&H being perceived as less valuable.

I've done customer care training twice or three times, don't need to do it again.

(Officer)

HR [told me to go on the training], which is again linked back . . . and get nothing out of it [the training]. If you are going on a course you are going to want to go on it and want to get something out of it, which is why these courses didn't work . . . well for me anyway.

(Technician)

I haven't been appraised since . . . yes [as it wasn't followed up it was a waste of time].

(Officer)

Other possible influences on perceptions of value include unmet expectations, lack of understanding of course objectives, lack of integration of training with organizational objectives and individual needs and perceptions that the focus of training is on the wrong disciplines.

> I would expect them [trainers] to give you a basic level training to get you into the job and then ... they can build on that to a different level ... so you can do basic management and then advanced management. This is what I thought would happen.
>
> (Assistant)

> Any training and development needs to constantly focus on organizational objectives.
>
> (Consultant)

> Staff need to be consulted about their needs.
>
> (Manager)

> There is currently inadequate training provided for dental nurses.
>
> (Consultant)

> They need to open it up ... some of them [training] is more geared to certain disciplines in the hospital.
>
> (Manager)

> It [PDP training] was grand. I don't see the benefits ... it seemed to be more of a confidence building thing.
>
> (Assistant)

Furthermore, not all respondents believed that so much time and money should be spent on training and development. Interestingly, while one consultant believed that training could help focus staff towards the care of patients, another respondent implied that expenditure on training and development could be spent elsewhere.

> You could say that this is a teaching hospital and a lot of resources are diverted towards these sorts of training programmes when surely the primary aim is to provide a good dental service as is possible.
>
> (Officer)

Two further accounts worth noting, which may explain why training may be perceived to be less valuable is in relation to the age of the employee and whether the training is delivered by an internal or external trainer.

> At 53 [years old], I am not terribly ambitious to take on a course and go out 2/3 nights as week for a year.
>
> (Officer)

The perception of the girls here was if there was an internal course they might know the person and say how can s/he be qualified to teach us something. There was an initial reluctance to internal training. This will eventually be glossed over. An external provider would get a plus from me.

(Administrator)

However, positive perceptions of the value of training and development emerged when a number of respondents volunteered specific examples of how they perceived training and development could be utilized to solve particular organizational and departmental problems.

The central focus needs to be on patients and the central ethos of the organization needs to be refocused on this. Top down change is needed and training and development can then help to cement this change.

(Consultant)

There is a need for team building between the two areas [X and Y areas of a department] as there is friction between certain personnel in these areas.

(Technician)

Value of training and development for reward and promotion

The lowest mean item rating was attributed to that on 'training and development enables employees to develop skills and knowledge that will help them to get rewarded and promoted.' The nature of the organization and the possibilities for promotion may partly explain the reason for this low rating; at least with respect to the promotion.

The roles are very defined and there isn't scope for promotion. Unless the departments expand which isn't going to happen with budgets in the health sector or unless me or two other team leaders leave . . . no one has guided us as to what is going to happen [in terms of how to develop her staff when faced with this problem].

(Manager)

Discussion and conclusions

This chapter highlights how various stakeholders – employees, line managers and senior management – within a health service organization perceived the philosophy, structure and operation of the HRD function. We specifically investigated strategic integration of the HRD function, participation, support and involvement of management and perceptions of value, effectiveness and quality and extent of participation in training activities.

We focused, in particular, on key literatures, which emphasized possible characteristics of HRD. The chapter is essentially based on the idea that while specific elements of context will influence the development of HRD in an organization, there exist a number of well-established principles or guidelines in the literature, which highlight particular features of a strategic HRD model.

The analyses overall reveals that organizational structural relationships supported HRD integration. Specific dimensions highlighted in this chapter indicate that there was a perception of strong commitment to HRD within the organization. Management espoused support for HRD and there appeared to be a corporate cultural commitment to HRD. However, it would seem, in many cases, that this support and commitment does not extend beyond; acting as a point of contact for information on training initiatives; authorizing attendance; and providing passive support. It was highlighted that while this was important and valued, it was not sufficient. The findings indicate that there are inconsistent perceptions regarding systems in place for learning transfer. However, the extent of management involvement and support distinguished between those who perceived the systems positively and those with negative perceptions. The analyses revealed that respondents both recognized and valued the systems in place for conducting level one evaluation and also recognized the need for systems to be developed to enable other levels of evaluations. The overall perception is that HRD is of value. However, a number of factors were identified related to the strategic integration, the systems and processes in place for pre-programme support, training needs analysis, programme design and post-programme support, which may diminish this positive perception.

The importance of senior and line management commitment is of considerable significance. The analyses indicated variation in perceptions between managers and non-managers in terms of what constitutes support. The qualitative analyses does suggest that where the respondents had positive perceptions concerning the levels of support, involvement and commitment of key organizational members, they were more likely to give more favourable evaluations of the effectiveness of training and development. If organizations are to achieve an effective strategic alignment of training and development then it is important that managers have positive attitudes towards HRD. As part of the decentralization of HRD, line managers are increasingly required to fulfil HRD activities. They must believe in the value of this type of activity, otherwise they are unlikely to perform these HRD activities. The analyses reveal that ambiguities exist regarding the role of line managers in involving and supporting employees in respect of HRD. Line managers appear not to be perceived as a barrier per se, however there is evidence that line managers may not act as proactive agents providing HRD. It is not sufficient alone to espouse policies that focus on the inclusion of line managers in the training and development process. They are not a guarantee that managers will follow up their words with actions.

The transition from a traditional training and development function with a strong focus on operational and tactical concerns to a more strategically integrated HRD function occurs at a number of different levels. At one level it is possible to talk about more superficial changes, which are more likely to involve the positioning of HRD within the overall managerial hierarchy and the nature of reporting relationships. These types of changes are of themselves insufficient. A more fundamental shift is required in the form of the core beliefs and values of managers and employees and particularly the actions of employees and managers in respect of training and development pre and post training. These latter elements usually prove more difficult to measure and understand. The decision to have a more strategically integrated HRD function will usually require that the organization make a number of superficial changes such as giving the HRD specialist an appropriate reporting arrangement. This alone, however, is inadequate. The HRD specialist must be committed to understanding the business, s/he must have a strong relationship with line managers. It is generally desired that the HRD professional has some experience as a line manager and a broad base of business knowledge.

The change process that has occurred within the study organization is still at a relatively early stage. It is important to emphasize that this transition process will continue to be emergent. It must be incremental given the complexity of the change that is desired, and the context within which the change is taking place. It takes time for key stakeholders to adapt to a new HRD philosophy and new HRD policies, structures, relationships and expectations. It is likely that the initial vision of a new approach to HRD may not actually emerge as anticipated and other unanticipated practices may develop. It is also likely that the reshaping of the HRD function in this organization was as much driven by pragmatism instead of a strong desire by the organization's leaders to bring about a new vision of HRD.

The study methods provided us with a detailed and rich understanding of the operation of the HRD function within a health sector organization. This methodology had a number of important advantages within the area of HRD. A mixed approach using quantitative and qualitative methods provides an important, intense understanding of key issues. The use of semi-structured interviews with key stakeholders allowed the researcher to explore the full range of factors that were relevant. The use of a cross-section of respondents allowed the researchers to gain insights into individuals who view HRD from inside as well as outside the HRD function. Interviews that are restricted to the HRD profession may produce a perspective on the value-based view of the contribution of HRD to the role of the HRD practitioner. The sample selected for interview provided a suitable cross-check of perceptions at various levels and a rich source of information. We assessed the value of HRD through the perceptions of the key stakeholders. This represents a different perspective on the value of training and development from that used by HRD practitioners. They typically refer to value in terms of the benefits that accrue to the organization. These benefits are typically measured through return on investment techniques. Respondents in this study measured the value of HRD in terms of whether they considered it time and money well spent and whether the learning was of value to their job and career.

A number of important findings concerning the management of HRD and the delivery of training and development activities are highlighted. The existence of a clearly formulated and well-articulated HRD strategy and policy will influence employees' and managers' perceptions and attitudes towards HRD. The existence of a well-articulated HRD strategy is in itself insufficient. These elements can be regarded as statements of intent. What employees look for is evidence of action. Lots of inconsistencies in perception concerning various aspects of HRD were highlighted. The way in which management communicate and practice HRD values and practices will have an important impact on the extent of diffusion of training and development practices. Managers need to pay close attention to the environment in which a particular training or learning intervention occurs. Various aspects of the workplace need to be given special consideration. These include providing learners with the necessary time, money, equipment, facilities and opportunities for the training. Deliberate steps should be taken to ensure that employees believe the resources provided are sufficient. Employees are less likely to value training and development where they perceive that insufficient resources are available. Employees must perceive that the training and development has value. These rewards may be intrinsic or extrinsic in nature.

A number of key learning points emerge from our discussions in this chapter.

- The term *strategic human resource development* is used broadly to signal the view that HRD activities should contribute to business effectiveness.
- HRD should be integrated both horizontally and vertically. HRD activities should be consistent with desired behaviours and competencies and these in turn should be consistent with the particular organizational context.
- The transition to a strategic human resource development model is incremental in nature. It requires a consistent and sustained effort.
- The strategic HRD model challenges the HRD professional. It requires a shift in perspective from being a provider of training and development to a partnership scenario where HRD professionals work cooperatively with key decision makers and with employees.
- Context plays a vital role in determining the effectiveness of strategic HRD. A variety of environmental conditions influence the approaches organizations use to develop their human resources. These aspects include features of the organization itself such as culture, work characteristics and characteristics of the workforce. It also includes consideration of external environmental conditions.

Notes

1 PDP is the Personal Development Planning programme. This programme is aimed at encouraging collaboration between employees and their managers for the purposes of identifying training needs. It aims to educate both parties on how to identify developmental needs, which benefit the employee and his/her job performance.

2 The HR manager stated that phase one of the plan for improving the training and development system in DDS&H was to offer a selection of training programmes which had been identified through a training needs analysis as required by the organization. Managers could then decide how many and what members of their staff to send on the programmes. As there was no culture of training and development in DDS&H, she found it difficult to get staff and managers to partake in training. To this end, she sometimes made it compulsory to send a specific number of staff. She hoped this would begin the introduction of a culture of training and development. One respondent did identify that her change in attitude towards training was due to being required to participate in the PDP training programme.

Personally for me yes [PDP training changed my attitude towards training]. Before that I didn't think about it much. (Administrator)

References

Baldwin, T.T. and Magjuka, R.J. (1991) 'Organizational training and signals of importance. Linking pre-training perceptions to intentions to transfer,' *Human Resource Development Quarterly* 2: 25–36.

Barney, J.B. (1991) 'Firm resources and sustained competitive advantage,' *Journal of Management* 17(1): 99–120.

Barney, J.B. and Wright, P.M. (1968) 'On becoming a strategic partner: the role of human resources in gaining competitive advantage,' *Human Resource Management* 37(1): 31–46.

Bates, R.A. (2001) 'Public sector training participation: an empirical investigation,' *International Journal of Training and Development* 5(2): 136–152.

Bates, R.A. (2003) 'Managers as transfer agents,' in E.F. Holton, III and T.T. Baldwin (eds) *Improving Learning Transfer in Organizations*, San Francisco, USA: Jossey-Bass, pp. 243–270.

Bates, R.A., Holton, E.F. III and Seyler, D.L. (1997) *Factors Affecting Transfer of HRD in an Industrial Setting.* Paper presented at the Academy of Human Resource Development Conference, Baton Rouge.

Blanchard, P.N. and Thacker, J.W. (2004) *Effective Training: Systems, Strategies and Practices*, 2nd edn, New Jersey, US: Prentice Hall.

Blanchard, P.N., Thacker, J.W. and Way, S.A. (2000) 'Training evaluation: perspectives and evidence from Canada,' *International Journal of Training and Development* 4(4): 295–304.

Block, P. (1999) *Flawless Consulting: A Guide to Getting Your Experience Used*, 2nd edn, San Diego: Pfeffer.

Blyton, P. and Turnbull, P. (1968) *The Dynamics of Employee Relations*, UK: Macmillan Press.

Brewster, C. and Soderstrom, M. (1994) 'Human resources and line management,' in A. Hegewisch (ed.) *Policy and Practice in European Human Resource Management: The Price Waterhouse Cranfield Study*, London: Routledge, pp. 50–67.

Brewster, C. and Larsen, H.H. (2000) 'Human resource management in Europe: evidence from ten countries,' *International Journal of HRM* 3(3): 409–433.

Brinkerhoff, O. (2005) 'The success case method: a strategic evaluation approach to increasing the value and effect of training,' *Advances in Developing Human Resources* 71(Feb): 86–101.

Brinkerhoff, R. (1997) 'Are you expecting enough from training?' http://self-management.com.

Brinkerhoff, R.O. and Gill, S.J. (1994) *The Learning Alliance*, San Francisco: Jossey-Bass.

Broad, M.L. and Newstrom, J.W. (1992) *Transfer of Training: Action Packed Strategies to Ensure Payoff from Training Investments*, Reading, MA: Addison-Wesley.

Brown, R.B. and Woodland, M.J. (1999) 'Managing knowledge wisely: a case study in organisational behaviour,' *Journal of Applied Management Studies* 8(2): 175–198.

Budhwar, P.S. (2000) Evaluating levels of strategic integration and devolvement of human resource management in the UK, *Personnel Review* 29(2): 141–161.

Carnevale, A. (1990) *Training in America*. San Francisco: Jossey-Bass.

Clardy, A. (2004) 'Toward an HRD auditing protocol: assessing HRD risk management practices,' *Human Resource Development Review* 3(2): 124–150.

Cohen, D.J. (1990) 'What motivates trainees?' *Training and Development* 36: 91–93.

de Jong, J.A., Leenders, A.J. and Thijssen, J.G.L. (1999) HRD tasks of first level managers, *Journal of Workplace Learning* 11(5): 176–183.

Deloitte (2004) *Improving Working Lives: Becoming and Employer of Choice in the Health Service*, Dublin, Ireland: Eastern Regional Health Authority.

Department of Health and Children (2002) *Action Plan for People Management in the Health Service*, Dublin, Ireland: Government of Ireland.

Donovan, P. (2000) 'Transferring learning,' *Arena* April: 18.

Dyer, L. and Holder, G. (1988) 'A strategic perspective of human resource management,' in L. Dyer and G. Holder (eds) *Human Resource Management: Evolving Roles and Responsibilities*, Washington, DC: The Bureau of National Affairs, pp. 1–48.

Finn, W. (1997) 'Training and development in the public sector,' *People in the Public Sector, Managing Your Organisation's Most Valuable Asset* 1(1): PMG.

Fomburn, C., Tichy, N. and Devanna, M. (1984) *Strategic Human Resource Management*, New York: Wiley.

Forrester, K., Payne, J. and Ward, K. (1995) *Workplace Learning*, Avebury, UK.

Fricker, J. (1994) 'Training for change: an investment in people,' in J. Prior (ed.) *Gower Handbook of Training and Development*, Hampshire, UK: Gower, pp. 21–31.

Garavan, T.N. and Carbery, R. (2003) *Who Learns at Work? A Study of Learners in the Republic of Ireland*, Dublin, Ireland: Chartered Institute of Personnel and Development (CIPD) with the University of Limerick, p. 38.

Garavan, T.N. and Heraty, N. (2001) *Training and Development in Ireland – Results 2001 National Survey*, Dublin: CIPD Ireland.

Gerber, B. (1987) 'It's a whole new ball game at BC Tel,' *Training* 24: 75–81.

Gillery, J.W. and Eggland, S.A. (1992) *Marketing HRD Programs Within Organizations: Improving the Visibility, Credibility, and Image of Programs*, San Francisco: Jossey-Bass.

Gilley, J.W. and Gilley Maycunich, A. (2003) *Strategically Integrated HRD: Six Transformational Roles in Creating Results-driven Programs*, 2nd edn, Cambridge: Perseus.

Guest, D., King, Z., Conway, N., Michie, J. and Sheehan-Quinn, M. (2001) *Voices from the Boardroom*, London: Chartered Institute of Personnel and Development (CIPD).

Holder Kunder, L. (1998) *Employees' Perceptions of the Status and Effectiveness of the Training and Development System and of the Value of Training and Development*, Falls Church, VA: Virginia Polytechnic Institute and State University.

Holton, E.F. and Baldwin, T.T. (2003) *Improving Learning Transfer in Organizations*, San Francisco: Jossey-Bass.

Huselid, M. (1995) 'The impact of human resource management practices on turnover, productivity an corporate financial performance,' *Academy of Management Journal* 38: 635–670.

Hyman, J. and Cunningham, I. (1998) 'Managers as developers: some reflections on the contribution of empowerment in Britain,' *International Journal of Training and Development* 2(2): 41–107.

Jones, E. (1995) *You Developed it: Can your Training Programs Survive the Reality Test?* Amherst, MA: HRD Press.

Kirkpatrick, D.L. (1994) *Evaluating Training Programs: The Four Levels*, San Francisco: Jossey-Bass.

Lawler, J. and Hearn, J. (1995) 'UK public sector organizations: the rise of managerialism and the impact of change on social services departments,' *International Journal of Public Sector Management* 8(4): 7–16.

Lee, C. (1988) Where does training belong? *Training* 25: 53–60.

Lee, M.B. and Chee, Y. (1996) 'Business strategy, participative human resource management and organizational performance: the case of South Korea,' *Asia Pacific Journal of Human Resources* 34: 77–94.

Lynton, R. and Pareek, U. (2000) *Training for Organisational Transformation: Part 1 for Policy Makers and Change Makers*, London: Sage.

Maguire, M. and Harrocks, B. (1995) *Employee Development Programmes and Lifetime Learning*, UK: CLMS.

Marchington, M. and Wilkinson, A. (2002) *People Management and Development*, 2nd edn, London, UK: CIPD.

Mavin, S. and Bryans, P. (2000) 'Management development in the public sector-what roles can universities play?' *The International Journal of Public Sector Management* 13(2): 142–152.

Maxwell, G.T. and Watson, S. (2004) 'Devolving HRM and HRD to line managers: the case of Hilton International's UK hotels.' Paper presented at the Academy of Human Resource Development, Austin, Texas.

McIntyre, T.L. (2004) 'A model of levels of involvement and strategic roles of Human Resource Development (HRD) professionals as facilitators of due diligence and the integration process,' *Human Resource Development Review* 3(2): 173–182.

Moller, L. and Mallin, P (1996) 'Evaluation practices of instructional designers and organizational supports and barriers,' *Performance Improvement Quarterly* 9(4): 82–92.

Mulder, M. (1992) Opleiden? ... Ook dat nog! Enkele gedachten bij het thema 'Managers als Opleiders' [HRD? ... Some thoughts to the issue 'Managers seen as trainers']. *Opleiding & Ontwikkeling* 5(3): 3–5.

Naquin, S.S. and Baldwin, T.T. (2003) 'Managing transfer before learning begins: the transfer-ready learner,' in E.F. Holton, III and T.T. Baldwin (eds) *Improving Learning Transfer in Organizations*, San Francisco, USA: Jossey-Bass, pp. 80–96.

Olsen, J.H. (1998) 'The evaluation and enhancement of training transfer,' *International Journal of Training and Development* 2(1): 275–282.

Poell, R.F., Pluijmen, R. and Van der Krogt, F.J. (2003) 'Strategies of HRD professionals in organising learning programmes: a qualitative study among 20 Dutch HRD professionals,' *Journal of European Industrial Training* 27(2/3/4): 125–136.

Rao, T.V. (1999) *HRD Audit*, New Delhi: Response Books.

Renwick, D. (2003) 'Line managers involvement in HRM: an inside view,' *Employee Relations: The International Journal* 25(3): 262–280.

Renwick, D. and MacNeil, C.M. (2002) 'Line manner involvement in careers,' *Career Development International* 7(7): 407–414.

Rossett, A. (1987) *Training needs Assessment*, Englewood Cliffs: Educational Technology Publications.

Rossett, A. (1992) 'Analysis of human performance problems,' in H.D. Stolovitch and E.J. Keeps (eds) *Handbook of Human Performance Technology: A Comprehensive Guide for Analyzing and Solving Performance Problems in Organizations*, San Francisco: Jossey-Bass.

Rossett, A. (1996) 'Training and organizational development: separated at birth?' *Training* April: 53–59.

Rossett, A. (1999) 'Analysis for human performance technology,' in H.D. Stolovitch and E.J. Keeps (eds) *Handbook of Human Performance Technology: Improving Individual and Organizational Performance World-wide*, San Francisco: Jossey-Bass, pp. 139–162.

Rummler, G.A. and Brache, A.P. (1992) 'Transforming organizations through human performance technology,' in H.D. Stolovitch and E.J. Keeps (eds) *Handbook of Human Performance Technology: A Comprehensive Guide for Analyzing and Solving Performance Problems in Organizations*, San Francisco: Jossey-Bass, pp. 32–49.

Rummler, G.A. and Brache, A.P. (1995) *Improving Performance: How to Manage the White Spaces on the Organizational Chart*, San Francisco: Jossey-Bass.

Schuler, R.S. (1992) 'Strategic human resource management; linking the people with the strategic needs of the business,' *Organizational Dynamics* 21(1): 18–32.

Sloman, M. (2003) *The Change Agenda – Focus on the Learner*, London, UK: CIPD.

Swanson, R.A. (1994) *Analysis for Improving Performance*, San Francisco: Berrett-Koehler.

Tannenbaum, S. and Yukl, G. (1992) 'Training and development in work organizations,' *American Review of Psychology* 43: 399–441.

Thijssen, J.G.L. (1997) 'Leren om te overleven. Over personeelsontwikkeling als permanente educatie in een veranderende arbeidsmarkt' [Learn in order to survive. About employee development as life-long education in a changing labour market]. Utrecht: Oratie.

Thornhill, A. and Saunders, M.N.K. (1998) 'What if line managers don't realise they're responsible for HR?' *Personnel Review* 27(6): 460–476.

Tjepkema, S., ter Horst, H.M., Mulder, M. and Scheerens, J. (2000) *The Role of HRD within Organisations in Creating Opportunities for Lifelong Learning: Concepts and Practices in Seven European Countries – Area II: Future Challenges for HRD Professionals in Europe*, Enschede, University of Twente: European Commission.

Tjepkema, S., ter Horst, H. and Mulder, M. (2002) 'Learning organisations and HRD,' in S. Tjepkema, J. Stewart, S. Sambrook, M. Mulder, H. ter Horst and J. Scheerens (eds) *HRD and Learning Organisations in Europe*, London: Routledge, pp. 8–19.

Torrington, D. and Hall, L. (1998) *Human Resource Management*, 4th edn, London: Prentice Hall.

Ulrich, D. (1997) *Human Resource Champions: The Next Agenda for Adding Value and Delivering Results*, Boston, MA: Harvard Business School Press.

Warr, P., Allan, C. and Birdi, K. (1999) 'Predicting three levels of training outcome,' *Journal of Occupational and Organizational Psychology* 72: 351–375.

Williams, J., Blackwell, S., Gorby, S., O'Connell, P.J. and Russell, H. (2003) *The Changing Workplace: A Survey of Employers' Views and Experiences*, Dublin, Ireland: National Centre for Partnership and Performance (NCPP).

Wognum, A.A.M. (1995) 'Effectiviteitsbepaling en opleidingsbeleidsvorming van bedrijfsopleidingen' [HRD effectiveness measurement and HRD policy making], in M. Mulder and W. de Grave (eds) *Ontwikkelingen in branche- en bedrijfsopleidingen {Developments in HRD}*, Utrecht: Lemma, pp. 189–205.

Wognum, A.A.M. and Mulder, M.M.(1999) 'Strategic HRD within companies,' *International Journal of Training and Development* 3(1): 2–13.

Yip, F., Kwong, W., Priem, R.L. and Cycyota, C.S. (2001) 'The performance effects of human resource managers and other middle managers involvement in strategy making under different business level strategies: the case in Hong Kong,' *International Journal of Human Resource Management* 12(8): 1325–1346.

Zimsky, R. and Iannozzi, M. (1996) 'A reality check: first findings from EQW National Employer Survey,' *EQW Working Papers*, University of Pennsylvania: The National Centre of the Educational Quality of the Workforce Issues.

4 Intraprelearning within the NHS

The tale of two Welsh trusts

Clair Roberts and Sally Sambrook

Introduction

This chapter explores the notion of learning and intrapreneurship within two Welsh NHS Trusts. It argues that attempts to enhance intra-corporate entrepreneuring (or 'intrapreneuring' for short) – translated into NHS discourse as creative, innovative and risk-taking behaviours – are closely linked to learning at the individual, team and organizational levels, hence the term *intraprelearning*.

The NHS is currently undergoing radical change to modernize its service for a twenty-first century Britain. At the heart of the NHS Plan (DoH 2000) is the commitment to work continuously at improving service quality and to support and value employees to achieve enhanced patient care (DoH 2000). Supporting employees in 'realizing their potential' is critical to the achievement of such commitments (WAG 2002; Wanless 2002) and is a phrase that is increasingly being used within NHS literature.

Furthermore, the limited financial, technical and human resources of NHS Trusts are being stretched by a multitude of external drivers including: the European Working Time Directive; the Government-enforced waiting-time targets; and consumers' demanding safer, cleaner hospitals. Such stretching of resources is demanding Trusts with increased capability to extend upon their operating and service capacities. Finding new and innovative ways of working through creative, innovative and [guarded] risk-taking activity (Burgelman 1983; Kanter 1983; Covin 1999) is one solution to increasing Trust capacity. Creative, innovative and [guarded] risk-taking behaviour is referred to in the literature by a number of labels (most frequent labels we noted were; corporate entrepreneuring, intra-corporate entrepreneuring, and intrapreneuring) and is also being encouraged at Trust level because of the valuable revenues that successful innovations may generate through intellectual property.

How can we build more of the NHS workforce capacity to be corporate entrepreneurs? With white papers such as the NHS Plan (DoH 2000), Well Being Wales (WAG 2002), and the establishment of agencies such as the Modernization Agency and NHS Innovations (England), it is certainly timely and valuable to explore if, how and what can be done. Accordingly, if we are to seek ways of increasing corporate entrepreneurial capability and therefore capacity, we need to know more about corporate entrepreneurship and we need to know more about how to develop corporate entrepreneuring capability through understanding the *changing* and *learning* experiences shaping Trust entrepreneurs and their organizations. We have labelled this *intraprelearning* (intra-corporate entrepreneurial learning).

Research into intraprelearning (that is research that explores the interrelationships between corporate entrepreneuring and organizational learning) is very much emergent. Developing a richer understanding of intraprelearning will have significant implications for practice, education and research, by providing us with an understanding of the content and context of successful intrapreneurial learning, and therefore providing us with the building blocks for developing intrapreneurial capability and capacity. Ultimately such research will support employees in realizing their potential and enhance the quality of patient care delivery.

Aims

In this chapter we have three aims. First, we contribute to the theoretical perspective of understanding intraprelearning through critiquing research literature from three broad organizational fields and through proposing a conceptualization of intraprelearning. Second, we describe and analyse an empirical context through ongoing research we are conducting within two Welsh NHS Trusts and highlight preliminary themes that are emerging. We map these initial findings onto our conceptualization and discuss these results. Our third aim is to explore the limitations and implications and make some recommendations for future research. First, we consider the theoretical context.

Theoretical context

In this section we hope to unpick some of the literature from the three broad fields that underpin intraprelearning that is; organizational learning (OL), corporate entrepreneuring (CE), and organizational change (OC). We argue how all three fields share similar themes and how the processes themselves require similar organizational conditions in which to flourish and, conversely, deteriorate. In light of this, we critique the emerging literature that explores the intraprelearning 'process(es)' at the macro (organizational) level, and to address our criticisms of this literature (Sambrook and Roberts 2005), we offer our conceptualization of intraprelearning within NHS Trusts.

Defining OL, CE and OC

As we noted in our introduction, in order to understand how we can increase entrepreneurial capacity within NHS Trusts, first we need to understand intraprelearning – that is, the intra-corporate entrepreneurial learning of Trusts – through the groups and individuals within. In order to understand intraprelearning, we need to explore the three broad organizational fields that underpin the concept – Organizational Learning (OL), Corporate Entrepreneuring (CE) and Organizational Change (OC). CE, OL and CE ideologies seek to provide solutions to problems associated with twenty-first century living in this empirical context, through building the NHS's capacity to modernize (Modernisation Agency 2005), providing safer care, supporting better use of existing resources (Wanless 2002) and developing skills and standards of the workforce (WAG 2002; DoH 2004). The next section briefly explores current definitions of OL, CE and OC.

Organizational learning

The capability of an organization to learn faster or better than its 'competitors' is believed by many to be the key to *long-term* success (Swieringa and Wierdsma 1992; Collis 1994; DoH 2004), and is the essence of OL. The NHS Plan recognizes the vital role learning plays in supporting change and improvement to service delivery. 'There is a tremendous appetite for change in the NHS. What holds back improvement everywhere is the lack of time and support to learn from others about what works' (DoH 2000: 20).

A topic frequently discussed by researchers within the field is the ambiguous use of the terms *learning organization (OL)*, *organizational learning (LO)* and *a learning organization (ALO)*. They are used interchangeably within the literature, but have different meanings. Sun (2003) argues that organizational learning 'refers to the learning process of an organization and by the organization in a collective (organizational) way' (Sun 2003: 156), whereas a learning organization can infer 'a concept functioning as a vision' (Sun 2003: 157) or 'a subject of scientific study and research' (Sun 2003: 158).

Some researchers have commented that literature within the field of OL concentrates on understanding the *learning processes* within organizational settings, whilst the literature within the field of LO is geared towards *creating an ideal type* (Easterby-Smith 1997; Tsang 1997). There also seems to be divisions in the 'type' of author behind contributions to the fields of OL and LO. Easterby-Smith and Araujo (1999: 8) describe two communities of authors; consultants and academic researchers. Those contributing to the LO literature tend to be represented by consultants, and those contributing to the OL literature tend to be academic researchers. Easterby-Smith and Araujo criticize the academic quality of contributions to LO literature. This, they argue, has been caused by the growing number of contributions from consultants who have identified the commercial significance of LO, inspired by a number of best selling books, such as Senge (1990) and Pedler *et al.* (1991, 1996).

Although these accounts are often very insightful, some may lack the critical objectivity of traditional academic work.

(Easterby-Smith and Araujo 1999: 2)

Another discussion point in the OL literature is the problem of *anthropomorphism* in OL (Popper and Lipshitz 1998), which means attributing human qualities to non-human entities. For example, March and Olsen (1976) state that learning implies thought and that the concepts of OL and LO attribute human characteristics to organizational structures.

Conversely, Hedberg (1981) contends that organizations are learning entities.

> Organizations do not have brains, but they have cognitive systems and memories. As individuals develop their personalities, personal habits and beliefs over time, organizations develop world views and ideologies. Members come and go, and leadership changes, but organizations' memories preserve certain behaviours, mental maps, norms, and values over time.
>
> (Hedberg 1981: 6)

However, there is some consensus in the literature, particularly in that OL is more than just the cumulative result of individual members' learning (Argyris and Schö 1978; Hedberg 1981; Dixon 1992).

> There is no organizational learning without individual learning, and that individual learning is a necessary but insufficient condition for organizational learning.
>
> (Argyris and Schö 1978: 20)

Corporate entrepreneuring

With assurances of regenerative outcomes, the field of CE has attracted audiences and contributions from across many business disciplines. Subsequently, definitions can vary considerably in their approach and desired outcome. Broadly speaking, there seem to be two types of definition. First, those that lean more towards a strategic management lens view corporate entrepreneurship as a form of strategic renewal. (We note that these definitions are usually associated with research that tries to explain corporate entrepreneurship through nomothetic methodologies; that is, they attempt to draw general laws or conclusions rather than study behaviours that make individuals unique.) Miller and Friesen (1983: 771) define 'entrepreneurial firms' through a strategic management lens.

> An entrepreneurial firm is one that engages in product-market innovation, undertakes somewhat risky ventures, and is the first to come up with 'proactive' innovation.

Second, those that lean towards an organizational behavioural lens try to explain the corporate entrepreneurship using ideographic methodologies. This means they appreciate that both individuals and groups help to shape the organizations within which they work through meanings, interpretations and social constructions.

> [Corporate] entrepreneurship is the organization's willingness to encourage creativity, flexibility and to support risk.
>
> (Morris and Paul 1987: 248)

However, the boundaries between these two streams are often blurred, and some definitions can fit partly into both. Covin (1999: 47) highlights that innovation is the single common theme underlying all forms (and definitions) of corporate entrepreneurship. However, he advises caution explaining that

> The presence of innovation per se is insufficient to label a firm entrepreneurial. Rather, it is suggested that this label be reserved for firms that use innovation as a mechanism to redefine or rejuvenate themselves, their positions within markets and industries, or the competitive arenas in which they compete.

Thomson and McNamara (2001) define corporate entrepreneurship drawing upon attributes identified by Stopford and Baden-Fuller (1994). These are *proactiveness* (strategic management lens), *aspirations beyond current ability* (based on the Schumpeter Innovation Concept), *team-orientation* (organizational behaviour lens), *capability to resolve dilemmas* (drawing from the Schumpeterian Innovation Concept) and *learning capability* (organizational behaviour lens). Based on this dynamic set of attributes, Thompson and McNamara provide the (private sector) field with one of the most complete definitions to date.

> Corporate entrepreneurship involves teams within a firm led by intrapreneurs or corporate champions who promote entrepreneurial behaviour inside large organizations, proactively engaging in risky projects that seek to create new, innovative, administrative procedures, products and services that facilitate organizational renewal and growth.
>
> (Thompson and McNamara 2001: 671)

Another label found within the CE literature is *'entrepreneurial posture.'* This describes organizations in which CE behavioural patterns are recurring (as does the learning organization for the organizational learning literature). We have noted that entrepreneurial posture is used interchangeably with the term *entrepreneurial organization*, within the research literature. We emphasize caution in using different labels to describe the same processes, as this can complicate literature searches, and could leave the field open to greater misinterpretation and fragmentation.

Earlier we described some differences between the nature of contributors and contributions to the fields of OL and LO. A similar pattern appears to be emerging within the field of corporate entrepreneuring – contributions from academic researchers that attempt to understand the corporate entrepreneuring process and associated behaviours (corporate entrepreneuring), and contributions from practitioners that attempt to prescribe a toolkit to achieve an entrepreneuring corporation. As with the learning organization, contributions from practitioners may lack the critical objectivity and academic robustness of those of academics who contribute to the corporate entrepreneuring sub-field.

Organizational change

The organizational change literature shares some similarities with the literatures of CE and OL, but also has some striking contrasts. Our first observation is that 'organizational change' is infrequently defined within the research literature; rather, the general concept of change is defined instead. However, Dawson offers a simplistic definition of *organizational change* as 'new ways of organizing and working' (Dawson 2003: 11) whilst Proehl (2001: 37) provides a more comprehensive description:

> In today's organizations we use the term change to describe activities ranging from transforming the organization's basic culture and values to introducing a new policy or system. Change can refer to external shifts in technology, political climate as well as to internal modifications in structure, policies, or personnel. Change can be initiated from the top or can sell up from front-line employees; it can be viewed as positive and exciting or negative and threatening.

Whereas the OL and CE literatures can be roughly separated into those contributors who are academics or practitioners and whose contributions are descriptive or prescriptive, the organizational change literature is more complex and interrelated. Traditionally, the organizational change literature has been predominately prescriptive in nature, regardless of its contributors. Beginning with its scientific management roots, and developing to include the human dimension of change in the late 1940s, OC literature has evolved through to the organizational development models (underpinned by the unfreezing-moving-refreezing work of Lewin, 1951) through to include the work of 'celebrity professors and practitioners' who were particularly prevalent in the 1980s and 1990s (Dawson 2003). From our observations, most of the earlier contributions are prescriptive in nature. However, more recently there has been a push towards learning about the processual and ongoing nature of organizational change through descriptive research and contributions are emerging from academics (Van der Ven and Huber 1990; Petti-grew 1990; Dawson 1994,1996; Ropo *et al.* 1997) who recognize the importance of descriptive research in understanding the dynamics of OC (Dawson 2003). Following from this, there appears to be no literature within the field that explores OC from an idealist state, as there is in the OL and CE literatures. The arguments against 'idealistic contributions' to the OL and CE literatures are strong and are based on the weak levels of acade-mic rigour underpinning existing contributions. However, if approached using high levels of academic rigour, the idealistic approach could provide all three fields with an alternative lens from which to view and explore the processes. We suggest that the viability of this approach is explored in more depth by academic practitioners within the three fields.

Types and levels of CE, OL and OC

After having explored some of the definitions of CE, OL and OC and com-mented on some similarities (and differences) between the nature of the con-tributions and contributors, we now highlight some similarities between the processes of CE, OL and OC.

The first similarity is that the literature tends to explore each 'process' in terms of three organizational levels; individual, team/group and organi-zational. Table 4.1 provides some examples of the different types of each process found within the research literature and relates them to the level from which they are said to occur.

Table 4.1 by no means offers a complete overview of all of the different types found. However, it does highlight some of the intra-field and inter-field overlap. For example, *intrapreneuring* is a CE and OC activity (we observe that the term is spelt intrepreneuring within the OC literature (see for example Dawson 2003). *Action-learning teams* are OL and OC activities (and although not illustrated in Table 4.1 in some cases may be CE activity). Some of these 'types' are descriptive labels, i.e. intrapreneuring, dialogic learning and industry rule bending and some are labels for prescriptive frameworks or activities, i.e. business process re-engineering and TQM. In addition some labels can represent both descriptive and prescriptive activ-ities, i.e. action learning teams and venture groups. Finally, CE and OC activities may be externally oriented (e.g. independent spin-offs), with many examples found of this at the organizational level (e.g. mergers). We could not find any examples of externally oriented OL activities, although we realize that activities such as mergers provide an indirect form of organi-zational learning at all levels.

Another set of similarities found between the three fields are the organi-zational factors that are common to facilitating all three processes. From an extensive literature search we have identified a number of similar supporting factors and present themes in Table 4.2.

Table 4.2 reiterates earlier observations that the three processes share

Table 4.1 Levels and labels of CE, OL and OC

	Occurring Level		
	Individual	*Team/Group*	*Organizational*
CE	Intrapreneuring Initiative from Below Independent Spin-Offs	Venture Groups Skunk Works Intrapreneuring	Organizational Transformation New Strategic Direction Joint Venture Industry Rule Bending Independent Spin-Offs Mergers & Acquisitions
OL	Instrumental Dialogic Self-Reflective Benchmarking Scanning and Noticing Vicarious/experiential/ congenital	Action Learning Teams Parallel Learning Cross-Functional Teams	Single/Double/Deutero Organizational Development Organizational Scanning TQM Six Stigma Business Process Re-engineering Business Process Redesign
OC	Individual Change Intrapreneuring	Team Change Group Change Action Learning Teams Cross Functional Teams	Business Process Re-engineering Business Process Redesign TQM Six Sigma Lean Management Mergers & Acquisitions

striking similarities. Mintzberg's (1973) entrepreneurial mode of *strategy* and Miles and Snow's (1978) prospector and analyser describe the strategic approaches that facilitate OL, CE and OC. A firm that follows the prospector strategy is highly innovative and constantly seeks out new markets and new opportunities and is oriented towards growth and risk-taking (Griffin 1999). The defender strategy is a strategy in which the firm focuses on protecting its current markets, maintaining stable growth, and serving current customers. The analyser strategy is 'a unique combination of the prospector and defender types' and 'a firm employing this strategy attempts to maintain its current business and to be somewhat innovative in new business' (Miles and Snow 1978: 68).

Structural themes for facilitating each process are also very similar with: flat, matrix structures (Kanter 1983; Covin and Slevin 1991; Lynskey 2002) with high centralization (although some CE literature argues towards low centralization, Lynskey 2002); structural integration not segmentation (Kanter 1988); and adaptive (Bennis 1969) organic (Burns and Stalker 1994) adhocracies (Toffler 1970).

Table 4.2 Facilitating conditions for OL, CE and OC

	Facilitating conditions for:		
	OL	**CE**	**OC**
Strategy	Entrepreneurial/Prospector/Analyser mode	Entrepreneurial/Prospector mode	Entrepreneurial/Prospector/Analyser mode
Structure	Flat/matrix structure Decentralized management Adaptive/organic adhocracy Structural integration	Flat/matrix structure High/low centralization Structural integration Flexibility Adaptive/organic adhocracy	Matrix Structure High centralization Structural integration Flexibility Adaptive/organic adhocracy
Communications	Open communication systems	Open communication systems	Open communication systems
Role Design	Autonomy Multi-disciplinary Teamwork	Low formalization of roles High specialization Flexibility Flexibility Multi-disciplinary Teamwork	Flexibility Multi-disciplinary Teamwork Collaboration
Culture	Fragmented culture Support/Achievement culture Openness Trust Shared Vision Commitment Tolerance Risk-taking Responsibility	Fragmented culture Power/achievement culture Openness Trust Commitment Tolerance Risk-taking Responsibility	Fragmented culture Power/Support culture Openness Trust Shared Vision Commitment Tolerance Responsibility Truth
Support	Mentor	Champion/Sponsor	Change Agent

The literature is full of examples reaffirming the need for *communication* to flow openly up and down organizational levels and across divisions, departments and teams, in order for each process to flourish. The matrix structure is often cited as supporting open communication systems in organizations (Davis and Lawrence 1977; Kanter 1983, 1988).

As with the other factors in Table 4.2, *role designs* that facilitate the three processes are similar, including flexibility, autonomy and multidisciplinary team work. Drawing from the work of Martin (1992), the desired facilitating *culture* is the same for each process (Martin identifies three types of culture; fragmentation, integration, or differentiation). However, in terms of a typology offered by Schein (1985), who proposes four different organizational cultures (power, achievement, support and role), there seem to be differences between what is desired in each instance. Finally, in terms of *support*, the research literature describes and prescribes middle-to-senior leaders as being critical in supporting the individuals or teams behind the process, and therefore the process itself.

The research literature provides many examples where OC, OL and CE (and their components) are discussed together, in synergy with one another. At the individual level a corporate entrepreneur is a change agent and an active learner. A change agent may be a corporate entrepreneur and may be a learner. A learner may be a corporate entrepreneur and a change agent. So how do these interrelationships work in practice, at the organizational (macro) team and individual (micro) levels?

The interrelationships between OL, CE and OC – intraprelearning

Supported by all of the evidence gathered from our critique of the research literature we set out to explore if there was any research that attempted to describe or conceptualize the links between all three processes. We have introduced the term intraprelearning to describe the possible interrelationships between the three processes of CE, OL and OE at all organizational levels. Intraprelearning has been derived from an abbreviation of the term intra-corporate entrepreneurial learning and (drawing from our literature review) describes a set of interrelationships that may occur at the individual, team or organizational level. Intraprelearning may be formal (and officially recognized by the organization in question) or may be informal (unofficial or unrecognized by the organization). Furthermore, intraprelearning may be externally oriented, or may be internally oriented. In all of these contexts intraprelearning incorporates change. Change may be the trigger to intraprelearning, it may be the result of intraprelearning, it may be incorporated within the corporate entrepreneuring and learning itself, and intraprelearning can be a complexity of any and many different combinations of the above. Change may be individual, team or organizational. At each of these levels, change may be planned or unplanned, and may be incremental or radical.

We were surprised to find a small number of contributions that fitted within our intraprelearning label and these can be critiqued. First, none of the contributions explore OL, CE *and OC*. We found two contributions that attempt to describe the relationship between OL and CE. Zahra *et al.* (1999) offer a cyclical model of corporate entrepreneurship, knowledge and organizational competence development for profit-making firms. Zahra *et al.* (1999: 1) recognize the important links between OL and CE.

> Some of the most profound contributions of corporate entrepreneurship activities may lie in its links with the organizational learning processes that increase an organization's competencies in assessing its markets or creating and commercializing new knowledge-intensive products, processes, or services.

Dess *et al.* (2003) propose a cyclical model that explores the relationships among corporate entrepreneurship *strategy*, organizational learning, knowledge, implementation and feedback. Dess *et al.*'s (2003) model draws heavily upon Zahra *et al.* (1999) work.

In both of these models two new labels of OL (acquisitive and experimental) are introduced, ignoring the significant work on the three levels of OL that has been discussed by key theorists such as Bateson (1973) and Argyris and Schö (1978) (single-loop learning, double-loop learning and deutero-learning). Using similar labels and meanings would help develop shared understanding between researchers exploring intraprelearning.

Furthermore, both models examine how CE may impact on OL, but as they are set within management science ontology, they neglect to explore how individuals' and groups' social constructions may impact upon and shape these interrelationships. We believe that framing future research within a social constructivist paradigm will help develop a richer understanding of the interrelationships between CE, OL and OC and therefore intraprelearning, through understanding the meanings individuals and groups attach to intraprelearning experiences. Having reviewed the literature, we now turn our attention to CE and intrapralearning within the NHS.

Defining NHS corporate entrepreneuring and intraprelearning

For our empirical study set within the context of the NHS, we have redefined corporate entrepreneuring to appreciate the unique requirements of *guarded* risk-taking required in health care; that is fostering corporate entrepreneuring without compromising safety (Thomas 2005).

Drawing from Thompson and McNamara (2001)'s definition of private sector entrepreneuring and from Greenhalgh *et al.*'s (2004a) definition of innovation in the NHS, we have developed a working definition of NHS corporate entrepreneuring. It is the process of proactively engaging in creative, ethical and guarded risk-taking behaviours, routines and ways of working that seek to create entrepreneurial behaviour that is:

a Perceived as new by a proportion of key stakeholders;
b Linked to the provision or support of health care;
c Discontinuous with previous practice.

which facilitates organizational redefinition and rejuvenation through improving administrative efficiency, cost effectiveness; the user experience; and ultimately leads to enhanced patient care.

NHS CE is engaged in by individual (or team) corporate entrepreneurs and supported by a sponsor or champion. NHS CE may be formal and official, may be informal and unofficial or both. Activities may be oriented within the Trust or externally to the Trust.

From our definition of NHS CE, our term intraprelearning becomes clearer. We can now provide a working definition of intraprelearning:

> Intraprelearning is any learning (individual/team/organizational) that facilitates CE (individual/team/organizational) through triggering change (individual/team/organizational). Intraprelearning may be tacit or explicit, may be single-, double- or meta-loop and may be formal or informal.

Empirical context

With these definitions in mind, and drawing on our earlier work (Sambrook and Roberts 2005), we redefined a set of conceptual frameworks that link the three processes. The original conceptualizations were set within the private sector and explored the interrelationships through four constructs; changing market environment, changing internal environment, OL and CE. To explore the NHS, we needed to recognize the different environment. Whereas private sector service industry counterparts promote some form of unique selling point or competitive advantage in order to win profits and market share, NHS Trusts are focused on meeting numerous standards and targets focused around providing a high quality of care to its patients.

The revised conceptual model consists of four constructs; CE, OL and External OC and Internal OC. The model (see Figure 4.1) shows CE at its centre (4a and 4b). We propose that CE represents all of the different types of CE (such as intrapreneurships, venture groups and independent spin offs), and can be formal/official (4a) or informal/unofficial (4b) in nature. OL (2) and (3) represents all types and forms of OL activities with (2) representing organizational-level learning, and (3) representing team and individual level learning. In either case, the OL may be intuiting, interpreting, integrating or institutionalizing (Crossan *et al.* 1999). Learning can be single-loop,

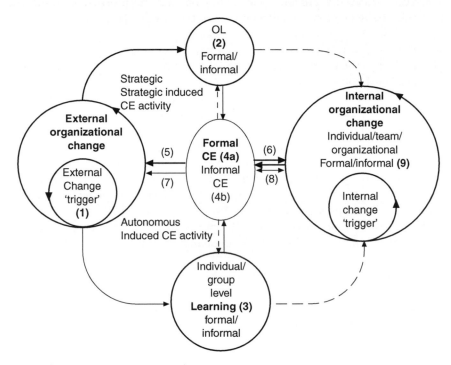

Figure 4.1 A conceptual model of NHS intraprelearning (CE).

double-loop or deutero learning (Argyris and Schö 1978) and may involve scanning and unlearning (Huber 1991).

There are two paths mapped out in the model. The bolder lines denote the path for official Trust innovation, whilst the black paths denote the unofficial innovation, or autonomous strategic behaviour (Burgelman 1983). To explain the model, we will begin the cycle when a change occurs in the external Trust environment, driven by an external trigger (1), although this may not be the start of the cycle in reality. We will use a hypothetical example based on the increased numbers of UK female smokers up to the 1960s (ASH 2000) to help explain how this model works.

Action on Smoking and Health (2000) shows that lung cancer in women has risen since the 1960s, and argues that this figure reflects the rise in female smoking that peaked in 1966. As that population has aged and continued to smoke, so the cancers associated with smoking have become evident. ASH (2000) argues that there is around a 30 year lag for the cancer rates that follow the rise of smoking in females up to the 1960s.

In the UK, smoking among women peaked in 1966 at about 46 per cent of adult women and has declined to around 26–28 per cent over the next three decades (26 per cent in 1998). The population smoking in

1966 would be the post-war baby-boomers and skewed towards the younger age group (older women were not taking up the habit, so the growth came from younger women). (ASH 2000)

Referring back to our model (Figure 4.1), external triggers of OC (1) within the NHS may include; Political factors, Economic influences, Sociological trends, Technological innovations, Ecological factors, or Legislative require-ments (Iles and Sutherland 2001: 29). Using the example of female smoking; a sociological trend in the 1960s – that is, increased female smoking has triggered a change in the external Trust environment (1), that is, an increase in the number of women aged 60 years old and above, with lung cancer in 2005.

For a NHS Trust to act upon an external change (1), some form of organi-zational learning must take place (2 and 3). In our hypothetical example on female smoking, this learning could be done at (2) the organizational level (e.g. statistics on the increased lung cancer rates in women, disseminated through a Department of Health white paper to a Trust's Board of Directors); at the team level (a cancer centre's increased waiting list for lung-cancer treatments is explored through a task group); or/and at the indi-vidual level (a cancer nurse observes an increase in lung cancer diagnoses of females over 60 years old).

Once learning has occurred, one of the ways a Trust, a team or individuals may react is through corporate entrepreneuring (4a and 4b). CE may occur from: the organizational level (for example the Trust sets up an innovative team to educate young adult females on the dangers of smoking); and/or the team- and individual-levels (a cancer nurse sets up an innovative support network for female lung cancer patients and their families). In the case of formal/official CE, once OL has occurred CE activities may be oriented exter-nally (5) (for example public education) or may be oriented internally (6) (for example a new lung-cancer treatment or service). In the case of unofficial autonomous CE (4a) these changes may also be externally oriented (7) (for example a nurse setting up a spin-off private hospice) or internally oriented (8) (doctor setting up smoking cessation hypnotherapy service).

Whether formal or informal, if the CE is externally oriented, it will have an effect on the present external environment and cause it to become differ-ent in some way. In our hypothetical example this can be illustrated as follows: educating the public on smoking (trace **CE (4a)** through to (5) on Figure 4.1) may reduce the numbers of smokers (sociological change in present external environment) and increase pressure on the Government to prohibit smoking in public places (political external trigger driven by soci-ological trend (1)) leaving children particularly exposed to passive smoking risks within the home (sociological trigger driving external organizational change (1)). So the cycle would begin again.

Tracing CE from 4a to 6, if the CE activities are internally oriented, then this will cause internal Trust change (9), such as new roles (for example a smoking cessation team). We argue that these changes would require further organizational learning support (2 and 3), and the CE spiral could begin again (4a or/and 4b).

The dashed lines in the model represent our acknowledgement that these cycles could not run as smoothly as described above. For example, externally oriented CE activities would probably induce internal Trust change, and vice versa. We also recognize that the act of OL (2 and 3) itself may cause internal Trust change (9), without the interaction with CE activities (for example smoking prohibited throughout the Trust site). Finally we recognize through the 'spiral effect' in the model, that both external Trust change (1) and internal Trust change (9) may arise without any CE or OL intervention.

Methodology

Having introduced our model, the next section explains our empirical research, which explores OL, CE and OC within two Welsh NHS Trusts (Trust A and Trust B). Influenced by our own ontological and epistemological standpoints, we argue that a qualitative approach to exploring intraprelearning is necessary since the topic is largely unresearched within any context, and this approach will facilitate the development of a rich descriptive research base. In terms of ontology, we feel that a qualitative approach will help us understand the ways in which individuals' differences and their social constructions of reality shape intraprelearning.

Our research questions were as follows:

1 Who are the corporate entrepreneurs within the Trusts?
2 How are they entrepreneuring?
3 Why are they entrepreneuring?
4 Who has supported and/or hindered them (individuals/groups/culture/leadership/power)?
5 What organizational conditions have supported/hindered them (strategy/structure/reward/resources/culture)?
6 How, where and when are they learning?
7 How are they agents of change and learning?
8 How has learning and change supported corporate entrepreneuring?
9 How are Trusts, and the individuals and teams within, intraprelearning?
10 What are the implications of the above for research, policy and practice associated with HRD, HRM, Clinical Governance and Strategic Policy?

Data collection

We collected data from two Welsh NHS Trusts starting with a key 'getting in' contact from each (Chairman of R&D – Trust A, and Deputy Director of

Nursing – Trust B). In order to collect the data, we had to achieve both ethical and R&D approval from each Trust. The ethical and R&D processes in both Trusts were time consuming and slow, taking over eight months from initial first contact to being granted honorary employment contracts.

During the proposal phase it became very clear that the terminology we were using (CE) was not clearly understood by health care staff. We revisited the academic literature and redefined CE using simple terminology such as creative, innovative and risk-taking behaviour. We also referred to recent literature (DoH 2000) and borrowed discursive resources such as *new and better ways of working*.

From our original two contacts, we conducted semi-structured interviews using purposive sampling and snowballing across and down each of the Trusts. We employed an inductive approach to our data collection. Participants emerged from word-of mouth referrals by others within the Trust, through the others' own interpretations and definitions of CE. We believe that this technique would help us to learn about meanings attached by individuals to CE (and subsequently OL, OC and intraprelearning).

Participants

Initial participants were strategic level employees (see Table 4.3 for roles of the strategic participants interviewed) and not the CEs themselves (11 from Trust A and ten from Trust B). Interviews typically lasted for half an hour and were semi-structured. Interviews were tape recorded, and notes were also taken to complement the recordings. These interviews provided rich information regarding the formal and informal culture, power and leadership structures within each of the Trusts, and also names of corporate entrepreneurs for subsequent interviewing.

The second set of participants were the corporate entrepreneurs. As stated previously, participating corporate entrepreneurs were identified through word of mouth referrals. Interviews were conducted until data saturation was reached, which amounted to 30 interviews with corporate entrepreneurs (16 Trust A and 14 from Trust B). Table 4.3 indicates the general roles of the corporate entrepreneurs interviewed from both Trusts. Interviews were semi-structured and included critical incident technique. Interviews generally lasted for an hour, were tape recorded, and notes were taken. This stage of research is current and ongoing, however some interesting initial themes are emerging, which we will discuss in the next section. First, we introduce one driver of change, used to focus our data collection.

The European Working Time Directive

During the initial phase of our data collection, we decided to trace CE activity down through each Trust using an external trigger of change (refer back to Figure 4.1). After initial discussion with senior representatives from Welsh

Table 4.3 Participants and their roles

Trust A	Trust B
Senior Participants	**Senior Participants**
SP 1 – Chief Executive	SP 1 – Head of Modernization
SP 2 – Head of Modernization	SP 2 – Deputy Medical Director
SP 3 – Human Resource Director	SP 3 – Director of Therapy
SP 4 – Head of Training	SP 4 – Head of Podiatry
SP 5 – Deputy Director of Nursing	SP 5 – General Manager of Surgery
SP 6 – Head of Nursing 1	SP 6 – General Manager of Mental Health
SP 7 – Head of Nursing 2	SP 7 – Intellectual Property Manager
SP 8 – Head of Nursing 3	SP 8 – Research and Development Manager
SP 9 – Research and Development Manager	SP 9 – Head of Nursing 1
SP 10 – EWTD H@N Coordinator	SP 10 – Head of Nursing 2
SP 11 – EWTD Medical Lead	
Specialist Nurse	**Specialist Nurse**
SN1 – Learning Disabilities	SN1 – Mental Health
SN2 – Team Leader: Accident & Emergency	SN2 – Day Surgery
SN3 – Accident & Emergency	SN3 – H Grade Nurse Practitioner
SN4 – Acute Pain	SN4 – Intensive Care
SN5 – Midwifery	SN5 – Nurse Practitioner on Secondment
SN6 – Thrombolysis	SN6 – G Grade Nurse Practitioner
SN7 – Cardiology	
SN8 – Midwifery	**Ward Manager**
SN9 – Night Nurse	WM1 – Day Surgery
	WM2 – Trauma & Orthopaedics
Ward Manager	WM3 – Care of Elderly
WM1 – Mental Health	WM3 – Care of Elderly & Renal
WM2 – Day Surgery	
WM3 – Theatre	**Allied Health Professional**
	AHP1 – Podiatry
Administrative	AHP2 – Physiotherapy
A1 – Librarian	
	Medical Consultant
	MC1 – EWTD Medical Lead
Nurse	
N1 – Learning Disabilities	**Nurse**
N2 – Coronary Care 1	N1 – Community Psychiatric Nurse
N3 – Coronary Care 2	

Trusts, we agreed upon the European Working Time Directive as the driver to follow. This would enable comparative analysis across the selected Trusts and provide examples of strategic induced (top-down) formal and informal CE.

The European Working Time Directive (EWTD) is a driver of change currently impacting on NHS Trusts. Driven by political factors, and sociological trends, the basic aim of the directive is the protection of employees' health and safety. It lays down minimum standards to protect the workers against the damaging effects of prolonged night work and shift work. In May 2000 the EU Member States agreed a staged implementation of the hours limits of the Working Time Regulation for junior doctors. Phasing in of this has already begun, and should be complete by 2012. The hours limits of the EWTD will not become limits on the hours of actual work for resident junior doctors but on the hours of actual duty. This therefore has implications on the Trust workforce as a whole.

> Compliance with the directive should be seen as a major driver for change ... The EWTD, and junior doctor's compliance with it has provided the impetus for change and gives rise to the opportunity to redesign service delivery and improve the work/life balance for NHS staff.
>
> (Welsh NHS Trust 2004: 15)

As the strategic-level interviews progressed it became apparent that there were a number of emergent issues surrounding our choice of driver of change (EWTD). The next section presents our findings.

Findings

This next section provides findings on five different themes; culture and leadership, the European Working Time Directive, the nursing stretch, corporate entrepreneur characteristics, and intraprelearning/critical learning experience. Analysis of the data from the senior lead participants focuses on the organizational context, the EWTD and the concept of nursing stretch. Analysis of the data from the corporate entrepreneurs focuses on their characteristics and their critical learning experiences.

EWTD as a driver of OC and CE

After conducting interviews with the strategic participants it became clear that the EWTD was not going to lead us to a rich selection of corporate entrepreneurs so we decided to open up the parameters of our research to include CE that had not necessarily been driven by the EWTD. This also enabled us to explore autonomous (bottom-up) CE.

The initial analysis of strategic interviews revealed a degree of ambiguity concerning the EWTD and its purpose, and this may have inappropriately influenced the identification of corporate entrepreneurs.

1   The impact that the EWTD has had or will have had on organizational-wide change.
2   The impact that the EWTD has had on staff other than the junior doctors within the Trust.
3   The impact the EWTD has had on driving Corporate Entrepreneurship.

Further to this, participants had different interpretations regarding the Hospital at Night (H@N) scheme, which was developed through the Department of Health's Modernization Agency to help address EWTD issues. H@N aims to redefine how medical cover is provided by hospitals during the out-of-hours period. The project is national, and requires a move from cover requirements defined by professional demarcation and grade, to cover defined by competency (Modernisation Agency 2003). H@N is versatile in that it provides numerous solutions and tools that Trusts can 'pick and mix' from. The scheme has been adopted differently by Trusts A and B to help solve their EWTD problem.

As stated previously, senior participants interpret and understand the H@Nscheme differently. Some perceive their use of the Hospital at Night scheme to be entrepreneurial, as would we, given our definition of NHS CE that highlights CE to be (a) perceived as new by a *proportion* of key stakeholders and (c) discontinuous with previous practice.

> We moved on a number of ways of working and we introduced the Hospital at Night which we pinched, we're happy to pinch ideas for our other things and then put our own version of it . . .
>
> (Trust A Chief Executive)

> The hospital at night project has been around for the last three or four years, and what we've been doing is taking up what is really quite a dry concept and starting to bring it alive.
>
> (Trust B Deputy Medical Director)

Others within the Trusts did not link the H@N scheme with creative, innovative and risk-taking behaviour:

> The Hospital at Night is a concept which facilitates our compliance with the EWTD and New Deal for junior doctors.
>
> (Trust A HR Director)

These findings suggest that strategic employees need to develop a clearer, mutual understanding of what NHS CE and innovation is. If there is lack of clarity at the senior levels then this may be compounded at the operational levels. An interesting observation from strategic participants is the pressure that has been put on other roles within Trusts A and B to enable junior doctor compliance.

The European Working Time Directive has never been fully engaged in the non-medical world.

(Trust B Deputy Medical Director)

We've no strategy yet for the EWTD for managers and everything, we've been so busy trying to sort out everything else ... what I would have to say as well is the silent group who've been constantly in breech of the EWTD are nurses, certainly in my career.

(Trust A Head of Nursing)

If the key principle underpinning the EWTD is the health and safety of staff (and subsequently patients) these comments suggest the need to include other non-compliant groups within EWTD compliance.

Culture and leadership

Emerging results indicate that trusts A and B have different cultures. Drawing from Harrison (1972), Handy (1979) and Williams *et al.* (1989), Trust A's culture seems to show more signs of being power-oriented, whilst Trust B seems to be more people-oriented. In the research literature power-oriented cultures are described as competitive, entrepreneurial and risk-taking, whilst people-oriented cultures feature consensus, mutuality and trust. However, successful examples of corporate entrepreneuring can be found within both Trusts. In addition, both Trusts provided examples of effective transformational leadership (Burns 1978) and more transactional oriented management.

The nursing stretch

Our findings highlight an emerging theme associated with a problem in nursing created by two drivers of change. The problem is the 'stretch' or tension created from the EWTD and the Fundamentals of Care (WAG 2003). The Fundamentals of Care is a Welsh Assembly Government initiative, similar to the English 'Essence of Care' (DoH 2001). 'Fundamentals of Care' present 12 fundamental aspects of health and social care that aim to improve the quality of care for adults (WAG 2003). However, this legislation requires nurses to focus on their basic tasks.

No financial support has been given to nursing to achieve compliance with WTD. Nurses have been encouraged to be more innovative and creative, however are being encouraged to get back to basics. Nurses are being stretched like elastic.

(Trust B Head of Nursing)

You're being asked to drive Fundamentals of Care, when you're asked to go back to basics, but on the other hand we've got no junior doctors, so the ward staff are doing bloods, ECGs, phlebotomies, they're trawling through lab results to make sure that when the consultants come they are there with all the information at their tips ... so we have created an absolute monster in all of this, so now we are been heavily criticized for not being at the patient's bedside.

(Trust B Head of Nursing)

Figure 4.2 illustrates the emerging nursing problem that requires nurses to stretch towards both ends of their competencies. At one end there is the EWTD which pulls nurses' competencies towards taking on more advanced roles, traditionally associated with basic junior doctor tasks, the other end is the Fundamentals of Care, which pulls nurses towards improving their basic beside skills. We suggest that at every point along this continuum there is an opportunity for some form of intraprelearning. Using the analogy of an elastic band being stretched, we ask at what point of stretch provides optimum learning, creativity and innovative output? And at what point will the elastic snap? We have not been able to address this issue within our study, but we recommend that further empirical research be conducted to address such questions.

Having presented themes from the strategic participants, we now turn to the corporate entrepreneurs themselves and explore some preliminary themes that are emerging from our research.

Corporate entrepreneurs' characteristics

Through interviews with the senior participants, 30 corporate entrepreneurs were identified and interviewed from Trusts A and B (16 Trust A and 14 Trust B). The majority of these entrepreneurs are based at the main acute hospital; however, four from Trust A and six from Trust B are located at other locations within the Trust's area. Corporate entrepreneurs were from a wide range of 'departments' including A&E, Cardiology, Intensive Care, Orthopaedics, Trauma Theatres, Day Surgery, Care of the Elderly and Mental Health. Many were nurses, but also included ward managers,

Figure 4.2 The nursing stretch.

medical consultants, allied health professionals and administrative staff. This suggests that CE is spread across the organization and professions.

Initial analyses of recordings and observation notes suggest that corporate entrepreneurs are *skilled communicators*. A range of techniques is used for example, some being very 'gentle-but-firm' in voice, some using humour, some being intelligently tactile (e.g. using an appropriate touch upon the hand to emphasize a point), and a number using metaphors during conversation.

> So you want to look like you're gliding along as a swan, but beneath the surface there's a lot of work and activity going on with the paddling, feet paddling, so you're still creating the energy and the action, but you're maintaining a calm gliding moving elegant appearance.
>
> (Trust B Head of Modernization)

> If you can imagine in a factory that's producing something, you can't turn the factory off, we shut down the NHS and go off line for 48 hours while we reconfigure, we still have to deliver things.
>
> (Trust B EWTD Medical Lead)

Reflecting back to the research literature there is little empirical research exploring the 'skills' and characteristics of corporate entrepreneurs. Some initial contributions have been found that begin to explore innovators, however, as we have implied earlier, corporate entrepreneurs are more than innovators, per se. In a recent literature review (Greenhalgh *et al.* 2004b) communication is identified as a key principle to the diffusion of innovations. This review is not unique and summarizes similar findings from empirical research spanning several research traditions, including communication studies, social network analysis, marketing and economics, and health promotion.

Within the field of OC, the theory on individual change focuses on resistance to change and coping with change. The corporate entrepreneurs interviewed seemed to enjoy the change experience, using discursive resources such as 'love,' 'like,' 'enjoy' and disliked organizational stagnation, as 'I get bored easily,' 'hate standing still,' and 'enjoy a new challenge.' Again this gives us an indication of a possible trait of the corporate entrepreneur. We recommend that further research be conducted into CE 'skills' such as communication and traits such as acceptance of change, as this may yield some insight into the diffusing and dissemination of CE within organizations.

The importance of *mentors* or champions in supporting the corporate entrepreneurs was evident within our research.

> The head of nursing there was very, very, very supportive but she said to me 'I don't care what you do if you can support the nurses if you can help them to identify their issues and improve it and I'm happy.' She

wasn't terribly interested in the process, which is fine 'cause she's an operational manager.

(Trust A Specialist Nurse, Team Leader: Accident & Emergency)

Few corporate entrepreneurs did not cite the help of a mentor or champion as being important in supporting their entrepreneuring. In some cases, a number of individuals had been important. The private sector literature highlights the key role of the champion in winning more funding and more time for projects (Pinchot 1985; Kanter 1989). In Trusts A and B the champion appears to provide legitimate power, political influence and business acumen to CE. Greenhalgh *et al.* (2004b: 2) suggest that individuals in an organization are more likely to adopt an innovation if key individuals have champions; however, they comment that there is remarkably little evidence on how to identify organizational champions and harness their energy.

In cases where acute hospital nurses were the corporate entrepreneurs, a number of champions have been those medical consultants newer to the post. Conversely, in some cases where nurses had experienced extreme resistance, the longer-serving consultants would often be the reason. In these cases, either the longer-serving consultant would retire, and so the project could continue, or the consultant would be won over by the newer consultants who were more supportive. In some instances the nurse entrepreneurs would have to work at different levels of autonomy for different consultants. For example;

> There's one who's very good and has helped us to develop project X, and there's one who's retiring who's very reluctant to do project X. I think he's allowing us to perform the procedures – he's the one who asked for us to train, strangely enough! He wants us to perform the procedures ... but doesn't want us to make any other decisions. Whereas the younger one, he will allow us to do the whole project.
>
> (Trust B G Grade Nurse Practitioner)

Critical learning experience

One of the key findings is the critical learning experience. Building on the work of Greenhalgh *et al.* (2004a) and setting it within a CE context, what is really interesting from our initial analysis is that most of the corporate entrepreneurs interviewed have had a *critical learning experience*, which has promoted an integrative view of their world. As Kanter (1983: 27–29) observes

> I found that the entrepreneurial spirit producing innovation is associated with a particular way of approaching problems that I call 'integrative'; the willingness to move beyond received wisdom, to combine ideas from unconnected sources, to embrace change as an opportunity to test limits. In the integrative mode [people] aggregate sub problems

into larger problem, so as to re-create a unity that provides more insight into the required action.

Our research has revealed examples of segmentalist (compartmentalizing and isolating) versus integrative pockets of intraprelearning thinking for example;

> It is about culture at the end of the day and the nursing staff are very much entrenched within their own culture, and they weren't aware of the bigger picture, and the bigger picture could be just outside [Ward X] not just the Trust or nationally, people don't see beyond their area of practice and it's about being aware.
>
> (Trust B Specialist Nurse, Day Surgery)

Corporate entrepreneurs in both Trusts have had some degree of integrative learning experience. For many, the undergraduate or postgraduate degree process provided a critical integrative learning experience, for others it occurred from several learning experiences;

> I try very much to find my boundaries and exceed them, I have training in [a holistic therapy], I have training in [psychotherapy], I have set up a couple of companies and I've also lived in a few countries as well – I mean these are all alternative ways of looking at life, if you like I have multiple caps, I can more naturally than most look at many ways of seeing a particular thing and obviously the more ways you look at something the more likely you are to find a use or see a solution in it.
>
> (Trust B EWTD Medical Lead)

As our data analysis proceeds we will be looking for more clues and insight regarding these critical integrative learning experiences. That integrative learning is experienced during undergraduate and postgraduate degree processes is an important finding, in that it highlights the value of such study, and presents an opportunity to identify what specific parts (context and content) of this study process encourage intraprelearning. It seems that once an integrative perspective has been formed, then the corporate entrepreneur is supported in creative, innovative and risk-taking behaviour. Other learning that supports this includes experiential learning and reflexivity. Having presented some key themes from our preliminary analysis, we now discuss the notion of intraprelearning.

Intraprelearning

Focusing on our key concept, intraprelearning, how do our preliminary findings fit onto our conceptual model? We have mapped some of our initial findings onto the intraprelearning model (see Figure 4.3). Small changes take into account some of the empirical evidence we have collected.

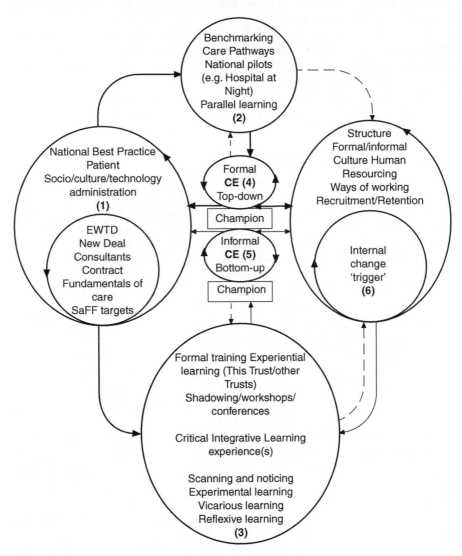

Figure 4.3 An empirical model of NHS intraprelearning (CE).

As with the scenario for Figure 4.1, we will begin by assuming an external trigger in (1) even though this may not be the case in reality. During our data collection, a number of triggers fitting into Iles and Sutherland's (2001) PESTEL factors were highlighted. These external triggers have driven numerous legislative policies and frameworks including; the EWTD, New Deal, Consultant's Contract, Fundamentals of Care, and Service and Financial Frameworks (SaFFs) target. There are many more triggers impacting upon Trusts A and B, and it is likely that more external drivers will be highlighted from our data as it is analysed further.

Some form of learning (2 and 3) took place for Trusts A and B to know about the aforementioned legislations and frameworks. At the organizational level (2) we found that this was done through National Pilots (i.e. the Hospital at Night scheme), the benchmarking of other Trusts, following National Care Pathways (developed by other Trusts), and parallel learning (forming shadow structures of main Trust). From our preliminary analysis, we feel that organizational level learning (2) tended to be single-loop learning.

At the team and individual level (3), learning was derived from a mixture of tacit and explicit knowledge (Nonaka 1991). We found examples of informal learning at both the team and individual levels. Drawing from the processual work of Huber (1991) informal learning included scanning and noticing, experiential learning, vicarious learning and reflexive learning. We also found examples of formal learning, particularly at the individual level, which included training, shadowing, attending workshops and conferences. Greehalgh *et al.* (2004a, b) have conducted a thorough review of the innovations literature and identified a large section on individual's tendencies to try out, adopt, and use innovations. These include personality traits such as:

- tolerance of ambiguity;
- intellectual ability;
- values; and
- learning style.

This builds on the work of Greenhalgh *et al.* (2004a) and sets it within a CE context.

Once learning has taken place (the Trust Board of Directors learn about the EWTD through the H@N scheme (organizational level), or an individual employee attends a conference and learns about a tension created by the EWTD (individual level), solutions are sought to the problem. One solution is to solve a change problem through CE (5 and 6).

From our study, CE that has been driven by individual and team level learning (3) appears to be more emergent and informal (5). Similarly, CE that has been driven by organizational level learning (2) appears to be more formal and planned (4). Contradictory to our initial conceptualization (Figure 4.1), it seems that individual and team level CE may be driven by both external and *internal* triggers. An example of an internal trigger is from a team in Trust A, who were driven to CE because their manager preferred a certain way of working, which limited their resources.

> Our line manager is dead against therapists working with condition X, which is very strange, so she was not proactive about doing anything, so we were being stopped from going on advanced training, so I was very aware that something had to be done – you just can't let things be,

whereas she was saying you're not meant to be doing anything. But I could see a definite gap, and the multidisciplinary task and finish group knew something had to be done, so we had to find a different solution.

(Trust A SN1 Senior Nurse; Learning Disabilities)

In our model, we have separated CE (4 and 5) into informal bottom-up CE (5) and formal top-down CE (4). This is to illustrate the role of the champion on our model. As shown, the champion is supportive in transforming the learned idea into an informal CE activity and also in formalizing informal CE activity. As with previous models, both informal and formal CE activities change the external and internal organizational environments. External changes (1) from Trusts A&B CE include new 'Best Practice' guidelines, changes in how and where clinic patients use certain facilities and technologies and changes in administrative systems that have been adopted across Wales. Internal changes (6) include reduction in sickness and absenteeism rates, decreasing waiting times for patients, more efficient and effective administration and significant changes to the hierarchy and culture.

Conclusions and critique

If we are to seek ways of increasing corporate entrepreneurial capability and capacity in NHS Trusts, we need to know more about intraprelearning at all organizational levels. The research literature underpinning intraprelearning can be broadly separated into three fields, corporate entrepreneurship (CE), organizational learning (OL) and organizational change (OC). We introduced the term intraprelearning to describe the possible interrelationships between the three processes of CE, OL and CE at all organizational levels.

From a search of the OL, CE, OC and intrapreneurship research literature, very few contributions were found that explored the interrelationships within intraprelearning. Those contributions that we did find were discussion based, and even though they provided foundations for further empirical research, we felt that they did not fully consider some significant contributions to the OL, CE and OC literatures offered by key theorists, and neglected the role of social constructions in their management science ontology. In order to address this gap, we reconceptualized our earlier models (Sambrook and Roberts 2005) and redefined CE in terms of the NHS. To explore the validity and utility of our conceptualization, we have mapped our initial findings from more than 50 semi-structured interviews in two Welsh NHS Trusts and have discussed some emerging themes.

From interviews with the senior participants, we observe that there are differing perceptions of the EWTD, H@N scheme and CE at the strategic level, which may be compounded at operational levels. However, given the small sample size and from only two Trusts, we are cautious not to generalize at this stage. Turning to the corporate entrepreneurs, an interesting theme regarding their 'skills' is emerging, in that they appear to be effective communicators, using techniques such as metaphors during conversation. The critical role of the sponsor in supporting CE is also emphasized. We have identified some of the organizational and individual level intraprelearning that is now emerging, most interestingly, the critical integrative learning experience(s).

Drawing from the work of Kanter (1983) we have observed how our corporate entrepreneurs have had this critical integrative learning experience, and how it has supported, or even triggered, their entrepreneurial capability. For integrative learning to be experienced from undergraduate and postgraduate degree processes is an important finding, in that it highlights the value of such study, and presents an opportunity to identify what specific parts (context and content) of this study process encourage intraprelearning. This area also provides a rich platform for future, useful research.

So what are the implications of our tale for HRD?

The implications for HRD can be summarized in the following key learning points.

- CE is not language that is used widely within the context of the NHS. Therefore, from a review of the research literature we have translated it into an NHS definition. It is the process of proactively engaging in creative, ethical and guarded risk-taking behaviours, routines and ways of working that seek to create entrepreneurial behaviour that is:

  a   perceived as new by a proportion of key stakeholders;
  b   linked to the provision or support of health care;
  c   discontinuous with previous practice.

  which facilitates organizational redefinition and rejuvenation through improving administrative efficiency; cost effectiveness; the user experience; and ultimately leads to enhanced patient care.
- There is a need to ensure a shared understanding of CE, whether clarified in documents, communications and/or education.
- The role of the sponsor or champion is key within CE activities. We need to understand more about how we can develop them.
- We have introduced and defined intraprelearning as any learning (individual/team/organizational) that facilitates CE (individual/team/organizational) through triggering change (individual/team/organizational). Intraprelearning may be tacit or explicit, may be single-, double- or meta-loop and may be formal or informal.
- We have described critical integrative learning events that appear to trigger CE thinking within our participants. How can we facilitate/prepare/capture and disseminate this form of intraprelearning?
- We have also explored issues such as culture and the nursing stretch. How can HRD support cultural changes that remove individuals out of

their silos, make them less resistant to beneficial change and support roles that are being stretched?

References

Argyris, C. and Schö, D. (1978) *Organisational Learning: A Theory of Action Perspective*, Reading, MA: Addison-Wesley.

ASH (2000) 'Lung cancer overtakes breast cancer as a killer of women,' Press release, 24 September 2000, www.ash.org.uk/html/press/000924.html accessed on 11 July 2005.

Bateson, G. (1973) *Steps to an Ecology of Mind*, London: Paladin.

Bennis, W.G. (1969) *Organization Development; Its Nature, Origins and Prospects*, Reading MA: Addison-Wesley.

Burgelman, R.A. (1983) 'Corporate entrepreneurship and strategic management: insights from a process study,' *Management Science* 29(12): 1349–1363.

Burns, J.M. (1978) *Leadership*, New York: Harper & Row.

Burns, T. and Stalker, G.M. (1994) *The Management of Innovation*, 3rd edn, Oxford: Oxford University Press.

Collis, D.J. (1994) 'Research note – How Valuable are Organisational Capabilities?' *Strategic Management Journal* 15.

Covin, J.G. (1999) 'Corporate entrepreneurship and the pursuit of competitive advantage,' *Entrepreneurship: Theory and Practice* 23(3): 47–64.

Covin, J.G. and Slevin, D.P. (1991) 'A conceptual model of entrepreneurship as firm behaviour,' *Entrepreneurship Theory & Practice* 16(1): 7–25.

Crossan, M.M., Lane, H.W. and White, R.E. (1999) 'An organisational learning framework: from intuition to institution,' *Academy of Management Review* 24(3): 522–537.

Davis, S.M. and Lawrence, P.R. (1977) *Matrix*, Reading MA: Addison Wesley.

Dawson, P. (1994) *Organizational Change: A Processual Approach*, London: Paul Chapman.

Dawson, P. (1996) *Technology and Quality: Change in the Workplace*, London: International Thomson Business Press.

Dawson, P. (2003) *Understanding Organizational Change: The Contemporary Experience of People at Work*, London: Sage.

DoH (2000) *The NHS Plan*, Department of Health Public Service Agreement.

DoH (2001) *The Essence of Care: Patient-focused Benchmarking for Healthcare Practitioners*, London: Department of Health Publications.

DoH (2004) *The NHS Knowledge and Skills Framework (NHS KSF) and the Development Review Process*, London: Department of Health Publications.

Dess, G.G., Ireland, R.D., Zahra, S.A., Floyd, S.W., Janney, J.J. and Lane, P.J. (2003) 'Emerging issues in corporate entrepreneurship,' *Journal of Management* 29(3): 351–378.

Dixon, N. (1992) 'Organisational learning: a review of the literature with implications for HRD Professionals,' *Human Resource Development* Quarterly 3(1) Spring.

Easterby-Smith, M. (1997) 'Disciplines of organizational learning: contributions and critiques,' *Human Relations* 50(9): 1085–1113.

Easterby-Smith, M. and Araujo, L. (1999) 'Organisational learning: the literatures' in M. Easterby-Smith, J. Burgoyne, and L. Araujo (eds) *Organizational Learning and the Learning Organization: Developments in Theory and Practice*, London: Sage.

Griffin, R.W. (1999) *Management*, 6th edn, Boston, USA: Houghton Mifflin.

Greenhalgh, T., Robert, G. and Bate, P. (2004a) *How to Spread Good Ideas; A Systematic Review of the Literature on Diffusion, Dissemination and Sustainability of Innovations in Health Service Delivery and Organisation*, London: NCCSDO.

Greenhalgh, T., Robert, G. and Bate, P. (2004b) 'Spreading and sustaining innovations in health service delivery and organisation,' *Briefing paper Change Management*, NCCSDO November 2004 accessed on 1 March 2005 www.sdo.lshtm.ac.uk/pdf/changemanagement_greenhalgh_briefingpaper.pdf.

Handy, C. (1979) *Understanding Organizations*, 2nd edn, Harmondsworth: Penguin Books.

Harrison, R. (1972) 'Understanding your organization's character,' *Harvard Business Review* 50(3): 119–128.

Harrison, R (1998) *Employee Development*, London: Institute of Personnel and Development.

Hedberg, B. (1981) 'How organisations learn and unlearn,' in P. Nystrom and W. Starbuck (eds) *Handbook of Organisational Design*, Vol. 1, Oxford: Oxford University Press.

Huber, G.P. (1991) 'Organizational learning: the contributing processes and the literatures,' *Organizational Science* 2(1): 88.

Kanter, R.M. (1983) *The Change Masters*, Great Britain: George Allen & Unwin.

Kanter, R.M. (1988) 'When a thousand flowers bloom: structural, collective and social conditions for innovation in organisations,' *Research in Organizational Behaviour* 10: 169–211.

Kanter, R.M. (1989) *When Giants Learn to Dance*, New York: Simon and Schuster.

Iles, V. and Sutherland, K. (2001) *Managing Change in the NHS: Organisational Change – a Review for Health Care Managers, Professionals and Researchers*, London: National Coordinating Centre for NHS Service Delivery and Organisational R & D (NCC/SDO).

Lewin, K. (1951) *Field Theory in Social Science*, New York: Harper & Row.

Lynskey, M.J. (2002) *Entrepreneurship and Organisation*, in M.J. Lynskey and S Yonekura (eds) Oxford: Oxford University Press.

March, J. and Olsen, J.P. (eds) (1976) *Ambiguity and Choice in Organizations*, Bergen, Norway: Universitetsforlaget.

Martin, J. (1992) *Cultures in Organizations: Three Perspectives*, Oxford: Oxford University Press.

Miles, R.E. and Snow, C.C. (1978) *Organizational Strategy, Structure and Process*, New York: McGraw-Hill.

Miller, D. and Friesen, P,H. (1983) 'Strategy making and the environment: the third link,' *Strategic Management Journal* 4: 221–235.

Mintzberg, H. (1973) 'Strategy-making in three modes,' *California Management Review* Winter, XVI(2): 44–53.

Modernisation Agency (2003) 'The Hospital at Night Scheme' accessed at www.modern.nhs.uk on 4 May 2005.

Modernisation Agency (2005) 'Innovation and Knowledge Group' accessed at www.modernnhs.nhs.uk/scripts/default.asp?site_id=24 on 4 May 2005.

Morris, M.H and Paul, G.W. (1987) 'The relationship between entrepreneurship and marketing in established firms,' *Journal of Business Venturing* 2: 247–259.

Nonaka, I. (1991) 'The knowledge creating company,' in *Harvard Business Review on*

Knowledge Management (1998), US: Harvard Business Review Paperback, 6th edn, President and Fellows of Harvard College.

Pedler, M., Burgoyne, J. and Boydell, T. (1991) *The Learning Company: A Strategy for Sustainable Development*, Maidenhead, McGraw-Hill.

Pedler, M., Burgoyne, J. and Boydell, T. (1996) *The Learning Company: A Strategy for Sustainable Development*, 2nd edn, Maidenhead, McGraw-Hill.

Pettigrew, A. (1990) 'Longitudinal field research on change: theory and practice,' *Organization Science* 1(3): 267–292.

Pinchot, G. (1985) *Intrapreneuring*, New York: Harper Row.

Popper, M. and Lipshitz, R. (1998) 'Organizational learning mechanisms: a structural and cultural approach to organizational learning,' *Journal of Applied Behavioural Science* 34: 161–179.

Proehl, R.A. (2001) *Organisational Change in the Human Services*, London: Sage.

Ropo, A., Eriksson, P. and Hunt, J. (1997) 'Reflections on conducting processual research on management and organizations,' *Scandinavian Journal of Management* 13(4): 331–335.

Sambrook, S. and Roberts, C.H. (2005) 'The inter-relationships between corporate entrepreneurship and organisational learning: a review of literature and the development of a conceptual framework,' *Journal of Strategic Change* 14: 141–155.

Schein, E.H. (1985) *Organizational Culture and Leadership*, San Francisco: Jossey-Bass.

Senge, P. (1990) *The Fifth Discipline: The Art and Practice of the Learning Organisation*, New York: Century Business.

Stopford, J.M. and Baden-Fuller, C.W.F. (1994) Creating corporate entrepreneurship, *Strategic Management Journal* 15: 521–536.

Sun, H. (2003) 'Conceptual clarifications for "organizational learning", "learning organization" and "a learning organisation,"' *Human Resource Development International* 6(2): 153–166.

Swieringa, J. and Wierdsma, A. (1992) *Becoming a Learning Organization*, Wokingham: Addison-Wesley.

Thomas, W.E.G. (2005) 'Fostering innovation without compromising safety,' *Clinical Governance Bulletin*, London: The Royal Society of Medicine Press Ltd 5(6).

Thomson, N. and McNamara, P. (2001) 'Achieving post acquisition success: the role of the corporate entrepreneurship,' *Long Range Planning* 34: 669–697.

Tofler, A. (1970) *Future Shock*, London: Pan Books.

Tsang, E.W.K. (1997) 'Organizational learning and the learning organization: a dichotomy between descriptive and prescriptive research,' *Human Relations* 50(1): 73–89.

Van de Ven, A. and Huber, G.P. (1990) 'Longitudinal field research methods for studying processes of organizational change,' *Organization Science* 1(3): 213–219.

Wanless, D. and The Health Trends Review Team (2002) *Securing our Future Health: Taking a Long-term View*, London: Public Enquiry Unit, HM Treasury.

WAG (2002) *Well Being in Wales*, Cardiff: Welsh Assembly Government Consultation Document.

WAG (2003) *Fundamentals of Care; Guidance for Health and Social Care Staff*, Cardiff: Welsh Assembly Government.

Welsh NHS Trust Medical Personnel Department (2004) *Outline Plan of Draft Document – V1 European Working Time Directive* (Internal Document).

Williams, A., Donson, P. and Walters, M. (1989) *Changing Culture: New Organisational Approaches*, London: Institute of Personnel Management.

Zahra, S.A., Nielsen, A.P. and Bogner, W.C. (1999) Corporate entrepreneurship, knowledge, and competence development, *Entrepreneurship Theory and Practice*, Spring: 169–189.

5 HRD and organizational commitment in health and social care organizations

Kenneth R. Bartlett

Health and social care organizations are increasingly realizing the extent to which they rely on their human resources. In an era of continued change and challenge, health and social care organizations are showing growing interest in two key human resource issues, namely Human Resource Development (HRD) and organizational commitment. The interest in HRD, including training, professional education, career development, and organization development, stems from the need to maintain a knowledgeable workforce able to provide quality service in the face of significant change within the entire health and social care sector. The interest in organizational commitment is driven by an increased understanding of the importance of this work-related attitude and its connection to a wide range of outcomes (Cohen 2003). Both of these issues exert considerable influence on the management and performance of health and social care organizations.

Introduction

The performance of the entire health and social care sector is noted as being critically dependent on human resources with health care delivery characterized as highly labor intensive (Franco *et al.* 2002). Reforms within health and social care delivery systems are now an international phenomena, although HRD issues associated with these changes are often overlooked. White (1991) suggested that the role of HRD assumes greater importance within the health service sector during times of restructuring and reform. As health and social care occupations become ever more complex in terms of the development of new technologies, treatment approaches, as well as new legal, regulatory, and financial management oversight requirements, the need for HRD is increasingly recognized. Added to this are requirements for ongoing training, leading to the achievement and maintenance of certification and accreditation of both individual employees and the health and social care organizations in which they work. This environment of increasing complexity and the escalating costs of managing health and social care organizations have focused attention on making HRD as effective as possible.

HRD is recognized as being able not only to develop skill and knowledge for improved job performance but also to foster and contribute to desired workplace attitudes and behaviors of employees (Meyer and Smith 2000; Bartlett 2001; Tansky and Cohen 2001; Benson *et al.* 2004). Furthermore, workplace attitudes have also been found to play a role in the attitudes, behaviors, and performance in HRD activities (Birdi *et al.* 1997). Among the many workplace attitudes studied, the construct of organizational commitment is singled out as an increasingly valued work-related attitude in health and social care settings. Organizational commitment is a term that refers to a person's type and strength of attachment to his or her organization (Arnold *et al.* 1998). The interest in organizational commitment is linked to issues such as retention, new requirements in job performance, and employee response to change, which demand the attention of health and social care managers.

Aims and objectives

The aim of this chapter is to define the concept of organizational commitment and to summarize current research on this increasingly valued workplace attitude. The theoretical context of organizational commitment will be described. Despite the prevalence of utilizing health and social care occupations for much of the existing literature related to organizational commitment, no summary of this research from a health and social care perspective has been conducted. This chapter aims to address this need. Furthermore, the state of research exploring the connection between various types of HRD and organizational commitment will be examined with an emphasis on those studies conducted in the health and social care settings. The implications and conclusions gained from this research will be presented and a range of examples of specific practices related to HRD will be provided to assist health and social care managers to foster the level of organizational commitment in their employees.

The theoretical context

The theoretical context of organizational commitment has received increased attention in recent years as a broader level of thinking has followed the expanding body of knowledge driven from empirical research. Much of the more recent work on the theoretical context of organizational commitment focuses on the employment relationship (Rousseau 1995; Baruch 2001), the recognition that commitment can take different forms, and that multiple commitment targets or foci exist around aspects of work (Reichers 1985; Randall and Cote 1991; Morrow 1993; Cohen 1999; Meyer *et al.* 2004). Yet, before the theoretical context is described, the concept or construct of organizational commitment needs to be defined.

Organizational commitment defined

Organizational commitment is one of numerous domains of life to which an individual may form an attachment. Yet, of all the life domains it is the attachment or commitment between an employee and their employing organization that remains the most studied. Numerous definitions of organizational commitment exist, reflecting that the concept has been the focus of more than 50 years of academic study (Cohen 2003). Adding to the difficulty in defining organizational commitment is the prevalence of related terms used in the business and popular press. The most frequently used are organizational affiliation, allegiance, loyalty, and attachment.

Meyer and Herscovitch (2001) listed many of the most prominent academic definitions in the literature, noting both points of agreement and disagreement in several. The two most often cited definitions of organizational commitment mirror the debate surrounding the issue of whether the construct is unidimensional or multidimensional in nature. The unidimensional approach advocates that commitment is a mind-set reflecting a level of desire to maintain membership in the organization, belief in and acceptance of the values and goals of the organization, and a willingness to exert effort on behalf of the organization (Porter *et al.* 1974).

The multidimensional approach suggests that individuals can have more than one mind-set that describes their psychological bind to an organization. The most widely recognized multidimensional conceptualization and definition of organizational commitment over the past several years has been that offered by Meyer and Allen (1991). They defined organizational commitment as comprising three components, which they labeled:

> *Affective commitment* refers to the psychological attachment to the organization, *continuance commitment* refers to the costs associated with leaving the organization, and *normative commitment* refers to a perceived obligation to remain with the organization.
>
> (Meyer and Allen 1991: 1)

These three components of commitment are alternatively described as 'the product of (a) emotional attachments (affective commitment); (b) the costs of leaving, such as losing attractive benefits or seniority (continuance commitment); and (c) the individual's personal values (normative commitment)' (Breif 1998: 38).

Meyer and Allen (1991) have suggested differences in the basis of employee behavior is the most important reason for supporting the multidimensional approach to organizational commitment. Although all three forms of commitment tend to bind the employee to the organization, the driver or reason for the attachment is different. Meyer and Allen (1991, 1997) cautioned researchers to consider affective, continuance, and normative to be components, rather than types, of commitment because an individual employee's relationship with an organization may vary across all three. Yet, it should be realized that common to all conceptualizations of commitment is the idea that commitment binds an individual to an organization (Meyer and Allen 1997). The overarching fact remains that those workers with strong commitment to the organization will be more valuable than those with weak commitment. As the body of research has grown, so too has support for the three-component model of organizational commitment. This chapter will primarily refer to the three-component conceptualization and definition of organizational commitment unless specified.

The empirical context

The number of studies on organizational commitment continues to accumulate at an increasing rate. Each year sees more of this research conducted internationally, or in multiorganizational contexts with an expanding range of diverse industry settings. Rather than provide a complete overview of this research, an illustrative sample of studies is highlighted, then studies of organizational commitment in health and social care settings are reviewed. Finally, the small but expanding body of literature exploring how HRD and organizational commitment are connected is considered, again highlighting those studies that have used data from health and social care organizations.

Research on organizational commitment

Much of the interest in organizational commitment stems from reports of positive consequences on employee behavior and desirable work outcomes. The business press has extolled the benefits of recruiting and retaining employees with high levels of organizational commitment as this leads to value creation in organizations (Elsdon 2003). Dessler (1993) argued that in a business environment of rapid change, committed employees give the competitive advantage to organizations. Jaffe *et al.* (1994: xii) stated that the 'demands on organizations today are so great that they cannot operate without high commitment from their employees.' Other writers of popular business books have suggested that 'employee commitment will become increasingly important in the coming decades because more and more companies are moving the decision-making processes farther down the organizational hierarchy, making it almost impossible for management to control performance directly' (Fink 1992: 3).

Over the past few decades a growing number of empirical studies have been conducted to determine if these proposed positive outcomes resulting from organizational commitment are indeed supported. This body of research could be summarized into three groups, comprising studies that have examined the causes or antecedents, the outcomes or consequences, and the relationships with correlate variables (Meyer and Herscovitch 2001). Correlate variables are those constructs that tend to be somewhat highly correlated with organizational commitment. It should be noted that frequently examined correlates such as job satisfaction, job involvement, and occupational commitment are correlated to organizational commitment, especially the affective component. Yet factor analytic and discriminate validity studies have repeatedly found that these correlate variables are distinct and distinguishable constructs from organizational commitment.

An additional key point to acknowledge is that different components of commitment are conceptually unique. The affective, continuance, and normative commitment components are thought to develop from different causes and result in different outcomes (Meyer and Allen 1991) and relationships with other types of workplace behavior can vary by the type of organizational commitment (Meyer *et al.* 2004). Research shows that affective commitment tends to produce the strongest relationships with desired work behaviors followed by normative commitment, whereas continuance commitment tends to be unrelated, or negatively related, to these behaviors (Meyer *et al.* 2004; Meyer and Herscovitch 2001).

An examination of antecedents is considered beneficial for exploring possible moderating variables that may influence organizational commitment (Mathieu and Zajac 1990) and to gain an understanding for managing for commitment (Meyer and Allen 1997). Studies examining the three components of organizational commitment and variables hypothesized to be its antecedents are often grouped into four categories: demographic variables, individual differences, work experiences, and the availability of job alternatives. In general terms, antecedents related to personal characteristics, demographic variables, and individual difference variables, produce very weak associations whereas previous work experiences and the availability of job alternatives play a greater role in developing commitment (Meyer *et al.* 2002). This suggests that employers should concentrate more on managing the experiences people have once employed rather than spending effort to recruit and select workers predisposed as being highly committed (Meyer *et al.* 1991).

While the antecedents of organizational commitment are frequently examined it is the outcomes or consequences of commitment that attract the most research attention. Major meta-analyses studies of Mathieu and Zajac (1990), Randall (1990) and Meyer *et al.* (2002) have confirmed the well-established positive relationships between organizational commitment and a series of organization-relevant and employee-relevant outcomes. As Meyer *et al.* (2002: 22) noted, 'until recently, organizational commitment theory and research has focused primarily on outcomes of relevance to employers. There is now a growing body of research examining the links between commitment and employee-relevant outcomes including stress and work-family conflict.'

Yet, arguably, the most studied and confirmed consequence of organizational commitment is the negative relationship with turnover as well as intentions to withdraw or voluntarily leave. Turnover researchers have long suggested that low organizational commitment levels were a key variable leading to thoughts of quitting an organization, intention to search for other employment, and finally the decision to stay or leave (Porter *et al.* 1974; Mobley *et al.* 1979). The most recent meta-analytic study examining the correlations between the three forms of organizational commitment and turnover conducted by Meyer *et al.* (2002) found that while all were negative, the magnitude of the correlations differed. The strongest relationships were found with turnover intention and affective commitment (−0.56), followed by normative (−0.33), and continuance commitment (−0.18). They noted that correlations with actual turnover behavior were weaker but showed the same pattern (−0.17, −0.16, and −0.10, respectively). The affective form of commitment is also negatively correlated with absenteeism, self-reported stress, and work–family conflict.

Much interest has centered on the relationship of organizational commitment and job performance. Meyer *et al.* (2002) showed that affective and normative commitment correlates positively whereas continuance commitment relates negatively with measures of job performance. Even stronger relationships are found between commitment and organizational citizenship behaviors (defined as a willingness of an employee to go above and beyond the scope of the job for the benefit of the organization).

The link between organizational commitment and employee effort towards the job and performance is potentially of great interest and use to managers. Several studies have shown that those employees with strong organizational commitment work harder at their jobs and perform better than those with weak commitment (Meyer and Allen 1997). In a study of Canadian food service managers, Meyer *et al.* (1989) found that affective commitment was positively related to performance ratings provided by the subjects' manager. In a separate study, a weak positive correlation was found between commitment and performance for a sample of 308 Singaporean life insurance agents (Leong *et al.* 1994). In studies using independent (and not perceptual) measures of performance, organizational commitment has been linked to measures such as sales figures (Bashaw and Grant 1994), the control of operational costs (DeCotiis and Summers 1987), and branch performance of German banks (Benkhoff 1997).

However, not all studies find a relationship between commitment and performance (e.g. Williams and Anderson 1991; Ganster and Dwyer 1995). Meyer and Allen (1997) offered four possible explanations for the variation and general weak association between performance and commitment. First, supervisory ratings of performance are subject to bias. Second, stated performance objectives are said to influence the direction of commitment (Shim and Steers 1994). In other words, 'commitment will most likely find expression in those aspects of job performance that employees believe are important to the organization' (Meyer and Allen 1997: 30). Third, the impact of commitment on performance is greatly influenced by employee-motivation and ability, and access to resources necessary to complete the job.

Fourth, and related to resource access, is that employees must have adequate control over the performance outcomes against which they will be measured. These four issues have important implications for the measurement of commitment and the relationship to in-role job performance. These four weaknesses in the commitment/performance relationship have prompted the examination of alternative measures of performance such as extra-role performance also referred to as organizational citizenship behaviors.

Organizational citizenship behavior first appeared in empirical studies in 1983 (Bateman and Organ 1983; Smith *et al.* 1983) to explore 'individual contributions in the workplace that go beyond role requirements and con-tractually rewarded job achievements' (Organ and Ryan 1995: 775). This construct is important to organizations because it 'represents contributions that do not inhere in formal role obligations' (Organ and Konovsky 1989: 157). Organizational citizenship behavior includes volunteering for extra job activities, helping others, and upholding workplace rules and procedures (Organ and Ryan 1995).

Organizational commitment is suggested as being an antecedent of organizational citizenship behavior because 'it reflects an employee's willing-ness to aid the organization even if direct reward is not contingent upon that aid' (Moorman *et al.* 1993: 211). Several empirical studies confirm this rela-tionship (Shore and Wayne 1993; Munene 1995). The meta-analysis of Organ and Ryan (1995) found a significant average relationship between organizational commitment and organizational citizenship behavior of $r = 0.23$. Meyer and Allen (1997) concluded their examination of organi-zational citizenship behavior and organizational commitment by suggesting that 'it appears, from these research findings, that the comment "It's not my job" is less likely to be heard from an employee with either strong affective commitment or strong normative commitment than one with weak commitment' (Meyer and Allen 1997: 35).

A growing number of studies have examined other consequences of organizational commitment. For example, Wahn (1993) found employees with high commitment levels less likely to engage in unethical behavior. Several studies have explored the relationship between commitment and work-related stress, suggesting that commitment has a negative correlation with self-reported measures of psychological and physical stress (Begley and Czajka 1993). Commitment was also shown to relate to satisfaction with career and measures of non-work life satisfaction in a sample of public employees (Romzek 1989).

Research on organizational commitment in health and social care

The construct of organizational commitment is noted as being of particular importance and relevance to public sector employment (Gould-Williams 2004) and especially within health care and social service organizations (McLean and Andrew 2000; Laschinger *et al.* 2001). Consequently, the existing body of literature on organization commitment has relied heavily on health and social care settings for empirical studies to test and advance theory. While the majority of the existing literature examining organizational commitment in health and social care organizations is composed of studies conducted in the United States and Canada, it is truly international in scope, including both individual and cross-cultural studies situated in nations as diverse as the United Kingdom (Baruch and Winkelmann-Gleed 2002), Finland (Kuokkanen *et al.* 2003), Israel (Cohen 2000), Malaysia (Pearson and Chong 1997); and New Zealand (Bartlett and Kang 2004).

The reasons for commitment researchers showing such interest in health professionals could include the often cited high turnover within health and social care occupations and the potential for commitment to explain why employees voluntarily depart work from one organization but remain in the profession. The importance of understanding the drivers of high turnover in the health care industry are supported with research findings that voluntary turnover is negatively related to cost effectiveness in hospitals (Alexander *et al.* 1994). Studies in the USA have carried titles such as 'the shocking cost of turnover in health care' (Waldman and Deane 2004) to convey the direct and indirect as well as the financial and non-financial impact of turnover to health care organizations. Waters (2003) discovered that full replacement costs for nursing staff are, on average, four-to-six times higher than most agencies typically estimate. Therefore, variables such as organizational commitment that help explain the turnover process are of considerable interest in the health and social care setting.

A massive study of almost 40,000 nurses from ten European countries has set out to uncover the reasons, circumstances, and consequences surrounding premature departure from the nursing profession (Halleslhorn *et al.* 2003). Preliminary results from this three year study are confirming the important role of organizational commitment in turnover (Stordeur *et al.* 2003). Organizational commitment scores were found to vary considerably across the ten European nations participating, with respondents from Italy having the lowest mean scores and Finland the highest. Organizational commitment also varied among nurses employed in different types of healthcare institutions with the lowest scores from nurses in hospitals, followed by those working in nursing homes and home care ranked equally, while nurses working in out-patient care facilities ranked highest. In concluding, the authors suggest that additional research is needed, including considering how workplace characteristics, including training and HRD, may influence organizational commitment (Stordeur *et al.* 2003).

One of the most often cited reasons for turnover in health and social care occupations is compensation, in that the lower levels of compensation that characterize many health and social care professions play a role in lowering commitment that eventually leads to voluntary departure. In a study of US nurses, Ahlburg and Mahoney (1996) found that the relative level of pay had a limited impact on retention, in that a 10 percent increase in relative wages increased the probability of continuing in the occupation by only 2 percent. A similar finding was reported in other public sector studies, drawing the conclusion that pay may have been overemphasized in research on turnover, with dissatisfaction at promotion and training opportunities found to have a stronger impact on intentions to quit (Bradley *et al.* 2004). A study on nurse intention to quit the British National Health Service found that dissatisfaction with promotion and training opportunities had a stronger impact than either workload or pay (Shields and Ward 2001). This is resulting in a rethinking of the role of compensation on commitment levels and the consideration of a far wider range of potential variables that might help understand what creates commitment in the hope of reducing high turnover.

The turnover issue is gaining increased prominence as it is compounding current and projected staffing shortages in most health-related occupations (Hudson 2003). This is not simply a USA and Western European issue, as many nations now confront the realities of a lack of trained health and social care employees (American Health Care Association 2003). This is prompting calls for further research on the commitment construct within health care settings (Zangaro 2001) with some suggesting that building organizational commitment among nurses and other health and social care workers is the key to alleviating projected staff shortages (McNeese-Smith 2001).

As health care organizations deal with turnover they are also faced with new demands placed on their frontline staff. These demands result from many different forces, such as new technologies and treatment approaches, changes to management systems and structures, and increased standards in the personal care of patients to improve patient satisfaction. This is, in turn, focusing attention on the context in which health and social care work is performed and on the interest in those aspects of the job which might influence or be related to organizational commitment. As Pearson and Chong (1997: 361) noted 'traditionally, nursing staff have enjoyed little discretion over many facets of their work activities, and often their roles have been structured to confine manifestation of the employment of their professional skills.' Their research showed that key factors of job design and job enrichment, including fostering feelings of autonomy, doing significant work, and receiving feedback have been found to be strongly related to organizational commitment levels in health care workers.

Research on HRD and Organizational Commitment

A small but growing body of literature has explored how certain management practices; including HRD, may influence organizational commitment (Iles *et al.* 1990; Tsui *et al.* 1997; Meyer and Smith 2000; Bartlett 2001; Gould-Williams 2004). Yet, the exploration of the relationship between HRD and organizational commitment is noted as still being in its early stages (Ahmad and Bakar 2003).

Although commitment can be considered as an outcome of HRD participation, previous research has also considered organizational commitment as a variable that influences various training and development activities. More specifically, higher levels of organizational commitment have been found to influence motivation for participation in training (Tannenbaum *et al.* 1991), levels of participant knowledge following a structured HRD program (McEvoy 1997), and the transfer of learning following training (Seyler *et al.* 1998). Regardless of whether it is considered as an antecedent or outcome of HRD, organizational commitment is acknowledged as influencing the training process (Meyer and Allen 1997).

The relationship between organizational commitment and a range of human resource management function areas, including incentive pay, benefits, performance appraisal, training, and career development, was explored by Canadian researchers Meyer and Smith (2000). Their results determined that career development practices were the best predictors of affective and normative commitment. They concluded that this was perhaps to be expected given that those 'organizations that take an active role in helping employees prepare themselves for advancement in the organization, and do so in a way that creates a perception of support, might foster a stronger bond to the organization' (Meyer and Smith 2000: 328). The authors of this study found the relationships to be mediated by perceptions of organizational support and fairness, leading to the conclusion that, 'although human resource management practices can be a valuable tool in the establishment and maintenance of employee commitment, their effects are neither direct nor unconditional' (Meyer and Smith 2000: 319).

In a study of employees from a manufacturing setting in the United Kingdom, Birdi *et al.* (1997) considered how different types of HRD activity may be related to organizational commitment. The results showed that four major categories of HRD – namely (1) required training courses undertaken in work time; (2) work-based development activities on work time; (3) voluntary job-related learning undertaken in employees' own time; and (4) career planning activities done either in work or own time – were all positively related to organizational commitment. A fifth category of HRD, voluntary learning activities with a non-job focus engaged in during employees' own non-work time, was not found to be related to commitment. This prompted the authors to state that this finding of the absence of an association between participation in voluntary learning and organizational commitment is notable because 'it is often assumed by managers that, as part of the "psychological contract," the provision of benefits to staff will enhance their commitment' (Rousseau and Wade-Benzon 1995: 855). The separation of different types of development activities was a major contribution of this study, suggesting to HRD managers that not all organizational sponsored learning will impact commitment levels in the same way.

Yet, of all the HRD activities that have explored links with organizational commitment, it is training that has been the focus for most studies. When considering how training may influence different types of commitment, a number of training-related measures have been used, including the availability for training, support for training, participant motivation for training, perceived benefits of training, and various aspects of the training environment. A study examining all five of these training-related variables in a white-collar work setting in Malaysia found significant relationships with affective and normative commitment (Ahmad and Bakar 2003). Fewer correlations were found with the continuance form of commitment leading to the conclusion that workers may not feel commitment based on a sense of obligation to remain in an organization that has made training available and supported participation in learning events. A number of studies have focused on training offered to new hires when organizational commitment is often a desired outcome of socialization and orientation programs (Klein and Weaver 2001). The results of a study of US Navy recruits (Tannenbaum *et al.* 1991) and entry-level accountants (Saks 1995) showed that organizational commitment was enhanced by participation in highly structured training programs designed for new members.

Other HRD-related practices have also been examined for their relationship to organizational commitment. As the prevalence, and cost, of non-work related employer-sponsored education has grown, so too have questions about the impact of tuition assistance and reimbursement programs. Such programs that support the general education of workers are usually offered to increase employee motivation, morale, and commitment levels. Yet, a recent study of the tuition assistance program of the US military found that those taking advantage of the program were more likely to leave the organization (Buddin and Kapur 2005). A different finding was attained by Benson *et al.* (2004) who found that commitment was high and turnover low while employees were still using tuition assistance and reimbursement programs, but turnover increased significantly after graduation or the awarding of an educational credential. Similarly, the offering of training agreements that stipulate the training an employee is to receive and the required return of service or return of expenditure have also been shown to do little to improve, and perhaps even negatively affect, organizational commitment (Story and Redman 1997). A recent confirmation of this general finding prompted Ito and Brotheridge (2005) to suggest that supporting HRD efforts to improve the career adaptability of employees may lead to both higher organizational commitment and higher turnover. Further research, especially studies using longitudinal designs, are needed in this area.

Mentoring is another area of HRD-related practice increasingly examined for its relationship to organizational commitment. In a longitudinal study of mentoring, Payne and Huffman (2005) found that both affective and continuance commitment levels were significantly higher among those with formal mentors. This outcome of mentoring was still found one year later, suggesting that mentoring serves additional roles beyond organizational socialization and career development. Furthermore, mentoring has been determined to provide benefits to both the mentor and mentee (protégé) with Colarelli and Bishop (1990) finding that mentoring relationships correlated strongly with career commitment for the mentor.

However, a strong caution to the organization of formal mentoring programs comes from the research of Raabe and Beehr (2003). Their study of mentoring outcomes, including organizational commitment and turnover intentions, asked whether mentees were more influenced by their supervisors and co-workers or their assigned mentor at least two levels senior. All mentors in this program had received training on the mentoring relationship. However, the results indicated that if organizations wish to affect commitment and turnover intentions then mentoring programs using supervisors and co-workers may be better than assigned formal mentors from higher up the organizational hierarchy.

Research on HRD and organizational commitment in health and social care settings

HRD in health and social care professions, and nurses in particular, have been utilized in previous research related to organizational commitment (Meyer *et al.* 1993; Hacket *et al.* 1994; Knoop 1995). Existing research has demonstrated that different management practices and organizational management systems play a role in the formation and maintenance of organizational commitment within the health care field (Nystrom 1993; Pearson and Chong 1997; Baker and Baker 1999). In a study of HRD and organizational commitment among nurses in US public hospitals, Bartlett (2001) found that perceptions of access to training opportunities were more strongly related to organizational commitment than either the number of training events attended or the number of hours spent in training during the past year. This suggests that creating an environment where health and social care workers feel that they have access and opportunities to participate in HRD may be more important than requiring a certain prescribed amount of time to be spent in training. Furthermore, Bartlett also found that organizational commitment was related to the perceived support for training from both senior staff and colleagues, personal motivation to learn, and the perceived benefits of training. The strongest relationships were with the emotional or affective component of organizational commitment.

Another study found that managers and supervisors of a large US metropolitan hospital who were satisfied with their employee development were more highly committed than those not satisfied with their employee development (Tansky and Cohen 2001). Furthermore, measures of perceived organizational support, defined as the extent to which the organization values employee contributions and cares about their well-being, were also found to be related positively with commitment. While this study is an important contribution to understanding the HRD/organizational commitment relationship it should be remembered that numerous concerns have been leveled at satisfaction measures of training and employee development (Holton 1996).

The health care profession has also provided an appropriate context to examine the relationship between various work-related practices and commitment, including leadership and HRD policies and practices (Corser 1998). The role of leadership on commitment levels of staff is considered especially important within the often hierarchal structures of many health care organizations. In a study of nurses from a large public hospital in Singapore, the important role of empowerment in the relationship between leadership and organizational commitment was highlighted (Avolio *et al.* 2004). The degree to which psychiatrists employed in the public sector believe their co-workers and administrators share similar ideas towards ideological and treatment approaches was also found to relate to organizational commitment (Baker and Baker 1999). This suggests that if health care professionals feel that they work with and for people with ideological differences towards treatment, then lower organizational commitment may result.

Mentoring has historically been, and remains, an especially salient HRD practice in the health care environment, especially in the nursing profession (Atkins and Williams 1995). A mixed-method study of informal mentoring (no formal mentoring programs were offered by the organization) in a public hospital in the USA found a direct effect on organizational commitment from mentor assistance in learning skills (Kalbfleisch and Bach 1998). In the qualitative part of this study a common theme emerged in which nurses felt that working hard and not having anyone notice, being frequently criticized and rarely rewarded, and being exposed to serious diseases were challenging and stressful aspects of nursing. In response, mentoring and organizational commitment were suggested as possible avenues for increasing the degree to which nurses feel that their job is rewarding (Kalbfleisch and Bach 1998: 388).

Within the social services profession, similar findings are found. Using data from the National Institute of Social Work Studies in the UK, McLean and Andrew (2000) found that job satisfaction, stress, and the amount of control over work were all significantly related to organizational commitment. In a profession where high levels of work-related stress are common, employers of social care workers frequently offer training in response. Yet, McLean and Andrew's findings suggest that affective commitment was associated more with intrinsic satisfaction, the freedom to choose working methods, the amount of responsibility, opportunity to use abilities, and the degree of variety in work. These are aspects of work that a HRD professional could assist with, but this requires more involvement than the offering of simply training to reduce stress. A study of social workers in public, not-for-profit, and proprietary institutions found employees in public organizations to be significantly lower in their organizational commitment and their commitment to the social service profession (Giffords 2003). This finding has implications for the recruitment, retention, and development of human resources in health and social care organizations as these services are increasingly moved from the public sector to alternative delivery systems.

Lastly, the fairly dramatic changes with the health care sector and within individual organizations have prompted a new wave of research examining the impact of change on levels of commitment (Narine and Persaud 2003; Thompson and Van de Ven 2002). A growing area of interest is the role of HRD during times of organizational change and the impact this may have on organizational commitment. Meyer *et al.* (1993b), noted that changes in the workplace, particularly those that result in a reduction in the size of the workforce, have the potential to impact all three forms of organizational commitment of those employees remaining. A Canadian study by Greenglass and Burke (2002) found that hospital restructuring contributed to greater burnout in nurses, although those higher in organizational commitment experienced lower levels of burnout. The growing trend of hospital mergers and acquisitions from umbrella corporations is now being examined from the viewpoint of impacts to health care employee commitment. In a study of a tri-hospital merger, Jones (2003) found that nurses in the acquiring hospital were significantly more committed to the corporate system than nurses from the acquired hospitals. Yet, nurses at all three hospitals showed greater commitment to their own hospital than to the umbrella corporate system.

More recent cross-national research has shown that commitment levels of nurses tends to be lower in nations that have undergone massive restructuring of their public health and social care delivery systems (Bartlett and Kang 2004). This study compared similar-sized hospitals located outside of major urban cities in the USA and New Zealand, finding significantly lower organizational commitment scores in New Zealand where major restructuring has occurred to the public health care system over the past two decades. The impact on organizational commitment could be made worse when investments in employees (e.g. HRD) are reduced. As the pace of change in the health and social care field appears to be showing no signs of slowing, the impact of various organization development and change practices on employee levels of organizational commitment is likely to create interest as the implications are examined in other public sector and for-profit settings.

Interpretations, conclusions, and critical analysis

Health and social care occupations worldwide seem to be experiencing a series of somewhat similar challenges. New demands placed on employees in health care related jobs are occurring at a time when the entire industry is dealing with repeated reform, restructuring, and reorganization, driven at national, regional, and organizational levels. Job stress, burnout, and turnover continue to be issues of great concern to health care managers faced with ongoing and future projected staff shortages. This is increasing the value of committed employees able to deliver health and social care in ever more demanding conditions. The body of theory and research that has grown around organizational commitment seems to suggest that HRD professionals should be aware of this work-related attitude.

Both the academic and practitioner literature have devoted considerable attention to the commitment levels of employees. A study by Shepherd and Mathews (2000) of human resource managers in the UK highlighted that there was widespread recognition of the desirability and benefits of organizational commitment, but clear disparity between the way academics and practitioners conceptualize and measure the construct. The authors concluded by suggesting that 'the subjective approach adopted by practitioners could inform the approaches of academics just as the structured objective approaches of academics should inform practitioners' (Shepherd and Mathews 2000: 555). As more studies are conducted on links between HRD and organizational commitment the same advice could be offered to HRD researchers and professionals.

While organizational commitment is a diverse construct with a large body of theoretical and empirical literature, HRD managers and organizational executives can focus on a few key elements. First, it appears that affective commitment is the most important component to foster within organizations. Previous research on the relationship with affective commitment and turnover intention, actual turnover behavior, and absenteeism supports the notion that efforts to foster affective commitment are desirable (Meyer and Herscovitch 2001). Second, HRD practitioners should focus on the job-related antecedents to commitment rather than personal or situational characteristics over which they have little control. Pinks (1992) provided a summary of relevant job-related and organizational antecedents of high levels of affective commitment that managers can influence. These have been adapted for HRD managers and include increasing job challenge, role clarity, participation in decision making about training, and communicating that the organization depends on the continued efforts of each employee. Pinks (1992: 11) concluded by stating that 'such efforts are likely to be associated with increasing levels of affective commitment.'

The finding that organizational commitment could be considered as a worthwhile outcome of HRD (Bartlett 2001) encourages the HRD professional to think of other meaningful outcomes that contribute towards the objectives of the organization. The almost exclusive focus on performance as the only outcome of HRD (Swanson 1995) has resulted in an overly narrow focus towards desired results from training. The findings from this growing body of literature may suggest that HRD professionals should adopt a broader perspective towards HRD outcomes. For example, HRD is one of many organizational programs that can assist in the development and maintenance of organizational commitment. HRD professionals can capitalize on the existing empirical work on commitment to demonstrate to organizational decision-makers that HRD contributes to commitment, which in turn relates to desired work place attitudes and behaviors, such as reduced absenteeism and turnover.

Some have argued that organizational commitment may be an outdated and redundant concept (Baruch 1998). This line of thinking is based on the changing employment relationship in which employers can no longer offer any form of guaranteed employment, resulting in employees wondering why they should offer any form of loyalty or commitment in return. However, employment in the public sector, and especially within health and social care related professions, has tended to attract individuals with a strong occupational or professional commitment. Meyer and Herscovitch (2001) have suggested that organizations might be able to benefit from efforts to foster occupational commitment without being concerned that they would be simultaneously undermining their employees' organizational commitment. The notion of dual commitments to the organization and the profession is now being explored in the health care arena (Hoff 2001) with training, and other HRD practices such as career development and leadership development, identified as key management actions that may shape dual commitment. The health care field may again take a lead role in commitment-related theory development and research as the complementary nature of dual commitments is explored.

While some HRD authors have suggested that HRD should be designed to achieve increased organizational commitment as an outcome (Lang 1992), it is worth remembering that despite an accumulating body of literature suggesting that HRD is connected to commitment, its regular use as an outcome measure is perhaps unlikely (Klein 2001). It must be remembered that organizational commitment is an attitude and not all HRD efforts are directed at attitude change. There is evidence that attitudes, in this case organizational commitment, do lead to important behavioral and performance outcomes, although far more research in this area is needed. The growing acceptance of multiple commitments (Cohen 2003) is an exciting area for HRD researchers to target their efforts at different types of commitment. An example provided by Klein (2001) suggested that team-building programs might be better focused on increasing commitment to the work team more than the organization.

As expenditures in HRD continue to increase (Association for Training and Development (ASTD) 2004) additional studies are needed to explore how a strategic approach to HRD for developing human capital and shaping organizational culture may impact organizational commitment. It must be highlighted that much of the research to date has employed correlational research designs so that causal influences cannot be made. Yet, the evidence to date suggests that future research examining HRD and organizational commitment could be valuable to HRD researchers and practitioners. Other variables associated with HRD policy and practice as well as employee attitudes towards HRD should continue to be further explored for their potential links to organizational commitment. Many of the unique aspects of health and social care work may mean that this setting is well placed to be at the forefront of future theoretical and empirical advancements on commitment and HRD.

Key learning points

- Organizational commitment is a work-related attitude that is increasingly valued by employers.
- Highly committed employees are valued for their ability remain with the organization while delivering health and social care in ever more demanding conditions.
- A growing body of literature does suggest that HRD is related to organizational commitment. Yet, the direction and ordering of the relations requires much additional study.
- Different HRD policies, practices, and activities should be targeted at different levels and types of organizational commitment.
- Health and social core occupations are ideal settings for examining emerging developments related to the HRD and organizational commitment link.

References

Ahlburg, D. and Mahoney, C. (1996) 'The effect of wages on the retention of nurses,' *Canadian Journal of Economics* 29: 126–129.

Ahmad, K.Z. and Bakar, R.A. (2003) 'The association between training and organizational commitment among white-collar workers in Malaysia,' *International Journal of Training and Development* 7(3): 166–185.

Alexander, J.A., Bloom, J.R. and Nuchols, B.A. (1994) 'Nursing turnover and hospital efficiency: an organizational-level analysis,' *Industrial Relations* 33: 505–520.

American Health Care Association (2003) 'Results of the AHCA nursing staff vacancy and retention study.'.

Arnold, J., Cooper, C.L. and Robertson, I.T. (1998) *Work Psychology: Understanding Human Behavior in the Workplace*, 3rd edn, London, UK: Financial Times.

Association for Training and Development (2004) 'The 2004 ASTD State of the Industry Report,' *Training* 36(10): 1–25.

Atkins, S. and Williams, A. (1995) 'Registered nurses' experiences of mentoring undergraduate nursing students,' *Journal of Advanced Nursing* 21: 1006–1015.

Avolio, B.J., Zhu, W., Koh, W. and Bhatia, P. (2004) 'Transformational leadership and organizational commitment: mediating role of psychological empowerment and moderating role of structural distance,' *Journal of Organizational Behavior* 25: 951–968.

Baker, J.G. and Baker, D.F. (1999) 'Perceived ideological differences, job satisfaction and organizational commitment among psychiatrists in a community mental health center,' *Mental Health Journal* 35(1): 85–95.

Bartlett, K.R. (2001) 'The relationship between training and organizational commitment: a study in the health care field,' *Human Resource Development Quarterly* 12(4): 335–352.

Bartlett, K.R. and Kang, D. (2004) 'Training and organizational commitment among nurses following industry and organizational change in New Zealand and the United States of America,' *Human Resource Development International* 7(4): 423–440.

Baruch, Y. (1998) 'The rise and fall of organizational commitment,' *Human System Management* 17(2): 135–143.

Baruch, Y. (2001) 'Employability: a substitute for loyalty,' *Human Resource Development International* 4(4): 543–566.

Baruch, Y. and Winkelmann-Gleed, A. (2002) 'Multiple commitments: conceptual framework and empirical investigation in the NHS,' *British Journal of Management* 13(4): 337–357.

Bashaw, E.R. and Grant, S.E. (1994) 'Exploring the distinctive nature of work commitments: their relationships with personal characteristics, job performance, and propensity to leave,' *Journal of Personal Selling and Sales Management* 14: 41–56.

Bateman, T.S. and Organ, D.W. (1983) 'Job satisfaction and the good soldier: the relationship between affect and employee citizenship,' *Academy of Management Journal* 26: 587–595.

Begley, T.M. and Czajka, J.M. (1993) 'Panel analysis of the moderating effects of commitment on job satisfaction, intent to quit, and health following organizational change,' *Journal of Applied Psychology* 78: 552–556.

Benkhoff, B. (1997) 'Ignoring commitment is costly: new approaches establish the missing link between commitment and performance,' *Human Relations* 50(6): 701–726.

Benson, G.S., Finegold, D. and Mohrman, S.A. (2004) 'You paid for the skills, now keep them: tuition reimbursement and voluntary turnover,' *Academy of Management Journal* 47(3): 315–331.

Birdi, K., Allan, C. and Warr, P. (1997) 'Correlates and perceived outcomes of four types of development activity,' *Journal of Applied Psychology* 82: 845–857.

Bradley, S., Draca, M., Green, C. and Mangan, J. (2004) 'Quits, separations, and worker turnover in the public sector: evidence from a competing risks analysis.' Unpublished working paper. Lancaster: The Management School, Lancaster University.

Breif, A.P. (1998) *Attitudes In and Around Organizations*, Thousand Oaks, CA: Sage.

Buddin, R. and Kapur, K. (2005) 'The effect of employer-sponsored education on job mobility: evidence from the U.S. navy,' *Industrial Relations* 44(2): 341–363.

Cohen, A. (1999) 'Relationships among five forms of commitment: an empirical examination,' *Journal of Organizational Behavior* 20: 285–308.

Cohen, A. (2000) 'The relationship between commitment forms and work outcomes: a comparison of three models,' *Human Relations* 53(3): 387–417.

Cohen, A. (2003) *Multiple Commitments in the Workplace: An Integrative Approach.* Muhwah, NJ: Lawrence Erlbaum Associates.

Colarelli, S.M. and Bishop, R.C. (1990) 'Career commitment: functions, correlates, and management,' *Group and Organizational Studies* 15: 158–176.

Corser, W.D. (1998) 'The changing nature of organizational commitment in the acute care environment: implications for nursing leadership,' *Journal of Nursing Administration* 28(6): 32–36.

DeCotiis, T.A. and Summers, T.P. (1987) 'A path analysis of a model of the antecedents and consequences of organizational commitment,' *Human Relations* 40: 445–470.

Dessler, G. (1993) *Winning Commitment: How to Build and Keep a Competitive Workforce*, New York: McGraw Hill.

Elsdon, R. (2003) *Affiliation in the Workplace*, Westport, CT: Praeger.

Fink, S.L. (1992) *High Commitment Workplace*, New York: Quorum Books.

Franco, L.M., Bennett, S. and Kanfer, R. (2002) 'Health sector reform and public sector health worker motivation: a conceptual framework,' *Social Science and Medicine* 54: 1255–1266.

Ganster, D.C. and Dwyer, D.J. (1995) 'The effects of understaffing on individual and group performance in professional and trade occupations,' *Journal of Management* 21: 175–190.

Giffords, E.D. (2003) 'An examination of organizational and professional commitment among public, not-for-profit, and proprietary social service employees,' *Administration in Social Work* 17(3): 5–23.

Gould-Williams, J. (2004) 'The effects of "high commitment" HRM practices on employee attitude: the views of public sector workers,' *Public Administration* 82(1): 63–81.

Greenglass, E.R. and Burke, R.J. (2002) 'Hospital restructuring and burnout,' *Journal of Health and Human Services Administration* 25(1): 89–114.

Hackett, R., Bycio, P. and Hausdorf, P. (1994) 'Further assessments of Meyer and Allen's 1991 three-component model of organizational commitment,' *Journal of Applied Psychology* 79: 1–9.

Halleslhorn, H.M., Tackenberg, P. and Müller, B.H. (2003) *Working Conditions and Intent to Leave the Profession among Nursing Staff in Europe.* Stockholm, Sweden: National Institute for Working Life.

Hoff, T.J. (2001) 'Exploring dual commitment among physician executives in managed care,' *Journal of Healthcare Management* 46(2): 91–109.

Holton, E.F., III (1996) 'The flawed 4-level evaluations model,' *Human Resource Development Quarterly* 7(1): 5–21.

Hudson, R.B. (2003) 'Emerging crisis: the geriatric care workforce,' *Public Policy and Aging Report* 13(2): 1–2.

Iles, P., Mabey, C. and Robertson, I. (1990) 'HRM practices and employee commitment: possibilities, pitfalls and paradoxes,' *British Journal of Management* 1: 147–157.

Ito, J.K. and Brotheridge, C.M. (2005) 'Does supporting employees' career adaptability lead to commitment, turnover or both?' *Human Resource Management* 44(1): 5–19.

Jaffe, D.T., Scott, C.D. and Tobe, G.R. (1994) *Rekindling Commitment: How to Revitalize Yourself, Your Work and Your Organization*, San Francisco: Jossey-Bass.

Jones, J.M. (2003) 'Dual or dueling culture and commitment: the impact of a tri-hospital merger,' *Journal of Nursing Administration* 33(4): 235–242.

Kalbfleisch, P.J. and Bach, B.W. (1998) 'The language of mentoring in a health care environment,' *Health Communication* 10(4): 373–392.

Klein, H.J. (2001) 'Invited reaction: the relationship between training and organizational commitment – a study in the health care field,' *Human Resource Development Quarterly* 12(4): 353–361.

Klein, H.J. and Weaver, N. (2001) 'The effectiveness of an organizational-level orientation training program in the socialization of new hires,' *Personnel Psychology* 53: 47–66.

Knoop, R. (1995) 'Relationships among job involvement, job satisfaction, and organizational commitment for nurses,' *The Journal of Psychology* 129(6): 643–649.

Kuokkanen, L., Leino-Kilpi, H. and Katajisto, J. (2003) 'Nurse empowerment, job-related satisfaction, and organizational commitment,' *Journal of Nursing Care Quality* 18(3): 184–192.

Lang, D.L. (1992) 'Organizational culture and commitment,' *Human Resource Development Quarterly* 3(2): 191–196.

Laschinger, H.K., Finegan, J. and Shamian, J. (2001) 'The impact of workplace empowerment, organizational trust on staff nurses' work satisfaction and organizational commitment,' *Health Care Management Review* 29(3): 7–23.

Leong, S.M., Randall, D.M. and Cote, J.A. (1994) 'Exploring the organizational commitment-performance linkage in marketing: a study of life insurance salespeople,' *Journal of Business Research* 29: 57–63.

Mathieu, J.E. and Zajac, D.M. (1990) 'A review and meta-analysis of the antecedents, correlates, and consequences of organizational commitment,' *Psychological Bulletin* 108: 171–194.

McEvoy, G.M. (1997) 'Organizational change and outdoor management,' *Human Resource Management* 36(2): 235–250.

McLean, J. and Andrew, T. (2000) 'Commitment, satisfaction, stress and control among social services managers and social workers in the UK,' *Administration in Social Work* 23(3/4): 93–117.

McNeese-Smith, D.K. (2001) 'A nursing shortage: building organizational commitment among nurses,' *Journal of Healthcare Management* 46(3): 173–187.

Meyer, J.P. and Allen, N.J. (1991) 'A three-component conceptualization of organizational commitment,' *Human Resource Management Review* 1(1): 61–89.

Meyer, J.P. and Allen, N.J. (1997) *Commitment in the Workplace: Theory, Research, and Application*. Thousand Oaks, CA: Sage.

Meyer, J.P. and Herscovitch, L. (2001) 'Commitment in the workplace: toward a general model,' *Human Resource Management Review* 11(2): 299–326.

Meyer, J.P. and Smith, C. (2000) 'HRM practices and organizational commitment: test of a mediation model,' *Canadian Journal of Administrative Sciences* 17: 319–331.

Meyer, J.P., Allen, N.J. and Smith, C.A. (1993a) 'Commitment to organizations and occupations: extension and test of a three-component conceptualization,' *Journal of Applied Psychology* 78: 538–551.

Meyer, J.P., Allen, N.J. and Topolnytsky, L. (1993) 'Commitment in a changing world of work,' *Canadian Psychology* 39(1–2): 83–93.

Meyer, J.P., Becker, T.E. and Vandenberghe, C. (2004) 'Employee commitment and *motivation*: a conceptual analysis and integrative model,' *Journal of Applied Psychology* 89(6): 991–1007

Meyer, J.P., Bobocel, D.R. and Allen, N.J. (1991) 'Development of Organizational commitment during the first year of employment: a longitudinal study of pre- and post-entry influences,' *Journal of Management* 17(4): 717–733.

Meyer, J.P., Paunonen, S.V., Gellatly, I.H., Goffin, R.D. and Jackson, D.N. (1989) 'Organizational commitment and job performance: it's the nature of the commitment that counts,' *Journal of Applied Psychology* 74: 152–156.

Meyer, J.P., Stanley, D.J., Herscovitch, L. and Topolnytsky, L. (2002) 'Affective, continuance, and normative commitment to the organization: a meta-analysis of antecedents, correlates, and consequences,' *Journal of Vocational Behavior* 61: 20–52.

Mobley, W.H., Griffeth, R.H., Hand, H.H. and Meglino, B.M. (1979) 'Review and conceptual analysis of the employee turnover process,' *Psychological Bulletin* 86: 493–522.

Moorman, R.H., Niehoff, B.P. and Organ, D.W. (1993) 'Treating employees fairly and organizational citizenship behavior: sorting the effects of job satisfaction, organizational commitment, and procedural justice,' *Employee Responsibilities and Rights Journal* 6(3): 209–225.

Morrow, P. (1993) *The Theory and Measurement of Work Commitment*, Greenwich, CT: JAI Press.

Munene, J.C. (1995) 'Not on a seat: an investigation of some correlates of organizational citizenship behavior in Nigeria,' *Applied Psychology: An International Review* 44: 111–222.

Narine, L. and Persaud, D.D. (2003) 'Gaining and maintaining commitment to large-scale change in healthcare organizations,' *Health Services Management Research* 16: 179–187.

Nystrom, P.C. (1993) 'Organization cultures, strategies, and commitments in health care organizations,' *Health Care Management Review* 18(1): 43–49.

Organ, D.W. and Konovsky, M. (1989) 'Cognitive versus affective determinants of organizational citizenship behavior,' *Journal of Applied Psychology* 48: 775–802.

Organ, D.W. and Ryan, K. (1995) 'A meta-analytic review of attitudinal and dispositional predictors of organizational citizenship behavior,' *Personnel Psychology* 48: 775–802.

Payne, S.C. and Huffman, A.H. (2005) 'A longitudinal examination of the influence of mentoring on organizational commitment and turnover,' *Academy of Management Journal* 1: 158–168.

Pearson, C.A.L. and Chong, J. (1997) 'Contribution of job content and social information on organizational commitment and job satisfaction: an exploration in a Malaysian nursing context,' *Journal of Occupational and Organizational Psychology* 17: 357–374.

Pinks, G.J. (1992), *Facilitating Organizational Commitment through Human Resource Practices*, Kingston, Ontario: Queen's University Industrial Relations Centre.

Porter, L.W., Steers, R.M., Mowday, R.T. and Boulian, P.V. (1974) 'Organizational commitment, job satisfaction and turnover among psychiatric technicians,' *Journal of Applied Psychology* 59: 603–609.

Raabe, B. and Beehr, T.A. (2003) 'Formal mentoring versus supervisor and coworker relationships: differences in perceptions and impact,' *Journal of Organizational Behavior* 24: 271–293.

Randall, D.M. (1990) 'The consequences of organizational commitment: methodological investigations,' *Journal of Organizational Behavior* 11: 361–378.

Randall, D.M. and Cote, J.A. (1991) 'Interrelationships of work commitment constructs,' *Work and Occupations* 18(2): 194–211.

Reichers, A. (1985) 'A review and reconceptualization of organizational commitment,' *Academy of Management Review* 10: 465–476.

Romzek, B.S. (1989) 'Personal consequences of employee commitment,' *Academy of Management Journal* 32: 649–661.

Rousseau, D.M. (1995) *Psychological Contracts in Organizations*, Thousand Oaks, CA: Sage.

Rousseau, D.M. and Wade-Benson, K.A. (1995) 'Changing individual/organizational attachments: a two-way street,' in A. Howard (ed.) *The Changing Nature of Work*, San Francisco: Jossey-Bass, pp. 290–322.

Saks, A.M. (1995) 'Longitudinal field investigation of the moderating and mediating effects of self-efficacy on the relationship between training and newcomer adjustment,' *Journal of Applied Psychology* 80: 211–225.

Seyler, D.L., Holton, E.F.I., Bates, R.A., Burnett, M.F. and Carvalho, M.A. (1998) 'Factors affecting motivation to transfer training,' *International Journal of Training and Development* 2(1): 2–16.

Shepherd, J.L. and Mathews, B.P. (2000) 'Employee commitment: academic vs practitioner perspectives,' *Employee Relations* 22(6): 555–575.

Shields, M. and Ward, M. (2001) 'Improving nurse retention in the National Health Service in England: the impact of job satisfaction on intentions to quit,' *Journal of Health Economics* 20: 677–701.

Shim, W. and Steers, R.M. (1994) 'Mediating influences on the employee commitment-job performance relationship,' Unpublished manuscript.

Shore, L.M. and Wayne, S.J. (1993) 'Commitment and employee behavior: comparison of affective and continuance commitment with perceived organizational support,' *Journal of Applied Psychology* 78: 774–780.

Smith, C.A., Organ, D.W. and Near, J.P. (1983) 'Organizational citizenship behavior: its nature and antecedents,' *Journal of Applied Psychology* 68: 453–463.

Stordeur, S., D'horse, W., van der Heijden, B., Dibisceglie, M., Laine, M., van der Schoot, E. and the NEXT-Study Group (2003) 'Leadership, job satisfaction and nurses' commitment,' in H.M. Halleslhorn, P. Tackenberg, and B.H. Müller (eds) *Working Conditions and Intent to Leave the Profession Among Nursing Staff in Europe*, Stockholm, Sweden: National Institute for Working Life, pp. 28–45.

Story, A. and Redman, T. (1997) 'Training agreements: resolving under-investment in training?' *International Journal of Training and Development* 1(3): 144–157.

Swanson, R.A. (1995) 'Human resource development: performance is the key,' *Human Resource Development Quarterly* 6(2): 207–313.

Tannenbaum, S.I., Mathieu, J.E., Salas, E. and Cannon-Bowers, J.A. (1991) 'Meeting trainees' expectations: the influence of training fulfillment on the development of commitment, self-efficacy, and motivation,' *Journal of Applied Psychology* 76(6): 759–769.

Tansky, J. and Cohen, D. (2001) 'The relationship between organizational support, employee development, and organizational commitment: an empirical study,' *Human Resource Development Quarterly* 12: 285–300.

Thompson, J.A. and Van de Ven, A.H. (2002) 'Commitment shifts during organizational upheaval: physicians' transitions from private practitioner to employee,' *Journal of Vocational Behavior* 60: 382–404.

Tsui, A.S., Pearce, J.L., Porter, L.W. and Tripoli, A.M. (1997) 'Alternative approaches to the employee-organization relationship: does investment in employees pay off?' *The Academy of Management Journal* 40(5): 1089–1121.

Wahn, J. (1993) 'Organizational dependence and the likelihood of complying with organization pressures to behave unethically,' *Journal of Business Ethics* 12: 245–251.

Waldman, J. and Deane, E. (2004) 'The shocking cost of turnover in health care,' *Health Care Management Review* 29(1): 12–17.

Waters, L.V. (2003) 'Overcome hidden expenses, migrating staff,' *Nursing Management* 34(5): 20–23.

White, D.B. (1991) 'The imperative of transcending routine HRD for OD in the health and human service sector,' *Organization Development Journal* 9(3): 44–49.

Williams, L.J. and Anderson, S.E. (1991) 'Job satisfaction and organizational commitment as predictors of organizational citizenship and in-role behaviors,' *Journal of Management* 17: 601–617.

Zangaro, G.A. (2001) 'Organizational commitment: a concept analysis,' *Nursing Forum* 36(2): 14–22.

Part II
Management development

6 Becoming a manager in the NHS

Learning styles and discourses

Nadine Bristow

Introduction/terms of reference

This chapter aims to describe an approach to the research and evaluation of action learning as an integral aspect of an NHS-based management development programme by addressing a series of research questions. It is hoped that the description will be of benefit or interest to all, or some, of the following;

- the academic community;
- professional associations, trainers and developers;
- managers and organizations;
- policy makers and regulators.

Coupled with the research questions are supporting references to the critical literature review and initial conceptual framework that I held. Discussion of the various academic fields appropriate to the research question are outlined for the reader via a reasoned selection. A synopsis of the critical review and evaluation of the literature is provided, which led to a set of working definitions of the key concepts used in the research.

A description of the organizational and managerial context of the research is detailed as an introduction to the identification of the research questions and their foundations in NHS organizational life.

The research questions are then discussed in light of their suitability for an interpretative report based on ethnographic research principles. A description of the ethical and political issues raised by the planned and implemented research schedule is provided. The structure of the research is outlined in order for the reader to contextualize and conceptualize the entirety of the piece of work. This foundation of knowledge will enable the reader to analyse the research findings and thereby critique the design and implementation of the research constructively.

Extracts from dialogue between several action learning participants, a co-facilitator and myself are provided to demonstrate how various responses provided by the research participants were analysed in light of the research questions. Detail of the main findings from the research, conclusions and a further developed formative conceptual framework are provided to demonstrate how additional ethnographic research to support the further development of this concept was designed.

The focus on an interpretative piece of ethnographic research has been provided with the desire to provide the reader with an opportunity to:

- explore the methodological implications of ethnographic research;
- consider the philosophical understandings of human agency and interpretation;
- view the nature of causal and interpretive understanding of the social world, in relation to the task and purpose of research;
- evaluate the approach described as a means of developing competence and judgement in ethnographic research and its interpretation;
- understand the philosophical issues surrounding claims to knowledge and understanding made as part of research;
- identify the skills associated with the design, implementation, interpretation and writing up of ethnographic research in the field of human resource development.

The empirical context

As an independent human resource development consultant I was commissioned during this period to design and deliver a number of management and leadership development programmes across the UK, on an in-house basis for NHS Trusts, and for business schools.

The programmes consisted of monthly workshops designed to provide participants with:

- opportunity for professional networking, discussion and debate;
- knowledge gained from guest speakers who were predominantly considered to be experts in their field from within the local health economy – e.g. Directors of Finance;
- skills practice via structured exercises;
- access to tutorial support;
- feedback from peers and tutors;
- facilitated action learning set meetings.

It was felt that the critical inclusion of action learning provided sustained peer/tutor interaction, enhanced group cohesion, encouragement for application of learning to the workplace, development of learning styles as well as many of the benefits as described by McGill and Beaty (1992: 31–32) such as '. . . making sense of that experience in a new way, leading to understanding. Understanding can lead to insights which allow for new plans, new strategies for action and new modes of behaviour.'

It was during this practitioner work that many questions about how to optimize action learning came to mind.

- Was there such a thing as a 'sleeper' effect with participants recognizing the value of the intervention post-programme?
- Could participation in an action learning set facilitate development of preference in terms of learning styles?
- Did participants feel more competent as learners and subsequently managers as a result of participation?
- How can human resource development practitioners effectively communicate the concept of action learning?
- Can the effectiveness of action learning be measured?

Bourner and Weinstein (1996) referred to 'ample evidence' that action learning can work and of there being 'lots of empirical evidence' to support this. I took heart and enthusiastically commenced a review of the literature, but concluded that this was not necessarily the case. Given that action learning has been a recognized model of development since the 1940s there was not the body of knowledge that one may anticipate could, or indeed should, be there.

Various other action learning practitioners that I worked with over the years had described a range of suggested admission criteria for set membership – the invitation to join the club so to speak. They included:

- vocational background;
- organizational background;
- gender;
- age;
- level of seniority in the organization;
- number of participants;
- voluntary membership;
- development needs etc.

Many colleagues did not clarify whether their recommendations were evidence-based. All appeared to imply that *similarity* was a positive for participants and their respective organizations.

Such recommendations for membership could equally be interpreted as the basis for diversity rather than similarity. It was interesting to note that Professor Revans 'the father of action learning' did not prescribe any criteria himself.

As a practitioner, I had previously structured action learning sets on the basis of diversity of preferred learning styles and vocational discipline as a means of practically dealing with the large numbers of staff entering leadership and management development programmes and the organizational culture shift that the NHS was attempting, in a bid to break down the sometimes real, sometimes perceived barriers between healthcare professionals. Multidisciplinary staff development was emphasized during the 1990s. On many occasions I observed a perception of elitism if programmes were uni-disciplinarian. Social inclusion was the order of the day, so to speak.

I considered the learning style of each participant to be a useful tool for pre- and post-course evaluation. It was essential data for the tutorial team to hold, particularly prior to the commencement of the programme, as it played a role in the initial assessment and personal objective setting stage of the management development process.

In a formative sense this information was similarly considered to be helpful to both my co-facilitators of the action learning sets and set members themselves. With this knowledge, all parties could be watchful for barriers to learning in individual learners and, potentially, access to such knowledge could influence fellow set members when devising questions aimed at providing critical insight into problems. This practitioner consideration became key when formulating the interpretative research questions.

Gradually, over a period of three years or so, my hypothesis emerged, based upon observation, that action learning set dynamics could potentially be anticipated on the basis of learning styles. This insight could then be utilized when planning the structure of the sets and subsequently increase the effectiveness of individual interaction and subsequent managerial and organizational development. Management of group dynamics is the domain of the facilitator and therefore a critical success factor. Obvious facets of the development of group dynamics were:

- the level of participation and disclosure provided by individual set members;
- the ability to present work-based successes and problems;
- choice of questions that will encourage critical insight into the presentations of other set members.

This social interaction is essential in order for the process of theorizing, concluding and planning of action to follow.

Could individual learning style influence the nature of issues disclosed within the set, the questions that a particular individual posed in such a forum and the personal action plan that they developed from this discourse? Or, more simply stated:
Could diversity of learning style at action learning set level lead to the development of other less preferred learning styles at individual level?

In an attempt to develop this idea further, first the learning styles of a sample group of 53 first and middle line managers (from a population group of 120, from across eight NHS organizations within the UK) were assessed both pre- and post-action learning. The diagnostic tool utilized was developed by Honey and Mumford (1982). This is a short self-administered questionnaire, comprising 80 statements. The results of the questionnaire enable categorization of preferred learning style across a range of four: Activist, Theorist, Reflector and Pragmatist. The objective of the exercise was to be able to pinpoint learning preferences and subsequently structure each set appropriately – i.e. on the basis of diversity. The statistical findings from this research were partially supportive of an experimental hypothesis that exposure to the action learning experience, whilst supported by fellow action learning set members who have differing learning style preferences, is beneficial.

Action learning is a phenomenological process and, as such, any aspects of its claimed effectiveness cannot alone be measured in such a manner – account has to be taken of the *personal* nature of action learning. Empirical research via self-report and introspection was relevant in the context of understanding and valuing the 'effectiveness' of action learning.

The theoretical context

Many books have been written about action learning. Action learning is essentially

> A continuous process of learning and reflection supported by colleagues, with an intention of getting things done. Through action learning individuals learn with and from each other by working on real problems and reflecting on their own experiences.
>
> (McGill and Beaty 1992: 21)

It is therefore a tool for organizational development via management development. Pedler *et al.* (1991) argue that, where action learning becomes a feature of the organization itself, the organization takes on some of the features of a 'Learning Company.' In my view it provides a more holistic approach to development.

Clark (1977: 42) claimed that listeners better understand texts if they have prior knowledge of the topic under discussion. Where there is no direct reference to the topic, one tends to fill the gap by making bridging inferences. This would support the premise that action learning participants require a similar concept of the human resource development strategy being deployed in order fully to engage with it and/or be able to evaluate it effectively at individual level. Questions such as 'What is action learning?' and 'What are learning styles?' need to be clarified at the outset.

This further developed the emerging concept that diversity of preferred learning styles was desirable within any action learning set, but that each individual should just as importantly have a *shared* concept of action learning or learning styles if they were to contribute to the evaluation process of such management development activity.

The search for a 'typical' concept of action learning is a natural integral and central part of cognition that helps us to make sense of many aspects of human resource development. Our ability to acquire new highly abstract concepts such as action learning is essential to us in developing our mental maps, but the purpose for which the representation is used and the difference in knowledge held by an individual both play a large role in how concepts are assimilated and represented.

Did a 'typical' concept of action learning and learning styles exist within the particular community of NHS managers participating in the programme?

According to Jacoby and Brooks 1984 (see Roth and Bruce 1995: 52) even the example of a relatively well defined, everyday object such as a cup or a glass may require an individual to store a mixture of representations for such a concept. Murphy and Wright, 1984 (see Roth and Bruce 1995: 59) confirmed the effect of expert knowledge in producing variations in how a given domain is represented. They compared and contrasted concepts of a variety of psychiatric disorders held by experts and novices – reporting that the experts' concepts were actually less distinctive and clear-cut, concluding that the greater knowledge held by the expert influenced a focus on the *shared*, rather than the distinctive features of the disorders.

Would this community hold a defined or fuzzy concept of action learning and learning styles? Would an experienced action learning set facilitator demonstrate a difference in their perception of the concept even with considerable exposure to the theory and model?

The work of Murphy and Wright (1984) may go some way to explaining any potential angst that individuals may feel (when new to action learning) that there is no definitive concept. Would more experienced practitioners use their underpinning background knowledge of other similar developmental processes, which are akin to action learning, to be more content with the prevailing ambiguity?

Further consideration of the various foundations of Revans' (1955) original thesis of action learning (which draws from different philosophies of learning and change) is relevant in explaining diversity in concepts of action learning.

Often action learning programmes can include a combination of approaches in their design and implementation, with practitioners adopting an eclectic methodology. This in turn can influence the perception of the intervention and the effectiveness of the process for both practitioners and participants, making subsequent evaluation both complex and difficult.

The conceptual framework influencing the research questions and design was shaped by three key models of human learning.

Honey and Mumford's (1982) four learning styles are represented in Figure 6.1.

However, we may also 'map' the model of action learning to this typology as shown in Figure 6.2 to demonstrate how I conceptualized the processes, theories and typology to make sense of the research questions.

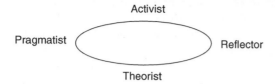

Figure 6.1 Honey and Mumford's (1982) learning style typology.

The 'action'	'Questioning'
Activist learner	Reflector Learner
Pragmatist learner	Theorist learner

'Programmed knowledge'   'Critical insight'

Figure 6.2 Honey and Mumford's (1982) learning style typology in relation to Revan's (1955) theory and process of action learn.

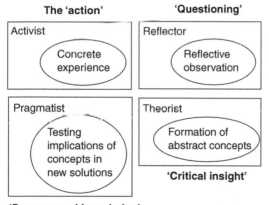

Figure 6.3 Honey and Mumford's (1982) learning style typology in relation to Kolb's (1995) experiential learning cycle and Revan's (1955) model and process of action learning.

In addition, we may 'map' the Kolb *et al.* (1995) experiential learning cycle onto this conceptual framework to highlight the role of further learning processes, as in Figure 6.3.

The three theories when overlaid illustrate the formative development of the primary cognitive framework behind the research questions. The need and value of diversity of preferred learning styles within the 'reflective observation' phase of Kolb *et al.*'s (1995) experiential learning cycle, i.e. the learning set meeting itself, can be interpreted as directly correlating with Revan's 'questioning' phase in the action learning process.

If all participants within an action learning set undertake this phase of the experiential learning cycle or action learning process with a similar learning style, it could be said that each could potentially derive a similar observation/reflective learning point from the experiences described within the previous phase.

If the process of reflection is not entirely varied and diverse, it could be argued that this does not add value to the learning process for each individual member of the action learning set meeting and therefore has consequences for the next phase of personal learning and indeed organizational development.

This appears to be the predominant phase of the process of experiential *or* action learning that is so critically dependent upon external influences. For example, the role of others and their questions is pivotal to the remaining phases on a continual, ever-evolving loop should we conceptualize learning in this way.

Research methods

The rhetorical question 'action learning: that's just learning by doing, isn't it?' is one that is no doubt frequently heard by practitioners. There are problems with the two concepts being used interchangeably.

The phenomenon to be investigated related to the development and change of learning styles amongst action learning participants as part of a wider management development programme and *how* individuals account for these changes. A non-representationalist epistemology was embraced in this research.

The intention was not to focus on explanations from Revans, Kolb, Honey and Mumford or any other theorist. It was to consider what experienced action learning participants and practitioners themselves recognize as the explanation for changes and developments in their own preferred learning style.

I was aware that I held a broad presupposition that generally participants would:

- View 'action learning' as 'learning by doing.'
- Suggest that learning styles can change, but only by a small amount.
- Interchangeably refer to learning style preference and cognitive styles.
- Directly attribute the changes in learning style preference post-programme to being directly and externally 'facilitated' in the development process

The research questions explicitly addressed were:

- What are action learning participants' and action learning facilitators' explanations and understanding of action learning – post-experience?
- What is their explanation and understanding of learning styles?
- What is their explanation for changes in learning styles, post-action learning experience?
- Do they feel that learning styles are fixed and rigid or something that can consciously be changed and developed and if so how?

The design of the research programme commenced with my wish to critique positivist epistemologies in an endeavour to explore the methodological implications of case-based and ethnographic research. In addition, the consideration of the philosophical understandings of human agency, interpretation and the nature of causal and interpretive understanding of the social world in relation to the task and purposes of research was of interest.

It was whilst reading and later reflecting upon the paper presented by Watson (1996), entitled 'Motivation: that's Maslow, isn't it?,' that an interpretative approach was considered. Watson had adopted this approach to both, 'tell a story about certain substantive issues as well as a story about the shaping of what we might call an ethnographic experiment' – a concept that represented a compromise between the phenomenological and positivist approaches, allowing great attention to 'control' to tackle the problem of 'going native.'

Watson (1996) faced a similar dilemma in his approach to research since he too represented a dimension of the body of knowledge that he was in effect asking participants to consider. In order to gain access to this group, he positioned himself as the new management lecturer undertaking a discussion with the aim of 'revisiting and evaluation' of the existing knowledge base of the cohort to ensure that this knowledge base could be developed further, rather than consolidated. He also explained to the discussion group participants that the notes taken to record their views would be used in a research project.

The method in both Watson's (1996) research and the research plan described in this chapter was simple and the broad procedure described was followed consistently.

First, Watson (1996) would introduce the session and then move into open questions designed to establish the knowledge base of the students, before progressing into a more probing style of questioning to encourage participants to expand upon their answers. The third stage of the experiment involved a leading question designed to provoke pragmatic responses. Lastly, the most open-ended stage was framed as an opportunity for participants to consider the responses that they had given in the previous three stages.

This approach was considered relevant in approaching an explanation through *understanding*. The research questions under investigation in Watson's (1996) study were considered at this point to be highly similar to those that I proposed to address, but within a different context.

Role conflict was also of concern – lecturer, tutor, assessor, facilitator and researcher. My relationship with participants and colleagues was multiple. This 'evaluative' approach allowed for the diversity described above to be effectively streamlined in an almost transparent way – thereby overcoming some of the potential ethical and pragmatic difficulties around 'going native.' I recognized that a postmodernist approach would help to encompass the mercuriality, variability and personal agency of the individuals involved – who indeed live and experience action learning in a predominantly phenomenological way and therefore required a flexible approach to the interpretation of their accounts.

The most obvious place to carry out this empirical investigation, and presumably find sources of such information, was indeed with the participants and practitioners themselves. Nevertheless, the problem of how this could be gathered in a way that was meaningful, relevant and motivational for the nominated research participants concerned was one that required careful analysis.

A decision was reached to build upon an already functional and developmental relationship. This would be economical in many ways, as well as practicable.

It was recognized that the principles of both ethnographic and participant observation could equally be applied to the working situation, i.e. the specific role of quality assurance related to the post-course evaluative processes for each programme. Therefore, participant ethnographic analysis of action learning and learning styles ensued, based within a pragmatic processual approach, which is described in the following section.

Participant ethnographic analysis of action learning as a tool for management development

The participant observer's role is described by Becker (1958) (see Watson 1996) in representationalist terms as 'gathers data by participating in the daily life of the group or organization . . .'

On this occasion there were numerous advantages to researching and theorizing in ethnography. There was a strong supportive working relationship, which was based upon well-defined processes developed over a period of time. In addition, there was also a strong contextualization for all parties involved. Specifically, the action learning participants and practitioners involved in the research were aware of the duplicity of roles and that this was an iterative relationship.

All of the action learning set members in the sets that I had worked with during the research period were aware from day one of the working relationship, i.e. that I was there as a participant observer. Obviously, this facet of the relationship had been previously negotiated at organizational level, but that did not guarantee agreement and cooperation from participants and especially those that I would go on to select to be included in a later phase of the research. A full, standard verbal briefing, i.e. an account of the research and my own involvement in the research process itself, was provided in order to begin the subsequent process of negotiation. The need for follow-up evaluative interviews with selected participants was made clear and this received full acceptance and support too. From that point onwards, every action-learning based discussion and interview was audio taped for subsequent analysis, becoming an accepted aspect of the 'custom and practice' associated with action learning and, equally as importantly, the participants' relationship with me. During a 12-month period, the ever-present audio tape recorder became the 'norm.'

In many ways this closeness allowed flexibility, openness and the vital credibility to ask questions. Positioning along the researcher continuum proposed by Gold (1958: 93) in the paper on participant observation, which suggested four 'ideal'-type researcher roles, ranging from 'complete participant' through 'participant as observer' and 'observer as participant' to 'complete observer' was varied during the sometimes long (12 month) relationship with the participants.

In order to take an ethnographic approach to the research, there must be a continuous process of 'negotiation and exchange' (Watson 2000) with the various parties involved, both formally and informally, in order to be provided with the necessary access, information and experiences that the research required. Examples of the type of bargains made with groups and individuals to ensure that the above criteria were met are as follows:

• One-to-one time to discuss personal development using the learning style inventory results, both pre- and post action learning experience to evaluate the 'effectiveness of action learning';
• On-site time with individuals to minimize disruption to their working schedule;
• Promises of follow up feedback regarding the outcomes of the research;
• Promise that the interview would not take longer than one hour maximum.

The philosophy of ethnography is often referred to as the study of 'the other' – a situation or group of people that are not familiar to the researcher. This can be, and often is, interpreted as the process of integrating oneself with a group in order to learn about them. However, my multifaceted role in this example can most definitely not be viewed as 'the professional stranger' (Agar 1980; see Watson 1996). As a facilitator of action learning, tutor, mentor etc, as stated earlier, there is an obvious differentiator here, namely that nobody else within the group performs these roles. So unlike Marsh *et al.* (1978), who became one of thousands of people within a group – all of whom shared the same role, i.e. football team supporter – this scenario was different, demonstrating that even within the classification of 'participant research' there can be a continuum.

A quasi-experimental method was designed to address a number of open questions and provide the catalyst for subsequent discussion regarding the effectiveness of action learning in producing a positive shift and development in learning styles. It was also deemed relevant to identify whether a shared concept of action learning and learning styles existed amongst the sample group.

The process would be repeated with a sample of four action learning set members from a broader research population, although again some scientific principles were adopted here within this selection process. For example, it was felt that at least two participants from a diverse action learning set and two participants from a randomly structured action learning set should be selected. To complement this, responses from one experienced facilitator would also be sought using the same approach, providing five sets of responses in total.

The discussion was introduced as a 'follow-up,' evaluative exercise to identify the impact of action learning as a tool for developing NHS-based managers. The need for this information was framed as 'useful information for both the organization and for research purposes.' An audio tape recorder was used to capture the information gleaned from these discussions.

Each of the five discussions followed the broad procedure as stated below.

I randomly selected one of the five participants and made telephone contact to arrange the meeting (having introduced the subsequent discussion along the lines explained above).

I arrived at the meeting time and place and again introduced the session, using the first in a range of semi-structured interview questions. Before the question was posed however, the participant was assured of anonymity and again permission sought to tape record the discussion. Participants were also reminded that 'there are no right or wrong answers to the questions, so just answer in your own words and be as honest as you can.'

The first question posed to participants was 'Can you, in your own words, describe to me your understanding of action learning? It may be helpful to assume that you are describing it to somebody who has never experienced it `and therefore has no knowledge base to work from.' It was only when the participant had clearly 'dried up' and no further suggestions were made that the next stage was moved to.

The second question posed to participants was 'What is your understanding of learning styles? It was during this stage that often a few more probing questions were required however – usually achieved by directing the participant to focus on their own preferred styles as a catalyst for discussion.

To build upon the answer provided to this previous question, participants were then asked 'Many participants experienced a change in their pre- and post-action learning experience learning style inventory scores. What do you feel may be an explanation for these changes – especially for yourself if you experienced a change?' Obviously in the case of the practitioner, this question had to be modified.

The fourth question posed to participants related to their second answer on learning styles and was really designed to validate the answers to this question by means of probing further to discover understanding. 'Do you feel that your learning styles are fixed and rigid or are they something that you can consciously set out to deliberately change and develop?' This question was an opportunity for me critically to examine the concept of learning styles, as opposed to cognitive styles.

The findings, interpretations, conclusions and critical analysis

Q: What do you know and understand of action learning?

Anecdotally, 'Action learning – that's learning by doing, isn't it?' was a typical response encountered when asking groups of applicants for management development (*pre*-action learning) what they already knew of action learning. What follows is a sample of the responses to the question offered by research participant's *post*-action learning (Reported verbatim).

> It is a pro-active type of learning rather than just sitting taking in theory, you take what you have learned into your own workplace and apply that to problems, tasks and other human resource issues. A totally holistic approach to how you deal with issues in the workplace not only when problems arise, but also for planning to minimize problems and how you manage.
>
> The interesting thing was you get to take this action learning and then come back into the classroom to discuss what you did, what you learned, things that you thought were useful, things you thought were less useful, and have a reflection on your own personal thinking. So it's actually bringing learning into the everyday workplace and everyday management.

Across all the five definitions gained, there were some shared component elements to the offerings, which can be broadly summarized as:

- Proactively participant focused;
- Focus on real work-based problems;
- Applied theoretical learning;
- Holistic;
- Group discussion based;
- Reflections on experiences;
- Balanced analysis of both positives and negatives;
- Supportive, sharing colleagues;

- Identical/similar learning agenda;
- Learning how to learn via self and others;
- Creative thinking.

It was identified that the quotes offered a highly consistent working definition of action learning in terms of the various aspects of the process; however, some participants chose to focus their definition upon the process in its entirety and some upon just one element of action learning.

For example, three of the five definitions provided referred specifically to all four of the essential components (clarified by Revans 1955; see Marsick and O'Neil 1999: 159–176), namely the action learning set meetings, the problem, the individual and the action (i.e. the work-based experiences). They referred to the entire process of action learning. They clearly framed their definition within this broad framework. Two of the participants interviewed did not.

It is interesting to note that the two individuals who did not provide definitions that referred to all four components, referred predominantly to one aspect, i.e. the action learning set meeting as being the phase where the critical reflection took place. The quote below, demonstrates this analytical point:

> ...whatever the theory or theories are of management styles, you are then taking them into the workplace and to try and draw from those theories into a practical application of it and then take it back to a group to reflect on that and to learn from other peoples' perception of how you have managed in a given situation.
>
> (Participant B)

In contrast to the predominantly focused quotes from two participants:

> To me, action learning is a group of people who have got together who are learning the same types of things, the same subject and they are pooling their resources and ideas. It's somewhere you can go...
>
> (Participant D)

> I would describe it as a vehicle which is supportive to a group in taking them through an opportunity in that environment to discuss strengths and particular issues, or successes ... the opportunity is that the members of the group can help them open up their thinking...
>
> (Participant E)

All five individuals quoted had been exposed to an identical verbal explanation of the process of action learning, which included emphasis (in both written and verbal terms) on the four key components of action learning. Equally, they were also made aware of Revans' original thinking that the 'action' identifies the 'problem' with the individual then seeking theory to aid the solution to the problem from themselves and others (the set), before re-visiting the 'problem' with further action. None made reference to this particular order, but often inferred that the theory came first and then was subsequently applied to the problem.

An important point to note in relation to the responses provided was the lack of reference to the meaning of the words themselves – i.e. 'action' and 'learning.' None of the participants queried what is actually meant by learning for example, which is obviously a complex concept.

However, participants did offer the kind of definitions that would help to relate the concept to everyday managerial practice in a very pragmatic sense. Their definitions were very action orientated. The point of definitions and the interpretation of these definitions will be discussed within this chapter.

Q: What do you know and understand about learning styles?

'Learning styles reflect your personality and the way that you process information' was a typical response encountered when asking groups of newly registered management development programme participants (*pre-action learning*) what they already knew of learning styles. What follows is an example of the response to the question offered by a participant *post-action learning* experience (reported verbatim).

> My understanding of learning styles is that we have preferred learning styles and that I would say comes from usually our experiences that we have had in terms of the type of learning we've had, that we feel comfortable with and probably some of that also is probably within us in terms of our own particular personality and learning styles can and do in fact change over a period of time and that can happen because of changes in work pattern which makes you have to learn in a different way or indeed in the learning that you are taking on board which is different from previously so you can modify, change and adapt your learning styles.
>
> (Participant E)

Again, across all of the five definitions, there were some shared component elements to the offerings that can be broadly summarized as:

* There are different types of learning styles;
* Categories of behaviours;
* Need to develop less predominant styles;
* Linked to learning environment;
* Linked to personality style;
* Can be changed and developed.

The quotes offered much deeper working definitions of learning styles when compared to those responses defining action learning. The range of common themes explicitly mentioned within the definitions was narrower, indicating a less ambiguous shared concept. The narrative was diverse in terms of many causal links identified. Again, interestingly, despite all respondents having been verbally briefed on the theory behind Honey and Mumford's work, there was no direct reference to the theorists themselves.

Two of the five definitions referred specifically to their own behaviour when describing and justifying different learning styles. Two of the five acknowledged the need to consciously develop less prominent learning styles, whilst three of the five responses suggested, both directly and implicitly, that individuals have one predominant learning style. None of the responses included direct naming of the four learning styles within this typology.

Causal effects that were listed as being influencers on learning style preference included:

- Previous experience;
- Comfort zones;
- Links to personality;
- Learning environment;
- The content or type of learning itself;
- Information processing/cognitive style;
- Intelligence quotient.

Of the seven influencers that were voluntarily offered, all but three suggest that learning styles are predominantly influenced by external environmental factors that can be controlled or managed. The three factors that do not fit neatly within this group are links to personality, intelligence and information processing/cognitive style, which (depending upon the theoretical base of personality you subscribe to) could be argued as internal to the individual, biologically determined and not therefore open to manipulation and change. In scientific terms they could be described as fixed variables.

Closer analysis of this discourse could lead one to anticipate that the sample of respondents could and would argue that learning styles are not fluid but constant – according to these responses. However, only one of the responses specifically mentioned the possibility of change.

Some highlighted quotes below, demonstrate this analytical point. (Words highlighted in bold reflect attribution to that individual participant's personal position regarding the fixed/fluid nature of learning styles and influencers).

> I understand now that people have different learning styles. . . . I think the assumption was, I understood **what my learning style was** (fixed) . . . people have different ways of approaching things, **some are quiet**, (personality) some are very active like me . . .
>
> (Participant A)

...how you personally have always thought (cognitive style) and project your own personality (personality) into how you manage ... if you were somebody who likes to think an awful lot (cognitive style) about what you are going to do...

(Participant B)

...if **information** (<u>information processing ability</u>) is presented to you in a way you are not used to dealing with, it is going to **make it harder for you to learn** (<u>cognitive style</u>) that topic...

(Participant C)

...highlighting **what kind of learner I was** (<u>fixed</u>) ... I haven't always got **the brains** (<u>intelligence</u>) to follow it up! I'm **not very good at reflective thinking** ... (<u>cognitive style</u>)

(Participant D)

In contrast there is the quote from the fifth participant:

...some of that also is probably within us in terms of our own particular **personality** (<u>personality</u>) and **learning styles can and do in fact change over a period of time** (<u>fluid</u>)...

(Participant E)

These responses should be compared and contrasted with the offerings given in response to the question below. The outstanding point to be drawn in this instance is that all of the respondents who had been action learning participants carried out a pre and post action learning experience analysis of their preferred learning styles. Statistically, all had experienced a change in either the strength of their preference or even in some cases a complete overhaul of their preferences. None of the four action learning set members who were asked the question made reference to the change that they had experienced within this stage of the research. The following stage assisted in the identification of some interesting links.

Q: What do you feel caused the changes and developments in your preferred learning style scores from pre to post action learning experience?

'They changed because they had to change, we were exposed to a range of different learning methods, so we had to just get on with it' was a typical response encountered when informally asking large groups of participants (post action learning experience) what they felt had caused a development or change in their style. What follows is the response to the question offered by one participant from the sample group, *post* action learning experience (reported verbatim).

I think part of the changes were because as you are going through the process of action learning and the ISM course, because it was structured in a way that you needed to take time out to reflect, then my score improved in that area because that was one thing that I know I am not so good at and it's partly because of having to take the time out to do it will reflect the kind of learning about reflection, reflection in action and reflection on action and the therapists are probably very good at reflecting as we are doing things in terms of sitting back later and reflecting on what you've done, it's a bit harder I think because of time constraints. I think that was part of why that improved because it was the process of going through and then the other thing that I think improved for me was the theorist side. Again I suppose the course itself presented information in a theoretical way that you then went away and applied practically, so I was simply learning kind of more about theories to support practice as well.

(Participant C)

The responses mirrored one another entirely. The predominant theme was that the changes in learning style preference were directly related to exposure to a range of different learning activities and methods, which accommodated the full range of learning styles.

Participant 'A' provided a response much along the same lines, but very much focused upon the action learning set activity itself, referring to a need to vary one's preferred learning style in order to facilitate learning in colleagues when working on a group basis. The participant argued that diversity within the action learning set meeting itself created a need to be fluid in terms of one's preferred learning style to prevent stifling another colleague's learning.

Conclusions

By virtue of the responses that participants provided to the questions, it was apparent that there was a consensus of opinion that their personal learning styles had changed. There was also an agreement that the action learning model itself created better learners – it provided an opportunity to develop one's style both consciously and unconsciously. In particular, the action learning set activity itself was deemed to be developmental in this sense – *providing* the criteria for membership was diversity of learning style preference. This arena was also perceived by some as useful for gaining positive reinforcement of their own approaches to learning and subsequently their learning style.

The interpretative analysis of the discourse presented within this paper demonstrates that this particular community of NHS managers and leaders did not share a 'typical' concept of action learning and learning styles. This supports the consideration of O'Neil (1999) in her point that action learning draws upon different philosophies of learning and change. She believes that the perceived lack of empirical evidence to support the effectiveness of action learning is due to this factor. Perhaps the same could also be said of learning styles.

Much of the diversity in concepts of action learning can be explained by existing knowledge held by individuals when they first encounter it, coupled with what they are explicitly told of the process and model. This would account for the diversity of common concepts held within this particular group of respondents, despite having received the same verbal explanation and briefing.

O'Neil's research across the US, UK and Sweden goes on to attribute this diversity to the varying schools of thought or 'faces of action learning.' She suggests all human resource development practitioners approach the design and implementation of action learning programmes in a different manner. These schools of practice are: Scientific, Experiential, Critical Reflection and Tacit.

In the *Tacit School*, participants are expected to learn incidentally when they progress with real work-based problems.

In the *Scientific School*, practitioners base their approach on Revans' model of problem solving – Systems Alpha, Beta and Gamma – which is intentionally biased towards learning, with questioning as a central part of the theory.

The *Experiential School* is the approach taken by those who believe that Kolb's experiential learning cycle is its theoretical base, which makes it different from Revan's approach because it has equal emphasis upon all points in the learning cycle, with no definitive starting point. In Revan's approach, however, action is defined as the starting point.

The *Critical Reflection School* of action learning offers a concentrated focus upon the closer examination of one's values and beliefs in order to change perspectives, as distorted perceptions of self can result in dysfunctional analysis of external problems and situations. This, it could be argued, can best be achieved by questions in the critical questioning phase of the process.

These four 'faces of action learning' can be referenced to assist practitioners in making sense of the various definitions of action learning provided by the participants in the research study.

It is important to note that this piece of interpretative research has been of value to me in considering which of the four schools of thought have been dominant in the design of the action learning programme that all research participants quoted had operated within. As stated earlier within this chapter, none of the responses contained reference to a particular *start point* for the action learning process. The lack of specific reference to 'the problem' being the start point (Revans 1955; see Marsick and O'Neil 1999) could easily be attributed to my own verbal presentation on the process of action learning delivered as part of the management development programme induction. Although the 'Scientific School' approach was described to the participants at the start, it was, on reflection, a highly eclectic model that followed.

Using O'Neil's typology to aid the retrospective pedagogical analysis of the explanation provided during the verbal presentation, it was identified that the model that was subsequently implemented for participants through facilitation was an 'Experiential School' approach. This did not require participants to explicitly consider where they should start on the learning cycle. There was also a strong emphasis upon the 'Critical Reflection' school of action learning, with dramatic leaning towards the importance of the evaluation of one's values and beliefs in order to change perspectives within the actual action learning set meetings themselves.

What can be identified though, as O'Neil has in her 'typology' of action learning, are common themes, similarities and consistent elements. These can be summarized and are included in the list below as:

- Focus on real, live problems which have no right answer;
- Participants that meet to engage in conversation about their problem and progress to date;
- Role of the group process;
- Learning how to learn.

O'Neil states that several underpinning educational theories are reflected in the action learning process, which are centred on the interaction of the person and the environment. 'Both understood that individuals learn as individuals, but that their experience is shaped and understood within social contexts.' If we are to say that practitioners adopt and agree on the common themes, similarities and consistent elements stated above, a starting point may be found upon which to base research.

One participant provided a particularly interesting point regarding the main catalyst for development and change in their learning style. The attribution was focused on the interaction within the action learning set with colleagues who had different learning styles to her own. The following quote is illustrative of how she framed the process of talk within this forum:

> When I first heard about action learning, I thought well this is going to be interesting, all sit around in a group and talk to each other but actually action learning is not about what you say, it's about the way you say it and watching the body language, it's not the words, it's the interaction between people and groups and if there is anything I have learned from action learning it is the hidden messages and it's about how people want you to perceive them. Its games, I mean it is very serious games but it is games.
>
> And one of the other things is bringing action learning back into the workplace because it makes you increase your listening skills because you can't do it if you don't have good listening skills. You cannot do action learning skills in a group without good listening skills. It also makes you

less judgmental because I think before action learning I was very judgmental. Someone would say something, and I would think get on with it,
you know? Whereas now, I am more prepared for people to find their own
way so it has made me less judgmental. I can still be very judgmental in
my own mind but I correct myself and the key element is . . .

(Participant A)

Participants have laid great emphasis upon their concept of action learning
being the action learning set meeting itself. This observation, coupled with
their predominant explanation of changes in their learning styles being attributed to talk with others who did not share the same learning style preference,
has led to the development of further research questions in the investigation of
the effectiveness of action learning. The focus upon participants' perception of
learning via language and the questioning process in particular has been
addressed within a further piece of ethnographic research that I undertook
concerning individual attribution style, explanatory style and action learning.

The preceding accounts of what happened to four action learning participants and one practitioner, presented as five small social experiments, offers a
range of diverse explanations of the key features of both action learning and
learning styles. The research was not carried out within the action learning set
environment itself, but within participants' own workplaces – their offices,
their classrooms, their therapy treatment rooms, hospital wards and clinics.

Key learning points

The focus on experimental semi-structured interviews had in some ways
almost forced the participants to engage in real, individual theorizing or
social construction. In a sense this intervention could be perceived as being
culturally based and therefore conducive to research outcomes. The interviews with the participants could be interpreted as a management development intervention in their own right – real teaching/facilitative sessions as
well as research events. As a questioner/interviewer the research questions
represented further learning.

As a practitioner I was partially responsible for the lack of a 'typical' definition of the concept. Action learning and any other management development facilitator should perhaps pay close attention to what 'they say' and
what 'they do.' As a result of this reflection one example of a practice-based
change has been to include a similar intervention at an earlier point in the
action learning experience in an attempt to heighten awareness and enhance
subsequent learning of the participants involved.

By presenting opportunities and challenges for action learning participants
to discuss their perceptions and definitions of the process at regular points a
deeper cognition of personal learning and evaluation of relevant influencing
factors on their learning may take place.

The challenge for all practitioners is to be continuously alive to opportunities to link evaluation into design and delivery if action learning is to gain increased confidence as a development tool of *choice*.

References

Agar, M.H. (1980) In: Watson, T.J. (1996) 'Motivation: that's Maslow, isn't it?' *Management Learning* 27(4): 449.

Becker, H.S. (1958) In: Watson, T.J. (1996) 'Motivation: that's Maslow, isn't it?' *Management Learning* 27(4): 449.

Bourner, T. and Weinstein, K. (1996) 'Just another talking shop? Some of the pitfalls in action learning,' *Employee Counselling Today, The Journal of Workplace Learning* 8(6): 54–65.

Clark, J. (1977) In: Greene, J. and Coulson, M. (eds) (1986) *Language Understanding, Current Issues*, 2nd edn, Open University Press, p. 42.

Gold, R.L. (1958) In: Bannister, P., Burman, E., Parker, I., Taylor, M and Tindall, C. (1994) *Qualitative Methods in Psychology – A Research Guide*, Open University Press, pp. 39.

Gold, R.L. (1958) 'Roles in sociological field observation,' *Social Forces* 36: 93.

Honey, P. and Mumford, A. (1982) *The Manual of Learning Styles*, Ardingly House, Berkshire: Peter Honey.

Kolb, D., Rubin, I.M. and Osland, J.S. (1995) *Organizational Behavior. An Experiential Approach*, New Jersey: Prentice Hall.

Marsh, P., Rosser, E. and Harre, R. (1978) *The Rules of Disorder*, London: Routledge and Kegan Paul.

Marsick, V.J. and O'Neil, J. (1999) 'The many faces of action learning,' *Management Learning* 30(2): 159–176.

McGill, I. and Beaty, L. (1992) *Action Learning – A Guide for Professional, Management and Educational Development*, Kogan Page, pp. 29, 31–32.

Murphy, G.L. and Wright, J.C. (1984) In: Roth, I. and Bruce, V. (1995) *Perception and Representation – Current Issues. Open Guides to Psychology*, 2nd edn, Open University Press, p. 59.

O'Neil, J. (1999) In: Marsick, V.J. and O'Neil, J. (1999) 'The many faces of action learning,' *Management Learning* 30(2): 159–176.

Pedler, M., Burgoyne, ?. and Boydell, T. (1991) *The Learning Company*, Maidenhead: McGraw-Hill.

Revans, R.W. (1955) In: Marsick, V.J. and O'Neil, J. (1999) 'The many faces of action learning,' *Management Learning* 30(2): 159–176.

Roth, I. and Bruce, V. (1995) *Perception and Representation, Current Issues*, Open University Press, pp. 52, 59.

Watson, J.T. (2000) 'Research methodology and the use of case and ethnographic methods presentation handout materials,' The Nottingham Trent University, Doctorate of Business Administration Course May/July 2000.

Watson, T.J. (1996) 'Motivation: that's Maslow, isn't it?' *Management Learning* 27(4): 447–464.

7 Environmental, organizational and individual influences on line managers' roles as facilitators of learning in social care voluntary organizations

Rona S. Beattie

Aims and objectives

The aim of this chapter is to explore the influence environmental, organizational and individual variables have on line managers' attitudes and behaviours related to their developmental roles and responsibilities.

The culture and values of voluntary organizations provide relatively unexplored and fertile territory for HRD research; as Dartington (1992: 30) indicates, 'voluntary organizations, even more than other organizations, have implicit not just explicit aims. One of these is providing opportunities for learning.'

Such exploration of voluntary sector managers helps address two significant deficits in HRD knowledge. First, it will enhance our understanding of this increasingly important socio-economic player. Second, it will provide evidence-based research into the role of line managers as facilitators of learning; a topic in which much current literature is normative and prescriptive (Hamlin *et al.* 2004; Beattie *et al.* 2004).

The objectives focus on the influence of the following factors on developmental relationships between line managers and employees and managerial behaviours:

- Environmental factors, including Care in the Community and increased regulation of social care;
- Organizational factors: organizational history; values, mission and strategy; structure; culture; HRD strategy, practice and line manager's roles; and.
- Individual factors: gender; learning style; motivation to learn; motivation to support learning; and educational and career background.

The theoretical context

The theoretical influences explored in this chapter are the interaction between current knowledge about line managers as facilitators of learning, and voluntary sector management theory.

Line managers as facilitators of learning

A growing literature recognizes the increasing devolution of HRD responsibilities to line managers (e.g. Mumford 1993; Bevan and Hayday 1994; Heraty and Morley 1995; Hamlin *et al.* 2004; Beattie *et al.* 2004). However, there has been limited empirical research into what line managers actually *do* to facilitate learning (Mumford 1993; Heraty and Morley 1995; IPD 1995; Horowitz 1999; de Jong *et al.* 1999; Ellinger and Bostrom 1999), a gap which this study attempts to address.

Heraty and Morley (1995) argue that line managers are well placed to assess training needs and deliver training in the workplace, whilst Higgins and Thomas (2001) have found that high levels of employee development can encourage employee commitment.

However, the capability of managers in supporting learning depends considerably on whether they have the appropriate knowledge, skills and attitudes (Leicester 1989; Heraty and Morley 1995; IPD 1995; Thomson *et al.* 2001). Concerns have also been expressed about the motivation of line managers to undertake developmental responsibilities, the insufficient training they have received for such roles and workload pressures (IPD 1995; Cunningham and Hyman 1999).

Bevan and Hayday (1994) identified three problems managers had with staff development. First, in relation to assessing employees, managers were reluctant to make medium or long-term predictions about employees' potential and felt they lacked the knowledge to do so. Second, there was the challenge of balancing devolution with a corporate view of HRD, for example letting their best staff progress to other jobs within the organization. Third, many managers found it difficult to talk to staff about their development needs as 'for many the appraisal interview often represents too much dialogue, so conducting an ongoing dialogue with individuals about their work preferences, development and career potential can be a low priority' (Bevan and Hayday 1994: 8–9).

Indeed, a significant minority felt threatened by such processes as 'actively developing some staff would amount to training subordinates to be better than them. This was, for some, a threatening notion, and one which HR managers had not seemed to recognize' (Bevan and Hayday 1994: 9).

The existing literature recognizes that line managers need support and development for their HRD roles and responsibilities (Cabinet Office 1993; Bevan and Hayday 1994), including exposure to management development for themselves (Mumford 1993; McGovern *et al.* 1997; Ellinger and Bostrom 1999; Buckingham 2000). Support can also be provided by having a coherent HR strategy that is clear about the role of line managers, by providing training to line managers for people management (McGovern *et al.* 1997; Cunningham and Hyman 1999), and by the HRD function acting as an internal consultant or partner to line managers. Thomson *et al.* (2001) also found that line managers are more likely to be involved in supporting development when the organization has a formalized strategy for development. This interaction is explored further in this study.

Although there is an extensive literature on developmental roles, such as coaching, much of this literature is normative (Horowitz 1999) and the view has been expressed that the 'developmental humanism' that underpins many normative HRM (and HRD) models is overcome by the short-term pragmatism of capitalist ventures (McGovern *et al.* 1997). It is argued here that voluntary organizations operating in the social care field may not be so susceptible to the capitalist pressures that may inhibit development.

Voluntary sector management

The voluntary sector provides a comparatively untapped domain for management researchers, as it has not been exposed to the same theoretical and empirical scrutiny as the public and private sectors, and therefore offers new perspectives on management issues and problems.

> The contribution of voluntary sector management to the development of management thinking and practice in general needs to be noted. There is a dawning realization that managing in voluntary and non-profit enterprises may provide useful insights into the definition of generic roles and competencies. Most immediately, the experience of voluntary sector managers is particularly relevant to managers operating in sections of the erstwhile public sector – in schools, colleges and hospitals ... for whom simple private sector models of management are woefully inappropriate.
>
> (Batsleer 1995: 225)

Within HRM/HRD specifically it has been argued that research in the non-profit sector is needed to redress the dominance in the literature of for-profit organizations (Kamoche 2001), and to evaluate the relevance of HRM for voluntary organizations (Cunningham 1999). A focus on the voluntary sector is rare in the HRM/HRD literature, an exception being a special issue of *Employee Relations* in 2001. In it, Cunningham (2001a) also noted that the UK voluntary sector literature is also bereft of any substantial bibliography of employment-related books. Moreover, employment-related articles in the internationally respected refereed academic journals, such as *Voluntas* and *Non-profit and Voluntary Sector Quarterly* are rare. As a consequence, we know little about people management in the voluntary sector (Cunningham 2001b). This is a matter of some concern given that staff in this sector care for the most vulnerable groups in our society, and the effectiveness of that provision is linked to the commitment (and skills) of those staff (Paton and Cornforth 1992).

There is no simple answer to the question 'what is different about managing voluntary and non-profit organizations?' However,

...managing in voluntary and non-profit organizations will often be different in significant ways and for good reasons when compared with many other organizations. The difficulty lies in expressing the nature and significance of those differences without getting caught up in, or reinforcing, the stereotypes, both positive and negative, of the different sectors. For every sector has its positive self-image and legendary figures – and its negative caricatures of the other sectors.

(Paton and Cornforth 1992: 45)

There are factors, which when combined, can make managing in voluntary organizations *'different'* (Paton and Cornforth 1992; Bruce and Raymer 1992; Leat 1993) including:

- Social goals – which make it more difficult to determine priorities and performance;
- Particular resource acquisition and management issues associated with independent, non-trading organizations;
- The nature and variety of stakeholders and their relationships with voluntary organizations;
- A 'way of doing things' or culture that emphasizes value commitments and participatory-democratic decision-making;
- Operation through small, informal units;
- The virtual absence of complex technological systems (although this is increasingly less the case); and,
- High lay involvement in policy-making and management.

Steane (1997) also argues that voluntary organizations are more likely to have greater emphasis on expressive rather than instrumental values, and as such are likely to be 'affiliative and human in their orientation and favour an ontological contribution to a person, that is, those values that are integral to being human or contribute to enhancing humanity' (Steane 1997: 6).

He continues that the ideal of value neutrality in human services is not feasible as these are 'a myriad of implicit and explicit beliefs about the world which contributes to conduct and preferences' (Steane 1997: 16).

Butler and Wilson (1990: 51) also argue that voluntary organizations have distinctive cultures that are 'dominantly moral, self-reflective, democratic, participative and altruistic.'

Paton and Cornforth (1992) suggest that these sectoral factors create three implications for managers in voluntary organizations.

i   A large proportion of managers in voluntary organizations need to be 'all rounders.'

ii There is a premium on personal sensitivity and influence in situations where managers cannot rely on the authority of their position or on incentives. These personal skills include the ability to handle intense value differences and to deal appropriately with people from different social or organizational worlds.

iii Managers must cope with considerable uncertainty and ambiguity. These may result from an unstructured work environment, insecure resourcing and need to accommodate a range of conflicting principles and expectations, both internally and externally.

In the late 1980s, Druker (1989) suggested that organizations in the future would be knowledge-based, composed largely of specialists, who manage their own work and bear little resemblance to the manufacturing sector which then dominated many management texts. He concluded that many voluntary organizations resembled this *future* and also argued that voluntary organizations have the best management practices.

This theme is developed further by Dartington (1992) who argued in the 1990s that private sector organizations were beginning to recognize management principles that had been long understood in the voluntary sector, such as:

i People value a sense of ownership of what they are doing;
ii Organization around task is more effective than organization around resources;
iii Authoritarian management has limited effect and potential compared with networking democratic management;
iv Individual initiative can be encouraged;
v The quality of work done is the most important indicator of effectiveness; and,
vi Intuition and creation are often more effective than going by the book.

Given the above discussion, it is argued here that the theoretical and applied implications emerging from this research include:

i Voluntary social care organizations provide an alternative perspective for HRD theory and practice.
ii There is enhancement of knowledge and understanding about both line managers as developers and voluntary sector management in the social care sector, thus contributing to the development of effective management education and development.
iii There is increasing inter-sector understanding given the growing prevalence and importance of partnership working in health and social care, arising from the likes of community care policy and the Joint Future agenda (Scottish Executive 2003).

The empirical context

The empirical research was conducted in two large Scottish voluntary social care organizations. Both organizations, Quarriers and Richmond Fellowship

Scotland (RFS), are highly regarded in their respective fields and have undergone considerable growth in recent years. At the time of the fieldwork both organizations employed close to 1000 staff each. This growth has been sustained and both now employ around 1500 staff each. At the time of the fieldwork both organizations had aspirations to be learning organizations and both had been recognized as Investors in People.

Whilst the author is a trustee of Quarriers and has provided consultancy services to RFS she adopted the role of academic researcher for this study (see Beattie 2002).

The research methods

The first phase of the study involved an initial period of ethnographic immersion (see Beattie 2002) to gain familiarity with the culture, language and operations of each organization. The second phase involved a series of intensive semi-structured interviews ($n = 60$), utilizing critical incident technique (Flanagan 1954), with senior line managers (SLM), first line managers (FLM), employees and key informants (KI), such as HRD managers and practitioners. Forty-one developmental relationships were explored.

Managers and employees were asked questions regarding managerial behaviours that facilitated or inhibited employee learning and organizational factors that might influence learning. The data were then analysed, utilizing a grounded theory approach, to identify the facilitative behaviours, the focus of this chapter, and inhibitory behaviours demonstrated by line managers and their interaction with workplace factors. Findings have been presented using the impersonal pronoun and codes to minimize identification of respondents.

The findings

Following cross-case analysis, the key environmental, organizational and individual influences on learning within the organizations and developmental relationships were identified. Developmental relationships are then explored by examining the nature, processes and content of developmental interactions. This analysis has enabled the identification of developmental manager behaviours.

Environmental influences

Political and economic

The voluntary sector is playing an increasing role in economic and social policy (Butler and Wilson 1990; Green 2000) because:

> ...when it comes to the 'softer' products such as health care, education and welfare, there are considerable problems in relying solely on the

marketplace for service provision since it relies so heavily on profitable returns.

(Butler and Wilson 1990: 11)

A key development for both organizations was the NHS and Community Care Act in 1990,[1] which had four elements impacting on the voluntary sector (Scott and Russell 2001).

  i   A shift from institutional to community care;
 ii   An emphasis on needs-led (user/carer preferences) services rather than supply-led ones;
iii   A decentralization of strategic responsibilities from central to local government; and,
 iv   The development of a mixed economy of care approach with independent for-profit and non-profit providers alongside, or instead of, state provision.

Community care enabled both organizations to grow rapidly from the mid-1990s. However this 'mixed economy of care' approach has seen the replacement of grants with contracts for the delivery of specific services and increased demands for accountability (SCVO 1999). Therefore, both organizations have had to develop services that provide both value-for-money and quality to address increasing government demands for 'best value,' which requires competition for contracts and tight performance standards (Cunningham 2001a; Alcock *et al.* 2004). This has resulted in both organizations developing more professional and managerial frameworks such as business planning, quality systems including EFQM, Investors in People (IiP), Scottish Vocational Qualifications, and strengthening traditional development approaches in social care, such as supervision.

Whilst both organizations acknowledged that they had to operate within the 'contract culture' climate they were keen to ensure voluntary sector values would not be lost. For example, Quarriers reflected this in their strategic aim for 'an agenda for independent action.' This aim is supported by the voluntary income that the charity raises.

The establishment of the Scottish Social Services Council (Scottish Office 1998) has increased the pressure on RFS and Quarriers, and other providers, to increase the numbers of qualified care staff and managers. As much of this increase in qualifications will be achieved through SVQs, line managers will be required to play an increasing role in facilitating workplace learning and assessing staff competency.

Societal and technological trends

A significant issue for the sector is the ageing population. This affects the sector's ability to recruit staff and volunteers, and more particularly means that voluntary organizations have to cope with ageing service users (Taylor 1996) whose problems become increasingly complex.

Investment in Information and Communications Technology has tended to lag behind the for-profit and public sectors due to cost. However, chief officers of Scottish voluntary organizations are increasingly recognizing the need to improve ICT knowledge and skills in the sector (Green 2000). Technology also has a valuable role to play in assisting communication with particular service user groups including people with learning disabilities.

Advances in medical technology including drug regimes, diagnostic processes and medical equipment have changed the way many service users are supported. For example, many individuals with mental health problems can be treated at home rather than having to be admitted to long-stay institutions. Such changes require employees to keep up-to-date with the latest changes in health and social care policy and practices, whilst employers need to address the challenges of managing and developing staff serving in dispersed workplaces such as service users' homes.

This dynamic environment, therefore, plays a crucial role in influencing priority learning needs at RFS and Quarriers, and can be seen by both organizations emphasizing the acquisition of qualifications for front-line staff, through workplace learning approaches, and management development.

Organizational influences

History

Despite their very different origins and long-term histories Quarriers' and RFS's recent histories have much in common. Both have grown rapidly since the mid-1990s and they have also diversified. Quarriers is no longer solely a children's charity, and RFS is no longer solely a mental health charity. Both are increasingly delivering services, such as support for people with learning disabilities, within individuals' communities rather than in large-scale projects. Key informants in both organizations believed that the organizations were at a critical point in their life cycles, following this period of rapid growth and diversification. The challenges now facing the organizations were retaining their innovation, whilst controlling the level of bureaucracy that inevitably accompanies growth.

Mission and strategy

Both organizations have similar missions – to help individuals who are disadvantaged to overcome or minimize those disadvantages. In particular, both emphasize that the needs and rights of individuals are the central focus of organizational activities. To achieve these missions the strategic policies of both organizations echo similar themes, such as quality, continuous improvement, and standards. Of particular relevance to this research were their aspirations to be learning organizations. This could be seen in the language used in policy documents, such as strategic plans and Annual Reports, and in respondents' statements:

> ... without learning and development services will stultify.
>
> (Chief Executive, RFS)

> It's a learning organization you are always learning.
>
> (Employee 4, Quarriers)

Their commitment to learning organization ideals heightened the role of line managers as developers.

Structure

Paton and Hooker (1990) found that organizations, such as RFS and Quarriers, with dispersed operations could have problems with staff development, as line managers may be at a distance from staff. This proved to be less of a problem for junior staff as their direct line manager was still geographically accessible, although it was going to be an increasing challenge with the move towards individual supported accommodation. There is, however, a challenge for senior managers, based at Head Office, developing first line managers based in projects. However, due to the commitment of senior managers this problem was minimized, although there was some acknowledgement that distance, and the time involved in travelling, was a potential barrier to development.

Culture

The culture of both organizations was heavily influenced by their commitment to social care models of practice and person-centred planning. That these values were translated into everyday practice was confirmed by respondents at all levels.

> The values that underpin our mission statement are values about the person-centred approach, about dealing with people in their place of need whatever that is and responding directly and therefore giving people a sense of hope for positive change.
>
> (HR Director Quarriers)

> I think the value base is person centred.
>
> (FLM2, RFS)

These cultures meant both organizations have been well placed to cope with the changes in the regulation of care in Scotland, the continued de-institutionalization of social care and the requirement to provide person-centred services.

In both organizations some concerns were expressed that the contract culture, rapid growth, and the consequent increase in bureaucratic process could threaten the idealism of both organizations and result in values being applied inconsistently.

> It has had to become contracting, outcome orientated ... to do with the culture that we bid for contracts. I think all voluntary organizations have to an extent lost the individuality they had.
>
> (Employee 10, RFS)

> I think they're expanding a great deal ... I feel the bureaucratic side of it is increasing.
>
> (FLM5, Quarriers)

However, a positive outcome of such growth was that it offered staff increased career development opportunities.

Of particular interest to this study was whether RFS and Quarriers transferred their human-centred approach to social care to the learning and development of employees (see Beattie 2004). Respondents confirmed that these social care values were indeed transferred to HRD.

> I think the culture is very much about being an enabling organization and enabling not only the clients that we come into contact with but also the members of staff.
>
> (SLM4, RFS)

> Putting the people we work with at the centre of our work is really important ... you can't separate how we work with staff from how we work with service users.
>
> (KI3, Quarriers)

The application of such values could be most clearly seen in the caring behaviours demonstrated by all managers in this study (see Table 7.1). These behaviours included managers being supportive, encouraging, reassuring and approachable, showing commitment to employee development and demonstrating empathy. Two examples are provided below.

The first is provided by an employee describing how their manager had helped them cope with a return to formal study late in life.

> ...because I had somebody *supporting* me ... I wasn't frightened if I made a mistake ... it wasn't like being back at school ... I think there is probably a confidence in FLM5 that I knew FLM5 would make it OK.
>
> (Employee 15, Quarriers)

Table 7.1 Facilitative behaviours

Category	Behaviours	Description
Caring	Supporting	To give aid or courage to
	Encouraging	Inspiring or instilling confidence
	Being approachable	Easy to approach
	Reassuring	To relieve anxiety
	Being committed/involved	Gives time
	Empathizing	Showing understanding of another's situation
Informing	Sharing knowledge	Transmitting information
Being professional	Role Modelling	Behaving in a manner that people respect and wish to emulate
	Standard-setting	Outlining or encouraging an acceptable level of performance or quality
	Planning and preparing	Organizing and structuring learning
Advising	Instructing	Directing an individual in a specific task
	Coaching	Discussing and guiding activity
	Guiding	Providing advice
	Counselling	Helping others take control of their own behaviour and solve problems
Assessing	Providing feedback and recognition	Letting someone know how they are performing and acknowledging their achievements
	Identifying development needs	Assessing what is required to enhance current performance or career development
Thinking	Reflective or Prospective Thinking	Process of taking time to consider what has happened in the past or may happen in the future
	Clarifying	Process of making something clearer or easier to understand
Empowering	Delegating	To give duties, responsibilities to another
	Trusting	Having confidence in someone
Developing developers	Developing developers	Stimulating the acquisition of skills and knowledge by employees to develop others
Challenging	Challenging	Stimulating people to stretch themselves

The second example demonstrates managers providing support beyond routine work by helping employees cope with service user bereavement, an event they will increasingly have to learn to deal with as the service user population ages.

> [I provided] a kind of emotional support ... I was there for the person on the day and the day after I spoke to [them]. I then followed up a week later ... and I made sure that the person supervising [them] discussed it at supervision again.
>
> (FLM1, RFS)

The transfer of values from social care to employee development could also be seen in organizational practices such as the supervision and appraisal processes that mirror person-centred planning, the development of learning and development plans, and learning portfolios. The power of such processes to support learning is demonstrated below.

> In my previous job I never got any supervision or reviews. I never had an opportunity to air my concerns or say anything at all about my job or about what I was doing or what I thought about anything I was doing. Since I came here it's been very in-depth ... 'how have you felt about this and are you clear about that?' ... I think it is really, really good.
>
> (Employee 3, Quarriers)

Links between culture and learning could be most clearly seen by Quarriers' Learning Organization experiment, which was seen to be impacting on managerial attitudes.

> Managers are understanding that learning is a cultural activity at the heart of service delivery, it's not separate.
>
> (HR Director, Quarriers)

> ...its commitment to learning, the Learning Organization stuff, the SVQs and now the Quality Standards ... having come from the health board ... I just saw there was a totally different environment, totally different commitment right from the word go and I think that in itself gives you the drive to see that happen with other people.
>
> (FLM1, Quarriers)

Finally, line managers were seen as having significant influence on culture and learning climate at a local level. For example, one manager used football as a metaphor to describe how they were trying to create a culture where their staff saw themselves as the best 'team' in the organization.

> It's about promoting a culture that we're the best. I think that's quite important because people feel good about going to their work and they're working for a joint cause. I always relate management to football management ... You're leading a team ... but you've got different positions and you're always going to have a star in every team but the rest of them have to work just as hard and everybody should be appreciated for the things they do.
>
> (FLM3, RFS)

This manager's employees provided corroborating evidence of this positive culture and it was also recognized by social work inspection reports.

HRD strategy, practice and line managers' roles

There were common themes emerging from the HRD strategies of RFS and Quarriers. These included the desire to maintain IiP accreditation, recognition of the role of line managers in HRD processes, encouragement of staff to take responsibility for learning and the expansion of workplace qualifications such as SVQs. There were also explicit links made between learning and quality, with both strategies aiming to support the continuous improvement of staff and ulti- mately services, indeed RFS has a joint learning and quality strategy. This link was reinforced in each organization's supervision and appraisal policy.

> To enhance individual performance in order to improve the quality of services, encourage professional and personal growth and increase accountability between the individual and the agency.
> (Quarriers Supervision Policy)

> Regular staff supervision and appraisal are essential to realising [RFS's] commitment to deliver the best possible high quality services.
> (RFS Staff Supervision and Appraisal Policy)

Another common feature was the language of the respective strategies emphasizing learning rather than training.

There are operational differences in the way Quarriers and RFS deliver their central HRD activities. Quarriers have a central training function and much of the formal training provision is delivered at HQ, although some local training is also provided. RFS have recently decentralized their train- ing function, and each geographical area has an Area Learning Coordinator (ALC) who works in partnership with local managers to identify, design and facilitate learning, as well as delivering core programmes.

In terms of central training courses, both organizations offer similar provi- sion covering social care, management and organizational policies. Staff in both organizations generally valued such courses not only for their content, but also for the opportunity to network with colleagues. Both organizations used core training courses, such as induction, to introduce and reinforce the values of the organization. Managers contributed to the delivery of these courses.

Both organizations are recognized SVQ assessment centres, which is important given the regulation of care in Scotland. Managers played an active role in the SVQ process, acting as assessors and/or internal verifiers. Staff also have access to external training and education where relevant to their jobs. In both organizations staff are encouraged to record their learning in individual portfolios.

Policy documents, key informants and senior managers articulated the central role that line managers play in the development of staff at Quarriers and RFS, and the overall development of the organizations.

> I think it is the most important role; it's crucial to what they do ... it forces thinking on them so that they consider their staff are the lynch-pin ... We're here for service users. What we're actually here to do depends on staff actually understanding what they're involved in doing.
>
> (SLM2, RFS)

> I increasingly think that project leaders have the key role in the organiza-tion ... and I think it is absolutely crucial that they give priority to staff development.
>
> (SLM1, Quarriers)

Quarriers, for example, outlined managerial responsibilities for development as including: assessment of training and development needs; induction; support and supervision; providing clear information; on-the-job instruc-tion, coaching and counselling; performance management; and offering positive role models to colleagues (IiP Storyboard 1998) These responsibil-ities are reflected in a range of developmental behaviours revealed in this study (see Table 7.1) such as: identifying development needs; supporting; informing; advising; providing feedback; and role modelling.

The labels for these behaviours were largely identified by the respondents and can be seen in some of the respondent quotes provided in this chapter. For example, 'challenging' behaviours were seen by respondents as managers trying to stretch employees out of their comfort zone, such as going for promotion and trying another role. The categories are also presented in terms of frequency of managers demonstrating these behaviours. All man-agers demonstrated caring behaviours; however, challenging behaviours tended to be demonstrated by more senior and experienced managers.

Managerial responsibility for learning is most clearly seen in managers' contributions to the supervisory processes of both organizations.

Supervision in social care provides a framework for line managers as developers and is a holistic approach to managing, teaching and supporting staff (Sawdon and Sawdon 1995). It is the pivotal element of an organi-zational system (see Figure 7.1) that links induction, quality standards, appraisal and learning opportunities.

Both organizations have explicit supervision policies stating the purpose and frequency of supervision, appraisal and training needs analysis. Critical incidents involving supervision showed individuals and managers identify-ing learning opportunities, and reflecting on and evaluating experience, all examples of good adult learning practice.

> I've been placing responsibility on both of us to look at learning opportunities that might help longer term career development.
>
> (SLM6, Quarriers)

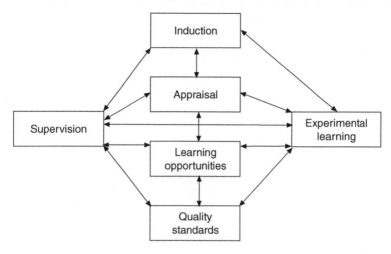

Figure 7.1 Organizational framework for supporting learning.

From the managers' perspective they saw clear links between staff development, the observation of organizational values and the achievement of standards. They also felt that sharing their knowledge would help to ensure that the standard of work in their services and/or attitudes towards service users would be appropriate.

> I'm doing something worthwhile to improve the standards of other people in their role.
>
> (SLM2, Quarriers)

One manager emphasized that they developed *all* their staff, through supervision, induction and on-the-job learning, to at least a minimum level of competency for the benefit of the project and service users.

> There should be a basic level that I am looking for within all of the staff and there's an expectation to get that within about 6 months ... I just don't like the idea that there's a difference. I think it causes barriers – 'I can do that and you can't'. Getting them all able to administer particular types of medicines/procedures ... all of these things are part of service users' care plans and if you have staff who can't do it basically what you are saying is that you can't work with that service user. So it's really good for the project that your staff are skilled to that level but I also think it's good for them and for morale.
>
> (FLM2, Quarriers)

This approach was corroborated by one of the manager's team leaders who admired how the manager developed staff, with no previous care experience, to a high standard of performance.

> [FLM2] doesn't skimp on anything, nothing is missed out, even how to fold sheets on a bed . . . [FLM2] can train these people . . . [so] that they can eventually be left with service users and know exactly how to handle it if somebody takes a seizure or takes ill.
>
> (Employee 6, Quarriers)

Support for line managers

Concern has been expressed that supervision has not fulfilled its potential due to managers lacking facilitative skills and having limited understanding of adult learning (Sawdon and Sawdon 1995; Hughes and Pengelly 1997). RFS and Quarriers addressed this by providing training courses for 'supervisors' such as supervision, appraisal, training for trainers and coaching and these were designed to maximize links with practice. Increasingly, these courses incorporated input on aspects of adult learning such as learning cycles and styles to:

> . . . help people see that people may be approaching things in a different way because of their learning style.
>
> (KI4, Quarriers)

Written guidance was also provided to managers. Managers in both organizations also reported that they had received individual support from the training function in addition to these formal processes. This was likely to increase in the future, particularly in RFS with the establishment of the ALC posts. Managers also had the opportunity to acquire SVQ D units to support the assessment and internal verification processes in both organizations.

Managers had also learnt how to be developers through experiential learning, for example by reflecting on how their own managers had facilitated their learning, including through supervision.

> I think what has been best for me has been having a manager myself who's been good at that. Who I have felt developed me, who's given me a chance to stretch my wings a bit and find out what I am capable of.
>
> (SLM1, RFS)

> When I was promoted I could not have done the job without [them]. I just felt that was somebody that I could trust to say 'look I don't know where I am going with this' and get advice.
>
> (FLM4, RFS)

Most managers recognized that they still required further development for their developmental roles. Such development included the need to acquire management qualifications and D units, training or further training in organizational processes such as supervision and appraisal, and being able to identify learning needs more effectively. Several managers at RFS suggested that the support of a mentor would enhance their developmental performance.

As well as the specific development opportunities provided for their developmental roles and responsibilities, managers in both organizations also had access to general management development. In RFS there was a 6-day Management Development Programme, which several managers commented on positively. RFS has also experimented with action learning sets, and those that focused on HR issues tended to be the most successful. Quarriers' managers could access internal training courses and a number of managers have been sponsored on the Certificate in Social Work Management.

In both organizations managers identified few barriers to their development roles, if anything they underplayed them. The main barriers were workload, time, financial and staffing resources, which could result in them giving insufficient attention to learning.

> . . . one of the struggles that line managers have in their developmental role are the other pressures that are around, so sometimes they are overwhelmed by just reacting to the situations. I think what sometimes happens is that instead of seeing it as an opportunity for development there is almost not the time and they're rushing on to the next thing . . . or the time for reflection is actually quite difficult to build in.
>
> (KI2, Quarriers)

> I think all my managers are genuinely concerned to do it and see the need for it. I think it is obviously harder for them because day to day they are frequently dealing with some of the major things like staff shortages which absorb a phenomenal amount of time and stress. So I think they feel pulled in a lot of different directions.
>
> (SLM3, RFS)

Increasing bureaucracy, including that generated by the HR function, was also cited as a barrier.

> You've got pressure coming from HRD . . . you've got development reviews to do. You've got this to do . . . and it's very, very hard to feel that you're being a developer and sometimes it feels just like a paper exercise.
>
> (FLM5, Quarriers)

Individual influences

Gender

Although two key informants suggested that women might be more natural developers than men there was no evidence to suggest that female and male managers in these organizations adopted different behavioural sets when facilitating learning. This is perhaps not surprising given that social care is likely to attract individuals with caring and nurturing qualities.

Learning style

The sample size of managers and employees was too small to offer statistically significant findings regarding learning styles (Honey and Mumford 1986). However, a clear finding that emerged about learning styles related to the interaction of learning styles, resulting either in complementarity or a potential for tension.

This interaction could be most clearly seen in critical incidents clustered under the thinking category. One incident demonstrated the potential difficulties between a 'reflector developer' and an 'active learner.'

> [SLM2] is very much a theory type person whereas I'm much more of a doer and I find it quite difficult.
>
> (FLM1, RFS)

However, another example demonstrated a 'pragmatist learner' recognizing the value of learning from a 'reflector/theorist developer.' In this second example, the learner, a more experienced and confident manager, recognized the difference in learning styles as a means to develop, emphasizing that 'it makes me think' (FLM3). Indeed they had asked a previous manager, a 'theorist,' to act as a mentor.

These findings suggest that learning styles should not be seen in isolation but should be considered as part of a holistic picture about the learner. Interestingly, one respondent felt that a downside of knowledge about learning styles was that individuals may act out the stereotypical behaviours associated with their identified style or use it to justify not participating in certain learning activities, and thus fail to benefit from a wider range of learning opportunities.

There was evidence that managers were becoming increasingly aware of the need to consider the possible interactions between learning styles. This could be seen by managers using Learning Style Questionnaires to identify individuals' preferred ways of learning.

Motivation to learn

Respondents revealed that individuals were encouraged to learn by a range of formal and informal processes, including induction, supervision, appraisal and two-way discussions with managers. Most engaged in learning activities ranging from training courses and education to informal learning, such as coaching by line managers.

'Developmental managers' were recognized by key informants as individuals who were engaged in learning both for themselves and to support their staff.

They're thinking of their own learning, are focused and have a grasp of how other people learn.

(KI4, RFS)

An outcome of their willingness to learn was that managers became role models for staff.

If I don't develop myself I'm not going to encourage others.

(FLM1, RFS)

Managers also demonstrated a willingness to learn from their staff, as well as from formal management development activities.

Most of my learning comes from the staff that I support by seeking their opinions about how we're doing and then reflecting with them.

(SLM2, RFS)

Motivation to support learning

Neither organization has performance-related pay, therefore the focus of the research was on the intrinsic factors that motivated managers to facilitate employee learning.

All managers accepted, and many welcomed, having some responsibility for facilitating learning. Indeed the role was seen as critical.

I really firmly believe *that* unless we know our staff and unless we know what their development needs are and the areas in which they excel and which could be utilized I really don't think we can provide a quality service.

(FLM4, RFS)

Two main motivators emerged. One was ensuring employees were meeting standards, and the second was the satisfaction of helping individuals develop.

It is important for me that the reputation of the organization is good and that's not just what I do but obviously is what the people that I am responsible for do as well. So it's important that I'm developing people.

(FLM5, Quarriers)

It was a really powerful thing as a supervisor to see [them] through that level when you have that gut instinct when you think people can do it . . . I get a lot of pleasure and satisfaction from seeing someone develop to that level.

(FLM5, RFS)

Educational and career background

Analysis of managers' qualifications revealed that they were generally well educated possessing qualifications ranging from degrees, professional qualifications (including CQSW or registered nurse), and HNDs. A number were continuing to study for further qualifications such as MBAs, Certificate in Social Work Management and SVQ4 in Social Care and Management. Several managers suggested that their professional training, in social care or nursing, had helped them as developers of others.

There was also evidence that career experience and level influenced some developmental behaviours. First, experienced managers were more likely to have the confidence to share information openly. They were also more able to delegate tasks to staff; an important element of experiential learning. In contrast, inexperienced managers had some difficulty with this.

> I think you come into the job thinking I need to know this and I need to be ready to answer this and they [staff] were very unsure of what was being asked of them . . . I carried an awful lot here on my shoulders and it was a case of I'll deal with it, I'll cope with it. I possibly inhibited some of their learning.
>
> (FLM6, Quarriers)

Second, from an employee perspective, first line managers appeared to be more approachable, perhaps a reflection on their closer physical proximity.

> Just being there, being approachable, being able to talk to [them]. If there's anything I want to know I can come and discuss it with [them] and [they'll] bring me back an answer.
>
> (Employee 17, Quarriers)

Developmental relationships and interactions

Prior to this study there was very limited research into the 'managing people' behaviours of voluntary sector managers. Those that have been identified include diplomacy, openness, effective listening and empathy (Cornforth and Hooker 1990). In this study, the facilitative behaviours were identified by analysing developmental interactions within developmental relationships by exploring their processes and content. Developmental interactions occurred within a range of situations, such as formal and informal supervisory sessions, discussions or through everyday work activities such as care of service users and meetings.

A common feature of developmental interactions was the security and comfort felt by many staff, particularly in those incidents within the caring cluster.

Table 7.2 Content of developmental interactions

Personal domain	Organizational domain	Personal-organizational domain

• Personal problems
• Study
• Adjusting to new roles
	• Work practice
	  Social care
	  Management
	• Understanding of the
	  organization
		• Career development

> FLM5 is the kind of person you can say anything to ... and [they're]
> not going to take offence at what you're going to say ... there's not a
> fear.
>
> (Employee 15, Quarriers)

The same employee also demonstrated the consequences of not providing
security for learning when describing working for a previous manager.

> ... by the time the manager left I felt I'm useless, I'm hopeless because I
> had been constantly told that everything was my fault.

The content of developmental interactions can be classified into three categories as seen in Table 7.2.

First, the personal domain saw consideration of personal problems that
impacted on performance and also affected readiness to learn.

> The support throughout this [period of long-term absence and return to
> work] I thought was tremendous because it shows how much you are
> valued. I was able to get myself back together.
>
> (Employee 5, Quarriers)

Second, the personal domain involved reassuring, particularly inexperienced
staff, undertaking study or training.

> 'Do you really think I'm up for it?' [FLM1] said 'yes you'll be fine, just
> go and do the course.' [FLM1] has confidence in you, which makes you
> feel good about yourself.
>
> (Employee 2, RFS)

Third, the domain saw managers helping staff adjusting to new roles.

> It's ... been coming to FLM6 and saying 'this is what is happening, this
> is what I've done and is it OK?'
>
> (Employee 19, Quarriers)

The organizational domain involved conversations and actions which concentrated on work practice, either in relation to social care or management duties.

> FLM5 is very good at modelling. FLM5 does a lot of direct work with service users so staff see FLM5 working with service users, related professionals and carers.
>
> (SLM3, RFS)

> FLM3 gives tips on how supervision should be. It's tips like obviously you can't supervise everybody in the same way; people don't learn the same way nor need the same support as the next person.
>
> (Employee 12, RFS)

Within this domain there was also evidence of managers helping more junior staff to understand the organization's cultures and practices.

> I helped SLM5 understand the different culture and perhaps less rigid regime than SLM 5 might have been familiar with.
>
> (SLM6, Quarriers)

The personal-organizational domain included interactions that focused on career development.

> ...[they've] taken quite a lot of time to do that [give feedback] ... as well as it being a priority for the project and the organization I can see that ... [they] also think along the lines of my development ... that makes me feel valued ... and inspires enthusiasm.
>
> (Employee 12, RFS)

Interpretations, conclusions and critical analysis

The results from this empirical research are now used to confirm, extend or challenge the existing theory and knowledge related to HRD, line managers as facilitators of learning and voluntary sector management.

This research has confirmed Thomson *et al.*'s (2001) argument that formal learning systems can encourage line managers to support employee development. Critical within Quarriers' and RFS's learning frameworks was the pivotal contribution of supervision in linking organizational and individual objectives.

The need for a partnership between the HRD function and line managers (Cabinet Office 1993; Bevan and Hayday 1994) to maximize workplace learning was recognized both by managers and HRD managers and practitioners. An important aspect of this partnership was the recognition of the need to develop managers, both in terms of their general development as managers and particularly as developers of their staff (e.g. McGovern *et al.* 1997; Ellinger and Bostrom 1999), thus addressing concerns about the competency of managers to adopt such roles (e.g. Heraty and Morley 1995; Hyman and Cunningham 1998).

This study has also provided clear evidence of the critical role that organizational culture plays in creating an environment conducive for learning; an environment that this study demonstrated managers contributing to through their behaviour. This culture was also underpinned by the values and ethics of current social care practice, and informed by adult learning theory. A challenge for the wider HRD field is whether such an approach can be transferred into environments that may be less sympathetic to these values. However, it is argued here that by providing an insight into HRD policies and practices in the voluntary sector this study has explored a research environment less dominated by the capitalist pragmatism of the corporate sector (McGovern *et al.* 1997) and has enabled HRD to be explored through a different contextual lens.

With regards to barriers to devolution whilst this study corroborated barriers such as time and the tension between operational and developmental

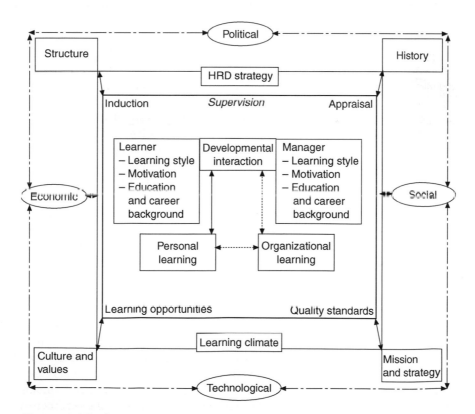

Figure 7.2 The developmental manager model.

duties, the findings challenged other barriers that have been identified in the literature (Bevan and Hayday 1994). For example managers in the two organizations received development for their developmental roles, and were comfortable in engaging in dialogue with their staff through the supervision process.

This study has therefore addressed the empirical deficit regarding our lack of knowledge into how devolution of HRD is translated into practice. By examining how devolution operates in a sector where line managers have had, and accepted, such responsibility for many years, through supervision, this study has provided lessons for other sectors that have recently engaged in or are about to embark on such devolution. It is therefore argued that the results of this research should be tested for wider applicability in other settings. Other caring environments, such as the NHS and education, would seem obvious sectors to test the behaviours, in particular to see if the caring behaviours are replicated. To enable such analysis the author suggests that the Developmental Manager model (see Figure 7.2) which emerged from this study could be applied in alternative organizational contexts.

The outer boundary of the model delineates the environmental influences that were driving the need for learning. The dashed arrows represent the ongoing dynamism of this environment. Organizational influences, such as history, mission and strategy, culture and values, and structure, are represented as cornerstones of the model, which are then integrated with the HRD strategy and learning climate of the organization. The highlighted central box represents the learning and development framework outlined in Figure 7.1 above, and the two-way arrows represent the interaction between learning and development processes and organizational variables such as strategy and culture. Supervision has been represented in bold because of its considerable influence on developmental interactions. Within this learning and development framework learners and managers participate in developmental relationships and these are influenced by individual variables such as learning style, motivation and educational and career background. The resultant developmental interactions enabled the author to identify the facilitative behaviours used by managers, as well as a range of personal and organizational learning outcomes. The arrows emanating from developmental interactions to organizational learning, and between organizational and personal learning are presented in dashed format to represent more tentative findings.

Key learning points

It is hoped that the results of this research can inform other health and social care organizations, particularly those in the public sector such as NHS hospitals, primary care providers and social work departments, as well as other voluntary organizations operating in the health and social care field. The key lesson for managers in these fields is to reinforce that they, after individuals themselves, are the most important influence on an individual's learning in the workplace. To enhance their performance is it suggested that managers

Figure 7.3 Hierarchy of facilitative behaviours.

need to be informed of and develop the behaviours that facilitate learning. One possible way of doing this would be by presenting them with a hierarchy of behaviours as shown in Figure 7.3. Behaviours, such as caring, informing and being professional, are at the foundation levels of the hierarchy because these are closest to the 'professional' backgrounds of the managers and thus it would be easier to help them to develop these behaviours. More sophisticated behaviours, such as empowering and challenging, are at the higher levels as these are behaviours that managers become more comfortable with as they gain more experience.

Finally, it is argued here that if health and social care organizations genuinely want to devolve HRD to line managers they must provide appropriate support and development opportunities to enable managers to carry out this increasingly important management and leadership responsibility.

Note

1 Since Scottish devolution, further legislation has been passed in this area, e.g. Community Care and Health (Scotland) Act 2002.

References

Alcock, P., Brannelly, T. and Ross, L. (2004) *Formality or Flexibility? Voluntary Sector Contracting in Social Care and Health*, London: NCVO.

Batsleer, J. (1995) 'Management and organization,' in J. Smith, C. Rochester and R. Hedley (eds) *An Introduction to the Voluntary Sector*, London: Routledge.

Beattie, R. (2002) 'Going native! Ethnographic research in HRD,' in J. McGoldrick, J. Stewart and S. Watson (eds) *Understanding Human Resource Development: A Research-based Approach*, London: Routledge. pp.

Beattie, R. (2004) 'Line managers, HRD, ethics and values: evidence from the voluntary sector,' in J. Woodall, M. Lee and J. Stewart (eds) *New Frontiers in Human Resource Development*, London: Routledge.

Beattie, R., Hamlin, R. and Ellinger, A. (2004) 'Managers as Facilitators of Learning: theory-building through comparative analysis,' *Fifth International Conference on HRD Research and Practice across Europe*, 27–28 May, University of Limerick, Republic of Ireland.

Bevan, S. and Hayday, S. (1994) *Towing the Line: Helping Managers to Mange People*, Brighton: Institute of Manpower Studies.

Bruce, I. and Raymer, A. (1992) *Managing and Staffing Britain's Largest Charities*, London: VOLPROF/City University Business School.

Buckingham, G. (2000) 'Same indifference,' *People Management*, 17 February: 44–46.

Butler, R. and Wilson, D. (1990) *Managing Voluntary and Non-Profit Organizations: Strategy and Structure*, London: Routledge.

Cabinet Office (1993) *Encouraging and Supporting the Delegation of Human Resource Development Responsibilities to the Line*, London: HMSO.

Cornforth, C. and Hooker, C. (1990) 'Conceptions of management in voluntary and nonprofit organisations: values, structure and management style,' in *Towards the 21st Century: Challenges for the Voluntary Sector*, Proceedings of the 1990 Conference of the Association for Voluntary Action Scholars, 16–18 July London: Centre for Voluntary Organisations, London School of Economics.

Cunningham, I. (1999) 'Human resource management in the voluntary sector: challenges and opportunities,' *Public Money and Management* April–June, pp. 19–25.

Cunningham, I. (2001a) 'Employment issues in the UK voluntary sector – guest editorial,' *Employee Relations* 23(3): 223–225.

Cunningham, I. (2001b) 'Sweet charity! Managing employee commitment in the UK voluntary sector,' *Employee Relations* 23(3): 226–239.

Cummingham, I. and Hyman, J. (1999) 'Devolving human resource responsibilities to the line: the beginning of the end or a new beginning for personnel,' *Personnel Review* 28(1/2): 9–27.

Dartington, T. (1992) 'Professional management in voluntary organizations: some cautionary notes,' in J. Batsleer, C. Cornforth and R. Paton (eds) *Issues in Voluntary and Non-Profit Management*, Wokingham: OU/Addison-Wesley.

De Jong, A., Leenders, F. and Thijssen, J. (1999) 'HRD tasks of first-level managers,' *Journal of Workplace Learning* 11(5): 176–183.

Druker, P. (1989) 'What business can learn from non-profits,' *Harvard Business Review* July–August: 89–93.

Ellinger, A. and Bostrom, R. (1999) 'Managerial coaching behaviours in learning organizations,' *Journal of Management Development* 18(9): 752–771.

Flanagan, J. (1954) 'The critical incident technique,' *Psychological Bulletin* 51(4): 327–359.

Green, S. (2000) 'Learning at the top: a report on the management development needs of chief officers working in the voluntary sector in Scotland,' Edinburgh: Scottish Council for Voluntary Organizations.

Hamlin, R., Ellinger, A. and Beattie, R. (2004) 'In support of coaching models of management and leadership: a comparative study of empirically derived managerial coaching/facilitating learning behaviours,' *Academy of Human Resource Development*, Austin, Texas, USA, 3–8 March.

Heraty, N. and Morley, M. (1995) 'Line managers and human resource development,' *Journal of European Industrial Training* 19(10): 31–37.

Higgins, M. and Thomas, D. (2001) 'Constellations and careers: toward understanding the effects of multiple developmental relationships,' *Journal of Organizational Behaviour* 22(3): 223–247.

Honey, P. and Mumford, A. (1986) *Using your Learning Styles*, 2nd edn, Maidenhead: Peter Honey.

Horowitz, F. (1999) 'The emergence of strategic training and development: the current state of play,' *Journal of European Industrial Training* 23(4/5): 180–190.

Hughes, L. and Pengelly, P. (1997) *Staff Supervision in a Turbulent Environment: Managing Process and Task in Front-Line Services*, London: Jessica Kingsley Publishing.

Hyman, J. and Cunningham, I. (1998) 'Managers as developers: some reflections on empowerment in Britain,' *International Journal of Training and Development* 2(2): 91–107.

IiP Storyboard (1998) Bridge of Weir: Quarriers.

IPD (1995) *Personnel and the Line*, London: IPD.

Kamoche, K. (2001) *Understanding Human Resource Management*, Buckingham: Open University Press.

Leat, D. (1993) *Managing Across Sectors: Similarities and Differences between For-Profit and Voluntary Non-Profit Organizations*, London: VOLPROF/City Business School.

Leicester, C. (1989) 'The key role of the line manager in employee development,' *Personnel Management* March: 53–57.

McGovern, P., Hope-Hailey, V. and Stiles, P. (1997) 'Human Resource Management on the line?' *Human Resource Management Journal* 7(4): 12–29.

Mumford, A. (1993) *How Managers Can Develop Managers*, Aldershot: Gower.

Paton, R. and Cornforth, C. (1992) 'What's different about managing in voluntary and non-profit organizations?' in J. Batsleer, C. Cornforth and R. Paton (eds) *Issues in Voluntary and Non-Profit Management*, Wokingham: OU/Addison-Wesley.

Paton, R. and Hooker, C. (1990) 'Managers and their development in voluntary organizations: trends and issues in the UK,' in *Towards the 21st Century: Challenges for the Voluntary Sector*, Proceedings of the Association of Voluntary Actions Scholars, 16–18 July, London: Centre for Voluntary Organizations, LSE.

Sawdon, C. and Sawdon, D. (1995) 'The supervision partnership: a whole greater than the sum of its parts,' in J. Pritchard (ed.) *Good Practice in Supervision: Statutory and Voluntary Organizations*, London: Jessica Kingsley Publishing.

SCVO (1999) *Working in the Voluntary Sector: a Report of Research to Map the Voluntary Sector Workforce and its Training Needs in Scotland*, Edinburgh: SCVO.

Scott, D. and Russell, L. (2001) 'Contracting: the experience of service delivery agencies,' in M. Harris and C. Rochester (eds) *Voluntary Organizations and Social Policy in Britain: Perspectives on Change and Choice*, Basingstoke: Palgrave.

Scottish Executive (2003) *Partnership for Care: Scotland's Health White Paper*. Edinburgh: Scottish Executive.

Scottish Office (1998) *Aiming for Excellence*, Edinburgh: Scottish Office.

Steane, P. (1997) 'Strategy across sectors – the influence of values,' a paper presented at *The second International Research Symposium on Public Services Management*, 11–12 September, Aston University, Birmingham.

Taylor, M. (1996) 'Influences on voluntary agencies,' in D. Billis and M. Harris (eds) *Voluntary Agencies: Challenges of Organization and Management*, Basingstoke: Macmillan.

Thomson, A., Mabey, C., Storey, J., Gray, C. and Iles, P. (2001) *Changing Patterns of Management Development*, Oxford: Blackwell.

8 Developing effective managers and leaders within health and social care contexts

An evidence-based approach

Bob Hamlin and David Cooper

Aim and objectives

With six objectives in mind we aim to address the important issue of managerial and leadership effectiveness within health and social care contexts in general and the British National Health Service (NHS) in particular. Our first objective is to explain why this topic should be considered of critical importance to HRD practitioners both in the UK, Europe and the USA. The second is to highlight the sparseness of research currently underpinning this field of study and practice, and the pressing need for practice-grounded research specifically designed to inform and support HRD initiatives and interventions aimed at improving the effectiveness of managers and leaders within the health and social care sector. Our third objective is to provide a summary of the empirical base that does exist in the UK, and in particular to describe in some detail the results of a recent study we have carried out into the criteria of managerial and leadership effectiveness applying within the Birmingham Women's Healthcare NHS Trust (BWHT). Our fourth objective is to provide insights into the way these BWHT research findings have been, and are being, used to bring about strategic change in the management culture of BWHT through research informed and evidence-based HRD, OD and HR interventions. Our fifth objective is to reveal the extent to which the BWHT research results have been found generalized to the findings of other researchers who have studied managerial and leadership effectiveness in the NHS, and to show how the results of these comparisons provide empirical support for 'universalistic' models of management and managerial leadership. Our sixth and final objective is to draw the attention of readers, particularly HRD practitioners striving to become more evidence-based in their own professional practice within health and social care settings, to the merits of the concept of 'HRD Professional Partnership' research as advocated by Jacobs (1997) in the USA, and as applied by Hamlin and Cooper (2005) in BWHT and previously by Hamlin *et al.* (1998) and Hamlin (2002a) in various other UK public sector organizations.

Background

In the UK, engagement with managerial and leadership effectiveness research ought to be of great interest and concern to all HRD professionals currently working in the health and social care sector in general and the NHS in particular, for two main reasons. First, because of the central importance the British Government is placing on leadership and leadership development as part of its ongoing modernization agenda for the UK public services, including the NHS. Second, because of the increasing application of evidence-based approaches to practice now prevalent and firmly established in medicine and most other healthcare-related professions. As Willcocks (1997) argues, the study of managerial effectiveness should be central to any [healthcare] organization but, as Zairi and Jarrar (2001) observe, although the NHS has witnessed a plethora of changes since its inception, particularly in the area of clinical outcomes and effectiveness, very little work has been undertaken in the area of managerial and leadership effectiveness. Nevertheless, with increasing importance being attached by government to the measurement and improvement of health service quality, efficiency and effectiveness (Proctor and Campbell 1999; Department of Health 2000), and the government's call for a 'new' style of management 'which needs to be facilitative and involving, not hierarchical and controlling' (Department of Health 2002: 14), the issue of managerial and leadership effectiveness research should be perceived as a 'hot' topic both by HRD scholars and HRD practitioners alike.

Expert opinion supports the government's call for new management and managerial leadership styles as part of its modernization agenda for the NHS, based on the fact that it has long been established that good leadership and management produces good healthcare, and that poor leadership and management generates poor healthcare (Kitson 1991; Pembrey 1980; Flowers *et al.* 2004; Michie and West 2002; Borrill *et al.* 2004). Drawing upon the work of Dye (2000) who studied leadership in healthcare within the United States, Zairi and Jarrar (2001: 884–885) suggest the NHS needs 'leaders who can rebuild trust, restore efficient processes and ensure quality through rough organizational transitions.' However, they note that 'being a health care leader today means being faced with daunting challenges, increasingly complex organizational structures, unfamiliar operational and strategic issues, rapid change and a lack of time,' and that overcoming these obstacles requires new managerial leadership competencies. Hartley and Allison (2000) also claim that, in conditions of increasing complexity and uncertainty, leadership is not so much about directing, but more about exercising developmental and influence skills. They conclude that models of leadership in the UK Public Sector (including the NHS) urgently need updating to reflect this. Such calls for new management and managerial leadership competencies have been echoed in the writings of other expert commentators (see Mullally 2001; Howatson-Jones 2004; Porter O'Grady 2003).

In our view, helping and supporting managers in the NHS and other parts of the health and social care sector to change their management and leadership styles from ones based predominantly on the 'traditional management paradigm' of command, control and coercion, to styles based predominantly on the 'new management paradigm' of empowerment, inclusion, support, development and influence, is likely to be a huge challenge for HRD professionals. This is because we perceive them facing three main hurdles, as follows.

i   The first hurdle is the fact that serious question marks have been raised both in the UK and the USA concerning the effectiveness of much management and leadership development (Hamlin 2002b; Smyth 2002; Collins and Holton 2004; Edmonstone and Western 2002; Alimo-Metcalfe and Alban-Metcalfe 2003a). Collins and Holton usefully draw attention to the fact that the comprehensive meta-analysis conducted by Burke and Day (1986) revealed managerial training as having been only moderately effective during the 1970s and 1980s. More recently, their own meta-analytic study of the effectiveness of leadership development programmes in the USA revealed a wide variety of programme outcomes – with some effective but others failing (Collins and Holton 2004). However, because of the limited number of studies into this issue, they argue 'the relationship between leadership development and organizational performance still remains unclear' (Collins and Holton 2004: 241). In the UK, Alimo-Metcalfe and Alban-Metcalfe (2003a and b) draw attention to the fact that despite massive investment by public and private sector organizations in leadership development, most initiatives have been regarded as failures.

ii A second hurdle confronting HRD professionals is the fact that there is a general lack of empirical research evidence available, both in the UK and USA, to inform, influence, shape and evaluate management and leadership development programmes and other HRD interventions (Fiedler 1996; Mumford 1997; Hamlin and Stewart 1998). As Fiedler laments, all the reviews of leadership training stress that we know little about the processes of leadership and managerial training that contribute to organizational performance, and at least one reason for the lack of knowledge is the scarcity of meaningful and rigorous research. Seeking to understand managerial and leadership effectiveness in the British NHS and wider public services sector, Flanagan and Spurgeon (1996) found little empirical evidence reported in the management literature. Since that time the only significant empirical studies carried out in the field have been those of Willcocks (1997); Alimo-Metcalfe and Alban-Metcalfe (2000, 2001), Barker (2000), Gaughan (2001), Hamlin (2002a; 2002c) and Hamlin and Cooper (2005) respectively. Even in the USA where a significant number of studies of management and leadership have been undertaken, few have focused on leaders, managers and administrators in healthcare. The most notable are those of Shipper (1991), Shipper *et al.* (1998) and Shipper and White (1999), but all appear to have been deductive survey-based studies using a pre-determined questionnaire based on a set of managerial behaviours originally identified over 25 years ago by Wilson (1978).

From the foregoing it will be clear to readers that the empirical base available to HRD practitioners in support of the training and development of managers and leaders in the health and social care sector is very limited both in scope and scale. Hence, much of what is offered by management trainers and developers is based more on their own personal values, belief systems and experiences, or on fads, fashions and the prescriptive views of 'gurus,' rather than on best evidence derived from good research. Consequently, as Alimo-Metcalfe and Alban-Metcalfe (2004: 50) observe, 'there is so much "spin" and "hype" around the topic of leadership that it is not surprising people [within the NHS] are turned off or totally confused with the subject.'

iii   A third significant hurdle that confronts HRD professionals working in the health and social care sector is the fact that evidence-based approaches to practice are becoming widely and firmly established. As Walshe and Rundell (2001) observe, the concept of evidence-based health care has already become part of the language of clinicians, managers, policymakers, and researchers in health services throughout the world, and is spreading to other fields outside health care including social care, education and the criminal justice field. This means that practising managers and leaders such as clinical directors, directors of nursing, and middle and first line managers of doctors, nurses, therapists, and social care professionals, are likely to resist HRD initiatives designed to bring about change in their managerial and leadership styles of behaviour, particularly if they perceive them not to be informed specifically by relevant best evidence.

Because medical and healthcare professionals are required increasingly to practise evidence-based medicine (EBM) and evidence-based healthcare (EBH), it is likely they will increasingly wish to incorporate evidence-based approaches into their everyday practice as managers and leaders, in line with the various calls in the management literature for evidence-based management (see Bury 1998; Axelsson 1998; Stewart 1998). Although some managers within healthcare, as in other sectors, will be particularly susceptible to management fads and fashions (Abrahamson 1996; Walston and Bogue 1999), the rise of evidence-based clinical practice has caused people to start questioning how health care managers and policy makers make decisions, and what role evidence plays in the process (Walshe and Rundell 2001). As Stephen M. Shortell of the University of California-Berkeley contends, 'we have to marry evidence-based medicine to evidence-based management to achieve sustainable improvement in the delivery, quality, cost and outcomes of care,' and 'an effective partnership between academics and practitioners is needed' to ensure relevant practice-grounded research is correctly translated for practising healthcare managers to use in their day-to-day activities (Grazier 2004: 74). This marrying of evidence-based practice in the health and social care sector is likely to result in similar questioning of how HRD professionals make decisions, and of the role that evidence plays in the training and development of managers and leaders. Without an adequate evidence base to inform and shape the content of their management and leadership development programmes, HRD practitioners could find themselves severely challenged by course delegates who happen to be exemplars, role models and strong advocates of EBM, EBH and evidence-based healthcare management. Interestingly, just as there have been calls in the literature for evidence-based management, there have also been specific calls for 'evidence-based' and 'research-informed' approaches to HRD practice (see Hamlin and Ash 2000; Brewerton and Millward 2001; Russ-Eft *et al.* 1997; Leimbach and Baldwin 1997; Swanson 1997; Hamlin 2002b; Holton 2004). In the US, Holton (2004) advocates a national movement as in mental health to embed evidence-based approaches to practice throughout the HRD business. In the UK, Hamlin (2002b) has defined and strongly articulated the case for 'evidence-based HRD' and 'research-informed HRD' respectively.

In light of the three hurdles outlined above, it is incumbent upon HRD practitioners working within the health and social care sector to be proactive in facing up to the challenge of becoming as evidence-based as their professional colleagues in medicine and the other health and social care professions. To help meet that challenge we intend now to illustrate one way this might readily be achieved.

The research

Despite the various calls in the British and American management literatures for evidence-based approaches to practice in the fields of management and HRD, limited progress has been made in closing the much talked about 'HRD research–practice gap.' Nevertheless, the experience of one of the authors suggests an efficient and effective means for HRD practitioners to become evidence-based is through the concept of the 'HRD Professional Partnership' as defined in the USA by Jacobs (1997) and strongly advocated and applied in the UK by Hamlin (2001, 2002b). In this type of 'partnership research' arrangement, HRD scholars and HRD practitioners collaborate in a common research programme, but enter the partnership with their own mutually exclusive yet complementary goals. Maintaining the integrity of both sets of goals for the common good is considered important. Thus, there is a dual goal to improve the organization through the application of academically rigorous applied research, whilst at the same time advancing the HRD field of unique knowledge. The research can be either practice-grounded internal research, or external research relevant to the organization. However, to date, only a few case histories of 'HRD Professional Partnership' research studies have been reported in the literature. These include, for example, those of Holton *et al.* (1998) in the USA, and Hamlin *et al.* (1998), Hamlin (2002a) and Hamlin and Cooper (2005) in the UK. In this chapter we present the findings of the Hamlin and Cooper (2005) HRD Professional Partnership study that was designed to identify the criteria of managerial and leadership effectiveness applying within the Birmingham Women's Healthcare NHS Trust (BWHT), which is part of the British National Health Service. We also report how the results have been used for the development of evidence-based and research-informed approaches to management development and HRD within BWHT, and reveal the generalized nature of the findings plus their potential for application to other NHS Trust hospitals and health and social care related organizations.

Problem statement

Organizational context

Despite the government's ambitious programme of modernization, which explicitly links management and leadership skills development to service reforms, as set out in its strategy document 'HR in the NHS Plan' (DoH 2002) referred to earlier in this chapter, little management development has been aimed at first line and middle managers in the acute hospital sector of the NHS. Within BWHT, and prior to the Hamlin and Cooper (2005) study, the little that had, had been relatively uncoordinated with providers and consultancies designing and delivering a range of ad hoc programmes predominantly focused on the general aspects of management. In light of this, BWHT concluded in 2003 that it needed to refocus its existing limited management development provision onto the training and development of managers in specific managerial leadership skills and behaviours essential for managing effectively within the changing environment of the NHS. However, whilst the existing traditional hierarchical and bureaucratic management practices were perceived no longer to be relevant, it was unclear which aspects of the management culture as manifested in the behaviour of managers should be discarded and which should be retained. Hence, it decided to initiate a programme of internal practice-grounded research in order to understand in greater depth the BWHT management culture. The aim was to obtain examples of managerial behaviour perceived and judged by people within the organization to be either most effective or least effective/ineffective, and thereby identify a set of managerial and leadership effectiveness criteria reflecting 'best practice' management within the organization. Furthermore, it was considered desirable also to assess the external generalizability of the findings in order to demonstrate if possible the relevancy and utility of the BWHT criteria for other specialist and acute NHS Trust hospitals.

Theoretical context

Over the past 40 years or so, substantial amounts of research have been conducted into the nature of management and leadership. However, few studies have focused on the issue of managerial or leadership effectiveness, or attempted to differentiate between what is 'good' or 'bad' management/leadership practice. Consequently, much research is regarded as lacking relevance, utility and generalizability, with little agreement about what constitutes and is meant by managerial and leadership effectiveness (see Cammock *et al.* 1995; Barker 2000; Kim and Yukl 1995). Another major criticism of most management and leadership research concerns the lack of generalizability across organizational settings, sector boundaries and cultures. For example, Axelsson (1998) claims that despite the volumes of management research studies that have been published, few have produced empirical results that can be generalized beyond particular organizational settings. A similar situation appears to exist in the field of leadership research. Kim and Yukl (1995) draw attention to the fact that not only is the number of studies on specific behaviors still small but different researchers have examined different sub-sets of behaviours, thus making it difficult to compare and contrast the findings from one study with another. House and Aditya (1997) suggest no pattern of leader behaviour has been found to be consistently associated with any criteria of supervisor or manager effectiveness. An explanation provided by Avolio *et al.* (1999) is that weaknesses in research design, such as the lack of central control over the consistency of procedures utilized in most management studies have been the cause of limitations on the generalization of findings. To rectify this they argue replica studies should be carried out using common research designs and methods. Despite the lack of empirical evidence, and the reported problems of generalizability, Thompson *et al.* (1996) claim that comparisons between existing lists of managerial competencies and overlaps point toward the existence of generic managerial competencies. In the field of leadership Bennis (1999) suggests some leadership competencies are universal. This lends support to the views of House and Aditya (1997: 453) who believe it is likely there are several 'generic leadership functions and universal/near universal effective leader behaviours.' They go so far as to suggest these are 'expected, accepted, and effective across organizations, industries, and cultures' and that 'the logic suggesting [the] universality of leader behaviors is compelling.' However, House and Aditya point out there is only sparse empirical evidence relevant to this issue, which as yet represents theoretical speculation that needs to be demonstrated empirically. In light of these calls for research into the generalizability and universality of management and leadership, and the advice of Avolio *et al.* (1999), it was decided a parallel aim of the BWHT professional partnership study should be to search for evidence of generic criteria of managerial and leadership effectiveness using identical, or as near as possible identical research methods as those used by other researchers who had studied managerial and leadership effectiveness within the NHS or other UK public sector organizations.

Empirical context

As already mentioned, few studies of managerial and leadership effectiveness have been reported in the management and HRD literatures. This section summarizes the findings of the most significant and relevant studies found by us in the British literature. In combination, these studies indicate the scale and nature of the empirical base currently under-girding the training and development of effective managers and leaders within the field of health and social care.

Alimo-Metcalfe and Alban-Metcalfe (2000, 2001), using repertory grid and factor analytic techniques, investigated the characteristics of 'nearby' transformational leadership based on the perceptions of male and female top, senior and middle-level managers and professionals working in two large UK public sectors, namely local government and the NHS. The NHS sample of participants comprised 23 chief executives/directors, 17 assistant directors and nine middle managers from a range of NHS Trusts. The behavioural data gathered were used to create a questionnaire that was then administered widely throughout the NHS. Factor analysis of the data so obtained yielded 12 factors that became the basis of the NHS version of their 'New Transformational Leadership Model.' The factors are as follows:

- Genuine concern for others
- Ability to analyse and think creatively
- Manage change sensitively and skilfully
- Decisiveness, determination, readiness to take risk
- Transparency (integrity)
- Empowers others to lead
- Inspirational communicator, net worker and achiever
- Charisma
- Accessibility, approachability and flexibility
- Ability to draw people together with a shared vision
- Encouraging challenges to the status quo
- Supporting a development culture

Barker (2000) investigated constructs of leadership held by a group of male and female chief executives and general managers ($n = 16$) from within hospice and specialist palliative care units in the UK using the repertory grid technique. Ten themes were identified as follows:

- Dynamic, entrepreneurial, proactively embraces change
- Political/environmental awareness, networking, strategic thinker, visionary, charismatic
- Good communication skills
- Develops, values and supports others
- Consultative, shares information, knowledge

- Integrity, fairness, honesty, respect, humility, responsiveness
- Professional, self-motivated, develops self, confident
- Self-awareness, openness
- Organizational skills, performance management
- Inspirational, takes the team with them

Gaughan (2001) explored the leadership behaviours required for members of the management boards of two Primary Care Groups. Using the repertory grid technique, data were collected from 12 professional people of mixed gender including general practitioners, nurses, health visitors and midwives, local authority professionals and general managers. Nineteen themes were revealed, as follows:

- Approachable and sociable
- Builds a team
- Challenges, innovative and opportunistic and flexible
- Clarifies roles and responsibilities
- Clear vision and direction
- Clinical background
- Communicates and shares a vision
- Delegates
- Develops partnerships and networks

- Develops and empowers people
- Drive and ambition
- Evaluation skills
- Influences and negotiates
- Integrity honesty
- Intellectual capacity and experience
- Political sensitivity and skills
- Time management
- Self-awareness and humility
- Valuing and supporting staff

In contrast to these researchers, *Hamlin (2002a)* investigated the issue of managerial and leadership effectiveness at the middle and front-line manager and supervisor levels of the management hierarchy within an acute NHS Trust hospital. The research was conducted as part of an 'HRD Professional Partnership' arrangement, and replicated previous studies of managerial effectiveness within other parts of the UK public sector, namely secondary education and HM Customs and Excise. Critical Incident Technique (CIT) was used to obtain concrete examples of effective and least effective/ineffective managerial behaviour. A representative sample of 45 managers out of a total population of 102 senior, middle and front line managers/supervisors were interviewed, plus 12 non-managerial staff. In total, 405 critical incidents were collected and used to create a behavioural item questionnaire (BIQ) which comprised 26 positive (effective) and 26 negative (least effective/ineffective) behavioural statements (items). The BIQ was administered widely throughout the NHS Trust hospital to different groups of people, and the different data sets so obtained were then subjected to factor analysis. A detailed comparative analysis of the various factorial solutions revealed high degrees of sameness, similarity, and congruence of meaning, and resulted in the identification of eight positive criteria (indications) and 11 negative criteria (contra-indications) of managerial effectiveness, as follows:

Positive criteria	Negative criteria
Organization and planning	Dictatorial/autocratic management
Active supportive leadership	Intimidating behaviour
Giving support to staff	Negative approach
Open and personal management approach and style	Undermining of others
Inclusive decision making	Avoidance and ignoring behaviour
Looking after the interests and needs of staff	Failing to inform other people
Empowerment and delegation	Not giving, receiving or using information
Informing people	Exhibiting poor organization
	Self-serving and uncaring management
	Lack of concern for staff
	Abdicating roles and responsibilities

As readers can deduce from the five research summaries outlined above, the overall empirical base underpinning the concept of managerial and leadership effectiveness within the health and social care sector in the UK is very limited.

The Birmingham Women's Healthcare NHS Trust study

Research aims and research questions

In light of the theoretical and empirical contexts as summarized in the previous sections of this chapter, we concluded that the research programme most suitable for providing a 'template' for the proposed BWHT replica HRD Professional Partnership research study was that of Hamlin (2002a). The primary aim and goal of one of us acting in the role of the HRD practitioner partner in this HRD Professional Partnership was to obtain results that would help BWHT to understand better its management culture, and subsequently to use the findings to inform, shape and evaluate future management development programmes and HRD initiatives designed to bring about organizational change and development within the hospital. In contrast, the primary goal of the other of us, acting in the role of the HRD scholar partner, was to obtain evidence of any external generalization of the BWHT findings that might support or challenge current debates concerning the 'universal' versus 'contingent' nature of management and leadership. To achieve these different but complimentary goals the study addressed two research questions as follows:

1   How are the criteria of managerial and leadership effectiveness manifested within the Birmingham Women's Healthcare NHS Trust hospital?
2   To what extent are these criteria held in common with those previously identified by the chosen 'template' NHS Trust hospital study?

Research methodology and methods

Adopting a constructivist ontology and interpretivist epistemology the research design comprised four stages using the following methods:

Stage 1. Concrete examples of specific behaviours characterizing effective and ineffective management and managerial leadership were generated using the well-established Critical Incident Technique (CIT) of Flanagan (1954) as previously applied by Hamlin (2002c). Forty-five managers randomly selected as a representative sample from a total of 110 senior, middle and junior managers drawn from both medical and non-medical departments were interviewed, plus 15 non-managers. In total, 467 CIs were collected, of which 35 were deemed unsuitable for further inclusion in the study. Of the remaining 432 CIs, 204 were examples of effective and 228 of ineffective management and managerial leadership behaviour.

Stage 2. The 432 usable CIs were reduced to a smaller group of discrete statements (items) of behaviour using a form of 'summarizing,' 'explicative' and 'structuring' content analysis to identify those CIs with a same or similar meaning (Flick 2002). A total of 50 discrete items were identified by this process of which 25 were examples of effective (positive) managerial behaviour and 25 least effective/ineffective (negative) behaviour.

Stage 3. This stage involved identifying criteria of managerial/leadership effectiveness through a process of reducing, classifying and grouping the effective and ineffective items into behavioural categories, using the 'retranslation' procedure of Smith and Kendall (1963). This involved scrutinizing the items in search of commonalities and grouping them into common clusters. The clusters were then explored, interpreted and classified using descriptive labels that encapsulated in essence the meaning held in common to all of the behaviours comprising each cluster.

Stage 4. The Stage 3 criteria were compared against the findings of the chosen 'template' acute NHS Trust study of Hamlin (2002a) in order to search for evidence of external generalization as indicated by the sameness, similarity and/or congruence of meaning found between the two sets of findings at both the criterion and behavioural item level. The method used was a variant of open coding applied inductively and deductively within a grounded theory mindset (Miles and Huberman 1994; Flick 2002). To ensure internal consistency and enhance the reliability and trustworthiness of the respective comparative analyses, a form of 'investigator triangulation' was adopted whereby two researchers initially worked independently of each other (Easterby-Smith *et al.* 1991). Overall there was general agreement regarding their respective judgments and perceptions regarding the commonalities existing between the respective sets of data. Minor discrepancies and inconsistencies were resolved through critical examination and discussion to reach a consensus.

Results and findings

From the Stage 3 findings, seven positive and nine negative criteria of managerial and leadership effectiveness were identified, as given in Table 8.1. These criteria suggest that for managers to be perceived as effective they need to exhibit strong skills and capabilities in organizing and planning, an approachable, supportive and personal management style, and inclusive decision making. This involves dealing with staff in a sensitive and caring way, and being accessible and approachable. In addition, managers need to listen to staff, adopt proactive approaches to taking staff ideas forward, and empowering staff to make effective changes to working practice. In order to avoid being judged as ineffective, managers need to guard against behaviours that staff perceive as non-listening, non-supporting, uncaring, undermining, avoiding and abdicating, failing to inform, failing to use information or communicate effectively, and lacking in organizational skills.

The results of the Stage 4 analysis are also revealed in Table 8.1. All of the BWHT behaviours were found to have some degree of commonality and congruence of meaning with the findings of the Hamlin (2002a) study. Those that were the same or identical have been typed in **bold italics,** and those that were near identical or similar have been typed in non-bold *italics*. As can clearly be seen there is a very high degree of commonality and congruence of meaning. Of the 36 positive behavioural items 25 (70%) were identical and 11 (30%) near identical/similar, and of the 45 negative behavioural items 28 (62%) were identical and 17(38%) near identical or similar. As illustrated in Table 8.2, of the 15 BWHT criteria of managerial and leadership effectiveness, the overall meaning of all seven positive criteria and six of the nine negative criteria are either near identical or very similar to the criteria identified by the Hamlin (2002a) study. As can also be seen in Table 8.2, a degree of alignment and some congruence of meaning exists between the other three BWHCT negative criteria (printed in italics) and various corresponding 'template' NHS Trust Study criteria. These results suggest the two studies mutually validate each other to a great extent with all of the positive and negative criteria obtained from the BWHT study being held in common to a greater or lesser degree with one or more of the Hamlin (2002a) criteria. Only one criterion identified by Hamlin

Table 8.1 BWHT criteria of managerial and leadership effectiveness and associated behaviours

Positive criteria	Negative criteria
Staff felt appreciated and looked after *Values work of team and acknowledges work completed to a high standard;* *Listens to staff when they are overworked and helps to provide solutions;* *Actively promotes work of staff and department; Makes time to talk to staff (e.g. engenders feeling of value in their work; showing an interest in their work;* *Supports staff in identifying and finding development opportunities;* *Deals with personal and difficult situations with sensitivity.*	**Abdication of responsibility** *Gives little or no support to staff;* *Makes poor decisions (e.g. applies blanket rule which disadvantages all staff instead of dealing with member of staff who is abusing system);* *Avoids making decisions (e.g. uses others to make decisions for them); Disregards policy (e.g. makes decisions to meet own needs); Refuses to recognize problems or deadlines (e.g. leaves tasks to last minute;* *Fails to follow policies and procedures.*
Leads by example and gives positive feedback *Assists other staff at busy times (e.g. prepared to get stuck in to alleviate work overload);* *Positively delegates work to staff (e.g. is fair in delegating work, not just dirty work);* *Values work of team and acknowledges work completed to a high standard;* *Publicizes and promotes good news stories to rest of Trust staff; Involves staff in decision making where appropriate (e.g. consults staff on changes to work patterns etc);* *Makes time to talk to staff (e.g. engenders feeling of value in staff by showing an interest in their work).*	**Ineffective communication, not passing on information** *Does not inform staff of changes that are to be made (e.g. does not consult on things, just implements them);* *Does not praise or give credit when it is due;* *Gives insufficient time to complete job (e.g. sits on job until it is critical and then demands job to be completed in rush);* *Does not consult when giving out additional work (e.g. just expects individual to 'drop everything' to complete a particular task);* *Fails to be open and honest with staff (plays one member of staff against another).*
Offers support to staff *Supports staff in identifying and finding development opportunities;* *Listens to staff on personal issues and acts to support the member of staff where appropriate;*	**Undermines others** *Fails to be open and honest with staff (plays one member of staff against another);* *Overrules decisions made by staff (e.g. humiliates member of staff who has*

continued

Table 8.1 continued

Positive criteria	Negative criteria
Recognizes and acts appropriately when things are going wrong; Listens to staff when they are overworked and helps to provide solutions; **Respond quickly to staff work problems.**	made decision); **In meetings criticizes or acts in negative way towards staff;** Does not support staff in difficult positions (e.g. will not back up staff member who was harassed by member of public).
Good organizational and planning skills Prepares well for meetings so that the meeting is run effectively and efficiently; **Plans ahead so that work can be carried out effectively.** Uses resources well (e.g. brings in people to assist in times of pressure, chooses best person for job); **Develops long term strategy with team members and communicates objectives to staff.**	**Lack of concern for staff** Criticizes members of staff in front of other members of staff; **In staff meetings humiliates members of staff (e.g. breaks confidential news)** Does not support staff in difficult positions (e.g. will not back up staff member who was harassed by member of public); Does not treat staff equally (e.g. unfairly praises staff when not appropriate, prepares rotas unfairly); **Refuses to admit mistakes or failings; Shouts staff down in public**
Approachable and supportive management style Publicizes and promotes good news stories to rest of Trust staff; **Responds quickly to staff work problems;** Deals with personal and difficult situations with sensitivity; Uses personal approach to leadership (e.g. develops sense of trust); **Develops trusting relationships with staff (e.g. does not break confidences of staff);** When problems occur deals with them quickly and fairly.	**Unfair treatment of staff** Does not treat staff equally (e.g. unfairly praises staff when not appropriate, prepares rotas unfairly); Shouts staff down in public; **In meetings, criticizes or acts in negative way towards staff;** Engages in bullying or harassing behaviour; Criticize members of staff in front of other members of staff; **In staff meetings humiliates members of staff (e.g. breaks confidential news);** Does not inform staff of changes that are to be made (e.g. does not consult on things, just implements them).

Looks to include staff in decision making, keeps staff informed
Keeps staff informed of trust business, e.g. regularly updates staff in matters concerning the Trust and how it applies/affects them;
Develops long term strategy with team members and communicates objectives to staff;
Gives staff freedom and flexibility in performing duties (e.g. self-rostering);
Involves staff in decision making where appropriate (e.g. consults staff on changes to work patterns etc).

Gives support and encourages staff to try new ways of working
Works with staff to support flexible working practice. (e.g. rearrange workload in line with staff members' personal circumstances);
Ensures staff have the confidence and ability to perform required tasks (e.g. supports staff who require additional skills);
Assists other staff at busy times (e.g. prepared to get stuck in to alleviate work overload);
Recognizes and acts appropriately when things are going wrong;
Actively promotes work of staff and department.

Fails to listen to staff suggestions
Is unwilling to listen to staff or unprepared to sort out staff problems;
Runs meetings ineffectively (e.g. allowing certain staff to dominate meeting);
Overrules decisions made by staff (e.g. humiliates member of staff who has made decision);
Refuses to recognize problems or deadlines (e.g. leaves tasks to last minute).

Uncaring attitude
Refuses to admit mistakes or failings;
Criticize members of staff in front of other members of staff;
Shouts staff down in public; Asks member of staff to stay late to complete task for deadline but is not prepared to stay over and help;
Engages in bullying or harassing behaviour.

Lack of support for staff
Does not praise or give credit when it is due;
Does not consult when giving out additional work (e.g. just expects individual to 'drop everything' to complete a particular task);
Fails to recognize when staff member is struggling with tasks;
Gives little or no support to developing staff;
Does not praise or give credit when it is due.

Lack of organizational skills
Runs meeting ineffectively (e.g. allowing certain staff to dominate meeting);
Gives insufficient time to complete job (e.g. sits on job until it is critical and then demands job to be completed in rush);
Does not control meetings effectively.

Table 8.2 Comparison of the BWHT and 'template' NHS Trust criteria

BWHT Study	NHS Trust Study
Positive criteria	
Staff felt appreciated and looked after	Looks after the interests and needs of staff
Leads by example and gives positive feedback	Active support leadership
Offers support to staff	Gives support to staff/Active supportive leadership
Good organizational and planning skills	Organization and planning
Approachable and supportive management style	Open and personal management approach or style
Looks to include staff in decision making and empowers staff	Empowerment and delegation/Inclusive decision making
Gives active support and encourages staff to try new ways of working	Inclusive decision making/Active supportive leadership
Negative criteria	
Abdication of responsibility	Abdicating roles and responsibility/ Avoidance and ignoring behaviours
Ineffective communication – not passing on information	Not giving, receiving or using information
Fails to listen to staff suggestions	
Undermines others	Undermining others
Lack of concern for staff	Lack of concern for staff
Uncaring attitude	Intimidation of staff/Self serving and uncaring management
Unfair treatment of staff	Self serving and uncaring management
Lack of support for staff	Avoidance and ignoring behaviour/self serving and uncaring management
Lacking in organizational skills	Exhibiting poor organization
	Dictatorial/autocratic management

in the acute NHS Trust hospital setting was found not to be manifested within the BWHT specialist hospital setting, namely the negative criterion labelled 'Dictatorial/autocratic management.'

Generalizability of the findings

As can be deduced from the comparative analyses outlined in the previous section, the BWHT findings are strongly generalized to Hamlin's acute NHS Trust hospital findings. Additionally, the BWHT findings have also been found to be strongly generalized to the 'Generic Model of Managerial and Leadership Effectiveness' offered by Hamlin (see Hamlin and Cooper 2005). Hamlin's 'generic model' was derived from replica managerial and leadership effectiveness studies carried out with various co-researchers within three different types of UK public sector organization, namely UK secondary schools, HM Customs and Excise (a then department of the British Civil Service) and the acute NHS Trust hospital 'template' study reported earlier in this chapter (Hamlin 2004). Interestingly, the findings used as part of the empirical evidence supporting Hamlin's 'generic model' are strongly generalized to the factorial and behavioural constructs comprising the 'NHS' and Local Government (LVG) versions of the 'New Model of Transformational Leadership' as offered by Alimo-Metcalfe and Alban-Metcalfe (see Hamlin 2002c). A detailed comparison has revealed a high degree of overlap and similarity between Hamlin's findings and seven of the nine 'LVG' factors plus eight of the 12 closely aligned 'NHS' factors comprising the Alimo-Metcalfe and Alban-Metcalfe 'new model.' It is interesting also to note that whereas their transformational leadership model was derived from examples of managerial leader behaviours obtained predominantly from top and senior managers working within healthcare and local government settings, Hamlin's 'generic model' was derived from concrete examples of managerial and leadership behaviours exhibited by middle and front line managers/supervisors in educational, central government and healthcare settings, as observed by their superiors, peers and subordinates respectively.

From these studies there appears to be a high degree of commonality across all the hierarchical levels of management within these different organizational contexts. This lends support to the view that both transformational and transactional leadership behaviours are widely distributed throughout the whole of the management structure of these organizations. In combination, the various comparative analyses have revealed a significant and coherent 'body of knowledge' that could act as a frame of reference for dialogue and debate concerning current management and leadership practice within health and social care contexts and the public sector at large. Furthermore, the research has added significantly to the available empirical base of 'best evidence' available to HRD practitioners for informing and underpinning future management and leadership development programmes. Additionally, the research provides empirical support for HRD initiatives designed to impact the management culture of public services and health and social care organizations, in particular the management culture of NHS Trust hospitals.

Application of the managerial and leadership effectiveness research findings

For the purpose of illustration, it is our intention in this section to provide examples of how the results obtained to date from the BWHT 'partnership research' study have been applied by one of us (David Cooper) to inform and shape HRD practice within his organization. As will be appreciated from the earlier part of the chapter, the BWHT partnership-research produced rich and reliable results. These have had significant potential for application not only within BWHT but also in other NHS Trust hospitals. The BWHT criteria of managerial and leadership effectiveness have been, and continue to be used by the organization to bring about significant strategic change in line with the national requirement to secure step changes in productivity improvement as set out in the government's NHS Plan (DoH 2000). As you will recall, one of the strategic imperatives of the associated 'HR in the NHS Plan' (DoH 2002) is radically to change the predominant NHS style of management, from the current 'traditional' bureaucratic style of command, control and coercion, to a more participative style of inclusion, involvement, empowerment, and openness identified with the much talked about 'new management paradigm.' This requirement posed a huge challenge to the senior management team of BWHT. The initial question facing David Cooper was how best to equip managers with the necessary 'change management' skills and competencies to enable them to effectively address the implications of the 'HR in the NHS Plan,' in particular the changes required to the way staff and resources were to be managed in the future, and to help them develop more appropriate styles of management. The obstacle he faced was the great difficulty of managers being released to undertake conventional time consuming off-the-job management development, particularly at a time of unprecedented levels of internal organizational change and external pressure to achieve performance targets set by the government, and the need to ensure the service to patients was carried out without damaging the quality of patient care. The first stage in his strategy for bringing about the desired changes was the creation of a 'behavioural competency framework' derived from the criteria of managerial and leadership effectiveness that had been identified through the HRD Professional Partnership research. The second stage was then to use this framework to inform and shape the proposed HRD intervention strategy, which had two strands, an OD strand and an MD strand.

For the OD strand the framework was used as a tool for holding up a 'mirror' to the organization through a series of OD workshops designed for the BWHT directorate and localized groups of departmental managers respectively. The first workshop was held for the directors and senior management team with the aim of reflecting back to them the research findings and securing their 'buy-in' to the proposed management culture change strategy. The new competency framework, which comprised both the 'positive' and 'negative' managerial behaviours associated with effective and ineffective management within BWHT was used to provoke thought and dialogue. In particular, the aim was to get these managers to discuss and confront those persistent behaviours identified with the traditional management style that the research suggested were no longer appropriate for managing effectively in the changing context of the organization. As a result of this OD workshop, it was possible to redefine with a high degree of clarity and precision the required changes in the management culture, namely those positive (effective) managerial leader behaviours that were to be valued, encouraged and developed, and those negative (ineffective) behaviours that needed to be curtailed and eliminated. At the time of writing a series of similar, yet somewhat different OD workshops was being planned for the departmental managers, with the idea of following these with a series of 'cascade' OD workshops to be facilitated by the departmental managers for the middle and junior managers using action learning principles. The aim of these workshops has been to get individual managers to reflect critically upon their own management style and that of their colleague managers using the competency framework as a 'benchmark,' to identify the extent to which examples of effective and ineffective management have been manifest in their part of the organization, and then to consider ways of changing and improving the situation as required.

For the MD strand, David Cooper used the insights gained from the early OD workshops to inform and shape a redesign of the formal BWHT Management Development Programme that was now to be based essentially upon the results of the managerial and leadership effectiveness research and the newly devised 'behavioural competency framework.' Several diagnostic tools to identify gaps in the management skills and competencies of individual managers have been developed, and various strategies formulated to develop 'bespoke' management development programmes and 'self help' learning and development initiatives. Plans are in place also to use the competency framework for the development of other competence-based HR and HRD systems, including revised approaches to selection and performance appraisal. The results of the BWHT partnership-research have been shared with HR/OD colleagues in other 'associated' NHS Trust hospitals in the local geographical area. The work has attracted much interest, so much so that plans have been put in place to replicate the research in several of these hospitals with the ultimate aim of carrying out a comparative study in search of commonalities and generalized findings that can be applied across the NHS region and beyond. Furthermore, consideration is now being given to pursuing the potential for sharing more HR/OD intelligence, and possibly developing shared management development programmes.

We believe the range of 'BWHT' evidence-based and research-informed HRD initiatives and interventions outlined above illustrate the particular organizational benefits to be derived from in-company practice-grounded research, the results of which tend to be perceived immediately both by line managers and staff to have practical relevancy and utility within the organization. They also illustrate the particular value of research conducted as part of an HRD Professional Partnership arrangement. The fact that the findings have been found highly generalized to each other suggests they have the potential to be used by other acute and specialist NHS Trust hospitals. However, a wide range of additional replica studies need to be carried out to validate the findings further. These would then make possible the development of a 'generic model of managerial and leadership effectiveness' for general application within the health and social care sector. It should be noted that Alimo-Metcalfe and Alban-Metcalfe (2003b) have discussed and illustrated how their 'New Model of Transformational Leadership' model has been used to create a 360° rating instrument which they claim provides 'precise data on what is being done well' managerially within the NHS.

Interpretation, conclusions and critical analysis

By responding to the call of Avolio *et al.* (1999) for replica studies using same methodologies, we have produced findings that go some way toward addressing the concerns regarding the paucity of research into the issue of managerial and leadership effectiveness and the lack of generalization of most research in the field.

From a theoretical perspective, the Hamlin (2002a) and Hamlin and Cooper (2005) research findings discussed above provide strong empirical support for those such as Thompson *et al.* (1996), House and Aditya (1997) and Bennis (1999) who believe in the 'universality' of management and leadership, including the existence of generic managerial/leadership competencies, generic leadership functions, and universal managerial leader behaviours. Conversely, the results challenge the thinking of those who subscribe to 'contingency models' of management and leadership believing managerial and leadership, effectiveness is contingent upon the organizational context, is situation-dependent and perspective-specific (Antonacapoulou and Fitzgerald 1996; Flanagan and Spurgeon 1996; van der Velde *et al.* 1999; Hayes *et al.* 2000; Shipper 2000; Garavan and McGuire 2001). However, it should be noted that the BWHT research as conducted and reported to date has had several limitations with regard to the methodology deployed. Although identical research methods to those used in the 'template' study were adopted for Stages 1 and 2 of the research programme, circumstances at the time prevented this for Stage 3. Hence, the Stage 3 behavioural construct used at Stage 4 was not a complete replica of the Stage 3 construct resulting from the 'template' study against which it had been compared. Another limitation has been the possibility that some subjective 'bias' could have crept into the interpretive judgements of the researchers, particularly during the Stage 3 'retranslation' process of deriving the effectiveness criteria. Because of these limitations, a larger scale Stage 3 study has been initiated using a statistical analytic technique for reducing and classifying the behavioural items, namely factor analysis as used by Hamlin (2002a) for his acute NHS Trust study. The results of this subsequent study have not yet been finalized and brought into the public domain through peer review. Consequently, no reference has been made to this specific work in this chapter.

From a practitioner perspective the BWHT findings demonstrate the benefits to be gained by HRD practitioners and scholars engaging in HRD Professional Partnership research. In particular, they illustrate how relevant research with strong academic credentials can become, as Jacobs (1997) claims, an 'essential counterpart to HRD practice,' and how HRD practitioners can advance their professional practice through organization-ally grounded 'backyard research' as advocated by Swanson (1997). The BWHT study also illustrates how HRD scholars can readily engage in acad-emically rigorous 'practice-grounded' research that produces results of suffi-cient quality to contribute to the body of HRD knowledge, and how these generalized findings have the potential to be used as 'best evidence' by evid-ence-based practitioners in other organizations. In summary, it exemplifies one way in which 'an effective partnership between academics and practi-tioners' can be created, as called for recently by Stephen M. Shortell, who is the Dean and Blue Cross of California Distinguished Professor of Health Policy and Management at the School of Public Health, and professor of organization behaviour at Haas School of Business, University of California-Berkeley (Grazier 2004: 73–74). From our experience we can strongly commend the concept of HRD Professional Partnerships to other HRD practitioners and HRD scholars.

Key learning points

The specialist BWHT hospital and 'template' acute NHS Trust hospital studies outlined above are good examples of the win:win benefits that can be derived from HRD Professional Partnership research, and demonstrate one way of effectively and efficiently bridging the HRD research-practice gap. They also illustrate one way of bridging what Adler *et al.* (2004: Preface) refer to as 'the challenges and opportunities faced by management science and management practice through the exploration of collaborative research approaches.' Several lessons can be drawn from these examples, not only by HRD practitioners and HRD scholars, but also by senior executives, organizational leaders and line managers within the health and social care sector as follows.

HRD practitioners

As change agents concerned with helping organizational leaders and senior executives bring about effective and beneficial organizational change and development, not least changes in the management style and culture of the organization, HRD practitioners operating as management trainers and developers and OD consultants would do well to recognize:

i   The need to develop an in-depth understanding of the organization and its management culture by having ready access to a sufficient amount of reliable data in order to interpret accurately what is actually going on deep inside the organization, in particular the managerial and leadership behaviours that can cause things either to happen or not to happen.
ii The particular relevance and utility of internal practice-grounded col-laborative research.

iii   The value of deploying particularly powerful HRD instruments and OD
      intervention tools derived from the findings of such academically rigor-
      ous and robust practice-grounded research for stimulating and bringing
      about transformational shifts in the management culture of an organi-
      zation.
iv   The fact that the stronger the foundation of research evidence used to
      inform, shape, and measure organizational change, the greater will be
      the chances for its long-term survival and success.
 v   The increasing need for HRD professionals to deploy proactively evid-
      ence-based and research-informed approaches to practice within health
      and social care contexts.

HRD scholars

A possible lesson for scholars of management as well as HRD scholars is to
recognize the potential for good academic research resulting from HRD Professional Partnership research between individual academics in universities
and practitioners in organizations. As Jacobs (1997) explains, such 'partnership research' differs from conventional full cost contract research through
'service agreements' where the scope for conducting academic research of
publishable quality can be restricted or even non-existent. By definition,
'partnership research' inevitably leads to win:win outcomes for both the academic and the practitioner.

Senior executives, organizational leaders and line managers

An insight for senior executives, organization leaders and line managers
within the health and social care sector, particularly those with specific
responsibilities for actively nurturing the training and development of
effective leadership capability and competence within the organization,
and for leading strategic change initiatives and projects, is the need to
develop an in-depth understanding of the organizational and management
culture and to gain the necessary insights for combating the inhibiting or
blocking effects of what Bate (1996) refers to as 'cultural lag.' This means
managers having ready access to reliable empirical data that tells them
what is actually going on deep inside the organization, particularly the
'soft' people issues and cultural factors such as the particular management
and managerial leadership attitudes and/or behaviours that either help or
hinder things from happening. To this end, HRD and management-
related professional partnership research could make an important contribution. In our view, evidence-based management and evidence-based
HRD, informed by the findings of sound internal and/or relevant external
practice-grounded research, are approaches to professional practice they
should be role modelling and actively encouraging throughout their
respective organizations.

References

Abrahamson, E. (1996) 'Management fashion,' *Academy of Management Review* 21(1): 254–285.

Adler, N., Shani (Rami), A.B. and Styhre, A. (2004) *Collaborative Research in Organizations Foundations for learning, change, and theoretical development*, London: Sage.

Alimo-Metcalfe, B. and Alban-Metcalfe, R.J. (2000) 'Heaven can wait,' *Health Service Journal* October: 26–29.

Alimo-Metcalfe, B. and Alban-Metcalfe, R.J. (2001) 'The development of a new Transformational Leadership Questionnaire,' *Journal of Occupational and Organizational Psychology* 74: 1–27.

Alimo-Metcalfe, B and Alban-Metcalfe, R.J. (2003a) 'Under the influence,' *Public Sector Reform* March: 31–35.

Alimo-Metcalfe, B and Alban-Metcalfe, R.J. (2003b) 'Stamp of greatness,' *Health Service Journal* 113(5861): 28–32.

Alimo-Metcalfe, B. and Alban-Metcalfe, J. (2004) 'The myths and morality of leadership in the NHS,' *Clinician in Management* 12: 49–53.

Antonacopoulou, E.P. and Fitzgerald, L. (1996) 'Reframing competency in management education,' *Human Resource Management Journal* 6(1): 53–62.

Avolio, B.J., Bass, B.M. and Jung, D.L. (1999) 'Re-examining the components of transformational and transactional leadership using the Multifactor Leadership Questionnaire,' *Journal of Occupational and Organizational Psychology* (UK) 72(4): 441–463.

Axelsson, R. (1998) 'Towards an evidence based health care management,' *International Journal of Health Planning and Management* 13(4): 307–317.

Barker, L. (2000) 'Effective leadership within hospice and specialist palliative care units,' *Journal of Management in Medicine* 14(5/6): 291–309.

Bate, S.P. (1996) 'Towards a strategic framework for changing corporate culture,' *Strategic Change Journal* 5(February): 27–42.

Bennis, W. (1999) 'The end of leadership: exemplary leadership is impossible without full inclusion, initiatives and co-operation of followers,' *Organizational Dynamics* 28(10): 71–80.

Borrill, C.S., West, M.A. and Dawson, J F (2004) 'The relationship between leadership and trust performance,' *Department of Health Report*, Aston University.

Brewerton, P. and Millward, L. (2001) *Organizational Research Methods*, London: Sage Publications.

Burke, M.J. and Day, R.R. (1986) 'A cumulative study of the effectiveness of managerial training,' *Journal of Applied Psychology* 71: 232–245.

Bury, T. (1998) 'Getting research into practice: changing behaviour,' in T. Bury and J. Mead (eds) *Evidence-based Healthcare: A Practical Guide for Therapists*, Oxford: Butterworth-Heinemann.

Cammock, P., Nilakant, V. and Dakin, S. (1995) 'Developing a lay model of managerial effectiveness,' *Journal of Management Studies* 32(4): 443–447.

Collins, D.B. and Holton, E.F. (2004) 'The effectiveness of managerial leadership development programs: a meta-analysis of studies from 1982 to 2001,' *Human Resource Development Quarterly* 15(2): 217–248.

Department of Health (2000) *White Paper the NHS Plan: Managing for Excellence*, Department of Health, 2000.

Department of Health (2002) *HR in the NHS Plan*, Department of Health, July 2002.

Dye, C. (2000) 'Leadership in healthcare; values at the top,' *Healthcare Executive* 15: 6–13.

Easterby-Smith, M., Thorpe, R. and Lowe, A. (1991) *Management Research: An Introduction*, London: Sage.

Edmonstone, J. and Western, J. (2002) 'Leadership development in health care: what do we know?' *Journal of Management in Medicine* 16(1): 34–47.

Fiedler, F.E. (1996) 'Research on leadership selection and training: one view of the future,' *Administrative Science Quarterly* 41: 241–250.

Flanagan, H. and Spurgeon, P. (1996) *Public Sector Managerial Effectiveness: Theory and Practice in the National Health Service*, Buckingham: Open University Press.

Flanagan, J.C. (1954) 'The critical incident technique,' *Psychological Bulletin* 51(4): 327–358.

Flick, U. (2002) *An Introduction to Qualitative Research*, 2nd edn, London: Sage Publications.

Flowers, C., Sweeney, D. and Whitefield, S. (2004) 'Leadership effectiveness: using partnership to develop targeted leadership training,' *Nursing Management-UK* 11(6): 23–27.

Garavan, T. and McGuire, D. (2001) 'Competencies and workplace learning: some reflections on the rhetoric and the reality,' *Journal of workplace Learning* 13(4): 144–163.

Gaughan, A.C. (2001) 'Effective leadership behaviour: leading "the third way" from a primary care group perspective,' *Journal of Management in Medicine* 15(1): 67–94.

Grazier, K.L. (2004) 'Interview with Stephen M. Shortell, PhD., FACHE, University of California-Berkeley,' *Journal of Healthcare Management* Mar/Apr 2004, 49(2): 73–79.

Hamlin, R.G. (2001) 'Towards research-informed organizational change and development,' in R.G. Hamlin, J. Keep and K. Ash (eds) *Organizational Change and Development: A Reflective Guide for Managers, Trainers and Developers*, Harlow: FT Prentice Hall.

Hamlin, R.G. (2002a) 'In support of evidence-based management and research-informed HRD through HRD professional partnerships: an empirical and comparative study,' *Human Resource Development International* 5(4): 467–491.

Hamlin, R.G. (2002b) 'Towards evidence-based HRD practice,' in S.J. Stewart, J. McGoldrick and S. Watson (eds) *Understanding Human Resource Development: A Research-based Approach*, London: Routledge, pp. 93–121.

Hamlin, R.G. (2002c) 'A study and comparative analysis of managerial and leadership effectiveness in the National Health Service: an empirical factor analytic study within an NHS Trust hospital,' *Health Services Management Research* 15: 245–263.

Hamlin, R.G. (2004) 'In support of universalistic models of managerial and leadership effectiveness: implications for HRD research and practice,' *Human Resource Development Quarterly* 15(2): 189–215.

Hamlin, R.G. and Ash, K. (2000) 'Toward evidence-based organizational change and development,' Paper presented at the *NHS-P Research into Practice Conference*. Birmingham, UK, 13 January.

Hamlin, R.G. and Cooper, D.J. (2005) 'HRD professional partnerships for integrating research and practice: a case study example from the British National Health Service,' *AHRD 2005 International Research Conference*. Estes Park, Colorado, February.

Hamlin, R.G. and Stewart, J.D. (1998) 'In support of evidence-based human resource development practice,' Lancaster-Leeds Collaborative Conference: Emergent Fields in Management-Connecting Learning and Critique, Leeds University.

Hamlin, R.G., Reidy, M. and Stewart, J. (1998) 'Bridging the HRD research-practice gap through professional partnerships,' *Human Resource Development International* 1(3): 273–290.

Hartley, J. and Allison, M. (2000) 'The role of leadership in the modernization and improvement of public services,' *Public Money and Management* 20(2): 35–40.

Hayes, J., Rose-Quirie, A. and Allinson, C.W. (2000) 'Senior managers' perceptions of the competencies they require for effective performance; implications for training and development,' *Personnel Review* 29(1): 48–56.

Holton, E.F. (2004) 'Implementing evidence-based practice: time for a national movement?' *Human Resource Development Review* 3(3): 187.

Holton, E.F. III, Redmann, D.H., Edwards, M.A. and Fairchild, M.E. (1998) 'Planning for the transition to performance consulting in municipal government,' *Human Resource Development International* 1(1): 35–55.

House, R.J. and Aditya, R.N. (1997) 'The social scientific study of leadership: quo vadis?' *Journal of Management* 23(3): 409–465.

Howatson-Jones, I.L. (2004) 'The servant leader,' *Nursing Management-UK* June 11(3): 20–24.

Jacobs, R.L. (1997) 'HRD professional partnerships for integrating HRD research and practice,' in R. Swanson and E. Holton III (eds) *Human Resource Development Research Handbook: Linking Research and Practice,* San Francisco: Berrett-Koehler, pp. 47–61.

Kim, H. and Yukl, G. (1995) 'Relationships of managerial effectiveness and advancement to self-reported and subordinate-reported leadership behaviors from the multiple-linkage model,' *Leadership Quarterly* 6(3): 361–377.

Kitson, A. (1991) *Therapeutic Nursing and the Hospitalized Elderly*, London, Scutari Press.

Leimbach, M.P. and Baldwin, T.T. (1997) 'How research contributes to the HRD value chain,' in R. Swanson and E. Holton III (eds) *Human Resource Development Research Handbook: Linking Research and Practice,* San Francisco: Berrett-Koehler, pp. 21–46.

Michie, S. and West, M.A. (2002) *Measuring Staff Management and Human Resource Performance in the NHS*, London: Commission for Health Improvement.

Miles, M.B. and Huberman, A.M. (1994) *Qualitative Data Analysis*, Thousand Oaks, CA: Sage.

Mullally, S. (2001) 'Leadership and politics,' *Nursing Management* 8(4): 21–27.

Mumford, A. (1997) *Management Development: Strategies for Action*, London: Institute of Personnel and Development.

Pembrey, S. (1980) *The Ward Sister: Key to Nursing*, London: RCN.

Porter O'Grady, T. (2003) 'A different age for leadership: new context, new content,' *Journal of Nursing Administration* 33(2): 105–110.

Proctor, S. and Campbell, J. (1999) 'A developmental performance framework for primary care,' *International Journal of Health Care Quality Assurance* 12: 279–286.

Russ-Eft, D., Preskill, H. and Sleezer, C. (1997) *Human Resource Development Review: Research and Implications*, Thousand Oaks, California: Sage.

Shipper, F. (1991) 'Mastery and frequency of managerial behaviors relative to subunit effectiveness,' *Human Relations* 44(4): 371–388.

Shipper, F. (2000) 'A cross-cultural, multi-dimensional, nonlinear examination of managerial skills and effectiveness,' Paper presented at the *Academy of Management Meeting*, Canada, August.

Shipper, F. and White, C.S. (1999) 'Mastery, frequency and interaction of managerial behaviors to subunit effectiveness,' *Human Relations* 52(1): 49–66.

Shipper, F., Pearson, D.A. and Singer, D. (1998) 'A study and comparative analysis of effective and ineffective leadership skills of physicians and non-physicians health care administrators,' *Health Services Management Research* 11(2): 124–135.

Smith, P. and Kendall, L.M. (1963) 'Retranslation of expectations: an approach to the construction of unambiguous anchors for rating scales,' *Journal of Applied Psychology* 47: 149–155.

Smyth, C. (2002) *Review of Leadership and Management Development Opportunities in the Personal Social Services: a First Class Service-PSS Training Strategy 2000–2003*, Belfast Northern Ireland Social Care Council.

Stewart, R. (1998) 'More art than science?' *Health Service Journal* 26 March: 28–29.

Swanson, R.A. (1997) HRD research: don't go to work without it!' in R.A. Swanson and E.F. Holton III (eds) *Human Resource Development Research Handbook*, San Francisco, Berrett-Koehler.

Thompson, J.E., Stuart, R. and Lindsay, P.R. (1996) 'The competence of top team members: a framework for successful performance,' *Journal of Managerial Psychology* 11(3): 48–67.

van der Velde, M.E.G., Jansen, G.W.E. and Vinkenburg, C.J. (1999) 'Managerial activities among top and middle managers: self versus other perceptions,' *Journal of Applied Management Studies* 8(2): 161–164.

Walshe, K. and Rundell, T.G. (2001) 'Evidence-based management: from theory to practice in health care,' *The Millbank Quarterly* 79(3): 429–457 (29).

Walston, S.L. and Bogue, R.J. (1999) 'The effects of reengineering: fad or competitive factor?' *Journal of Healthcare Management* 44(6): 456–474.

Willcocks, S.G. (1997) 'Managerial effectiveness in the NHS: a possible framework for considering the effectiveness of the clinical director,' *Journal of Managerial Psychology* 10(1): 16–21.

Wilson, C.L. (1978) 'The Wilson multi-level management surveys: refinement and replication of the scales,' *JCAS: Catalog of Selected Documents in Psychology* 8 (Ms. No. 1707), Washington: American Psychological Association.

Zairi, M. and Jarrar, Y.F. (2001) 'Measuring organizational effectiveness in the NHS: management style and structure best practice,' *Total Quality Management* 12(7/8): 882–888.

9 Management development in healthcare

Exploring the experiences of clinical nurse managers in Ireland

Laura Purcell and Brigid Milner

Introduction

The dramatic reforms in the health service in recent years, arising from both strategy and review, have and will continue to have a significant impact on the way in which the health service in Ireland is managed. Whilst structural change is cited as a key element in the furtherance of delivery of a quality, people-centred service, the management of health service human resources will also prove critical in ensuring success. This chapter will provide a brief review of health service change in an Irish context, focusing particularly on the management development activities of clinical nurse managers in line with the generic and specific competencies identified to fulfil the clinical nurse manager role.

Empirical health service context

The recent proposals for the transformation of the health service have arisen from strategies such as *Shaping a Healthier Future* (Department of Health and Children 1994) and *Quality and Fairness*, (Department of Health and Children 2001). A period of unprecedented economic growth, together with a changing demography and a national demand for a first-class health service that can support the growing population, are cited as significant drivers for change and modernization of the Irish health service. These in turn are coupled with macro-environmental influences such as politics, socioculture, economics, and technology all of which had and will continue to have a varying impact. Machell and Nixon (2003: 5) capture this by suggesting 'rapid technological advance, rising consumer expectation/demand, accompanied by wide ranging demographic and social change, are creating a turbulent and uncertain environment for those working in healthcare systems.' O'Hara (1998: 3) with reference to the problems facing the Irish health service, suggests that, 'the solution to many service delivery problems often depends on first understanding the structural and organizational arrangement of the health system.'

The health service reform programme

Several high level reports have addressed the need for reform. *The Report of the Commission on Health Funding* (Department of Health and Children 1989: xi) states, 'the solution to the problem facing the Irish health services does not lie primarily in the system of funding but rather in the way that services are planned, organized and delivered.' Sixteen years later and the issue of health service spending is still a topic of much debate (Lawlor and McCarthy 2003; Barrett 2003; Wren 2004 and O'Reardon 2004). Wren (2004: 47) argues that 'some of the black hole"arguments are exaggerated and based on inappropriate comparisons.' It is her view that health spending should occur within the wider context of health sector reform. Shaping a Healthier Future (Department of Health and Children 1994) emphasized quality, equity and accountability as the underlying principles for enhancing health service delivery. Health Service improvement would be based upon three elements, one of which was to develop the organizational and management structures of the health service. In a similar vein, *Quality and Fairness* (Department of Health and Children 2001) was the blueprint upon which the transformation and modernization of the health service should occur, based upon the principles of equity, people-centredness, quality and accountability. Six frameworks for change were identified to enable the four national goals to be fulfilled. Of particular significance are the frameworks of organizational restructuring, developing human resources and reform of the acute-care hospital sector.

In relation to organizational restructuring, the *Prospectus Report: Audit of Structures and Functions in the Health System* (Department of Health and Children and Watson Wyatt 2003) revealed a service that had been relatively unchanged for the past 30 years and as such was 'becoming unmanageable' (Kelly 2003). Duplication of agencies and multiplication of roles had led to tensions in terms of both the management and organization of the health service. In addition, pressures to accommodate local and national agendas had proved difficult and, as such, a complex, bureaucratic organization was seen to be the resultant outcome. *Prospectus* (Department of Health and Children and Watson Wyatt 2003) indicated that more than structural change would be required if the ambitions outlined in *Quality and Fairness* (Department of Health and Children 2001) were to be fulfilled. Four major reforms were proposed, in which the development of supporting processes and legislation to underpin the new consolidated structure is of particular importance. *Prospectus* (Department of Health and Children and Watson Wyatt 2003) in its findings, argues that there is no single, centralized function of human resources. The risk of duplication of human resource roles and functions was suggested to be high, with the implication being that change will be managed differently by the current agencies in place, namely the Health Service Employers Agency and the Office for Health Management. In order to enhance health service capability and performance, management development was cited as a potential key lever and the formation of a Health Service Executive as a result would enable the repositioning of the management development agenda to a national arena.

Finally, the Commission on Financial Management and Control Systems in the Health Service, otherwise known as the Brennan Report (Department of Health and Children 2003: 5) while also reinforcing the need for a consolidated health structure, indicated that there was 'inadequate investment in information systems and management development.' The Report also highlighted a degree of urgency in the implementation of management development programmes to address this deficiency.

Nursing reform

In relation to the reform of the acute-care hospital system, recommendations outlined in the Hanly Report (National Task Force on Medical Staffing 2003) may have a significant influence upon the organization and management of acute hospital services. Although Hanly's main focus is on the reduction of Non-Consultant Hospital Doctors' (NCHD's) working hours in line with the European Working Time Directive, the impact upon other sectors such as nursing is identified as being considerable. The Report recommended an increase in the frequency of multidisciplinary working and an enhanced management remit for nurses, both of which are likely to have an overall influence on the role.

The role of nursing can be examined in relation to increasing demands to act in both a clinical and management capacity. Following the publication of *The Report of the Commission on Nursing* (The Commission on Nursing 1998), changes affecting the nursing role can be classified into three groupings, namely, changes in relation to nurse management; the continuing professional development of nursing and developments in clinical practice (Rush et al. 2004).

In order to reflect the significant role nursing management has and will have to play within the nursing profession, a new nursing structure was developed with resulting changes in job titles. *The Report of the Commission on Nursing* (The Commission on Nursing 1998) in its ambitions to reform the nursing profession, proposed a new management structure for nurse managers, 'The Commission recommends the development of first line nursing and midwifery management to fulfill the functions of professional leadership, staffing and staff development, resource management and facilitating communication. The title of first line nursing and midwifery management should be changed to clinical nurse manager or clinical midwife manager' (The Commission on Nursing 1998: 6).

A three-step management ladder was established for both first-line nursing and midwifery management. The Clinical Nurse Manager 1 reports to a Clinical Nurse/Midwife Manager 2. The Clinical Nurse/Midwife Manager 2 is in charge of a ward or unit of care. In relation to a Clinical

Nurse/Midwife Manager 3, their remit is departmental. This structure is illustrated in Appendix 1 with reference to its relationship to the traditional structure of nursing. *The Report of the Commission on Nursing* (The Commission on Nursing 1998), also recommended 'that first-line nursing and midwifery managers should have management training before taking up a post and be required and supported in continuing to develop management skills' (The Commission on Nursing 1998: 134).

The Report indicates that management development may also facilitate the culture change that is sought within the health service. Evidence to support this assertion may be found in many areas of the Report such as, 'there appears to be a culture in certain areas of the health service of retaining information ... the greater dissemination of information and a culture within a health service provider which encourages and supports an open flow of information is essential to an effective communications system ... it will be necessary to train, encourage and support all levels of management in communications' (The Commission on Nursing 1998: 125).

Health service human resource development

The development of human resources was a key priority and challenge outlined in *Quality and Fairness* (Department of Health and Children 2001). A lack of strategic human resource management (HRM) had resulted in a system where essential functions of HRM were relatively ignored, where, 'too often the emphasis is almost solely on industrial relations, to the detriment of many other aspects, including personal development, education and training and a range of HR issues affecting quality of working life and job satisfaction' (Department of Health and Children 2001: 121). Securing a qualified workforce and becoming an 'employer of choice' are amongst the ambitions articulated in *Quality and Fairness* and, following on from this, the *Action Plan for People Management* (Department of Health and Children *et al.* 2002). *The Action Plan* explored how the various human resource aspects of the health service could be developed. Amongst these reforms, management development and initiatives to improve quality of work life were identified as needing to play key roles, coupled with the implementation of management competency frameworks to orchestrate the necessary culture change within the health service. The first annual progress report has recently been published in relation to the implementation of the recommendations of *Action Plan for People Management* (Office for Health Management and The High Level Group on Empowerment of Nurses and Midwives 2002) in which the introduction of management competency frameworks are cited as having some success where, 'many employers have undertaken initiatives to implement the management competency frameworks locally' (Office for Health Management *et al.* 2004: 4).

Management development and health service strategy

The strategic implications of the utilization of training and development and within this, management development, as a means to fulfil the ambitions outlined in *Quality and Fairness* (Department of Health and Children 2001) and related reports are worth exploring in further detail. *The Report of the Commission on Nursing* (The Commission on Nursing 1998); *Quality and Fairness* (Department of Health and Children 2001); *Action Plan for People Management* (Department of Health and Children *et al.* 2002) and the *Audit of the Structures and Functions in the Health System* (Department of Health and Children and Watson Wyatt 2003) emphasize the important contribution that training and development can have in the management and implementation of change within the health service. This is consistent with the literature in which training and development is viewed as a vehicle for change. Hussey (1988) outlines the relationship between training and development and corporate strategy and suggests that training could make an impact upon the following areas such as strategy formulation; strategy implementation; policy implementation, corporate culture, environmental change and problem solving. Likewise, Mabey and Salaman (1995) provide some contribution to the debate surrounding the strategic rationale for training. They suggest that some may see training purely as a means in which skill deficiencies may be addressed, but additionally, training and development may also be viewed as 'catalyst for change' for those seeking to shift the organizational culture (Mabey and Salaman 1995: 143). The recurring theme that the purpose of any management development programme should be to facilitate a culture change is further illuminated within the forward of the *Report on an Evaluation Study of Leading an Empowered Organization Programme (LEO) for Clinical Nurse Managers 1* (Centre for the Development of Nursing Policy and Practice University of Leeds 2003: 3) which comments 'in time, this [development] should lead to a cultural shift in nursing management with the emphasis on empowering and valuing people, team working and interprofessional collaboration.'

Theoretical context

Multiple meanings have been proffered in relation to the term management development. A cross-section of definitions gives an insight into a complex process. Mumford (1997: 6) defines management development as 'an attempt to improve managerial effectiveness through a learning process.' Harrison (1997) argues that management development is 'the planned process of ensuring through appropriate human resource (HR) processes and learning environment the continuous supply and retention of effective managers at all levels to meet the requirements of an organization and enhance its strategic capability' (Harrison 1997: 355). This is concurrent with Jansen *et al.* (2001) who purport that management development (MD) is defined as 'the system of personnel practices intended to ensure that an organization can rely on timely availability of qualified and motivated employees.'

While the above definitions are linked to the general area of human resource management, it must also be noted that definitions on organization development-based management development are also contained within the literature. An organization development-based definition of management development is posited by Molander (1986) and cited in Jansen *et al.* (2001) as 'a conscious and systematic process to control the development of managerial resources in the organization for the achievement of goals and strategies.' Harrison (1997) made a further distinction between 'manager development' and 'management development,' the latter encompassing organizational and cultural development, 'management development, (meanwhile), concerns building a shared culture and enhanced capability across the whole management group in order to improve the organization's ability and capacity to survive, innovate and advance in its environment' (Harrison 1997: 356). This definition enunciates the rationale of *Quality and Fairness* (Department of Health and Children 2001) and subsequent reports of using training and development as a means of transforming and modernizing the health service.

There is an increasing body of literature that challenges the overall strategic effectiveness of management development activity. Preston (1993) goes so far as to suggest that management development is often a 'form of brain-washing' for managers, while others view management development activity as some form of control mechanism imposed by the upper echelons of management (Clarke 1999). Kamoche (2000) questions the overall contribution that management development can make to organizational performance and suggests that 'the difficulty of establishing such a linkage has led some to accept the value of management training and development as an act of faith' (Kamoche 2000: 278).

Defining competency-based management development

A competency-based approach to management development, as outlined in Irish health service statements of strategy, merits further exploration. (Antonacopoulou and FitzGerald 1996) suggest that 'the term competency has ended up as another word in the management literature which is widely known and used, yet unclear and confusing in its definition and purpose.' *The Action Plan for People Management* (Department of Health and Children *et al.* 2002: 10) indicates that the purpose of implementing competency frameworks in the Irish health service is,

> To assist the organization in identifying the managerial knowledge, skills and attributes which are needed to deliver a quality service to clients and to recruit and develop managers accordingly. There is evidence of a gap between the skills and competencies perceived as most

critical to delivering today's health service and those actually possessed by managers.

This rationale is evident in the competency literature, where the implementation and use competency frameworks, 'provides a set of performance criteria at organization and individual levels, and identifies the expected outcomes of achieving those criteria' (Marchington and Wilkinson 2002: 385).

The Report of the Commission on Nursing (The Commission on Nursing 1998) recommended that competencies be developed to reflect the role of nurses in management capacities. As a result, the Office for Health Management developed a set of generic and specific competencies relating to the top, middle and lower levels of nursing management. The intention is that these competencies will drive future development activities within the health service, 'we intend that any management development initiatives commissioned for nurse managers in the future should be informed by these competencies' (Rush *et al.* 2000: 1).

Management development activity

The 'Empowerment of Nurses and Midwives Steering Group – An Agenda for Change' was established in 2000 and a 'Management Development Subgroup' explored the various ways in which nurse and midwife managers could further be empowered using the medium of management development. The subsequent publications such as *Guidance on the Commissioning of Nursing Management Development Programmes* (Office for Health Management 2002); the *Evaluation of Nursing Management Development Programmes* (Faulkner and McMahon 2002) and the *Report on an Evaluation Study of the Leading an Empowered Organization Programme (LEO) for Clinical Nurse Managers* 1 (Centre for the Development of Nursing Policy and Practice University of Leeds 2003) review the way in which management development is viewed and implemented within the Irish health service. The LEO programme, according to the Centre for the Development of Nursing Policy and Practice, is seen as being successful in the development of nurse managers in the UK and US, and is identified as the vehicle by which to develop the management skills of Irish Clinical Nurse/Midwife Managers. It is also widely recognized in the UK and USA for its 'quality and relevance in the development of nurse managers (Centre for the Development of Nursing Policy and Practice University of Leeds 2003: 3). The LEO programme, as a national management development initiative, is in the initial implementation stages although on a regional level, historically, health service structures have offered other management development alternatives, such as the Frontline Management Programme. As LEO is in its infancy in Ireland and the bulk of the literature surrounding LEO programme effectiveness is UK based (Smith and Edmonstone 2001; Faugier and Woolnough 2003) there is a need to undertake a review of the current state of play surrounding the issue of management development within the Irish health service.

While some of the changes envisaged for the health service can be easily examined, other changes, such as those related to management development and culture change, are not readily measured. If the rationale adopted is one that management development is initiated to facilitate a culture change, the success of management development and management development programmes should therefore be explored on the basis of their impact on facilitating this change. This rationale may be seen as two tiered. First, there is a need to investigate whether the positive skills, attitudes and behaviours enhanced on a management development programme are transferred into the workplace setting. Second, there is need to investigate the effects of management development activities upon the culture of the health service, and exploring the impact of management development activities upon quality of work life may provide insight into whether a culture change has occurred. Quality of work life satisfaction can be directly influenced by management style, resources and communication, and organization structure (Graham 1992; Lewis *et al.* 2001; Robertson Cooper 2003). In the context of the health service Gifford *et al.* (2002) argue that 'unit organizational culture does affect nurses' quality of work life factors.'

Transfer of training

Transfer of training may be defined as 'the application of knowledge, skills and attitudes learned from training on the job and subsequent maintenance of them over a certain period of time' (Cheng and Ho 2001). While this definition appears limiting in the assumption that training occurs on the job, Tannenbaum and Yukl (1992) provide a more holistic view in which transfer is defined as 'the extent to which trainees effectively apply the knowledge, skills and attitudes gained in a training context back to the job.' Riggio (2003) has also suggested transfer of training will more likely occur if the 'work environment supports new behaviours that are learned and if the work environment allows the trainee opportunity to use those newly learned behaviours' (Riggio 2003: 157).

In exploring transfer, the issue of positive and negative transfer must be taken into consideration. Garavan *et al.* (2003) suggest that positive transfer will take place if trainees are able to make the transition from the training environment back to the workplace. They detail two forms of transfer:

- Specific or Pure Transfer – the skills or tasks learned can be repeated precisely as they were performed during training;
- Generalizable Transfer – occurs when the skills learned can be similarly repeated but not identically repeated, as was the case during training. This form of transfer is of particular relevance in the acquisition and training of interpersonal skills (Garavan *et al.* 2003: 527).

Learning transfer can be affected by a number of factors. Garavan *et al.* (1995) argue that two principle factors influence the transfer of learning: organizational and social factors. In relation to organizational factors, pay and promotion policies as well as environmental pressures will have an effect. The social factors influencing transfer of learning include the support of supervisors, peers and the trainer (Garavan *et al.* 1995, 2003). Supervisory support can range from support for development, benefits of development articulated to staff and support to the extent that working conditions and situations are altered to facilitate development (Garavan *et al.* 2003). Peers can provide the necessary support by coaching and encouraging the transfer of knowledge, skills and behaviours learned during training back into the workplace. Other views have been put forward by Belling *et al.* (2004) who identified seven impediments and four supports relating to transfer. Barriers such as lack of peer support, the perceptions of the trainee on the relevance of the programme itself and a lack of organizational support, all impact transfer of training. Support from supervisors and peers can also be perceived as increasing transfer of training.

The UK experience – the NHS

In attempting to implement change through management development, it may prove useful to draw on an international comparison. The National Health Service (NHS) in the UK has undergone a similar modernization to that which the Irish health service is currently experiencing. The publication of the Griffiths Report (DHSS 1983) resulted in a renewed emphasis on the importance of business management and development within the health care context. Arising from these and subsequent publications, a competency-based approach to management development was implemented with varying degrees of success. Loan-Clarke (1996) and Smith (2000) outline the successes associated with such programmes such as increased confidence and awareness of the organization's goals and activities. However, the problems encountered with implementing a management development programme also need to be acknowledged. Currie (1999) for example, highlighted the failure of a competence-based management development programme to fulfil organizational objectives and suggests that given the uniqueness of the hospital environment, it is often difficult to incorporate generic management competencies. The Office for Health Management's publication, *Learning from the NHS in Change* (Office for Health Management 2003) also analyses the pitfalls and successes encountered by the NHS in implementing change and the implications for Ireland. One of the recommendations is to 'concentrate on getting the "ways of working" right; avoid a preoccupation with structure. Recognize the potential of restructuring to destabilize and focus on rebuilding processes, systems, relationships' (Office for Health Management 2003: 24).

Research methodology

The current state of practice regarding management development in nursing within the context of the Irish health service will be explored, along with the subsequent impact of management development activities on management style and quality of working life. The research objectives can be summarized in the form of three questions.

1   What is the current state of practice regarding management development in nursing within a health service structure?
2   To what extent is the implementation of management development activities successful in terms of facilitating culture change?
3   How does management development initiatives impact upon quality of work-life issues?

The Centre for Management Research in Healthcare and Health Economics was established with a remit to investigate management and organization issues affecting the health system in Ireland. The Centre works on a collaborative basis with a regional health service structure and, as such, the research findings have both regional and national implications. The research adopted a questionnaire approach in its first phase, incorporating a number of Likert scales and open-ended questions, facilitating the generation of data that had both depth and breadth and that was both qualitative and quantitative in nature.

A census approach was utilized and the first phase of the methodology involved the administration of questionnaires to all 141 Clinical Nurse/Midwife Managers at the three grades (Clinical Nurse/Midwife Manager 1s, 2s and 3s) in five acute-care hospitals within the regional health structure. The approach was deemed appropriate as the highest density of all three Clinical Nurse/Midwife Manager grades occurs within an acute care setting. Clinical Nurse/Midwife Manager contact details were accessed from the Director of Nursing in each acute care hospital. This in turn reduced the possibility of non-response in terms of eliminating unsuitable grades from the study such as Clinical Nurse Specialists. The Clinical Nurse/Midwife Manager list also reduced the possibility of 'deadwood' within the sample. An internal email was then sent from each Director of Nursing in advance of the questionnaires, which were sent via the internal post of the hospital in question. Attached to the questionnaire was a covering letter explaining the basis of the research, the confidential nature of questionnaire responses and a stamped addressed envelope in which the respondents could return their completed questionnaires. Non-response measures also consisted of ensuring complete confidentiality and anonymity in returning the questionnaire. An additional section of the questionnaire provided respondents with an opportunity for further participation in an in-depth interview at a later stage in the research process. The questionnaire investigated issues in relation to

Table 9.1 Response rates of Clinical Nurse Managers

Category	Response rate (%)
Clinical Nurse/Midwife Manager 1	49
Clinical Nurse/Midwife Manager 2	43
Clinical Nurse/Midwife Manager 3	69

Table 9.2 Response rates of acute-care hospitals

Category	Response rate (%)
Hospital A	42
Hospital B	44
Hospital C	55
Hospital D	37
Hospital E	78

work environment, management competencies, management development activity and the post-management development environment. The initial piloting of the questionnaire brought to light management development issues that were further investigated in the final questionnaire.

Findings and discussion

A total of 67 questionnaires from the five acute-care hospital sites were returned, giving a response rate of 48 per cent. The findings will be discussed in relation to the groupings Clinical Nurse/Midwife Manager 1s, 2s and 3s. Table 9.1 represents the response rates of each Clinical Nurse Manager Grade.

Table 9.2 provides a more detailed breakdown of response rates per acute-care hospital in the region.

Management development activity

Competency-based management development

The competency-based approach to management development enunciated in the Report of the Commission on Nursing (The Commission on Nursing 1998) and also in Rush *et al.* (2000) is well articulated and communicated within the five research sites. Ninety-one per cent of respondents strongly agreed and agreed that they were aware of the generic and specific competencies for their role as a Clinical Nurse Manager. High ratings of strongly agree and agree were also applied to the statement on whether these competencies were a true reflection of the knowledge, skills and attitudes required for the role of Clinical Nurse Manager (70 per cent). Whilst the issue of awareness is important to investigate, it is also necessary to explore to what extent these competencies are driving management development activity, 'we intend that any management development initiatives commissioned for nurse managers in the future should be informed by these competencies' (Rush et al. 2000: 1). Fifty-two per cent of respondents strongly agreed and agreed that they were always made aware of these generic and specific competencies when attending any management development programmes. Table 9.3 details a breakdown of results per hospital, which indicates a degree of uncertainty felt by respondents.

The existence of formal policy documents is debated throughout the literature. Although Mabey (2002) argues 'that such policy documents often represent statements of intent rather than actual practice.' Heraty and Morley (2003) purport 'organizations with actual policies on personnel/human resource strategy and on management development have higher levels of management development activity.' Table 9.4 provides a brief summary by hospital in terms of policy awareness. It is evident that there are high rates of uncertainty and disagreement amongst the majority of the five acute-care hospitals examined.

Table 9.3 I am always made aware of these generic and specific competencies when attending management development programmes

Category	Strongly agree (%)	Agree (%)	Uncertain (%)	Disagree (%)	Strongly disagree (%)
Hospital A	–	50	50	–	–
Hospital B	10	20	60	10	–
Hospital C	12	40	32	12	4
Hospital D	13.3	46.7	20	6.7	13.3
Hospital E	28.6	42.9	14.3	–	14.3

Table 9.4 There is a policy for management development, which is well-documented and communicated to staff

Category	Strongly agree (%)	Agree (%)	Uncertain (%)	Disagree (%)	Strongly disagree (%)
Hospital A	25	25	50	–	–
Hospital B	–	27.3	54.5	18.2	–
Hospital C	3.8	23.1	57.7	11.5	3.8
Hospital D	6.7	33.3	33.3	13.3	13.3
Hospital E	28.6	42.9	28.6	–	–

The key issue is not whether a policy exists, but the intent and subsequent communication on the hospital's behalf of its commitment to the development of its employees. Fifty-seven per cent of respondents strongly agreed and agreed that they were aware of the various management development activities that can contribute to their development as a clinical nurse manager.

In relation to management development programme attendance, 70% of respondents had attended a formal management development programme. Further analysis by location and grade revealed that a significantly lower proportion of Clinical Nurse Manager 1s had attended management development programmes. This was consistent across all hospitals.

The Report of the Commission on Nursing (The Commission on Nursing 1998: 134) stated 'that first-line nursing and midwifery managers should have management training before taking up a post and be required and supported in continuing to develop management skills.' It is evident that despite this recommendation, 58 per cent of Clinical Nurse Manager 1s still had not had any formal management development training at the time the research was conducted (Figure 9.1).

As outlined in the literature, the management development of clinical nurse managers within the health structure studied, rests with the implementation of the LEO programme, a programme that has had success in the UK and US. Fifty-two per cent of respondents still have not attended the programme. It must be understood that the LEO programme is in its infancy in Ireland, and the limited places and other constraints, both personal and professional all play contributing factors. As one clinical nurse manager 2 indicated, 'It is impossible to go to educational days because I have to be replaced.'

A number of factors were cited as preventing Clinical Nurse Managers accessing or engaging in formal management development activity, 'Lack of development programmes, funding/replacement issues and support from senior management' (CNM 2) were cited as particular barriers to nurse manager development. It is evident that some of the barriers detailed by respondents are issues concerning work environment, some of which can be remedied.

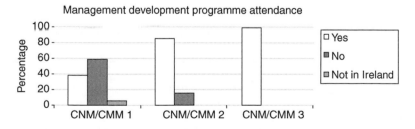

Figure 9.1 Management development programme attendance, breakdown by grade.

Keeping a record or plan in terms of a personal development plan or portfolio appears to be an infrequent activity with 31 per cent of respondents keeping a personal development plan and 36 per cent of respondents keeping a personal development portfolio. In terms of how management development is planned, 26 per cent of the respondent population indicated that management development is mainly a self-directed activity, with no assistance from the line manager. Twenty-three per cent of respondents reported that management development was planned in consultation with their line manager and in relation to organization needs. It is interesting to note that 90 per cent of respondents strongly agreed and agreed with the statement, 'I am responsible for determining my management development as a clinical nurse manager.' Although the findings suggest that management development is mainly a self-directed activity, the line manager does play a role, with 49 per cent of respondents strongly agreeing and agreeing that their line manager is instrumental in their management development as a clinical nurse manager. An explanation for this may be the fact that the line manager may act in a 'gate-keeping' capacity in terms of the Clinical Nurse Manager being afforded time off and support to attend management development programmes. As one CNM 2 suggested:

> the hospital I work in has supported me in undertaking the LEO programme but I feel at a loss as to my options for further study that would contribute to my professional development while being compatible with the demands placed upon me in my current post.

The lack of clearly defined roles for Clinical Nurse Managers was an issue that came to light in the pilot questionnaire and was further probed in the final questionnaire. In a similar vein, Rush *et al.* (2000) acknowledges that 'further work needs to be done on the definition and specification of clear role profiles within the three levels of nursing management before the full benefits of competency-based development are realized.' Table 9.5 provides a breakdown of responses by clinical grade.

Closer inspection of the clinical nurse manager 1s response rates revealed a difference of opinion surrounding the clinical nurse manager role. One CNM 1 argued that 'the CNM 1 role can be confusing, one day I run the ward, the next I'm not able to make decisions.'

Table 9.5 I have a clearly defined job role/description – a breakdown by clinical grade

Category	Strongly agree (%)	Agree (%)	Uncertain (%)	Disagree (%)	Strongly disagree (%)
CNM 1	8.3	41.7	12.5	25	12.5
CNM 2	17.6	47.1	11.8	14.7	8.8
CNM 3	–	50	12.5	37.5	–

Another CNM 1 detailed the conflicting roles and functions of the clinical nurse manager, 'The Clinical Nurse Manager 1 role is not as clear as it should be ... It can be a difficult role as one has to oscillate between a staff nurse's role and that of an autonomous manager (only when doing locum for the CNM 2). CNM 1 needs redefinition in my opinion.'

Perhaps the difference of opinion hinges upon the willingness of nurse managers to embrace the ever increasing management role, as an acting CNM 2 illustrated:

> 'A CNM 1 is a no job and if anything it is frustrating. Most of my CNM 1 colleagues agree with this. You have no voice you are neither a nurse nor manager.'

A CNM 2 argues 'Clinical Nurse Managers should always have a clinical focus, i.e. working directly with patient. As in nursing when a person is promoted they are taken further away from the patient. Thus, the patients loses out on an experienced nurses perspective, i.e. CNM 2 – CNM 3. CNM 3 – administrative role'.

It is worth contemplating that the issue does not lie in defining the clinical nurse manager role but the it is the inherent tension between the 'management' and 'clinical' aspects of the role that must be addressed 'The clinical component of the role does not allow for time to develop the "manager" element of the title as you are expected to part of the "working quota" on the ward' (CNM 2). The willingness to embrace the ever-increasing management role that clinical nurse managers must now play in the reformed health service was an issue that was further investigated in subsequent in-depth interviews.

The questionnaire also sought to investigate the range and number of supports offered by the health structure in relation to management development. The most popular supports provided were study leave (79 per cent), financial support for further education and training (60 per cent) and off-the-job management training (40 per cent). One CNM 1 commented:

> I have found the Irish system appears to put obstacles in our way rather than facilitating our development – I have experienced greater financial, time and personal support when working overseas.

While support for management development does have some presence, an issue of being supernumerary comes to the fore, as one CNM 2 argued:

> Clinical Nurse Managers should be supernumerary. It is very difficult to manage a ward if you are part of the numbers on the ward, e.g. during break times I am one of two on the ward. It is impossible to go to educational days because I have to be replaced.

E-learning has also been cited as a current and ever-increasing influence in the area of management development (Mumford and Gold 2004). In an Irish context, the Office for Health Management (TOHM) has developed an online learning centre. One CNM 2 purported:

> I have found access to the TOHM e-learning website a valuable resource. However, this presupposes computer literacy and Internet access. Therefore, computer training/internet training should be supported for Clinical Nurse Managers who are currently excluded from availing of all potential learning resources by this deficit.

Work environment

The work environment section sought to elicit the views of clinical nurse managers in relation to their immediate work environment and the contribution management development activities had made in the hospital. The perspectives generated were not contingent upon respondents' attendance on a management development programme.

Management style

Fifty-eight per cent of total respondents strongly agreed and agreed that there had been a positive change in management style in their hospital. Further analysis revealed some variance per hospital as illustrated in Table 9.6. The results would appear to suggest that the extent to which a positive change in management style has occurred is contingent upon each hospital, with some acute-care hospitals embracing the said structural and cultural shifts more than other acute-care hospitals in the region.

Moreover, the requisite culture change outlined in such strategy statements such as the *Report of the Commission on Nursing* (The Commission on Nursing 1998) may be falling short in some hospitals. Fifty-seven per cent of total respondents strongly agreed and agreed that there was a culture of collaboration and trust between departments/units in the hospital while 80% strongly agreed and agreed there was a participatory management

Table 9.6 Positive change in management style, a breakdown by hospital

Positive change in management style per hospital	Cumulative response rate: strongly agree and agree (%)
Hospital A	71
Hospital B	40
Hospital C	48
Hospital D	66
Hospital E	100

Table 9.7 Indicators of management change

Indicators of a change in management style	Strongly agree (%)	Agree (%)	Uncertain (%)	Disagree (%)	Strongly disagree (%)
Increased top/down communications	24.2	45.2	9.7	16.1	4.8
Increased bottom/up communications	19.7	41	24.6	9.8	4.9
Increased delegation	20.6	52.4	12.7	12.7	1.6
Devolution of power	13.8	25.9	32.8	27.6	–
Positive change in work-life culture	12.7	36.5	27	19	4.8

Table 9.8 Work-life culture, response rates per hospital

Positive change in work-life culture per hospital	Response rate, % uncertain	Response rate, % disagree	Response rate, % strongly disagree	Cumulative percentage
Hospital B	50	20	10	80
Hospital C	38.5	23.1	3.8	65.4

style. Other indicators of management style change were also investigated and are outlined in Table 9.7.

A further breakdown of the statement investigating the extent to which there was a devolution of power within each hospital, revealed a level of uncertainty experienced by some respondents, where 44 per cent of respondents in Hospital B were uncertain and 42 per cent of respondents in Hospital C disagreed that a devolution of power has occurred.

In relation to a positive change in work-life culture, there appeared to be a significant difference of opinion per hospital. While 71 per cent of respondents in Hospital A, 69 per cent of respondents in Hospital D and 86 per cent of respondents in Hospital E strongly agreed and agreed that they have seen a change in work–life culture, levels of uncertainty and disagreement were felt by respondents in the other hospitals. This is outlined in Table 9.8.

Work life environment

While also investigating management style and culture, the questionnaire also explored issues in relation to work environment. Table 9.9 outlines a brief number of statements in relation to the work environment.

Seventy-six per cent of respondents indicated that they do have the authority and autonomy to make decisions. While this may the case, a CNM 2 added:

the current lack of autonomy and empowerment make development difficult. The theory in programmes attended is useful but difficult to implement in present culture. Lack of information regarding formal education, postgraduate study not as well supported by [health structure] as diploma/degree. Nominated to attend training rather than encouraged to attend training of relevance. PDPs [personal development plans] done by some individuals but not formally supported.

Post management development – transfer of learning and work environment

The Report on an Evaluation Study of the Leading an Empowered Organization Programme (LEO) for Clinical Nurse Managers 1 (Centre for the Development of Nursing Policy and Practice University of Leeds 2003: 3) proposed that 'in time, this [development] should lead to a cultural shift in nursing management with the emphasis on empowering people and valuing people, team working and inter-professional collaboration.' The extent to which management development activity has and is facilitating a culture change within the health service is explored in further detail. A number of statements examined attitudes and behaviours following the respondents' attendance at a management development programme. Seventy-seven per cent of respondents strongly agreed and agreed that they were empowered to incorporate new skills, knowledge, behaviours and ways of working back into the workplace following management development training. Despite agreeing to this statement, one CNM 1 noted that her 'CNM 2 does not want change and prefers me to take on clinical workload and leave ward running to her.'

In terms of support offered post management-development, 60 per cent of respondents strongly agreed and agreed that their immediate work colleagues support them in utilizing the new skills, knowledge and behaviours learned on a management development programme. Figure 9.2 illustrates a breakdown of the results by clinical grade. While 50 per cent of clinical nurse managers 1 strongly agreed they were supported in transferring new skills and behaviours,

Table 9.9 A selection of responses concerning work environment

Work environment	*Cumulative response rate %: strongly agree and agree*
I work in an environment where there is a spirit of cooperation and teamwork	89
My relationships with colleagues are good	94
I work in an environment where others treat me as a professional – with courtesy and respect	85
I have the authority and autonomy to use my judgement and make decisions	76

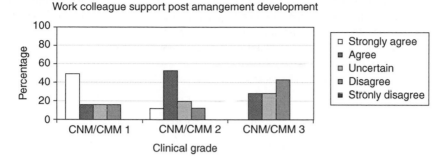

Figure 9.2 Work colleague support in the utilization of new skills, knowledge and behaviours learned on a management development programme.

it must be noted that 43 percent of Clinical Nurse Managers 3 disagreed with the statement regarding work colleague support. As one CNM 2 noted:

> The role of Clinical Nurse Managers has changed so much in the past 5 years with the new style of management I feel the role of CNM 2 is too far removed from the patient. The extended role has made huge demands on the CNM 2 without a support system.

The issue of work colleague support merited further investigation. Forty per cent of respondents strongly agreed and agreed that they received feedback from immediate work colleagues in relation to their management effectiveness post management development. Despite the apparent lack of support from work colleagues, particularly at Clinical Nurse Manager 3 level, the ability to transfer new skills, knowledge and behaviours post management development was rated highly. Seventy-eight per cent of respondents strongly agreed and agreed they were able to transfer skills and behaviours learned back to their role as clinical nurse manager. One CNM 2 argued:

> The most frustrating aspect is having the theory and development opportunities but not having the autonomy or structure to carry out the job as successfully as is possible. Due to not being supernumerary my colleagues suffer a greater burden of clinical workload if I am carrying out non-clinical administrative work . . . Better collaboration and agreement of priorities is essential – priorities for me on a clinical level are not necessarily the same as those for my line managers. I also find it difficult to cope with excessive control of ward running issues at the next level of management structure.

In investigating the ability of management development programmes to facilitate culture change, the question had be posed as to the extent management development programme participants have modified their own behaviour post management development. While some amount of reflexivity is involved, the statement aimed to explore the efficacy of management development in changing behaviour. Ninety-two per cent of respondents strongly agreed and agreed they have changed their behaviour towards others post management development.

Interpretations, conclusions and critical analysis

A number of issues have arisen from the questionnaire findings that merit further investigation. The use of in-depth interviews will facilitate and generate a more detailed picture of management development activity within this regional structure. The findings have illustrated varying degrees of success in terms of cultural change and management development activity. *The Report on an Evaluation Study on the Leading an Empowered Organization Programme (LEO) for Clinical Nurse Managers 1* (Centre for the Development of Nursing Policy and Practice University of Leeds 2003: 3) suggests that 'LEO is not a substitute for the broad-based programme of management skill needed to develop the nursing management competencies identified for front-line nursing managers.' While the Irish health service looks to its UK and US counterparts in terms of nurse manager development, it maybe prudent on the part of the regional health structure not to disregard other development initiatives or to examine the LEO programme success in an isolated fashion. While Currie (1999) acknowledged the importance of health service context when implementing a competency-based management development programme, it is hoped that this study has successfully explored the management development activities of Clinical Nurse Managers with reference to the context and work environment within which they operate.

Key learning points

- Management development is an important element of HRD within health service organizations, whether through formal (competency-based) or informal activities.
- This research has investigated the management development activities of Clinical Nurse Managers and the impact of management development activities on management style and quality of working life. Clinical Nurse Managers are an important group to investigate as they are responsible for nurses, one of the largest groups of professionals in health services.
- The findings have illustrated some of the tensions between clinical and managerial roles, and ambiguity in managerial levels, suggesting greater role clarification is required. The development levels of Clinical Nurse Manager 1s are a cause for concern and an issue that must be addressed in the future.

- Similarly, the extent to which the LEO programme alone is effective in initiating culture change is challenged, as is the willingness to embrace such change initiatives by Clinical Nurse Managers. Findings suggest varying degrees of success in terms of cultural change and management development activity.
- It is important to acknowledge the health service context when implementing any competency-based management development programme, and it is hoped that this study has successfully explored the management development activities of clinical nurse managers with reference to the context and work environment within which they operate.

Appendix 1: nursing structure

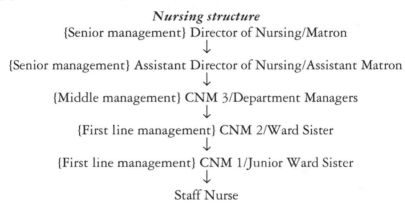

Nursing structure
{Senior management} Director of Nursing/Matron
↓
{Senior management} Assistant Director of Nursing/Assistant Matron
↓
{Middle management} CNM 3/Department Managers
↓
{First line management} CNM 2/Ward Sister
↓
{First line management} CNM 1/Junior Ward Sister
↓
Staff Nurse

(Reproduced with the guidance of Caroline Murphy, Project Manager, Nursing Department, School of Health Sciences, Waterford Institute of Technology.)

Appendix 2: nursing competencies

TOP LEVEL
1 Strategic and System Thinking
2 Establishing Policy, Systems and Structures
3 Leading on Vision and Values
4 Stepping up to the Corporate Agenda
5 Development Approach to Staff

MIDDLE LEVEL
1 Proactive approach to Planning
2 Effective Co-ordination of Resources
3 Empowering/Enabling Leadership Style
4 Setting and Monitoring Performance Standards
5 Negotiation Skills

FRONT LINE LEVEL
1   Planning and Organization of Activities and Resources
2   Building and Leading the Team
3   Leading on Clinical Practice and Service Quality

GENERIC COMPETENCIES
1   Promoting Evidence-based Decision Making
2   Building and Maintaining Relationships
3   Communication and Influencing Relationships
4   Service Initiation and Innovation
5   Resilience and Composure
6   Integrity and Ethical Stance
7   Sustained Personal Commitment
8   Practitioner Competence and Professional Credibility

(Source: Rush *et al.* 2000).

References

Antonacopoulou, E. and FitzGerald, L. (1996) 'Reframing competency in management development,' *Human Resource Management* 6(1): 27–48.

Barrett, S.D. (2003) 'The task of Irish Health Service Reform,' *Irish Banking Review* Winter: 18–30.

Belling, R., James, K. and Ladkin, D. (2004) 'Back to the workplace,' *Journal of Management Development* 23(3): 234–255.

Centre for the Development of Nursing Policy and Practice University of Leeds, Management Development Sub-group and Empowerment of Nurses and Midwives Steering Group – An Agenda for Change (eds) (2003) *Report on an evaluation study of the Leading an Empowered Organisation Programme (LEO) for Clinical Nurse Managers 1*. Dublin Office for Health Management.

Cheng, W.L.E. and Ho, C.K.D. (2001) 'A review of transfer of training studies in the past decade,' *Personnel Review* 30(1): 102.

Clarke, M. (1999) 'Management development as a game of meaningless outcomes,' *Human Resource Management Journal* 9(2): 38–49.

Currie, G. (1999) 'Resistance around a management development programme: negotiated order in a hospital trust,' *Management Learning* 30(1).

Department of Health and Children (1989) *Report of the Commission on Health Funding*, Dublin: The Stationery Office.

Department of Health and Children (1994) *Shaping a Healthier Future: A Strategy for Effective Health Care in the 1990s*, Dublin: Stationery Office.

Department of Health and Children (2001) *Quality and Fairness: A Health System for You*, Dublin: The Stationery Office.

Department of Health and Children (2003) *Commission on Financial Management and Control Systems in the Health Service*, Dublin: The Stationary Office.

Department of Health and Children, Health Service Employers Agency and Health Services National Partnership Forum (2002) *Action Plan for People Management in the Health Service*, Dublin Department of Health and Children.

Department of Health and Children and Watson Wyatt (2003) *Audit of Structures and Functions in the Health System*, Dublin: The Stationery Office.

DHSS (1983) *NHS Management Inquiry (Griffiths Report)*, London: HMSO.

Faugier, J. and Woolnough, H. (2003) 'Lessons from LEO,' *Nursing Management* 10(2): 22–25.

Faulkner, P., McMahon, K., The Management Development Sub Group, The High Level Steering Group and Empowerment of Nurses and Midwives, (eds) (2002) *Evaluation of Nursing Management Development Programmes – Front Line and Middle Level Nurse Managers*, Office for Health Management.

Garavan, T., Costine, P. and Heraty, N. (1995) *Training and Development in Ireland: Context, Policy and Practice*, Dublin: Oak Tree Press.

Garavan, T., Hogan, C. and Cahir-O'Donnell, A. (2003) *Making Training and Development Work: A Best Practice Guide*, Cork: Oak Tree Press.

Gifford, B.D., Zammuto, R.F., Goodman, E.A. and Hill, K.S. (2002) 'The relationship between hospital unit culture and nurses' quality of work life,' *Journal of Healthcare Management* 47(1): 13–26.

Graham, J. (1992) 'Quality of working life and total quality management,' *International Journal of Manpower* 13(1): 41–58.

Harrison, R. (1997) *Employee Development*, London: Institute of Personnel and Development.

Heraty, N. and Morley, M.J. (2003) 'Management development in Ireland: the new organizational wealth?' *The Journal of Management Development* 22(1): 60–82.

Hussey, D. (1988) *Management Training and Corporate Strategy – How to Improve Competitive Performance*, London: Pergamon.

Jansen, P., Van Der Velde, M. and Mul, W. (2001) 'A typology of management development,' *The Journal of Management Development* 20(2): 106–120.

Kamoche, K. (2000) 'Developing managers: the functional, the symbolic, the sacred and the profane,' *Organisation Studies* 21(4): 747–774.

Kelly, M. (2003) *The Health Service Reform Programme*, Department of Health and Children.

Lawlor, J. and McCarthy, C. (2003) 'Browsing onwards: Irish public spending in perspective,' *Irish Banking Review.*

Lewis, D., Brazil, K., Krueger, P., Lohfeld, L. and Tjam, E. (2001) 'Extrinsic and intrinsic determinants of quality of work life,' *International Journal of Health Care Quality Assurance* 14(3): ix.

Loan-Clarke, J. (1996) 'Health-care professionals and management development,' *Journal of Management in Medicine* 10(6).

Mabey, C. (2002) 'Mapping management development practice,' *Journal of Management Studies* 39(8): 1139–1160.

Mabey, C. and Salaman, G. (1995) *Training and Development Strategies* in C. Mabey and G. Salaman (eds) *Strategic Human Resource Management*, UK: Oxford; USA: MA: Blackwell.

Machell, S., Nixon, G., Management Development Sub-group and Empowerment of Nurses and Midwives Steering Group – An Agenda for Change (eds) (2003) *Report on the Diagnostic Exercise for Directors of Nursing/Equivalent Nursing Management Grades*, Office for Health Management.

Marchington, M. and Wilkinson, A. (2002) *People Management and Development*, 2nd edn, Wiltshire: Cromwell Press.

Molander, C. (1986) *Management Development*, Bromley: Chartwell-Bratt.

Mumford, A. (1997) *Management Development: Strategies for Action*, 3rd edn, London: Chartered Institute of Personnel and Development.

Mumford, A. and Gold, J. (2004) *Management Development: Strategies for Action*, 6th edn, London: CIPD.

National Task Force on Medical Staffing (2003) *Report of the National Task Force on Medical Staffing*, Dublin Department of Health and Children.

Office for Health Management (2003) *Learning from the NHS in Change – A Study on the Management of Major Structural Change in the NHS*, Dublin Office for Health Management.

Office for Health Management and The High Level Group on Empowerment of Nurses and Midwives (eds) (2002) *Guidance on the Commissioning of Nursing Management Development Programmes – Front Line and Middle Level Nurse Managers*, Dublin Office for Health Management.

Office for Health Management, HSEA and Health Service National Partnership Forum (2004) *Implementation of the Action Plan for People Management – 1st Annual Progress Report 2004*, Office for Health Management.

O'Hara, T. (1998) *Current Structure of the Irish Health Care System – Setting the Context*, in A.L. Leahy and M.M. Wiley (eds) *The Irish Health System in the 21st Century*, Dublin: Oak Tree Press.

O'Reardon, C. (2004) 'Improving the Irish public services,' *Irish Banking Review.*

Preston, D. (1993) 'Management development structures as symbols of organizational culture,' *Personnel Review* 22(1): 18–30.

Riggio, R.E. (2003) *Introduction to Industrial/Organizational Psychology*, New Jersey: Pearson Education.

Robertson Cooper (2003) *Quality of Working Life Audit-Health Board Results*, Robertson Cooper.

Rush, D., McCarthy, G. and Cronin, C. (2000) *Report on Nursing Competencies*, Dublin Office for Health Management.

Rush, D., McCarthy, G. and Cronin, C. (2004) *Management Competency User Pack for Nurse and Midwife Managers*, Dublin: Office for Health Management.

Smith, P. (2000) 'Introducing competence-based management development: a case study of a university-hospital partnership,' *Journal of Workplace Learning: Employee Counselling Today* 12(6): 245–251.

Smith, S. and Edmonstone, J. (2001) 'Learning to lead,' *Nursing Management* 8(3): 10–13.

Tannenbaum, S.I. and Yukl, G.A. (1992) 'Training and development in work organisations,' *Annual Review of Psychology* 43: 399–441.

The Commission on Nursing. Department of Health and Children (ed.) (1998) *Report of The Commission on Nursing – A Blueprint for the Future*, Dublin: The Stationery Office.

Wren, M.A. (2004) 'Health spending and the black hole,' *ESRI Quarterly Commentary.*

Part III

HRD and workplace learning

10 Tailoring learning programmes to everyday employee learning

Customisation strategies of HRD practitioners in healthcare

Rob F. Poell and Ferd J. Van der Krogt*

Aims and objectives

Customisation is an important activity in the design and delivery of learning programmes. In the literature, tailoring consistent sets of learning activities to the characteristics of the learner is usually approached from the perspective of HRD practitioners (designers, developers, trainers, educators). They customise to the extent that the learning programme is tuned to, for example, the learner competencies already acquired, their learning style, needs, and so forth. Various types of methods and instruments have been developed within HRD to achieve such customisation, including task analysis, training needs assessment, transfer enhancing measures, etc. From the perspective of the learners themselves, however, a (formal) learning programme is basically a disruption of the way they (informally) learn from work on an everyday basis. If this is a beneficial disruption, it can provide learners with fresh impetus to solve work problems in the future. From this perspective, the effectiveness of a learning programme increases with the extent to which HRD practitioners attune it to the everyday learning activities undertaken by the participants.

Both approaches to customisation reserve an important role for HRD practitioners. In the first one, they are designers and deliverers of didactically sound training programmes. In the second one, HRD practitioners provide employees with advice on how to learn more systematically during work. Integrating these two roles, what exactly can HRD practitioners do to create tailored learning programmes? This question is central to the current chapter, which combines theoretical and empirical insights on the subject. Not much is known as yet about the strategies employed by HRD practitioners in 'real life' learning programmes. However, practice-based knowledge about the ways in which customisation takes shape is necessary to develop further the instrumental repertoire of HRD practitioners. Alternative perspectives on customisation and the action opportunities derived from these can benefit their further professionalisation.

The chapter first presents theory on customisation from the perspectives of both the HRD practitioner and the learning employee. It then describes an analytic framework for studying customisation of learning programmes, based on a combination of both perspectives. Next, extensive empirical results obtained using this framework in the healthcare sector are presented. The chapter finishes with conclusions and implications for further research on customisation.

The theoretical context

Two different perspectives on customisation are identified.

- *Tailoring training programmes*, focusing on the activities of the HRD practitioner in tuning training to learner characteristics;
- *Connecting learning programmes to everyday learning*, focusing on employee work-related learning activities and the ways in which HRD practitioners can foster those.

The former perspective has been elaborated rather extensively in literature, whilst the latter is much less widespread. Both approaches will be presented consecutively below, after which it is intended to combine them into an analytic model for customised learning programmes.

Tailoring training programmes

Six measures can be derived from educational and HRD literature for HRD practitioners to tailor training to learner characteristics.

- *Performing training needs and task analyses.* Analysing employees' learning needs is a familiar part of training design (Swanson 1994), as is gathering information about problems and changes in work (Robinson and Robinson 1989). These are intended to attune better the training to the organisation. Tailoring here involves adapting the training content to the work situation and the participants.
- *Taking into account learning styles.* Riding and Sadler-Smith (1997) identified three ways to adapt a training design to the different learning styles of participants.
    - Adaptive training design, where the designer adapts the presentation and structure of the training programme to individual learning styles.
    - Balanced training design, where participants can choose from a broad and well-balanced set of possibilities to select the information most appropriate to them.
    - 'A strategy approach, which encourages trainees to develop strategies to make learning tasks easier by using the strength of their styles'

(Riding and Sadler-Smith 1997: 203). Participants themselves play a key role here, since they are expected to attune their learning styles to the task at hand.

- *Individualisation and programme flexibility.* Educational scientists have long studied the ways in which educational programmes can adapt to individual differences among students. Key words here are individualisation (Dochy *et al.* 1989) and programme flexibility (Bell *et al.* 1997). Flexible programmes offer individuals many opportunities to create their own learning route. Flexibility can pertain to programme content (e.g. through modularisation), didactic approach (e.g. through variation in work methods), and guidance (e.g. in establishing an individual route).
- *Facilitating self-directed learning.* Facilitation here refers to creating conditions that encourage learning, within which employees can direct their own learning process (Brookfield 1986). In this way, they can ensure that what they learn is relevant (to them). HRD practitioners need to create the necessary preconditions, for example, provide employees with insight into their learning capability and into available learning opportunities in the workplace. This means that the HRD practitioner shares an important part of programme ownership with the employees.
- *Continuous adaptation of the training programme.* Evaluation can indicate that a training programme is not running the way it was planned. If this happens at the end of a programme, it can be adapted for the next time around. However, it is also possible for the HRD practitioner to evaluate and modify the programme as it is running (cf. the Japanese concept of kaizen, continuous improvement; de Lange-Ros 1999). Tailoring here means establishing the possibilities of the participants during programme execution and continuously adapting its content and shape accordingly. Participants play an important role in this process as well, for example, by providing feedback.
- *Transfer enhancing measures.* Transfer of training refers to the extent to which participants use in the workplace what they had learned in a training programme. Transfer enhancing measures can be targeted at the training programme itself (e.g. include assignments based on actual work problems) or at the work situation (e.g. make arrangements with the direct supervisor of the participants). Initially, much attention was paid to adapting the training content to the work situation (Broad and Newstrom 1992). During the 1990s, influencing the work situation itself became a key interest (Holton *et al.* 2000).

Connecting learning programmes to everyday learning

The starting point of the second approach is that employees learn continuously within their organisation. This everyday learning, which is mostly unintended and unstructured, happens incidentally during work as people solve their daily problems. However, employees can also initiate their own learning activities intentionally through, for example, engaging in self-study, enrolling in a training programme on their own initiative, consulting an expert or a job coach. When such activities are combined over time, an individual learning path comes into being, which can differ among employees in terms of content and structure.

Sometimes, however, employees will want to learn with others in a more systematic and intensive manner. They then jointly create a temporary learning programme. In part, such a learning programme continues the normal, 'old' way of learning characteristic of the employees' individual learning paths. On the other hand, it also has its own dynamics and contents, which result from the collective efforts of those involved in the temporary learning programme (Poell and Van der Krogt 2003a). The idea is that a joint learning programme gives fresh impetus to individual learning paths, such that employees can organise their own learning paths better and build upon the experiences and contacts gained during the temporary learning programme.

There are several distinctions between individual learning paths of employees and the temporary learning programmes in which they can enrol. Individual learning paths indicate continuous learning processes, whereas learning programmes represent a certain period in time. Learning paths are individual processes, albeit in a social context, whereas learning programmes are usually a group activity guided by an HRD practitioner. Individual learning paths involve highly implicit learning, whereas learning programmes are intentional in nature. A temporary learning programme can be regarded as a disruption of the individual learning paths of employees. It is up to the HRD practitioner as well as to the employees to connect the two in meaningful ways.

The HRD practitioner can play an important role in a learning programme by making it more systematic, for example, by supporting employees and adapting the programme halfway through. HRD practitioners bring added value when they succeed in bringing fresh impetus to the individual learning paths of the participants in the learning programme. The latter are most likely to benefit from the programme if they are able to connect it with their individual learning paths. Thus, an experiment with the production of a job aid as part of a learning programme can lead to a different way for employees to start shaping their individual learning path – using job aids more often if the experiment was successful, maybe never again if they found out that asking an expert to tell them about optimal working methods was far more efficient. An HRD practitioner who can bring about such reflection on the part of employees in a learning programme introduces new elements into their normal learning paths and thereby offers added value.

In the course of a learning programme the HRD practitioner and the participants can engage in customisation in various ways. At the outset, participants can put forward their own desires and expectations as to the contents and organisation of the programme. Towards the end they can engage in additional action planning with a view to continuing their individual learning paths. In making customisation concrete, important questions are: to what extent can participants learn in accordance with their own learning capabilities and learning styles; and, is the evolving programme well enough attuned to their existing competencies?

Thinking in terms of tuning temporary learning programmes to the individual learning paths of the participants is not as widespread as the measures (discussed in the previous sub-section) that the educational literature has produced around training customisation. The next section intends to combine the two perspectives into a joint analytic framework for studying tailor-made learning programmes.

Analytic framework

Combining the two perspectives outlined above yields the framework presented in Figure 10.1. The upper part shows individual learning paths (ILPs – horizontal arrows) of four employees brought together for a joint temporary learning programme (TLP – dark rectangular). The lower part shows six customisation strategies that HRD practitioners can use to tune a learning programme to the individual learning paths of the employees. The first two strategies (performing learning needs and task analyses, and taking into account employee learning styles) take effect mainly at the start of the learning programme, disrupting the individual learning path. Hence, the left vertical arrow points at the transition from ILPs to TLP. The next three strategies (individualisation, facilitating self-directed learning, and continuous adaptation) are expected to occur during the learning programme, with

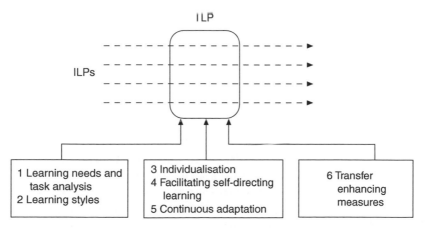

Figure 10.1 Analytic framework to study customisation strategies of HRD practitioners.

individual learning paths going on as ever. Therefore, the middle vertical arrow points at the TLP. The final strategy (transfer enhancing measures) marks a return from the learning programme to the four individual learning paths of the employees. Hence, the right vertical arrow points at the transition from TLP to ILPs.

These six customisation strategies can be regarded as measures that HRD practitioners can take to tailor a learning programme to the individual learning paths of participating employees. The next section describes an empirical study that investigated which of these strategies (or any others not described in the literature) were actually employed by HRD practitioners.

The empirical context

The study, which drew upon the analytic model described above, took the shape of an action-research project in which the researchers collaborated with HRD practitioners from the Dutch healthcare sector. Its first aim was to use joint reflection on the practices of the HRD practitioners explicitly to improve their self-understanding. Second, the project aimed to broaden the researchers' insight into the customisation strategies employed by HRD practitioners. Healthcare was chosen because the broad nature of its primary processes yields a possibly wide range of learning-programme types. To facilitate comparisons, participant selection focused as much as possible on the primary work process of the organisation as opposed to its management layers. In the selection of learning programmes for the study, the emphasis lay on those with participants around the higher vocational education level. Two learning-programme cases were selected for each HRD practitioner. Each case was analysed for elements of customisation strategies using the analytic framework described above, first in individual interviews and later on in the project in joint reflection sessions.

Research methods

The action-research project with the HRD practitioners took place throughout 2001 and 2002 in four phases: selection, description, analysis, and reflection (cf. Poell and Van der Krogt 2005).

Selecting the participants and learning programmes

Two learning groups were established consisting of HRD practitioners. Snowball sampling was used to find HRD practitioners from the Dutch healthcare sector who worked with employees at least at the secondary vocational education level. Potential participants were asked to take part in an action-research project-cum-learning programme about customisation strategies. Eventually a useful and complete data set was acquired from seven participants, among them six men. They worked as HRD practitioners in or for large (psychiatric) hospitals, and in or for medium-sized nursing homes and institutes for home care or for mentally handicapped people. Most participants were very well informed within the healthcare sector and had extensive experience with educational consultancy and training. Two introduction sessions were held with the participants at the start of the study in order to familiarise them with theory about learning programmes and customisation.

Describing the learning programmes conducted

An especially developed checklist ('Customised Learning-Programmes Checklist': CLPC, see below) was used to interview each participant twice about two different recent learning programmes they had organised. Useful learning programmes had a core theme to do with the quality of care or service and lasted at least a month with two plenary sessions. One participant had only one useful learning programme, accounting for a total number of 13 cases on which the analysis was based. The interviews were conducted in Dutch. In total, five researchers were involved in conducting the interviews, including an initial analysis, operating in ever changing pairs. Table 10.1 contains a general overview of the cases.

Table 10.1 HRD Practitioner (not their real names), Learning-Programme Theme, and Participants and Organisation per Case.

	HRD practitioner	*Learning-programme theme*	*Participants and organisation*
Case 1	Ed	Methodical treatment	Community supervisors in an institution for problem youths
Case 2	Ed	Therapeutic action	Community supervisors in a residence for youth assistance
Case 3	Harry	Systems methodology	Nurses in a psychiatric institution
Case 4	Harry	Client participation	Nurses in a psychiatric institution
Case 5	Jacco	Restricted actions	Intensive-care nurses in a hospital
Case 6	Jacco	Thorax draining	Nurses in a hospital
Case 7	Johan	Day-care improvement	Activity coaches in an institution for mentally handicapped
Case 8	Johan	Supervisor–client collaboration	Community supervisors in an institution for mentally handicapped
Case 9	Pascal	Respectful treatment	Helpers, attendants, and nurses in a nursing home
Case 10	Pascal	Vision development	All employees of a nursing home
Case 11	Trudy	Networked care	Managers and employees of four nursing homes
Case 12	Trudy	Client allocation	Managers in an institution for home care
Case 13	Uri	Doing research	Nurses in a hospital

Analysing the learning programmes described

During the interviews the researchers summarised the answers of the participants at the end of each separate section of the CLPC in order to check whether their interpretations fitted with the intentions of the participants. Tape recordings, full transcripts, interview notes, and the CLPC as completed during the interview were used to make a four to six-page summary of each interview. This was sent to the participants for verification and additions, together with the version of the CLPC that was completed during the interview. All 13 summarised case descriptions were returned to the researchers with corrections. These corrected versions were used for the initial case analyses, which were carried out by different pairs of researchers for each learning-programme case using the N-Vivo software package for qualitative analysis. An interpretation and diagnosis were made of the customisation strategies employed in each learning programme. All 13 case analyses were discussed and commented on by the other three researchers in two or three rounds, leading to a number of changes in the interpretation of some cases. The analysis was aimed at gathering information about preselected categories, although an effort was also made to find 'new' customisation strategies beyond the ones already singled out. At the end of this phase, the individual case analyses were used as input for a learning programme with the HRD practitioners and for a comparative multiple case analysis that was discussed with the participants during the last meeting of the programme.

Reflection on the learning programmes and case analyses

The descriptive and analytic phases of this action-research project contained some activities that could also encourage HRD practitioners' learning about the organisation of learning programmes. In the final reflection phase, their learning was intensified by forming two learning groups. The action-learning project in this phase consisted of four workshops and reflective discussions about the backgrounds to the choices made by the HRD practitioners in their respective cases. The researchers and other participants gave individual HRD practitioners suggestions to improve the way they organise learning programmes. The action-learning project ended after the participants had used the CLPC to improve an existing learning programme, or design a completely new one, from their own work practice. Participants were invited to think about how to continue the action-learning project individually in their own organisation. A final meeting was held with all HRD practitioners to evaluate the action-learning project for learning effects and impact on their work situation.

The Customised Learning-Programmes Checklist (CLPC)

Before the action-research project took place, a draft Customised Learning-Programmes Checklist was designed, which was piloted in interviews with six HRD practitioners (not the same group) to increase its validity, and adapted accordingly. During the action-research project the CLPC was employed to guide the interviews, but using it has also yielded many concrete ideas for customising learning programs (see Poell and Van der Krogt 2003b). HRD practitioners can draw upon these to determine to what extent, and how, they operationalise the vast array of possible customisation activities. It also provides them with a range of alternative ways to tailor their learning programmes to the organisation and its employees.

As an interview guide, the CLPC contains 52 open questions spread across five categories. First, there are 14 questions about the organisational context where the learning programme took place. The core of the interview is about the activities of the HRD practitioner and the learning-programme participants in the orientation phase (13 questions), learning and optimising phase (13 questions), and continuation phase (eight questions). The final category comprises four questions about the customisation strategy of the HRD practitioner. Time for completion in the 13 cases ranged from an hour and a half to two-and-a-half hours. Half this time was usually needed to achieve a general picture of the learning programme in its organisational context, the other half to complete the CLPC on the basis of the information provided with some specific additional questions.

The findings

Table 10.2 contains the main results of the analysis. The six columns to the right indicate to what extent the various customisation strategies were employed in each particular case. An 'X' means that the customisation strategy was found in that case at least once (e.g. an HRD practitioner who offered a programme both in the daytime and at night would receive a score on the third strategy, individualisation). An '**X**' (bold) indicates that the customisation strategy was the dominant one besides one or more secondary ones (e.g. Trudy in case 11 used mainly the fourth strategy, besides the third and fifth ones). A '−X' means that the customisation strategy was employed implicitly rather than explicitly (e.g. if HRD practitioners found out that they always used practical assignments as part of a programme 'because nurses are real doers,' that is some indication for implicitly taking into account their learning styles).

The main customisation strategies as apparent from Table 10.2 are individualisation and transfer enhancing measures, with learning styles being taken into account to a lesser extent. Facilitation of self-directed learning and continuous adaptation both occur infrequently, although the HRD practitioners in our sample did not put much effort into learning needs and

Table 10.2 Customisation strategies of seven HRD practitioners in 13 learning programmes

	HRD practitioner	Customisation strategies					
		1	2	3	4	5	6
Case 1	Ed		−X	X			**X**
Case 2	Ed			X		X	−X
Case 3	Harry		−X	−X	**X**		**X**
Case 4	Harry		X				X
Case 5	Jacco						
Case 6	Jacco		−X				
Case 7	Johan	X	−X		X		X
Case 8	Johan		X	X			
Case 9	Pascal		−X	X		**X**	**X**
Case 10	Pascal	X	**X**	**X**			X
Case 11	Trudy			X	**X**	X	
Case 12	Trudy	X	−X	X	X	X	X
Case 13	Uri			X			X

Note
For legend see Figure 10.1.

task analyses either. Also, very few 'new' customisation strategies (not covered in literature) other than the six specified upfront came to the fore in the interviews and reflection sessions. Only one learning programme (case 12) featured all six strategies, whilst one other case (5) had none at all. It is also clear from Table 10.2 that some HRD practitioners use more different customisation strategies than other colleagues.

Interpretations, conclusions and critical analysis

The first conclusion of this action-research project in the Dutch healthcare sector is that HRD practitioners used relatively few customisation strategies in the 13 sample cases. Although the main aim of the project was to find out how exactly HRD practitioners create tailor-made learning programmes, customisation turned out to be a topic that was not very high on their agendas. They did, however, employ certain rules of thumb to work with distinctive groups ('nurses are real doers, so the activities should be practical') and come up with a suitable programme. The customisation strategies described in the literature were found in organisational practice to a limited extent only, although a number of interesting examples did emerge (Poell and Van der Krogt 2003b). This finding is in line with earlier research, which showed the design and delivery of training programmes to be rather unsystematic (Sels 2002; Van der Klink 1999, Nijhof 2004; Overduin et al. 2002; Wognum 1999).

Another conclusion of the study is that individual learning paths of employees played only a very minor role in the design and delivery of the learning programmes investigated. Everyday learning activities of employees were not given much attention (Berings *et al.* 2005). HRD practitioners found these very hard to take into account, especially at the outset and at the end of a learning programme (cf. Poell *et al.* 2003). This means that the second approach to customisation, too, was hardly found in practice.

The HRD practitioners in our sample indicated that they are largely unable to influence the learning that goes on in their organisations (cf. Van der Krogt 2002). A learning programme usually gets its basic structure quite early on, when the HRD practitioner talks to the manager who is commissioning it. Few measures to encourage customisation turn out to be possible throughout that important first phase. During programme execution HRD practitioners often do have a picture in mind of the capabilities of the participants, which they use to adapt the programme if necessary (e.g. scheduling some extra practice sessions instead of theoretical elaboration, after it turned out that more than half of the participants 'hadn't got it yet'). It seems that through years of experience the HRD practitioners have developed a practical action repertoire, which they use in learning programmes when such problems with participants occur.

Some limitations of the present study need to be taken into account in interpreting these conclusions. The sample was limited to seven HRD practitioners in one sector, who self-selected to participate in an action-research project. Results may not be generalised to wider constituencies without careful consideration. The CLPC instrument was newly developed for the current study and, although it was deemed very useful in the healthcare context, may not be appropriate to every other research sector without amendment.

For further research it is necessary, in the first place, to realise that employee strategies may be much more important for actual learning practices in the organisation than measures conceived by HRD practitioners (and managers). It is impossible to force employees to learn something in general, let alone force them to learn something specific. Starting from their own learning views and interests, as apparent from their individual learning paths, therefore seems a fruitful strategy for establishing customised learning programmes. It is necessary in this connection to be able to analyse and make better use of the existing learning opportunities in the workplace. Research into these topics is unfortunately still in its infancy.

Second, the emphasis in the transition from a learning programme to the individual learning paths of the participants is still very much on the activities of the HRD practitioner. It is necessary to find out which possibilities the participants themselves have at their disposal to engage actively in the continuation of their learning. Reflection on the way in which prior learning programmes have helped them to solve work problems can give participants a clearer picture of the opportunities of various learning-programme types for individual customisation. It is likely that this will benefit the effectiveness of learning programmes, although more research is needed in this area as well.

A final consideration refers to the fact that many of the customisation strategies found in the literature put rather heavy demands on users (HRD practitioners, employees, and managers). They usually include elaborate analyses to establish work problems, learning styles, needs, effects, and so forth. Less intensive ways of data collection and analysis get little attention in the literature. It may be worthwhile to develop easier (less time and expertise consuming) ways for users to gain the relevant information necessary to come up with suitable learning programmes. A simple checklist for users to find out how employees use existing workplace learning opportunities within their individual learning paths would certainly help them to build upon in an ensuing learning programme. The examples of customisation from the Dutch healthcare sector can offer inspiration for such a checklist (Poell and Van der Krogt 2003b).

Key learning points

- Six measures for HRD practitioners to tailor training programmes to learner characteristics can be distinguished: (1) training needs and task analysis; (2) learning styles; (3) individualisation and flexibility; (4) facilitating self-directed learning; (5) continuous adaptation; and (6) transfer enhancing measures.
- From the perspective of the learner, however, a learning programme is mainly a disruption of their individual everyday learning path.
- HRD practitioners in this study used relatively few customisation strategies and paid little explicit attention to individual learning paths of employees in the design and delivery of learning programmes.
- HRD practitioners in this study seemed to have little impact on employee learning going on in their organisations.
- Further research should focus on understanding the individual learning paths created by employees as part of their everyday work activities.
- Strategies of HRD practitioners need to be better attuned to these employee learning strategies; research should also aim to develop less demanding instruments for the former to analyse and influence employee learning.

Note

The authors wish to thank the Foundation for Corporate Education for awarding them a research grant, which made this study possible in part.

References

Bell, C., Bowden, M. and Trott, A. (eds) (1997) *Implementing Flexible Learning*, London: Kogan Page.

Berings, M.G.M.C., Poell, R.F. and Simons, P.R.J. (2005) 'Conceptualizing on-the-job learning styles,' *Human Resource Development Review* 4(14): 373–400.

Broad, M.L. and Newstrom, J.W. (1992) *Transfer of Training: Action-packed Strategies to Ensure High Pay-off from Training Investments*, San Francisco: Addison-Wesley.

Brookfield, S.D. (1986) *Understanding and Facilitating Adult Learning: A Comprehensive Analysis of Principles and Effective Practices*, Milton Keynes: Open University.

de Lange-Ros, D.J. (1999) 'Continuous improvement in teams: the (mis)fit between improvement and operational activities of improvement teams,' PhD thesis, University of Twente, Netherlands.

Dochy, F.J.R.C., Wagemans, L.J.J.M. and De Wolf, H.C. (1989) *Modularisation and Student Learning in Modular Instruction in Relation with Prior Knowledge*, Heerlen, Netherlands: Open University.

Holton, E.F., Bates, R.A. and Ruona, W.E.A. (2000) 'Development of a generalized learning transfer system inventory,' *Human Resource Development Quarterly* 11: 333–360.

Nijhof, W. (2004) 'Is the HRD profession in the Netherlands changing?,' *Human Resource Development International* 7: 57–72.

Overduin, B., Kwakman, F. and Metz, B.J. (2002) 'De performancebenadering in Nederland: Een onderzoek onder HRD-afdelingen' [The performance approach in the Netherlands: a study among HRD departments], *M&O Tijdschrift voor Organisatiekunde en Sociaal Beleid* 56: 36–51.

Poell, R.F. and Van der Krogt, F.J. (2003a) 'Project-based learning in organisations: towards a methodology for learning in groups,' *Journal of Workplace Learning* 15: 217–228.

Poell, R.F. and Van der Krogt, F.J. (2003b) 'Maatwerkstrategieë van opleiders: Naar een checklist voor het leveren van maatwerk in leertrajecten' [Customisation strategies of HRD practitioners: towards a checklist for tailored learning programs], *Handboek Effectief Opleiden* 33: 1–21.

Poell, R.F. and Van der Krogt, F.J. (2005) 'Customizing learning programs to the organization and its employees: how HRD practitioners create tailored learning programs,' *International Journal of Learning and Intellectual Capital* 2: 288–304.

Poell, R.F., Pluijmen, R. and Van der Krogt, F.J. (2003) 'Strategies of HRD professionals in organising learning programmes: a qualitative study among 20 Dutch HRD professionals,' *Journal of European Industrial Training* 27: 125–136.

Riding, R. and Sadler-Smith, F. (1997) 'Cognitive style and learning strategies: some implications for training design,' *International Journal of Training and Development* 1: 199–208.

Robinson, D.G. and Robinson, J.C. (1989) *Training for Impact*, San Francisco: Jossey-Bass.

Sels, L. (2002) 'More is not necessarily better: the relationship between the quantity and quality of training efforts,' *International Journal of Human Resource Management* 13: 1279–1298.

Swanson, R.A. (1994) *Analysis for Improving Performance: Tools for Diagnosing Organizations and Documenting Workplace Expertise*, San Francisco: Berrett-Koehler.

Van der Klink, M.R. (1999) 'Effectiviteit van werkplekopleidingen' [Effectiveness of workplace training], PhD thesis, University of Twente, Netherlands.

Van der Krogt, F.J. (2002) 'Managers en werknemers creëen leersystemen? De lastige positie van HRD'ers' [Managers and employees create learning systems? The awkward position of HRD practitioners], in P. Blirs, H. Dekker, R.F. Poell, S. Tjepkema and S. Wagenaar (eds) *Organiseren van de HRD-functie {Organising the HRD Function}*, Alphen aan den Rijn: Kluwer.

Wognum, A.A.M. (1999) 'Strategische afstemming en de effectiviteit van bedrijfso-pleidingen' [Strategic alignment and the effectiveness of corporate training], PhD thesis, University of Twente, Netherlands.

11 What and how do nurses learn on the job?

Similarities and differences among nurses in on-the-job learning

Marjolein G.M.C. Berings, J.P.T.M. Gelissen and Rob F. Poell

Introduction

Researchers, hospital directors, professional associations of nurses and defenders of nurses' interests as well as HRD professionals all agree that nurses need to learn continuously and that on-the-job learning is significant if this is to be achieved. The aim of this study is to investigate what and how nurses learn on the job.

The main reason for the need for continuous learning by nurses is that the context of health care is constantly changing and nurses need to learn to adapt to new working situations. The development of new technologies, as used in nursing equipment for example, changing disease patterns and the shift from internal medical care to care that is, at least partly, provided externally means that there is a growth in the complexity of the knowledge and skills required. There has been a shift from task-centred nursing to patient-centred nursing and the boundaries between the work carried out by nurses and that of junior hospital doctors are shifting as well. All these changes imply an increase in the number of times that a nurse is faced with making a choice and with ethical dilemmas. Nurses require knowledge and intellectual skills for critical thinking. They need to be decisive and to work as competent and autonomous caretakers and as members of multi-disciplined and multi-professional teams (Clark 2001), something which they often experience as difficult (Eliens and Strijbol 2001). Another reason for the need for continuous learning for nurses is that the nursing profession will remain more attractive to nurses if they are given greater learning opportunities. Research in the Netherlands (Dik and van Splunder 2002) has shown that there is a clear relationship between a lack of learning possibilities and nurses leaving the profession.

Although hospitals can provide education and training to enable individual learning, these opportunities are not always available. Moreover, in many situations training or education has several disadvantages: it does not have impact unless it is well timed, transference of what has been learned to the daily work situation often seems difficult, and it is expensive (van Woerkom 2003). In addition to formal training and education, the most significant sources of learning are the challenges of the work itself and interactions with other people in the workplace (Eraut *et al.* 1998; Mumford 1995; Tannenbaum 1997). On-the-job learning overcomes the problems of training and education that have been mentioned above so that it would appear to be useful to put more effort into improving this method of learning. At present, however, little is known about methods that can be used for this improvement.

Berings *et al.* (2005) suggest that a useful way of improving nurses' on-the-job learning could be to make them aware of their on-the-job learning styles. On-the-job learning styles can be regarded as the tendency to use a particular combination of implicit and explicit learning activities that a person can and likes to perform on the job. The person adapts the combination of learning activities differently to each situation. The particular combination is called the actualized learning strategy (Berings *et al.* 2005). Knowledge about their own and other possible on-the-job learning styles can make nurses aware of their choices of learning behaviour. More knowledge about this subject is needed to help nurses become aware of their own on-the-job learning styles and alternative possibilities.

An on-the-job learning style may be regarded as a personal characteristic so this phenomenon can only be studied by observing or inquiring about the actual on-the-job learning behaviour of the nurse in relation to the different learning situations in which this behaviour occurs. The concept of an on-the-job learning situation includes many different factors, such as task and learning content, information environment, social work environment (Onstenk 1997), and learning climate (Baars-van Moorsel 2003). The learning content is continuously changing, in contrast to the other factors. Therefore, this study will relate the actual on-the-job learning behaviour of the nurses to the content of what is learned in order to gain insight into the relationship between the on-the-job learning behaviour shown by the nurses and the on-the job learning situation.

Aim and objective of the study

The aim of this study is to investigate what and how nurses, seen from their perspective, learn on the job. The relationship between the content of learning (what) and the process of learning (how) will be explored further.

Most literature dealing with on-the-job learning focuses on similarities in the overt learning processes of different employees (e.g. Gerber 1998; Eraut *et al.* 1998). In contrast, learning style research focuses on the mental learning process and differences among employees (Allinson and Hayes 1996). This study, following Berings *et al.* (2005), considers how similarities and differences in on-the-job learning among different nurses, in both mental and overt learning activities, contribute to the nurses' awareness of their on-the-job learning style. Further, most literature dealing with on-the-job learning focuses on types of learning content or learning processes only and does not relate them to one another (Collin 2002; den Boer and Hövels 2003; Gerber 1998; Eraut *et al.* 1998; Heikkila and Makinen 2001), whereas this study will pay attention to this relationship.

The results of this study provide suggestions for the development of an instrument that can be used to identify nurses' on-the-job learning styles. This could be used by HRD professionals to improve nurses' on-the-job learning.

Research methods

Twenty highly educated and qualified nurses from different departments of a general academic hospital in the Netherlands were observed during their work activities and afterwards interviewed about their on-the-job learning. These departments included three outpatient departments, six wards and one intensive care unit. The supervisors of the departments selected both novice and experienced nurses for participation in the research project. Six nurses were male and 14 were female. The respondent group included five nurses with leadership and/or development tasks. Table 11.1 shows relevant background information about the interviewees.

The observations were used as a trigger for making learning processes explicit in the interviews (cf. Berings *et al.* 2006) and were also used to question nurses about authentic work and learning situations. Furthermore, the observations were used as a validation method, facilitating the interpretation of the interview data. The nurses were observed for four hours, sometimes in the first part and sometimes in the last part of their shift. Sixteen nurses were observed during their day shift, three during their evening shifts and one during her night shift.

At the end of the shift the nurses were interviewed about their on-the-job learning activities for about 45 minutes. These semi-structured interviews were partly stimulated recall, using the observations, and partly more general. The researcher (the first author) asked questions about the nurses' learning activities after they had completed their initial nursing training. Questions were asked first about the variation in their work activities, followed by questions about what kind of knowledge, skills and attitudes the nurses thought they needed or would need in order to perform these work activities well. The discussion was initially restricted to general comments about these topics and then followed by more specific questions about three learning domains – the technical, social and organizational learning domains. The grounded theory research approach used in this study meant that the literature was not used to specify learning domains and methods of learning in the interview approach. However, this classification into learning domains, which is derived from nursing tasks as specified in job descriptions from different hospitals and from qualification levels for registered nurses in

Table 11.1 Background information about the participating nurses

N	Department	Specific information	Sex	Age	Years of working experience in nursing	in department	Hours per week
1	ward		female	37	16	12.5	24
2	ward		male	43	20	19	32
3	ward	ambition for development tasks	male	31	7	4	36
4	ward		male	34	4	4	36
5	ward	team leader, ambition for development tasks	female	38	15	13.5	32
6	ward		female	25	3	3	30
7	ward		female	42	20	5	24
8	outpatient department	ambition to become a team leader	male				
9	outpatient department		female	38	10	0.5	28
10	ward	development tasks	female	33	10.5	10	28
11	outpatient department	specialized nurse	female	40	8	3	32
12	ward		female	29	2	2	30
13	Intensive Care unit	team leader	female	39	13	5	32
14	outpatient department	development tasks	female	39	17	9	36
15	ward		female	34	10	0.5	32
16	ward		female	23	1	1	36
17	ward		female	44	12	6	22
18	ward	replacement team leader	male	48	22	10	32
19	Intensive Care unit		female	27	3.5	2.5	32
20	Intensive Care unit		male	48	28	13	36

the Netherlands (Commissie Kwalificatiestructuur 1996) was used to stimulate variety in the examples the interviewees used in their answers to the questions. In addition, the interviewees were stimulated to go beyond these three domains by asking more general questions. Finally, the nurses were asked about how they had achieved the required knowledge, skills and attitudes or how they thought they could acquire these in the future. The interviews focused on the nurses' actual learning behaviour, not on their preferences or intentions. The interviews were to establish prepositional (knowledge about), procedural (knowledge of how) and dispositional (values and attitudes) objects of learning (Billett 1993). The interviews were recorded, transcribed and analysed using Atlas-ti and a grounded theory approach.

The grounded theory approach is a qualitative research method that uses a systematic set of procedures to develop an inductively derived, grounded theory about a phenomenon (Strauss and Corbin 1998). The intention in this study was first to map the various on-the-job types of learning content and processes as reported by nurses during the interviews, and then to relate the learning content and learning processes to each other. Relevant categories which illuminated these two basic dimensions or core categories and which fitted the qualitative data had to be developed first. The grounded theory approach is a research method that is aimed expressly at achieving these goals.

This research method was applied as described below. Two core categories or main dimensions were identified in the first stage of analysis: on-the-job learning content and on-the-job-learning processes. Two broad questions based on these core categories were formulated to assist in the analysis of the data: (1) what do nurses, seen from their perspective, learn on the job? and (2) how do they learn on the job?

In the second stage, two coders (the first and second authors) independently read the transcripts of the interviews reflectively with these two core questions in mind, and identified fragments that were related to the two core dimensions. These two coders also assigned open codes to fragments that they believed were relevant. These open codes were intended to indicate the more general or conceptual idea shown in a given fragment. The coders also used memo-writing during this stage of analysis as a means of immediately recording all thoughts and difficulties relating to the coding process, to be used to continue the research process later on. At the end of this first stage the procedure of consensual validation was applied to evaluate the validity of the categories that emerged from the data. In particular, the codes used were compared critically and all the differences in fragments and codes identified between the coders were discussed. Where differences were identified, the relevant parts of the transcripts and memos were read again and discussed extensively in order to evaluate clearly their relevance to the two main dimensions. Where doubt remained about a code it was not incorporated into the final coding scheme.

In the third stage, the relationships of the categories identified in the open coding procedure were explored by making connections between them. In particular, in this stage the interest of the researchers was in exploring the more general categories or code families of the types of on-the-job learning content and on-the-job-learning processes that had been defined as being significant to interviewees, and of which the codes identified in the open coding stage could be seen as subcategories. Consensual validation was sought by critically discussing which particular codes could be assigned to each code family. This procedure resulted in the identification of six main categories of learning content and six main categories of learning processes. Each conceptual model of learning content and the learning processes was then compared with existing theories on these issues in order to validate the findings theoretically.

Data displays (Miles and Huberman 1994) were used to report the results. Cross-case data matrices were used to analyse and conveniently report the main findings for each respondent, and also allowed the relationships between the two core dimensions of this study of on-the-job learning content and on-the-job-learning processes to be described. These findings are presented in the next section.

Findings

What nurses learn on the job

Nurses tended to speak about socio-emotional skills and attitudes, such as contact with patients and colleagues, collaboration, empathic treatment, dealing with aggressive people and diplomacy when answering general questions about the content of their learning. This is in line with previous studies of nurses' views on important skills and behaviour (see Bjørk 1999).

All nurses mentioned technical-practical skills as well, but mostly in a cursory way as if they found this information trivial. Remarkably, none of the nurses mentioned basic nursing care, such as washing patients, distributing food, making beds, etc as a content of on-the-job learning. However, they all mentioned these issues when they explained their task in the first part of the interview. Evidently, they consider that they already possess these skills, having learnt them as part of their initial nursing training.

All the types of learning content nurses mentioned in the interviews are categorized in Table 11.2. This table also includes examples of each subcategory.

The division of tasks into technical tasks, social tasks and organizational tasks as used in the interviews is clearly visible in the categorization, with technical-practical, socio-emotional and organizational skills being found. These categories also cover all the learning content found by den Boer and Hövels (2003) in their recent study of Dutch health care. However, the results allowed these categories to be refined and additional categories were found.

Nurses mentioned many skills and attitudes that they need to learn concerning a proactive attitude to work, such as work ethic (e.g. working fast), decision-making and flexibility. For example, a nurse told us:[1] 'We work under terrible pressure, you need to start at eight and be ready with basic

Table 11.2 Categorization of nurses' on-the-job types of learning content

Categorization of nurses' learning content		Examples
1 technical-practical skills (20)	(a) general skills (5)	computer skills, administrative skills
	(b) nursing skills (20)	technical nursing skills, methodological acting, following protocols
	(c) knowledge of technical nursing (14)	knowledge of pathology, knowledge of medication
	(d) information transfer to patients (11)	information transfer, answering questions, forwarding, writing brochures
	(e) information transfer to colleagues (18)	answering questions, teaching clinical classes, reporting, elaborating protocols
2 socio-emotional skills (20)	(I) with respect to others	
	(a) socio-emotional contact with patients and family	empathy, empathic treatment, patience, dealing with aggressive people, emotional support
	(b) socio-emotional contact with colleagues (11)	emotional support, collaboration, diplomacy, giving feedback
	(c) daring to communicate (17)	assertiveness, honesty, prioritizing, drawing the line; tranquil, enthusiastic
	(d) how you appear to others (4)	
	(II) with respect to oneself (14)	
	(e) personal coping (14)	putting things in perspective, work–family balance, self-confidence, physical position
3 organizational skills (19)	(a) task-management skills (14)	planning, elaborating nursing schemes, structured working
	(b) coordinating tasks (12)	offering guidance, leadership, structuring meetings, performance assessment of team members
	(c) role and environment skills (10)	transcending one's own tasks, understanding different roles in the organization, critical reflection on the organization
4 developmental skills (17)	(a) learning and collecting information (15)	collecting information, asking questions, formulating learning objectives, studying learning opportunities
	(b) self-knowledge (8)	knowing your own weaknesses and strengths, knowing your own boundaries
5 proactive attitude to work (13)		work ethic, decision-making, practical support to colleagues, independent work attitude, flexibility

Note
The number of nurses who mentioned the learning content within each category is shown in brackets ($N = 20$).

care at ten. It just has to be ready then, and therefore you have to help each other.' This category can partly be compared with cultural-normative competences that Onstenk (1997) distinguished as an element of broad professional skills, including involvement, work ethic, motivation and willingness to achieve.

Another additional category found was that of developmental skills. The first subcategory distinguished here, learning and collecting information, can be compared with the category knowledge resources and how to access these distinguished by Eraut *et al.* (1998) and Onstenk's (1997) learning competencies. The second subcategory found in the data, however, is not mentioned in the literature. Aspects of developmental skills, such as knowing your own strengths and weaknesses and knowing your own boundaries, were categorized as self-knowledge. As one nurse said: 'you need to know what your abilities and disabilities are. You need to know your weaknesses precisely.' In on-the-job learning, nurses generally have to formulate their own learning objectives, and therefore self-knowledge is required.

Some noticeable subcategories were also found within the expected categories of socio-emotional and organizational skills. Skills such as socio-emotional contact with patients, their families and colleagues are well documented in the literature (e.g. den Boer and Hövels 2003; Eraut *et al.* 1998; Onstenk 1997). The nurses in this study often mentioned the socio-emotional skills of daring to communicate and how you appear to others, which required emphasis in the categorization used here. For instance, one nurse told us about her interrelationship with doctors:

> I have learnt to behave more independently, now I dare to interfere with their policy if necessary. Like this morning, on their visiting round, when they did not want to make a new appointment with my patient, I tried to behave more forcefully.

Another nurse told us the following about how she appears to others:

> Um, I should be more peaceful. I mean, I can be so active and full of energy that I may seem chaotic. But I am usually not chaotic, just fast, and that may seem very careless to other people.

Nurses also mentioned skills and attitudes that help them to remain mentally healthy in their job. These socio-emotional skills with respect to themselves, skills for coping personally, included for example, putting things in perspective and maintaining an appropriate work–family balance. For instance, a nurse told us:

> We have patients with very poor prognoses, who will die within a year..., then you need to behave lightly, telling yourself yes, it is grave today, but you have had major achievements.

As well as aspects of organizational skills that are common in the literature such as task-management skills and coordinating tasks, an additional category, role and environment skills, was found which can be compared with a competence that Mansfield (1991) found and described as understanding, working in and using the physical, organizational and cultural environment. Nurses in this study mentioned, for example, transcending one's own tasks and understanding different roles in the organization. For example, a nurse noted:

> You need to learn about the system here. I mean, there is a cluster and within this cluster are different departments; who is responsible for what, you need to know this just so that you can mention something.

How nurses learn on the job

The interviewees mentioned many ways in which they had learnt, or are still learning, in their job since they had graduated from nursing school. All these ways of learning are categorized in Table 11.3.

When the nurses were asked about how they had learnt their learning content, in general they put most emphasis on a phenomenon they call 'experience.' They all seemed to feel that experience is the most significant factor of learning on-the-job. Further questioning revealed that this concept covered a large range of learning processes, such as observing others, repeating successful behaviour, averting unsuccessful behaviour and practising. In fact, except for the categories checking media, attending information meetings and taking courses, all categories shown in Table 11.3 were mentioned in this respect. The subcategory work experience used in our categorization is much less well defined and therefore requires clarification. This category means learning through work activities and experiencing whether these activities are performed well or not well. Sometimes nurses did not manage to specify what they meant by experience, as one nurse remarked when asked to explain what she meant:

> I notice progression in my work, but I can't say how and why it has taken place. I suppose I've just carried on with my job and therefore been able to pick up new things.

The categorization derived from the data shows many similarities, but also differences, with categorizations found in the literature (e.g. Bolhuis 2000; Gerber 1998; Heikkila and Makinen 2001; den Boer and Hövels 2003; Collin 2002; Koopmans *et al.* 2006). Bolhuis (2000), for example, distinguishes learning by direct experience, learning by social interaction, learning by theory and learning by reflection. Her first type, learning by direct experience, resembles the first two categories used here, namely learning by performing one's regular job and learning by applying something new in the

Table 11.3 Categorization of nurses' ways of learning on the job

Categorization of nurses' learning processes		Examples
1 learning by doing one's regular job (20)	(a) work-experience (18)	learning by doing, learning from mistakes
	(b) contact with patients and	empathy, observing, conversation with patients and family (12)
	(c) observing colleagues (13)	learning from negative or positive colleague behaviour (nurses, doctors or colleagues in other disciplines)
	(d) practising (7)	practising, trying out, skills dummy
	(e) helping others with learning (12)	preparing and teaching clinical classes, answering colleagues' questions, student supervision
2 learning by applying something new in the job (12)	(a) broadening tasks (4)	doing other peoples' jobs, searching for new situations
	(b) job rotation (10)	working in different departments, temporarily doing something else's job in one's own department
3 learning by social interaction with colleagues (20)	(a) asking questions (17)	asking questions in or outside one's own department or organization of nursing colleagues, students, doctors or colleagues in other disciplines
	(b) asking for feedback (9)	asking for feedback from nursing colleagues, students or colleagues in other disciplines
	(c) obtaining feedback (13)	obtaining feedback from nursing colleagues, students, patients, doctors or colleagues in other disciplines
	(d) exchanging knowledge and experience (17)	brainstorming together, conferring, casuistry meetings, patient meetings, team meetings
4 learning by theory or supervision (19)	(a) checking media (18)	books, specialist journals, the Internet, protocols (on the intranet)
	(b) visiting information meetings (15)	symposiums, congresses, clinical classes
	(c) taking courses (15)	courses, workshops, training
	(d) direct supervision (15)	practising with supervision, supervision during introduction, annual performance assessment interviews
5 learning by thinking about work experiences (16)	(a) structuring one's thoughts (12)	reasoning, logical thinking, creating sttep-by-step plans, writing down
	(b) reflection (16)	retrospective, concurrent and prospective, at home or at work
5 learning through life outside work (6)	(a) life-experience (6)	having children, death in the family, personal conversations

Note
The number of nurses who mentioned the learning processes within each category is shown in brackets ($N = 20$).

job, which are also distinguished by Koopmans *et al.* (2006) and Collin (2002). These categories also resemble Heikkila and Makinen's (2001) category learning by doing/learning in action, which they found in their study on nurses and describe as learning from experience in continuously changing work environments.

The third category, learning by social interaction with colleagues, is related to but more specific than Bolhuis' (2000) second type of learning, social interactions. In contrast to Bolhuis (2000) and Heikkila and Makinen (2001), social interaction with patients is regarded here as a subcategory of the first main category, learning by doing one's regular job. Therefore, the category of social interaction with colleagues, which includes nursing colleagues, students, doctors or colleagues from other disciplines, is specified. This division resembles Collin (2002). The fourth category, learning by theory or supervision, is related to Bolhuis's (2000) category of learning by theory, but the term learning by supervision is added explicitly. Learning by theory includes checking media, attending information meetings and taking courses. The last two subcategories are particularly closely related to learning by supervision. In all situations another person is explicitly helping with the learning process. Koopmans *et al.* (2006) combined learning by social interaction with colleagues and learning by theory or guidance into two other categories: information seeking and exchanging information, based on whether the information exchange was one-way or two-way. Collin (2002) distinguishes learning through formal education only and Heikkila and Makinen (2001) distinguished searching for information, organized training and social interaction among their categories. The label of their first category overlaps the latter two and is therefore problematical.

The fifth category, learning by thinking about working experiences, is related to Bolhuis' (2000) and Heikkila and Makinen's (2001) category of learning by reflection and the retrospective part of reflection resembles Collin's (2002) learning through evaluating work experiences. Moreover, structuring one's thoughts was explicitly added as a subcategory. This category was mentioned by twelve of the interviewees and seemed an important way of learning on the job. For example, a nurse noted:

> Sometimes I just need to write down a step-by-step plan of all medical caring activities I need to undertake with a specific patient.

Even though there are many similarities between the findings of this study and the findings of den Boer and Hövels (2002) and Gerber (1998), their categorizations were not used in the above comparison since they appear to be rather random and are not very well organized, as is the case with many categorizations in this field in the literature. Neither their categorizations nor the categorizations that were explicitly compared with the categorization used in this study included the sixth category found here, that of learning through life outside work. This category was mentioned by six of the interviewees, who regarded this way of learning as a significant contribution to learning related to their job. For example, a nurse remarked:

> I became more emotional when I became a father, which made it easier to show empathy to patients. I don't mean tears and crying, but I do dare to show compassion. Before I had children I kept more of a distance.

This category is similar to the category of life outside work that Eraut *et al.* (1998) distinguish and, to some extent, Collin's (2002) category of learning from contexts outside work, but the latter only includes subcategories that are still very much related to work contexts.

The relationship between what and how nurses learn

Tables 11.4 and 11.5 show the relationship between the type of learning content and the learning processes. In the interviews, nurses mentioned many learning processes in a general way, without relation to a specific learning content. All examples of learning processes that the interviewees related to a specific learning content are summarized in the tables. Table 11.4 shows the relationship for all subcategories of learning processes and Table 11.5 summarizes the relationship for the main categories. Note that the figures given in the subcategories of Table 11.4 are not identical with those given in Table 11.5, since the figures show the number of nurses that mentioned certain relationships and many nurses mentioned more than one.

Nurses believe that they learn content in all the different main categories distinguished in this study, except the proactive work attitude, through work experience and reflection. The interviewees did not explain how they learnt skills that promote a proactive work attitude at all.

Technical-practical skills are learnt by all methods of learning distinguished in this study. It is remarkable that despite the fact that the interviewees only cursorily mentioned acquiring skills in a technical-practical learning content, they explained in detail how they learnt these skills. These skills are probably learnt more consciously than others. Socio-emotional skills with respect to others are also learnt by all the learning methods distinguished, except for visiting information meetings. The ways of learning other types of content are less varied.

Table 11.6 shows the different combinations of learning content and learning processes for the individual nurses. Many differences between the individual nurses can be seen in this overview. Some of the nurses show similar patterns of combinations of learning content and learning processes, but it is not immediately clear what causes these similarities. However, the findings in the table also show that substantial variation in nurses' on-the-job learning content and processes exists. A proactive attitude to work has been left out of the table since none of the nurses mentioned how they had been learning a proactive attitude to work.

Table 11.4 The relationship between what and how nurses learn for the main categories in 'what' and the subcategories in 'how' nurses learn

How / What		(1) doing one's regular job					(2) applying something new in the job		(3) social interaction with colleagues				(4) theory or supervision				(5) thinking about work experiences		(6) life outside work
		a	b	c	d	e	a	b	a	b	c	d	a	b	c	d	a	b	a
1 technical-practical		11	7	7	5	6	3	5	16	3	2	9	17	9	11	12	4	9	1
2 socio-emotional	I	6	7	8	1	2	1	1	6	2	4	10	3	0	4	4	12	7	5
	II	2	0	0	0	0	2	0	0	0	0	0	0	0	1	3	0	4	2
3 organizational		8	0	4	0	2	0	3	2	1	3	4	1	1	3	4	4	5	0
4 development		3	0	0	0	3	0	0	1	0	1	1	0	0	0	3	1	2	0
5 proactive work attitude		0	0	0	0	0	0	0	0	0	0	0	0	0	0	0	0	0	0

Note
Each cell shows the number of nurses that mentioned the particular relationship ($N = 20$). The headings in the rows correspond with those used in Table 11.2 and the headings in the columns correspond with those used in Table 11.3.

Table 11.5 The relationship between what and how nurses learn for the main categories

How What		(1) doing one's regular job	(2) applying something new in the job	(3) social interaction with colleagues	(4) theory or supervision	(5) thinking about work experiences	(6) life outside work
1 technical-practical		19	7	17	19	10	1
2 socio-	I	14	2	12	8	7	5
emotional	II	2	2	0	4	4	2
3 organizational		12	3	6	7	7	0
4 development		5	0	2	4	3	0
5 proactive work attitude		0	0	0	0	0	0

Note
Each cell shows the number of nurses that mentioned the particular relationship ($N = 20$).

Interpretations, conclusions and critical analysis

The aim of this study was to investigate what and how nurses, seen from their perspective, learn on the job and the relationship between these two phenomena. Six main categories and 16 subcategories of nurses' learning content (what) and six main categories and 18 subcategories of nurses' learning processes (how) were found (see Tables 11.2 and 11.3). The categories can be seen as hierarchically ordered to some extent, but this should be regarded as tentative only since it was not possible to construct a strictly hierarchical categorization (see also Collin 2002).

The findings were compared with categorizations in the literature, with some resemblances, but also some differences, being found. The categorization used here seems the most complete and most refined and would appear to overcome some of the overlap problems in existing categorizations. Further, in contrast to other studies, the analyses show the relationship between what and how nurses learn. Many similarities, but also many differences, were found between individual nurses; which supports the existence of different on-the-job learning styles within the nursing profession.

Qualitative research methods, which are often criticized in the literature for their lack of validity and reliability controls, were used in this study. However, many methods were used for this purpose. The categorizations were compared with categorizations described in the literature for the purposes of theoretical validation. Interpretative validity was improved by making observations prior to the interviews and by using two coders who compared and reflected on their independent findings. This procedure also improved the inter-coder reliability. Memo-writing as a procedure was used

Table 11.6 The relationship between what and how nurses learn for individual nurses

Nurse	Technical-practical skills						Socio-emotional skills												Organizational skills						Developmental skills					
							With respect to others						With respect to oneself																	
	1	2	3	4	5	6	1	2	3	4	5	6	1	2	3	4	5	6	1	2	3	4	5	6	1	2	3	4	5	6
1	x	x	x	x			x																				x			
2	x		x	x					x										x		x		x						x	
3		x		x	x		x		x								x					x	x							
4	x		x	x	x		x		x																				x	
5	x		x	x	x		x												x		x	x								
6	x		x	x			x		x			x		x		x	x	x										x		
7							x		x			x				x		x												
8	x	x	x	x			x		x	x	x								x	x	x		x					x		
9	x		x	x	x		x												x											
10	x	x	x	x	x		x		x	x									x	x	x	x	x				x			
11	x		x	x	x	x		x	x				x				x		x	x	x	x	x		x					
12	x		x	x	x			x	x	x									x		x		x		x				x	
13	x	x	x	x	x		x		x	x	x								x	x										
14	x		x	x	x					x	x									x										
15	x		x	x	x					x	x								x			x								
16	x	x	x	x			x		x	x	x					x			x	x	x	x	x		x			x		
17	x		x	x			x		x		x	x		x					x			x			x					
18	x			x						x			x				x													
19	x	x	x	x			x				x	x				x			x						x			x		
20	x	x	x	x			x					x																		
Total	19	7	17	19	10	1	14	2	12	8	7	5	2	2	0	4	4	2	12	6	7	7	7	0	5	0	2	4	3	0

Note
Each cell shows whether (x) or not ( ) the individual nurses mentioned the particular relationship (N = 20). The headings in the columns correspond with those used for the main categories in Table 11.3. The headings in the rows correspond with those used for the nurses in Table 11.1.

to continue the research process later on. Finally, for content validation, several nurses and researchers in the field of HRD were asked if they recognized the categorization used here and their comments confirmed the categorization used.

In future, it would be helpful to ask the interviewees to read the researchers' interpretations and ask them if they recognize themselves in the descriptions. Further, to improve external validity it would be valuable to confirm the findings in different hospitals. The nurses in this study work in different departments in the same, large, academic hospital. It is not expected that many differences would be found in other hospitals, except for, possibly, the number of different learning processes used by the individual nurses. There may well be more possibilities for learning in academic hospitals than in general hospitals.

The data collection technique used in this study had a number of limitations. Although a broad variety of types of learning content and processes of nurses were identified, it is still questionable whether all of them were found. It is conceivable that the interviewees did not remember the most salient examples of learning content and processes (Koopmans *et al.* 2006). Therefore, they might not have mentioned those that hardly ever occur or the ones that occur so often that they have become self-evident. Although the interview strategy was aimed at deriving both explicit and implicit learning activities, it is still conceivable that some activities have not been made explicit. Leading questions are needed to reveal implicit learning activities, but they must be used very carefully since they must not influence the results of the study. Therefore, such questions were not used very extensively. It should be noted, therefore, that if a nurse has not mentioned a specific learning content or process this does not mean that they do not take place. This means that the figures showing how many nurses have mentioned particular types of learning content and processes in the categorization (Tables 11.2 and 11.3) should be viewed with caution.

The figures shown in Tables 11.4, 11.5 and 11.6 should also be viewed with a great deal of caution. In the interviews, the nurses were first asked what they had learnt and later on how they had learnt this knowledge, these skills or this approach. Since a referral strategy was not used, many learning processes (how) were mentioned in a general way and were not always related back to specific learning content. Therefore, not all the information about the types of learning content and processes could be used in the analysis of the relationship between these two concepts. In particular, the unexpected categories of personal coping, developmental skills and proactive work attitude suffered from this defect in the design of the interview. For example, Tables 11.4, 11.5 and 11.6 do not show any relationship with learning processes for the category of proactive work attitude.

Finally, it should be noted that the observations made prior to the interviews were not as useful as expected for stimulated recall during the interviews. The nurses referred to episodes during the observation period several times during the interviews, which was very useful, but references made by the interviewer to certain episodes were not always remembered. Nevertheless, the observations were also very helpful for the interpretation and validation of the interview data, and for the creation of a confidential atmosphere which probably resulted in increased data being obtained, so that the observations can still be regarded as forming a valuable component of this study.

Key learning points

- There are six main categories of nurses' learning content: technical-practical skills, socio-emotional skills with respect to others and with respect to oneself, organizational skills, developmental skills and a proactive attitude to work.
- There are six main categories of nurses' learning process: learning by doing one's regular job, learning by applying something new in the job, learning by social interaction with colleagues, learning by theory or guidance, learning by thinking about work experiences and learning through life outside work.
- There are many differences between individual nurses.
- The results of this study provide more insight into nurses' on-the-job learning processes and outcomes and can offer opportunities for research into these phenomena in other professions.
- This study provides valuable insight in nurses' overt learning processes and offers supportive information on mental learning processes. However, the latter needs to be further explored, using more intensively structured interviews.
- It has been possible to explicate the existing multi-dimensionality of the types of learning content and learning processes as reported by nurses by grounding our classification in the data. This will presumably allow an encompassing structured instrument for identifying nurses' learning styles to be constructed, which does justice to the complexity and diversity of on-the-job learning by nurses. HRD professionals can use such an instrument to improve nurses' on-the-job learning.
- A better understanding of the differences between nurses needs more intensively structured data collection techniques. Understanding the differences between nurses can facilitate nurses' awareness of their on-the-job learning styles and consequently help them to improve their on-the-job learning.

Note

1 The interviews were conducted in Dutch. The examples were translated into English for use in this paper.

References

Allinson, C.W. and Hayes, J. (1996) 'The cognitive style index: a measure of intuition-analysis for organisational research,' *Journal of Management Studies* 33: 119–135.

Baars-van Moorsel, M. (2003) 'Leerklimaat: De Culturele Dimensie van Leren in Organisaties. [Learning Climate: The Cultural Dimension of Learning in Organisations],' PhD Thesis, Tilburg University, Delft, The Netherlands: Eburon.

Berings, M.G.M.C., Doornbos, A.J. and Simons, P.R.J. (2006) 'Methodological practices in on-the-job learning research,' *Human Resource Development International* 9(3): 333–363.

Berings, M.G.M.C., Poell, R.F. and Simons, P.R.J. (2005) 'Conceptualizing on-the-job learning styles,' *Human Resource Development Review* 4(4): 373–400.

Billett, S.R. (1993) 'Authencity and a culture of practice,' *Australian and New Zealand Journal of Vocational Educational Research* 2: 1–29.

Bjørk, I.T. (1999) 'What constitutes a nursing practical skill?' *Western Journal of Nursing Research* 21: 51–70.

den Boer, P. and Hövels, B. (2003) *Leer- en Loopbaanmogelijkheden in de Zorgsector {Learning and Career Possibilities in Health Care} (OSA Publicatie ZW41)*, Tilburg, The Netherlands: OSA.

Bolhuis, S. (2000) *Naar Zelfstandig Leren: Wat Doen en Denken Docenten? {Towards Self-directed Learning: What do Teachers Do and Think?}*. Leuven, Belgium: Garant.

Clark, J. (2001) Academisch Medisch Centrum, May 8th 2001, Anna Reyvaanlezing, *{Anna Reyvaan Lecture}*, Amsterdam, The Netherlands.

Collin, K. (2002) 'Development engineers' conceptions of learning at work,' *Studies in Continuing Education* 24: 133–152.

Commissie Kwalificatiestructuur (1996) *Gekwalificeerd voor de Toekomst: Kwalificatiestructuur en Eindtermen voor Verpleging en Verzorging. {Qualified for Future: Qualification Structure and Final Terms for Nursing Care}*. Zoetermeer, The Netherlands: Ministerie van VWS en OC&W, Hageman BV.

Dik, M.M. and van Splunder, R. (2002) 'Employability Leeft Onvoldoende in Nederland. [Concern of Employability in the Netherlands is Low],' *Tijdschrift voor Arbeidsvraagstukken* 18.

Eliens, A.M. and Strijbol, N.C.M. (2001) 'Naar een Toekomst voor Verpleegkundigen. [Towards a Future for Nurses],' in H.P.J.M. Habets (ed.) *Inspiratie. Jaarboek Verpleegkunde 2001*, Dwingelo, The Netherlands: Kavanah.

Eraut, M., Alderton, J., Cole, G. and Senker, P. (1998) *Development of Knowledge and Skills in Employment*, East Sussex, UK: University of Sussex.

Gerber, R. (1998) 'How do workers learn in their work,' *The Learning Organization* 5: 168–175.

Heikkila, K. and Makinen, L. (2001) 'Different ways of learning at work,' *Proceedings of the 2nd International Conference on Researching Work and Learning*, pp. 406–413, Calgary, Canada: University of Calgary.

Koopmans, H., Doornbos, A.J. and Van Eekelen, I.M. (2006) 'Learning in interactive work situations: it takes two to tango; why not invite both partners to dance?' *Human Resource Development Quarterly* 17(2): 135–158.

Mansfield, R. (1991) 'Deriving standards of competence,' in E. Fennel (ed.) *Development of Assessable Standards for National Certification*, London, UK: Department for Education and Employment.

Miles, M.B. and Huberman, A.M. (1994) *Qualitative Data Analysis: An Expanded Sourcebook*, Thousand Oaks, CA: Sage Publications.

Mumford, A. (1995) *Effective Learning*, London, UK: Institute of Personnel and Development.

Onstenk, J. (1997) *Lerend Leren Werken: Brede Vakbekwaamheid en de Integratie van Leren, Werken en Innoveren. {Learning to Work in a Learning Way: Broad Occupational Competence and the Integration of Learning, Working and Innovating}*, PhD Thesis, Katholieke Universiteit Nijmegen, Delft, The Netherlands: Eburon.

Strauss, A.L. and Corbin, J. (1998) *Basics of Qualitative Research: Techniques and Procedures for Developing Grounded Theory*, Thousand Oaks, CA: Sage Publications.

Tannenbaum, S.I. (1997) 'Enhancing continuous learning: diagnostic findings from multiple companies,' *Human Resource Management* 36: 437–452.

van Woerkom, M. (2003) 'Critical reflection at work: bridging individual and organisational learning,' PhD Thesis, Enschede, The Netherlands: Twente University.

12 Workplace learning in UK hospices

Nicholas Clarke

Aims

This chapter discusses the significance of workplace learning for healthcare organizations and draws upon research examining workplace learning in UK hospices to illustrate some of the key issues affecting healthcare organizations adopting more workplace-oriented learning approaches. Although hospices are not technically part of the public sector NHS (they are normally considered part of the voluntary sector in the UK) they do nonetheless employ both medical and nursing staff and often work closely with NHS organizations in providing specialist palliative care services. Specifically, the chapter aims to:

1   Identify the current policy context influencing the drive towards a greater use of workplace learning methods within healthcare organizations.
2   Review some of the key findings from research that has examined the significance of workplace learning within healthcare, and specifically in relation to caring for the dying.
3   Present and discuss findings from a national survey examining the utilization of workplace learning within UK hospices identifying the range of methods used and factors influencing the use of workplace learning within these healthcare environments.
4   Analyse findings from qualitative data obtained following the survey to identify how and in what ways research and practice in workplace learning can improve in order to enhance the use of workplace learning within healthcare settings.

Introduction

At both the levels of policy and practice there has been significant support for the concepts associated with workplace learning within the healthcare field in the UK. Indeed it has been closely associated both with the government's modernization agenda (DoH 1999; 2000a, b; 2001) and drives towards clinical excellence (DoH 1999). As a result it now occupies a central part of the NHS lifelong learning strategy (DoH 2001). This chapter examines the significance of workplace learning for healthcare staff and particularly as it relates to staff working in UK hospices. Drawing upon both survey and follow up qualitative data, the significance of workplace learning and also issues influencing the use of workplace learning methods are identified. Some of the key findings that emerged from the study were the significant role that workplace learning methods play for developing the professional skills and knowledge required for caring for the dying. However important issues regarding the need to develop the evidence-base of workplace learning were raised as chief concerns as to whether workplace learning methods would be given priority within these healthcare settings. These findings are discussed and considerations for developing a more evidence-based agenda within workplace learning research identified.

Background to the study: the empirical context

Perhaps one of the most important drivers of HR policy within healthcare in Britain, has been the recognition that workplace learning is more effective at providing healthcare staff with the types of skills and knowledge required for working in today's demanding work environments (DoH 2001). In particular, that workplace learning is likely to facilitate more effective problem solving and decision-making in relation to clinical matters (Clarke and Wilcoxson 2001; David *et al.* 2003), and that through greater reflection on practice and team-based learning, clinical skills are better acquired. Of most significance in this respect, research continues to show that formal learning activities do not compensate for that gained through workplace learning (Eraut *et al.* 1998; Yuen 1991; White *et al.* 1998; King 1991). Specifically, within hospices and specialist palliative care in the UK, training, learning and development has been recognized as critical to ensuring good quality service provision as well as supporting the philosophical values and goals of the hospice movement (MacLeod 1994). Importantly, a number of studies have identified the importance of workplace learning methods as occupying a central role in providing specialist palliative care and dealing with issues associated with terminal illness. MacLeod (2001) for example identified the limitations associated with formal medical education for preparing doctors for the task of caring for someone dying, and that this was only possible through developing close relationships and learning on the job from people who are dying themselves. Lloyd-Williams (2002) also identified the emphasis on experiential learning within hospice environments along with the central role played by doctor's informal networks both for support and learning. In relation to nursing, Rosser and King (2003) identified the significant part played by mentoring in ensuring the transition of qualified nurses to hospice nursing, particularly in dealing with the variety of emotional responses to death and dying and the development of specialist palliative care knowledge and skills. Jones (2003) too has identified the importance of group clinical supervision, or work discussion groups as providing hospice nurses with a more effective format for exploring issues concerning professional practice, learning from each other, and, importantly, as a mechanism for containing anxiety.

The theoretical context

For many healthcare practitioners the notion of workplace learning may at first sight be very familiar, especially if it is assumed to be simply another term for learning on the job. Indeed, workplace learning methods that combine reflection on practice have long been seen as key to the development of professional competence within the healthcare professions. Perhaps chief amongst these include the notion of clinical supervision as a cornerstone of effective professional practice and the use of preceptorship within nursing has been commonplace for some time. Significant theoretical developments regarding the nature of learning in organizations increasingly supported by empirical research, however, are enabling us to better understand the complex processes that might be associated with workplace learning. Particularly important in this respect have been contributions from theorists who perceive learning not merely as something singularly associated with the individual, but recognize learning as arising from the social context in which it takes place (Lave and Wenger 1991; Brown and Duguid 1991; Blackler 1995). This perspective sees learning as occurring as a result of participation in groups or networks of practitioners. It is only through identifying with, and being part of these groups or networks, combined with engaging in professional practice, that any meaningful learning can be gained. Knowledge then only has significant meaning for healthcare professionals in the context of their own professional practice (Eraut *et al.* 1998). From this perspective, learning is something that is most effective when it takes place simultaneously with performing the job itself, and where opportunities exist for making sense of this learning within professional networks or teams. In this sense, learning is 'situated' in the context of professional practice (Lave and Wenger 1991; Wenger 1998). As Billett (1999) states:

> ...learning is structured by the everyday activities and goals of the workplace. Given that these activities are necessarily important to the workplace, these learning experiences and their outcomes cannot be considered to be incidental, ad hoc or informal. Rather, they are authentic and rich opportunities to reinforce and extend individuals' knowledge. Importantly, workplaces also provide ongoing direct and indirect guidance which can assist learning in ways quite different from what happens in educational settings.
>
> (Billet 1999: 151–152)

Supporting these important insights into the nature of learning has been a number of studies specifically within healthcare settings. One particular study, for example, that undertook a qualitative analysis of the knowledge used by general practitioners during their consultations, showed how GPs reached their clinical decisions based on information from four different sources: the medical literature, their colleagues, the patient and his or her family, and the doctor's own memory and experience. Their learning was situated within the specific consultation that took place and significantly influenced by the social context (Robinson and Heywood 2000). So too in relation to nursing, Benner (1984) some while ago suggested that knowledge is highly embedded in the work practices of nurses. The implications are that the most significant form of learning that takes place is that which occurs as a result of undertaking the job itself and through interaction with peers and colleagues. Empirical support has been found for precisely this by Eraut and his colleagues (Eraut *et al.* 1998). Other studies too in healthcare, are providing insights into the highly contextual nature of learning that takes place, in particular the extent to which it is influenced by the specific socio-cultural circumstances in which it occurs (Dowie 1996; Hunter 1991; Robinson *et al.* 2003; Schmidt *et al.* 1990). These theoretical and empirical developments draw our attention not only to the importance of providing opportunities for learning on the job, which may be familiar to many healthcare staff; far more than that, they suggest we need to: (1) consider how social interactions, particularly through participation in teams and networks, can best be supported to maximize learning; and (2) focus just as much on how the social or workplace environment influences whether learning occurs or is effective. As healthcare professionals increasingly view themselves as each part of key networks responsible for the delivery of different components of their job, these networks need to be recognized as important and integral sites for learning (Conner 2001). Professionals in these networks are types of learning communities or what are often referred to as 'communities of practice' (Lave and Wenger 1991). It is within the context of these social arrangements that healthcare practitioners make sense of their knowledge and enact it, or use it in the context of the work practice that has meaning to them. Through a better understanding of how learning takes place in such networks, we can also gain new insights into how to maximize clinical effectiveness. In relation to the work environment, we need to understand far more how different workplace conditions influence the learning that takes place there, and studies are beginning to highlight how particular aspects of the work environment may actually support or hinder workplace learning (Clarke 2005a; White *et al.* 1998).

There are a number of implications that arise from these developments in terms of how workplace learning needs to be developed and supported. First, there are responsibilities on managers and the organization for providing effective mechanisms and conditions to support ongoing learning (Flanagan *et al.* 2000). These include, for example, organizational support for effective teamwork, senior management leadership for learning and the provision of appropriate resources (Wilson-Barnett *et al.* 1998). Second they require an understanding of how the work environment, (including organizational culture, systems, policies and procedures) is (a) inextricably linked to learning and (b) is highly influential on determining the quality of learning that takes place (Matthews and Candy 1999). Recently for example, White *et al.* (2000) investigated the impact of a policy of managed care on nurses' informal learning in a US health management organization, and found that their need for informal learning increased as a result of this service change. Based on nine group interviews involving nurses working in both community and hospital based settings, they demonstrated the close relationship between work design and the need for particular types of learning. Dovey (2002) has also provided some key insights in his case study examining work-based learning partnerships in the South African state health sector. He argues the importance of healthcare managers as coaches that are able to:

> mediate power across hierarchical barriers and facilitate networks that traverse work roles and narrow partisan interests, in focusing the collective effort on the attainment of shared interests as articulated in the organizational mission.
>
> (Dovey 2002: 521)

His work is important in showing how workplace learning and, in particular, factors that support it – such as collaborative working, empowerment and leaders adopting the roles of coaches – were able to have a significant impact on a range of clinical problem areas within district health management teams. Yet although there is a growing body of research demonstrating the importance of workplace learning in healthcare, there still remains a dominant focus on formal education and training within much of the healthcare field in the UK (Audit Commission 2001; Dowsell *et al.* 1998). Furthermore, despite the exhortations to adopt workplace learning strategies within British healthcare policy guidance within the past few years, we actually know very little about the extent to which such approaches are being adopted by healthcare organizations. Nor indeed what sorts of factors may either assist or impede their use or effectiveness within these settings. This chapter provides some insights into these questions as they relate specifically to healthcare staff working in hospices within the UK. A study was undertaken between 2003–04, utilizing both survey and follow up qualitative data to investigate (a) the use of workplace learning methods within these healthcare settings (b) factors associated with their effectiveness, and (c) issues influencing the shift towards a greater use of workplace learning by healthcare professionals and organizations. In addition to providing new data regarding workplace learning in these highly specialized healthcare organizations, the study has enabled the particular perspectives from hospice staff regarding this approach to staff development to be identified. This chapter therefore adds an important dimension to our understanding of how best to support workplace learning within healthcare by considering the views of healthcare professionals themselves. The most significant of these concern the need for healthcare professionals to be presented with far more evidence regarding the value of workplace learning over more traditional forms of education and training. Implications of this are discussed in relation to the different issues and demands raised by continuing professional education and development and workplace learning. Finally recommendations are put forward as to how workplace learning might be integrated with a more evidence-based approach to employee development.

The research study

The overall aims of the study were:

1 To investigate the extent to which hospices utilize different sources of workplace learning and factors that are associated with the use of these sources.
2 To identify the extent to which hospices assess either formal or informal learning in their organizations.
3 To examine the importance of particular organizational factors in supporting the assessment of informal learning in hospices.
4 To examine how different aspects of a hospice's learning climate are related to differing learning outcomes.

Both survey and follow-up qualitative data were obtained as part of the study. Hospices were chosen since they are smaller, self contained organizations with comparatively more centralized training and education functions. This both facilitated data collection and suggested that respondents were more likely to possess a more accurate knowledge of employee development systems within the whole organization. The aim of the survey was to collect data on the extent of workplace learning and the characteristics of the training and development infrastructure present. A total of 161 questionnaires were sent to hospices throughout Britain, together with a covering letter explaining the aims of the research and a guarantee of anonymity. One hundred and twenty questionnaires were returned; a response rate of 74 per cent. Questionnaires were addressed to either the chief executive or the director of nursing requesting that a member of the senior management team with either responsibility for, or knowledge of, training and development within the organization respond. Of those completing the questionnaire, 37.5 per cent (45) were nursing directors, 27.5 per cent (33) were chief executives, 4.2 per cent (5) were medical directors, 10 per cent (12) were HR personnel and 21 per cent (25) categorized themselves as other (such as education/training specialists). Twelve per cent (14) were male and 88 per cent (105) were female. The mean age of respondents was 47 (SD 8.36).

Qualitative data

Following analysis of the survey results, letters were sent again to all 161 hospices, containing a brief summary of the findings and an invitation to attend a half-day workshops to discuss the findings. The workshop took place 12 months after the survey data were collected. Twenty-two participants from 20 different hospices took part. Of these, 67 per cent (14) were involved in education/training, 27 per cent (6) were clinical nurse specialists, and 6 per cent (2) identified themselves as managers. The workshops took the form of a presentation of the survey findings followed by a two and a half hour discussion facilitated by the author. The format of the discussion was non-directive and based on a loose structure that had three headings to guide the interaction (Miles and Huberman 1984). These were (1) how do these findings relate to participants' understanding of their own organizations? (2) How can the survey findings be explained? (3) Where should research be directed next? The aim was for the discussion to be as free-flowing as possible with the facilitator making as little intervention as possible in order to minimize bias. The workshops were videotaped and the discussions subsequently transcribed. The data were initially analysed by reading through the whole transcripts identifying common themes and looking for areas where there was agreement between participants. These themes then formed the initial basis for coding excerpts of conversations which were then revised further through an ongoing iterative process as further sub-themes and commonalities were identified (Miles and Huberman 1984). Throughout the workshop discussion, verification of meaning was sought by the researcher where there seemed to be common agreement, in order to check understanding. Shorthand notes were also taken by a second researcher who summarized the key points that had emerged at the end of the workshop, again to maximize the trustworthiness of the data through verification (Swanson *et al.* 1997).

Key findings

The findings from the study presented here relate to data collected that addressed the first aim of the research study – examining the use of workplace learning methods within hospices and factors that influence the use of these methods. Other key findings from the research study that address additional aims can be found elsewhere (Clarke 2004, 2005).

Findings from the survey suggested the widespread use of workplace learning methods within hospices. Table 12.1 shows the results when survey respondents were asked to rate the extent to which they relied on each of the 12 different sources of employee development. Significantly, when the range of different methods of workplace learning were taken together as a whole, the survey found a greater reliance on workplace learning methods for staff development compared to more formal learning methods, such as training and education programmes. A mean score of 68 per cent (SD 14.31) was

Table 12.1 Major sources of learning (employee development) in hospices

Source of learning	Mean (%)	SD
Training	16.99	8.45
Education	13.55	6.77
Supervision	12.24	8.07
Team activities	10.70	4.75
Mentoring	9.05	4.75
Observation	8.54	4.82
Learning forums	6.92	5.53
Self-directed	6.82	3.77
Special projects	5.78	4.00
Job shadowing	4.12	3.54
Trial and error	2.97	3.28
Job rotation	2.66	3.46

Note
$N = 120$.

obtained for the overall use of workplace learning methods. However, hospices still relied considerably on formal education and training programmes as the most important individual sources of learning that are drawn upon in staff development. This would seem to be reinforced by the finding that staff received significant support to attend off-the-job training and education activities. Here, the survey found that 66 per cent of staff received leave to attend five or more days off-the-job staff development and 19 per cent received seven days or more.

Factors associated with the use of workplace learning

The role of HR policies to support workplace learning?

Within much of the HRD literature there has been an emphasis on the development of effective HR policies and procedures to support informal and formal learning. However, it is not known whether the presence of such policies and procedures are associated with the use of workplace learning within organizations. The survey asked respondents to indicate the extent to which particular HR policies were present in hospices. The study found positive support for the widespread presence of many of the policies examined.

Specifically, 98 per cent (117) of those surveyed indicated they had organization-wide staff appraisal, and 81 per cent (86) utilized staff personal development plans. Seventy-six per cent (81) indicated that they possessed a training and development policy and 70 per cent (66) stated that they had an organization-wide training and development strategy. Ninety-seven per cent (102) also had a policy on providing paid study leave for staff. Staff to specifically support policy implementation were also common, with 73 per cent (77) stating that a senior manager had responsibility for employee development and 66 per cent (70) indicating that they employed training/education staff. The findings also indicated that 52 per cent (55) of those surveyed incorporated workplace learning methods within their overall training and development policy. A number of statistical analyses were undertaken to determine whether any of these HR policies were associated with the use of workplace learning methods (Clarke 2006b). Only the presence of training staff in the organization was found to be significant in relation to the use of workplace learning methods, and this was found to be negatively associated with it. A number of possible explanations might be put forward to account for this. First, it may well be that the absence of training staff in hospices may mean that these organizations rely far more on the use of informal learning in order to meet their developmental needs. Alternatively, it might reflect a predilection on behalf of training staff to meet learning needs through formalized learning methods such as internal training courses rather than informal learning. It certainly may suggest that training staff within hospices may need to consider the extent to which they are making full use of the range of workplace learning methods. However, none of the other HR policies were found to have any influence on the use of workplace learning. Importantly, the presence of an organization wide training policy, and senior management responsibility for training and development were found to have no relationship with the use of workplace learning.

These results raise important questions regarding the complexities that may be associated with actually implementing HR policies within organizations. The presence of organizational policies does not tell us much about how they are actually enacted in practice. Indeed, findings from this research would seem to suggest that there are a number of key factors that influence whether HR policies such as these are able to have a significant influence in supporting workplace learning within these hospices and potentially within healthcare organizations more widely (Clarke 2006b). These were identified as (1) The Dualism of Competence and Professionalism; (2) The Conflicting demands of Business-led Employee Development; (3) Professional Values; (4) Bureaucratic Discretion; and (5) Learning and Knowledge. The dualism of competence and professionalism referred to the considerable ambiguity and contradictions that seemed to exist regarding how to undertake staff development. This arose due to the conflicting and sometimes competing demands of the multiplicity of approaches that employee development was supposed to meet. In particular, the study found that the use of competence-based frameworks for continuing professional development often conflicted with the lack of recognition given to workplace learning, often due to the absence of any formal accreditation.

Workplace learning methods were seen as valuable, particularly in relation to developing professionalism, but the pressures to meet professional competencies and standards often meant such methods were seen as secondary to more formally recognized and accredited development activities. This was further influenced by the view that training and development should be strategic, which was interpreted as meaning business-led. An important consideration here was the need to demonstrate the value of employee development to the organization. This was argued as being far easier to demonstrate when there were clear learning outcomes associated with staff development that were often associated with more formal type training or education programmes. It was also of note that over a third of those hospices surveyed (34 per cent, 41) stated that they had achieved Investors in People (IiP) Accreditation, which is the UK government sponsored standard for excellence in training and development (Alberga *et al.* 1997). A further 30 or 25 per cent indicated that they were actively working towards achieving the standard. These findings would seem to be mutually supportive, in that the IiP standard places considerable emphasis on organizations possessing those training and development policies and practices that were contained in the survey as part of the process of gaining accreditation. Professional values also played a part. Within the healthcare professions, it was also acknowledged that codified knowledge that was often the preserve of formal education and training was generally held to be of higher status. Indeed the claim to a specific body of knowledge was seen as a major determinant of professionalism. Professional values were such that, again, more formally accredited development programmes were often preferred. For staff responsible for professional development and education, the need to meet the demands arising from the various approaches to employee development that existed within the hospices, particularly competence-based frameworks in continuing professional education and business-led, often meant that their activities were more directed towards formally recognized programmes. This suggests that the decisions made by key staff involved in staff development in terms of where resources and learning opportunities are made available, will be significant in determining the support given to workplace learning and how HR policies are used in this respect. This gives rise to the importance of bureaucratic discretion as a further factor in determining how HR policies may actually be enacted within these organizations, despite what aims they may have.

The role of workplace learning for professionalism and care for the dying

Despite the range of factors that appeared to militate against the use of workplace learning methods, there was considerable recognition of these methods' importance both in terms of developing professionalism and specifically in relation to enabling healthcare staff to provide effective care for the dying. A key theme to emerge was the extent to which opportunities for workplace learning, particularly through undertaking practice and participating in professional networks, were seen as far more significant in enabling healthcare staff to develop the expertise that they associated with the idea of professionalism. Although difficult to define, it was seen as very different from the requirements of simply meeting professional competencies:

> Well how do you capture competencies to work in a hospice? It's a bit odd really ... there are really important questions about what constitutes a competence in that way, when a lot of it comes from experience. The issue is not so much about measuring competencies but how you appraise staff and record the level of experience or the softer skills that are so important to the job. And that's what I guess we're talking about.

> Well, I mean, if you look at one of Van Gogh's paintings, you don't say, oh, what competencies did he have to paint this picture, I mean you can be competent but practice transcends competence, its far more than competence. But I just don't think we're thinking that way in terms of professional development when you're working within competence-type practices.

> I think the problem I see is in relation to whether the only driving force for assessment is in relation to competencies, where if you like, hidden or unrecognized skills or knowledge is not recognized in professional competencies, because it's not valued or seen as important, and therefore is not going to be assessed ... and so you are actually in danger of missing so much that's actually key to practice, that's why reflecting on practice is so important. But I don't think we actually purposefully record it, you know in a way that's being suggested.

> My feeling is that the more focused we become on competencies, perhaps the less we are focused on actual learning, or the less learning is actually in place. We're in danger of missing so much.

Given the focus of the study within hospices it was of particular interest to note the value that staff placed on workplace learning in terms of enabling them to perform their roles within these emotionally demanding environments.

> ...how important all this is [workplace learning] to what we do ... Well, certainly in this sort of environment where your having to deal with so much ... emotionally as well as professionally ... its something to do with how learning can lift you, or you know provide some sort of inspiration, especially when things are difficult or, really are so demanding, and you can sense it.

You build up a close and often intense relationship with people who are often spending time both in and out of the wards . . . and visiting them at home, so you get to know how they're feeling from one day to the next . . . and so you hope you can do what you can, to make things that much better each time by responding in the right way.

The weekly team meetings have a vital role to play in dealing with anxiety, and emotion, they're a safety valve as much as anything else or a learning opportunity. It's about enabling people to work through their own emotions and it tends to work for people differently, I guess depending upon the sorts of relationships they have with other staff and their managers.

Yeah . . . it's quite powerful, that time to think on what you've done and how you've done something . . . talking through how to manage your anxiety and your feelings, and of course how you've coped with situations . . . especially where you learn from each other about how you've dealt with situations in the past.

But we are different, the type of work we do, patients who may be dying and need a different approach to their care. We need to rely far more on our intuitive skills in terms of how to deal with situations. I mean each person and their families are different, and you need to read every situation, to determine what's best, right from type of care to the type of support the family will need . . .

Ward rounds offer fantastic opportunities for learning and discussion, and sharing ideas and problems, rather than locking it into any sort of formal mechanism . . . but you've also got to think about how to get people to participate and share learning because some people tend to not say much, I suppose its about different levels of experience and being given permission . . . knowing that's its safe you know.

The need for an evidence-based approach

One of the major themes to emerge from the qualitative research was the emphasis these healthcare practitioners placed on the need for far more research-based evidence demonstrating the impact of workplace learning on professional development:

> . . . it seems to me that we need to focus on practice . . . and making improvements there and that's what we need to concentrate on . . . whether that's about formal or informal learning or whatever . . . it's still about how we motivate staff to take part and want to continue to develop themselves professionally. Its about getting them involved and

them wanting to be involved ... And, I suppose the more we know what impact informal types of learning have the more staff will recognize how important this all is.

...there's room for having multiple approaches ... as long as in a way, you have a learning aim at the top, rather than say, we should expect people to all go down one path. We should allow people to choose which path they want to take ... and that means looking at how different methods suit different people. But whatever it is, you've got to have something credible that people recognize as being effective, and that's seen as professional.

Well, I've just taken up my new role in [hospice], and my job is to try to develop a more strategic outlook for training ... I mean to look to see where training and development is needed and to ensure we have the right priorities. I need to find out about how workplace learning or informal learning fits in with all that ... it's a bit different I guess in emphasis ... and what, or how do you plan for it ... and its also about looking at the evidence-base to a lot of this.

We have to look at the context of a business, whether charitable or otherwise, and that requires accountability and efficiency, to survive as a business. You have to adopt that kind of mentality ... although we have important care values in relation to death, dying, we still have to look at where resources need to go, and that's the same for training or other types of staff development. What is the most effective?

Discussion

The survey findings from this research have revealed the significant extent to which hospices in the UK rely on workplace or informal learning methods to develop their employees, but that formal learning approaches still dominate within these healthcare settings. The qualitative data presented here were obtained from two focus groups comprising only a small self-selecting sample of healthcare organizations. There are then problems with generalizability beyond this specific sample of organizations. Nonetheless, findings from this aspect of the research have provided some interesting insights into those factors influencing the use of workplace learning that would appear to have important implications if workplace learning is to be better supported within these work settings. Workplace learning methods were seen as important for the development of professionalism (Conlon 2004), but were given special prominence in these particular healthcare organizations, also due to the role they played in helping these practitioners to develop the expertise and capacity for caring for the dying. This finding supports previous research regarding the significance of learning, both experientially on the job and through participating in professional networks, as being particu-larly prominent mechanisms for developing coping skills, specialist know-ledge, and as an effective means for dealing with stress and anxiety specific to this type of health care. This would seem to support the view that one of the key contributions of workplace learning methods is their capacity to generate and assist with the transfer of knowledge and skills that are highly contextualized and related to the particular nature of the job itself.

Elsewhere, Clarke (2005) has argued that workplace learning should be distinguished from other forms of learning based on its capacity for gener-ating and sharing procedural knowledge. This is defined as knowledge relating to 'knowing how,' which is often embedded deep within the work practices of staff, and can be difficult to articulate and often is not publicly available or documented. This type of knowledge is more hidden, but perhaps more accessible through the learning that takes place while in the workplace, observing and interacting with others, and reflecting on and discussing experiences within professional networks. This is distinguished from codified knowledge, or knowledge that is associated with facts, and is often far more accessible through documentation or education and training programmes. The significance of workplace learning for developing profes-sionalism has received quite widespread support within the literature, both theoretically and empirically (Eraut *et al.* 1998; Eraut 2000). What has received far less attention however, is the major role such methods play in developing particular coping skills within the context of different profes-sions. Certainly within the context of care for the dying, this appears to be particularly significant relating to the impact of workplace learning. Such methods may facilitate feelings of psychological safety within the work-place, and facilitate stronger professional identities that then promote feel-ings of greater perceived control or self-efficacy, the belief that one can deal with life events and stressors (Bandura 1977). In this sense, opportunities for workplace learning may, in addition to providing key practice skills, also be far more effective at either fostering empowerment (Clarke 2001a) or indeed Emotional Intelligence (EI) (McQueen 2004; Zeidner *et al.* 2004).

The concept of Emotional Intelligence has become of increasing import-ance within the field of organizational psychology as a number of writers from a variety of disciplines join an enlarging body of literature, arguing that it offers a new and unique dimension of psychological functioning. Levels of EI differ between individuals and have been found to be associated with a wide range of work-related outcomes (Dulewicz and Higgs 2000; Zeidner *et al.* 2004). This has resulted in a range of publications that have suggested emotional intelligence to be important for successful management and leadership (Goleman 1998; Zeidner *et al.* 2004), as well as particularly important within the health and caring professions (Akerjorder, and Sev-erinsson 2004; Bharwaney and Paddock 2003; Elam 2000; Freshwater and Stickley 2004). Specifically within healthcare, there has been a considerable deal of interest shown in the concept of EI. Cadman and Brewer (2001) for example, in relation to nursing, suggest that EI:

> encompasses the human skills of empathy, self-awareness, motivation, self-control and adeptness in relationships, all of which are recognized as being central in effective clinical practice.
>
> (Cadman and Brewer 2001: 321)

Given such support, it is unsurprising that many writers in the healthcare field have argued that an individual's emotional intelligence might usefully serve as a meaningful indicator of suitability for the caring professions, as well as a target for development in relation to developing professional competencies in nursing (Cadman and Brewer 2001; Freshwater and Stickley 2004), medicine (Carrothers *et al.* 2004; Lewis *et al.* 2004) and pharmacy (Latif 2004). It is the close identification of EI with both the disposition and skills required for caring that appears to have captured the attention of writers in the field of healthcare. McQueen (2004) discusses the significance of EI as being closely associated with the concept of emotional labour, which has previously received a great deal of attention, especially within the nursing literature. Emotional labour recognizes the elements that contribute to providing care for patients, which involve both physical and emotional dimensions. Here, emotions and feelings are seen as forming part of the complex pattern of exchanges that develop within a caring relationship. Importantly, this level of intimacy and emotional involvement is suggested as both having positive outcomes for patients, through ameliorating anxiety, as well significant outcomes for healthcare practitioners ranging from personal and job satisfaction (Luker *et al.* 2000; McQueen 2004) to, potentially, stress or burnout (Benner and Wrubel 1989). For the caring professions then, the value of EI is clear, both as a means to provide more effective care and as a means for better managing the emotional stresses and demands that come from a caring role. Although a number of writers have suggested that human resource development programmes may be important in developing emotional intelligence (Dulewicz and Higgs 2004; Opengart 2005; Slaski and Cartwright 2003; Weinberger 2002), there is very little empirical evidence regarding the relative efficacy of particular interventions (Clarke 2006b). Certainly the findings from this study would appear to suggest that workplace learning methods may potentially be far more effective at developing EI than perhaps more traditional forms of training (Clarke 2006c).

However, despite a recognition of the important role that workplace learning occupies in hospices, there were a number of factors that appear to suggest it remains of secondary importance to more formal, or accredited types of staff development. Indeed, the failure to find any positive support for the role of HR policies in influencing the use of workplace learning within these healthcare environments suggests that such factors may exert particularly strong effects (Clarke 2006a). In particular, this study suggests that dominant approaches to employee development within these organizations, associated with a competence-based model for continuing professional development, appears to impede the greater use of workplace learning within a healthcare context. This would appear to support previous findings both within healthcare organizations and more generally regarding the nature of CPE (Bierema and Eraut 2004). In order for organizations to adopt more workplace learning methods, this may require moving away from previously defined business-case notions of 'strategic' human resource development (Walton 1999), to those that are able to integrate a more learning organization framework (Raper *et al.* 1997). However, this will require a far more consolidated effort on demonstrating the value of workplace learning to the development of professional 'competence,' especially in knowledge intensive sectors such as healthcare. This is an area where further research is needed and would seem to be a chief concern of hospice staff themselves in this study. One of the clear findings to emerge here was that healthcare staff needed far more information regarding the effectiveness of workplace learning and its impact if it was to be seen as valuable as formal, often accredited, education and training programmes. Perhaps unsurprisingly, given the extent to which evidence-based practice now permeates healthcare, concerns were raised regarding the evidence-base underpinning workplace learning. In so doing, these practitioners are joining the chorus of criticism that continues to be laid at the door of HRD more widely:

> The alternative to having a second theoretical and disciplinary base for the HRD profession in the present state of rudderless random activity ... This present state celebrates short-term perceptions of success without having deep understanding or the ability to replicate results.
> (Swanson, 2001: 307)

What would seem obvious from the findings here, is that the absence of a more unified approach within the HRD field to developing a more evidence-based agenda is unlikely to assist with healthcare organizations making greater use of workplace learning methods. There are obvious reasons why professionals working within HRD in health and social care organizations should be particularly sensitized to asking questions regarding the research upon which increasingly popularized HRD interventions and activities are based. Evidence based practice (EBP) has its origins within healthcare and in particular within the field of medicine, although it now has come to exert considerable influence on most of the health and social care professions. The sentiment underpinning evidence-based practice is fairly straightforward, in that it advocates that professional practices should be based as far as possible on evidence from well-conducted research into the effectiveness of interventions (Ovretveit 1998; Walshe and Rundall 2001). Perhaps unsurprisingly, given the extent to which EBP has come to dominate health policy within both the UK and USA, a number of writers have begun to ask whether such an approach should not also be applied in relation to the management of healthcare organizations and the managerial practices that underpin it (Young 2002; Hewison 1997; Stewart 1998).

Axelsson (1998) argues that such an approach may well serve to reconnect management theory and research to practice which, he suggests, has increasingly become centred on the descriptive and rarely considers the generalizability of research for practical use as a central aim of the endeavour. As a result, the number of empirical studies examining management within healthcare in growing, although to date these studies have been primarily concerned with decision-making processes (Davies *et al.* 2000; Dixon *et al.* 1997; Harries *et al.* 1999; McCarthy 1998; Stocking 1995). By contrast, the number of studies within the wider management literature adopting an evidence-based approach has been relatively few (Homa 1998). From a HRD perspective, calls for an evidence-based approach have been far more limited (Clarke 2001b; Hamlin 2001). However, primarily through the influence of the medical and nursing fields, a number of writers have argued the importance of adopting an evidence-based approach with respect to education and training (Harden *et al.* 1999), which would appear to be influencing the role of HRD practitioners working in these arenas. Indeed, as far as social care is concerned, the policy document *Modernising the Social Care Workforce* (TOPPS 1999), states that 'a key component of a social care human resource strategy must be a commitment to evidence-based practice,' (TOPPS 1999: 9).

For the fields of management and HRD however, importing the concept of evidence-based practice as it has been applied within the healthcare professions has been subject to significant criticism even within the healthcare field itself (Booth *et al.* 1997; Hewison 1997; Rycroft-Malone *et al.* 2004). For most, this centres on the problems associated with the assumed superiority of positivistic research investigations that rely upon the control of variables, compared to phenomenological approaches that many argue are far more appropriate for researching the complex problems often associated with the management of organizations. As Walshe and Rundall (2001) remind us:

> Overall, the ... research base for many clinical professions provides a strong and secure foundation for evidence-based practice and lends itself to a systematic process of review and synthesis and to the production of guidelines and protocols. In contrast, the loosely defined, methodologically heterogeneous, widely distributed, and hard to generalize research base for healthcare management is much more difficult to use in the same way. There are real methodological and conceptual problems involved in framing research questions, searching the literature, appraising studies, and synthesizing or combining their results, which make the development of evidence-based management more challenging.

However, for many writers who have advocated adopting more evidence-based approaches to the varying fields within management, such challenges have not been seen as necessarily requiring a complete rejection of some of the key aspects that might constitute an evidence-based agenda (Hamlin 2001; Ovretveit 1998; Young 2002). Indeed, most have offered alternative expositions of EBP that might lend themselves far more readily to the management and HRD fields. A far more evidence-based approach within the field, potentially may offer a means to realize the aspirations of HRD professionals that their expertise and efforts can make a difference to individual, group and maybe organizational performance. Hamlin (2001) sets out the parameters here when he defines evidence-based practice in HRD as being derived from:

> a combination of good quality research; consensus of recognized professional experts and/or affirmed professional experiences that substantiates practice; quality improvement, operational or evaluation data; and the systematic feedback of opinions or preferences of client managers.
>
> (Hamlin 2001: 98)

Within this approach, good quality research does not necessarily mean research that is within the positivist tradition, but appropriate research methodologies applied to solving the sorts of organizational issues facing HRD practitioners with which they have a major stake in understanding and attempting to address. An evidence-based approach here attempts then to reconnect HRD to the concerns of key stakeholders within organizations. In the context of the findings here from HRD practitioners, this would appear particularly poignant as far as workplace learning is concerned, especially in light of the new CPD guidance for healthcare (HSC 1999). HSC (1999) sets out a new approach to staff development with the following core principles. It stresses that CPD should be: (1) purposeful and patient centred; (2) participative; (3) educationally effective; (4) cross boundary; (5) designed to build on previous knowledge and skills; and (6) part of a wider organizational development plan that supports local and national objectives. However, a key objective here is that CPD should *align training funds towards development activities that have been found to be effective.*

Within such a policy context, the focus on 'evidence' to underpin organizational support for workplace learning is arguably an issue that should be taken up within the wider HRD literature more vociferously. Indeed, the sentiments expressed by these healthcare professionals involved in HRD, would suggest that we need to undertake a far more rigorous evidence-based research agenda within the field. There is, however, at first sight what might seem an interesting paradox here. Workplace learning recognizes the extent to which both knowledge and learning are often contextualized. Evidence-based practice by contrast has been argued to assume that practice is decontextualized, and readily transposes from one situational context to another. Many writers have challenged this latter assumption and indeed research is beginning to examine the nature of the context in which 'evidence' is both judged and informs practice. However, this does not detract from the extent to which building a coherent body of research findings that together lend themselves more to particular conclusions than others, but which may be subject to particular contingencies, may offer considerable benefits for informing practice. Indeed, arguably it is far more preferable than the post-modernist view of organizations as being in such a constant state of unpre-dictability that it becomes pointless to attempt to determine the results of any interventions in order to underpin future practice. Hamlin (2001) has previously suggested that adopting an evidence-based approach to HRD can be facilitated by greater recognition of research findings by HRD practition-ers, but also a greater emphasis on research partnerships between HRD researchers and practitioners. However, what is also needed is far more research that is practice driven and that seeks to not only understand why certain events occur within organizations, but attempts also to predict the consequences of HRD interventions. There is also a desperate need for more systematic reviews of such research findings that can then be communicated to HRD practitioners within a range of accessible formats, including practi-tioner as well as the more academic oriented publications. In so doing, perhaps some of the difficulties identified by hospice staff here in adopting a more comprehensive approach to workplace learning might be overcome.

Conclusions

This study has found positive support for the use of a wide range of informal or workplace learning methods within hospices in the UK. However, formal education and training programmes remain the most dominant methods sponsored and supported by the organization. A number of factors were found to contribute to this. The most important being the extent to which competence-based frameworks for continuing professional development and education, alongside the need to demonstrate the 'value' of staff develop-ment, militate against the use of learning methods where gains may be far more difficult to determine. The hospice staff taking part in the qualitative aspect of this study identified a need for far more 'evidence' regarding the impact of workplace learning as a means to facilitate and encourage the greater use of such approaches. This has implications both in terms of driving a more practitioner-oriented empirical agenda in HRD research, but also in considering how best to make findings from research available to healthcare staff. Given the increasing emphasis within the education and training arenas within healthcare for a more evidence-based approach, such requirements are likely to become of increasing significance for HRD researchers working within healthcare contexts.

Key learning points

- Encouraging the greater dissemination of research findings specifically within healthcare practitioner journals is likely to be of considerable benefit in encouraging a greater adoption of workplace learning within healthcare organizations.

- Of chief importance though is much more research that demonstrates the value of workplace learning in healthcare. In this respect the finding from this study concerning the recognition of workplace learning as a key means for developing professionalism requires far more research and explanation. In particular, far more comparative studies are needed that identify the learning gains achieved through workplace learning methods such as mentoring, team learning and practice compared to training and educational programmes.
- In this respect one of the key findings here regarding the potential role that workplace learning may play in developing emotionally significant competencies for caring is one such area that requires far more in-depth investigation.

References

Akerjorder, K. and Severinsson, E. (2004) 'Emotional intelligence in mental health nurses taking about practice,' *International Journal of Mental Health Nursing* 13(3): 164–170.

Alberga, T., Tyson, S. and Parsons, D. (1997) 'An evaluation of the Investors in People Standard,' *Human Resource Management Journal* 7: 47–60.

Audit Commission (2001) *Hidden Talents. The Education, Training and Development of Healthcare Staff in NHS Trusts*, London: Audit Commission.

Axelsson, R. (1998) 'Towards an evidence based health care management,' *International Journal of Health Planning and Management* 13: 307–317.

Bandura, A. (1977) *Social Learning Theory*, Upper Saddle River, NJ: Prentice Hall.

Benner, P. (1984) *From Novice to Expert: Excellence and Power in Clinical Nursing Practice*, Menlo Park, CA: Addison-Wesley.

Benner, P. and Wrubel, J. (1989) *The Primacy of Caring*, London: Addison-Wesley.

Bharwaney, G. and Paddock, C. (2003) 'Emotionally intelligent helping,' *Competency & Emotional Intelligence Quarterly* 11(1): 27–32.

Bierema, L.L. and Eraut, M. (2004) 'Workplace learning: perspective on continuing professional education and human resource development,' *Advances in Developing Human Resources* 6(1): 52–68.

Billett, S. (1999) 'Guided learning at work,' in D. Boud and J. Garrick (eds) *Understanding Learning at Work*, London: Routledge, pp. 151–164.

Blackler, F. (1995) 'Knowledge, knowledge work and organisations: an overview and interpretation,' *Organisation Studies* 16: 1021–1046.

Booth, K., Kenrick., M. and Woods, S. (1997) 'Nursing knowledge, theory and method revisited,' *Journal of Advanced Nursing* 26(4): 804–811.

Brown, J.S. and Duguid, P. (1991) 'Organizational learning and communities of practice: toward a unified view of working, learning and innovation,' *Organization Science* 2(1): 40–57.

Cadman, C. and Brewer, J. (2001) 'Emotional intelligence: a vital prerequisite for recruitment in nursing,' *Journal of Nursing Management* 9: 321–324.

Carrothers, M.A., Gregory, S.W. and Gallagher, T.J. (2004) 'Measuring emotional intelligence of medical school applicants,' *Academic Medicine* 75: 456–463.

Clarke, C. and Wilcoxson, J. (2001) 'Professional and organisational learning: analysing the relationship with the development of practice,' *Journal of Advanced Nursing* 34(2): 264–272.

Clarke, N. (2001a) 'Training as a vehicle to empower carers in the community: more than a question of information sharing,' *Health and Social Care in the Community* 9(2): 79–88.

Clarke, N. (2001b) 'The impact of in-service training within social services,' *British Journal of Social Work* 31: 757–774.

Clarke, N. (2004) 'HRD and the challenges of assessing learning in the workplace,' *International Journal of Training & Development* 8(2): 140–156.

Clarke, N. (2005) 'Workplace learning environment and its relationship with learning outcomes in healthcare organisations,' *Human Resource Development International* 8(2).

Clarke, N. (2006a) 'Why HR policies fail to support workplace learning: the complexities of policy implementation in healthcare,' *International Journal of Human Resource Management*.

Clarke, N. (2006b) 'Emotional Intelligence Training: a case of caveat emptor,' *Human Resource Development Review* 15(4): 1–20.

Clarke N. (2006c) 'Developing emotional intelligence through workplace learning: findings from a case study in healthcare,' *Human Resource Development International* 9(4): in press.

Conlon, T.J. (2004) 'A review of informal learning literature, theory and implications for practice in developing global professional competence,' *Journal of European Industrial Training* 28(2/3/4): 283–295.

Conner, M. (2001) 'Developing network-based services in the NHS,' *International Journal of Health Care Quality Assurance* 14/6: 237–244.

David, D., Evans, M. and Jadad, A. (2003) 'The case for knowledge translation: shortening the journey from evidence to effect,' *British Medical Journal* 327: 33–35.

Davies, H.T.O., Nutley, S.M. and Smith, P.C. (eds) (2000) *What Works? Evidence-Based Policy & Practice in Public Services*, Policy Press.

Department of Health (DoH) (1999) *Continuing Professional Development: Quality in the new NHS*, London: Department of Health.

Department of Health (DoH) (2000a) *The NHS Plan*, London: HMSO.

Department of Health (DoH) (2000b) *A Health Service of All the Talents: Developing the NHS Workforce*, London: Department of Health.

Department of Health (DoH) (2001) *Working Together – Learning Together. A Framework for Lifelong Learning in the NHS*, London: Department of Health.

Dixon, S., Booth, A. and Perrett, K. (1997) 'The application of evidence-based priority setting in a District Health Authority,' *Journal of Public Health Medicine* 19(3): 307–312.

Dowsell, T., Hewison, J. and Hinds, M. (1998) 'Motivational forces affecting participation in post-registration degree courses and effects on home and work life: a qualitative study,' *Journal of Advanced Nursing* 28(6):1326–1333.

Dovey, K. (2002) 'Leadership development in a South African health service,' *The International Journal of Public Sector Management* 15(7): 520–533.

Dowie, J. (1996) 'The research practice gap and the role of decision analysis in closing it,' *Health Care Analysis* 4: 1–14.

Dulewicz, V. and Higgs, M.J. (2000) 'Emotional intelligence: a review and evaluation study,' *Journal of Managerial Psychology* 15(4): 341–368.

Dulewicz, V. and Higgs, M. (2004) 'Can emotional intelligence be developed?' *International Journal of Human Resource Management* 15(1): 95–111.

Elam, C.L. (2000) 'Use of emotional intelligence as one measure of medical school applicants noncognitive characteristics,' *Academic Medicine* 75: 445–446.

Eraut, M. (2000) 'Non-formal learning and tacit knowledge in professional work,' *British Journal of Educational Psychology* 70: 113–136.

Eraut, M., Alderton, J., Cole, ?. and Senker, P. (1998) *Development of Knowledge and Skills in Employment*, Research Report No. 5, University of Sussex Institute of Education, Brighton.

Flanagan, J., Baldwin, S. and Clarke, D. (2000) 'Work-based learning as a means of developing and assessing nursing competence,' *Journal of Clinical Nursing* 1 9(3): 360–368.

Freshwater, D. and Stickley, T. (2004) 'The heart of the art: emotional intelligence in nurse education,' *Nursing Inquiry* 11(2): 91–98.

Goleman, D. (1998) *Working with Emotional Intelligence*, New York: Bantam.

Hamlin, B. (2001) 'Towards evidence-based HRD practice,' in McGoldrick *et al.* (eds) *Understanding Human Resource Development*, London: Routledge, pp. 92–121.

Harden, R.M., Grant, J., Buckley, G. and Hart, I.M. (1999) 'BEME Guide No. 1: best evidence medical educational, *Medical Teacher* 21(6): 553–562.

Harries, U., Elliott, H. and Higgins, A. (1999) 'Evidence-based policy making in the NHS. Exploring the interface between research and the commissioning process,' *Journal of Public Health Medicine* 21(1): 29–36.

Hewison, A. (1997) 'Evidence-based medicine: what about evidence-based management?' *Journal of Nursing Management* 5: 195–198.

Homa, P. (1998) 'What's your evidence?' *Health Management* 2(6): 18–21.

HSC (1999) *Continuing Professional Development: Quality in the new NHS*, (HSC 1999/154), London: Department of Health.

Hunter, K.M. (1991) *Doctors' Stories: The Narrative Structure of Medical Knowledge*, Chichester: Princeton University Press.

Jones, A. (2003) 'Some benefits experienced by hospice nurses from group clinical supervision,' *European Journal of Cancer Care* 12: 224–232.

King, B. (1991) 'Learning needs of registered nurses,' *Australian Nurses Journal* 11(3): 42–43.

Latif, D.A. (2004) 'Using emotional intelligence in the planning and implementation of a management skills course,' *Pharmacy Education* 4(2): 81–89.

Lave, J. and Wenger, E. (1991) *Situated Learning: Legitimate Peripheral Participation*, Cambridge University Press.

Lewis, N., Ress, C. and Hudson, N (2004) 'Helping students identify their emotional intelligence,' *Medical Education* 38: 545–576.

Lloyd-Williams, M. (2002) 'Senior house officers' experience of a six month post in a hospice,' *Medical Education* 36: 45–48.

Luker, K.A., Austin, L., Caress, A. and Hallett, C.E. (2000) 'The importance of "knowing the patient": community nurses' constructions of quality in providing palliative care,' *Journal of Advanced Nursing* 31(4): 775–782.

MacLeod, R.D. (1994) 'Education in palliative medicine: a review,' *Journal of Cancer Education* 8: 309–312.

294   *Nicholas Clarke*

MacLeod, R.D. (2001) 'On reflection: doctors learning to care for people who are dying,' *Social Science & Medicine* 52: 1719–1727.

Matthews, J.H. and Candy, P.C. (1999) 'New dimensions in the dynamics of learning and knowledge,' in D. Boud and J. Garrick (eds) *Understanding Learning at Work*, London: Routledge, pp. 47–64.

McCarthy, M. (1998) 'The contracting round: achieving health gain or financial balance?' *Journal of Public Health Medicine* 20(4): 409–413.

McGoldrick, J., Stewart, J. and Watson, S. (2001) 'Theorizing human resource development,' *Human Resource Development International* 4(3): 343–356.

McQueen, A. (2004) 'Emotional Intelligence in nursing work,' *Journal of Advanced Nursing* 47(1): 101–108.

Miles, M. and Huberman, A. (1984) *Qualitative Data Analysis: An Expanded Sourcebook*, London: Sage.

Opengart, R. (2005) 'Emotional intelligence and emotion work: examining constructs from an interdisciplinary framework,' *Human Resource Development Review* 4(1): 49–62.

Ovretveit, J. (1998) *Evaluation Health Interventions: an Introduction to Evaluation of Health Treatments, Services, Policies and Organizational Interventions*, Buckingham: Open University Press.

Raper, P., Ashton, D., Felstead, A. and Storey, J. (1997) 'Toward a learning organisation? Explaining current trends in training practices in the UK,' *International Journal of Training and Development* 1(1): 9–21.

Robinson, P., Purves, I. and Wilson, R. (2003) 'Learning support for the consultation: information support and decision should be placed in an educational framework,' *Medical Education* 37: 429–433.

Robinson, P.J. and Heywood, P. (2000) 'What do GPs need to know? The use of knowledge in general practice consultations,' *British Journal of General Practice* 50: 56–59.

Rosser, M. and King, L. (2003) 'Transition experiences of qualified nurses moving into hospice nursing,' *Journal of Advanced Nursing* 43(2): 206–215.

Rycroft-Malone, J., Seers, K., Titchen, A., Harvey, G., Kitson, A. and McCormack, B. (2004) 'What counts as evidence in evidence-based practice?' *Journal of Advanced Nursing* 47(1): 81–90.

Schmidt, H.G., Norman, G.R. and Boshuizen, P.A. (1990) 'A cognitive perspective on medical expertise: theory and implications,' *Academy of Medicine* 65: 611–621.

Slaski, M. and Cartwright, S. (2003) 'Emotional intelligence training and its implications for stress, health and performance,' *Stress and Health* 19(4): 233–239.

Stewart, R. (1998) 'More art than science?' *Health Service Journal* 108(5597): 28–29.

Stocking, B. (1995) 'Why research findings are not used by commissions and what can be done about it,' *Journal of Public Health Medicine* 17(4): 380–382.

Swanson, B.L., Watkins, K.E. and Marsick, V.J. (1997) 'Qualitative research methods,' in R.A. Swanson and E.F. Holton (eds) *Human Resource Development Research Handbook*, San Francisco: Berrett-Koehler, pp. 88–113.

Swanson, R.A. (2001) 'Human resource development and its underlying theory,' *Human Resource Development International* 4(3): 299–312.

Training Organisation for the Personal Social Services (TOPPS) (1999) *Modernising the Social Care Workforce*, London: Department of Health and Social Services.

Walshe, K. and Rundall, T.G. (2001) 'Evidence-based management: from theory to practice in health care,' *The Millbank Quarterly* 79(3): 429–457.

Walton, J. (1999) *Strategic Human Resource Development*, Harlow: Prentice-Hall.

Weinberger, L.A. (2002) 'Emotional intelligence: its connection to HRD theory and practice,' *Human Resource Development Review* 1(2): 215–243.

Wenger, E. (1998) *Communities of Practice: Learning, Meaning and Identity*, Cambridge: Cambridge University Press.

White, J.P., Armstrong, H., Armstrong, P., Bourgeault, I., Choiniere, J. and Mykhalovskiy, E. (2000) 'The impact of managed care on nurses' workplace learning and teaching,' *Nursing Inquiry* 7: 74–80.

White, J.P., Eagle, J. and McNeil, H. *et al.* (1998) 'What are the factors that influence learning in relation to nursing practice?' *Journal for Nurses in Staff Development* 14(3): 147–153.

Wilson-Barnett, J., Butterworth, T., White, E., Twinn, S., Davies, S. and Riley, L. (1998) 'Clinical support and the Project 2000 nursing student: factors influencing this process,' *Journal of Advanced Nursing* 21(6): 1152–1158.

Young, S.K. (2002) 'Evidence-based management: a literature review,' *Journal of Nursing Management* 10: 145–151.

Yuen, F. (1991) 'Case study of learning mileu: the modifying effect of the workplace,' *Journal of Advanced Nursing* 16: 1290–1295.

Zeidner, M., Matthews, G. and Roberts, R.D. (2004) 'Emotional intelligence in the workplace: a critical review,' *Applied Psychology: An International Review* 53(3): 371–399.

13 Human resource development and continuing professional development of physical therapists

Alice J. Salzman and Kathy D. Hall

Introduction

Healthcare in the United States has been in a period of upheaval since the 1990s when the focus moved from providing the highest quality of care regardless of cost to a managed care system that concentrates on providing cost-effective services. Recent newspaper articles described decreased government funding for people in nursing homes (Japsen 2004) and a class-action lawsuit brought against hospitals charging that they were failing to provide the charity care required to retain their non-profit status (Kaiser 2004). Meanwhile, physicians continue to be plagued by the increasing cost of malpractice insurance (Illinois State Medical Society 2004). The chaos in health care has an impact on individuals' ability to provide services to patients and to grow as professionals. This chapter will focus on the challenges facing one group of health professionals, physical therapists.

Physical therapists are health professionals who are 'experts in the examination and treatment of musculoskeletal and neuromuscular problems that affect peoples' abilities to move the way they want and function as well as they want in their daily lives' (Guccione 1999: 12). Physical therapists work in a variety of settings and organizations, including non-profit hospitals, publicly traded healthcare corporations, colleges and universities, privately owned clinics, and the public school system. Physical therapists are licensed by the state in which they practice following graduation from an accredited physical therapy education program and passage of a national licensure examination. Participation in continuing professional education (CPE) is required to maintain licensure in 30 of the 50 states (Federation of State Boards of Physical Therapy 2002). The scope of physical therapy practice, which grew throughout the twentieth century, is defined by each state. In order to increase consumers' access to cost-effective health care physical therapists in the United States have been seeking the legal right to provide services to patients and clients without physicians' referrals.

Continuing Professional Development (CPD) is the process through which professionals modify and enhance their knowledge and skills throughout their careers. The changes in the healthcare climate and in the profession require practicing physical therapists to be effective lifelong learners who can develop and follow effective, well-structured CPD plans that include a variety of learning experiences and assist them to adjust to change (Cervero 2000; Chartered Society of Physiotherapy 1994; Eraut 1994; Knox 1993). One frequently used CPD strategy is participation in continuing professional education, or formal, organized short courses for practicing professionals.

Even though their focus is different, Human Resource Development (HRD) and CPE both contribute to CPD (Dirkx *et al.* 2004). HRD practitioners in health care organizations emphasize enhancing the productivity of the organization, while CPE has traditionally focused on improving individual professionals by updating their knowledge and skills or teaching new information. Within organizations, CPE and HRD often compete for the same limited resources (Jeris and Daley 2004). Consumers and healthcare organizations will benefit if HRD and CPE are able to work together to assist physical therapists to provide effective services during this time of health care crisis.

The purpose of this chapter is to describe continuing professional development among physical therapists, one group of health professionals. The questions that guide the chapter are:

1 What lifelong learning (LLL) experiences contribute to CPD for physical therapists?
2 How can HRD practitioners and CPD providers work together to provide professional development opportunities for physical therapists?

Context – physical therapy education

Physical therapy education in the United States is also in a period of change. In the early 1900s, physical therapists received training in programs that lasted less than a year and offered certificates in physical therapy. By the middle of the twentieth century, the training programs became formal educational programs housed in colleges and universities that offered baccalaureate degrees (Pinkston 1989). Since 2002, only post baccalaureate degree educational programs have been accredited because of the depth and breadth of knowledge required to enter the practice of physical therapy (American Physical Therapy Association [APTA] 2005a). Currently, 117 of the 205 accredited physical therapist education programs offer the doctorate of physical therapy as the entry-level degree (APTA 2005b). Practicing physical therapists who received other degrees are encouraged to obtain further formal education (APTA 2005a).

Physical therapy education occurs in academic and clinical settings. In the majority of physical therapy programs, coordination of the off-campus clinical component of physical therapy education is primarily the responsibility of one or two people, the Academic Coordinators/Directors of Clinical

Education (ACCEs/DCEs). In addition to teaching in the classroom, ACCEs/DCEs find appropriate sites for clinical education, assist clinical faculty to evaluate student performance and solve problems that arise during clinical education, facilitate professional growth in clinical educators through presentations on topics related to clinical education, counsel students on issues related to clinical education, and participate in scholarly activity (Strickler 1990, 1991). The majority of ACCEs/DCEs come to academia from clinical positions, where teaching, advising and meeting other patient- or student-related needs were emphasized (Ford 1990). To be successful in academia, ACCEs/DCEs must adjust to the culture of the academy and develop new skills.

Conceptual framework for professional lifelong learning

Professional development, the process of developing and changing one's professional skills and abilities throughout one's career (Daley 2001), requires the ability to be an effective lifelong learner. Establishing LLL capabilities and expectations during initial professional education (IPE) is considered by many to be the foundation for successful professional development (Cervero 1988; Houle 1980; Mott 2000). Professional LLL activities include formal learning activities, such as CPE courses (Cervero 2000), informal learning activities, such as networking or consulting with colleagues (Marsick and Watkins 2001), and non-formal learning activities, or organized activities that occur outside of the formal educational system, such as hospital in-services (Alheit and Dausien 2002). Professional LLL activities result in growth in practice-related knowledge, skills, and performance ability (Queeney 2000). In general, the goal of continued professional learning is to improve the quality of service provided to clients or patients (Daley 2001; Maggs 1996).

Effective practice of a profession requires the ability to acquire and use many types of knowledge. In the United States, the scientific method has been the predominant means of knowledge creation in the professions since the early 1900s (Rice and Richlin 1993). Knowledge developed through the scientific method has been called 'technical knowledge' (Schön 1983), 'declarative knowledge' (Cervero 1992: 94), or 'codified knowledge' (Eraut 1994, 2000). Schön (1983) linked the prominent use of the scientific method to the epistemology of technical rationality, which describes the work of professionals as solving well-defined problems by selecting and applying techniques grounded in theories developed through basic science research. Declarative knowledge can be obtained through reading and attending CPE.

Because the problems faced by physical therapists are complex, uncertain, and unique rather than clearly defined (Schön 1983, 1987), physical therapists also need practical knowledge to be effective (Cervero 1988, 1990, 1992; Shepard and Jensen 1990). Practical knowledge, also known as procedural or tacit knowledge, is time-bound and situation-specific. Practical knowledge is obtained as physical therapists struggle to solve successfully the problems faced in daily practice and reflect on the outcomes of their actions. Because procedural knowledge is gained through practice, it cannot be separated from practice (Polyani 1958, 1966).

Eraut (1994, 2000, 2001) described four types of knowledge used in professional practice: propositional knowledge, or fact; process knowledge, or knowing how to accomplish a task; know-how, or knowing how to get things done; and personal knowledge, which is the knowledge that a professional gains through practice. He reported that personal knowledge is acquired through learning to use public codified knowledge and from personal experience, reflection, and social interaction. To facilitate the development of professionals who are lifelong learners, Eraut (1994) argued for experience and practical relevance to have a more prominent place in IPE. In his opinion, IPE programs need to model the expectations for, and provide opportunities to practice, learning strategies used for CPD.

Professional development of physical therapists occurs through a variety of learning experiences. Formal learning experiences include IPE, post-professional education, and participation in CPE and professional meetings (Daley 1997, 2001; Karp 1992a, 1992b). Daley (1997, 1999, 2000, 2001) explored the methods professionals use to construct the knowledge base they use in daily practice. She found that information gained from CPE becomes meaningful only when it is connected to the knowledge of daily practice. The process of linking new and old information is 'recursive [and] transforming . . . rather than a simple, straightforward transfer of information from one context to another' (Daley 2001: 50). The end result is a change in both the old and the new information. Interactions with clients had a strong impact on the meaning-making process, and the meaning created by the linking together of the old and new knowledge was related to the nature of a professional's work and the structure of the organization in which they were working.

Physical therapists also learn through a variety of non-formal and informal methods. Similar to other professionals, the learning methods used by physical therapists often involve interactions with professional peers and colleagues (Case-Smith 1999; Daley 1999; Eraut *et al.* 2004). They may have mentors who assist them with projects, introduce them to influential individuals, or sponsor them for positions in professional organizations (Hansman 2001; Jensen *et al.* 1999). Additionally, physical therapists learn through professional reading (Slotnick 1999), interacting with colleagues (Daley 1999), solving work-related problems (Benner 1983), and reflecting on their professional practice (Cervero 1992; Schön 1983). Non-formal and informal learning experiences are more meaningful because they are more likely to occur simultaneously with practice and result in practical knowledge (Cervero 1992; Daley 1997, 1999). Physical therapists' learning experiences allow them to increase their knowledge, improve their clinical skills, and adapt to changes in the profession and in healthcare.

Several investigators and educational theorists support the importance of establishing LLL behavior early in the professional development of clinicians (Cervero 1988; Houle 1980; Knox 2000; Mott 2000). Within the workplace, HRD practitioners can facilitate effectiveness of the organization and aid professionals in their development by offering meaningful learning activities while creating an appropriate learning environment. In addition to traditional formal learning activities, effective HRD planning supports a variety of learning methods, including informal and non-formal self-directed learning activities (Ellinger 2004), within an environment that expects and encourages professionals to grow and change throughout their careers (Eraut *et al.* 2004; Sim *et al.* 2003).

Research methods

Data used in this chapter were gathered through two research studies and a review of current literature. Using a professional learning inventory, one study surveyed a random sample of 600 physical therapists in the United States to determine the professional LLL strategies they were most likely to pursue for the purposes of CPD (Hall 2005). Preferred LLL strategies and demographic variable data were collected from 229 physical therapists. The second study used a comparative, qualitative case study design to explore professional development among successful ACCEs/DCEs (Salzman 2003). Six successful ACCEs/DCEs participated in the study. Data were collected through semi-structured, face-to-face interviews using an interview guide. Information in the written transcripts was analyzed through coding by categories using a process of open coding (Creswell 1998) and the constant-comparative method of data analysis (Glaser and Strauss 1967). Concept maps were prepared to organize and structure the data pertaining to each participant (Beissner *et al.* 1994). The concept maps were used to prepare a summary for each case. Cross-case analysis was conducted to answer the research questions for this chapter.

Results

According to the survey of physical therapists, demographic factors that appeared to influence physical therapist clinician CPD choices included employment position (administrator or staff clinician), highest degree attained, association with physical therapy academic program, and membership in the American Physical Therapy Association (APTA). Continuing professional development activities that physical therapist clinicians in the United States are most likely to participate in include attending continuing education courses, communicating with peers, attending in-services and grand rounds, consulting with a colleague after working with a client, attending departmental staff meetings, and using the Internet.

Administrators were more likely than staff clinicians to participate in departmental staff meetings, attend professional regional or state meetings, present lectures to colleagues, students or community groups, and to participate in professional CPD activities outside of work time. Physical therapist clinicians with degrees beyond the entry-level baccalaureate degree are more likely to contribute to platform or poster presentations at professional meetings and to participate in professional CPD activities outside of work.

Physical therapist clinicians who have an association with a physical therapy academic program were more likely to participate in CPD activities outside of work. Some of these activities include attending professional association regional/state meetings, serving on professional committees, and serving as a clinical instructor/mentor. Finally, membership in the APTA also had a significant influence on strategies selected by physical therapist clinicians for their CPD. Professional association members were more likely to read professional journals, use electronic information systems, attend professional association regional/national/international meetings, and network with colleagues than non-members. Overall, APTA members were more likely than non-members to pursue professional CPD activities outside of work.

Cross case analysis in the study exploring the CPD of ACCEs/DCEs showed that their professional development included a web of interconnected experiences. The participants had focused on different aspects of their professional development at different times in their lives, and their professional development was closely tied to their personal development. Even though all were successful ACCEs/DCEs, the picture of success was different for each, based on their personal interests and the mission of the university where they worked.

Discussion

The results of the two studies were analyzed and compared to prepare this chapter. The studies' findings were summarized and illustrated in a concept map (Figure 13.1). The map shows that formal, non-formal, and informal LLL strategies contribute to the CPD of physical therapists. Physical therapists begin their professional development during IPE and continue participating in formal, CPE courses following licensure. Informally, interactions with colleagues and peers are frequently used learning methods. Interactions with colleagues can occur locally, in the workplace, or during physical therapy professional meetings. For physical therapists, professional LLL results in CPD. Understanding the CPD strategies that physical therapists are most likely to participate in may facilitate HRD and CPD providers' ability to make available professional development opportunities that are mutually beneficial for the client, physical therapists, and employer.

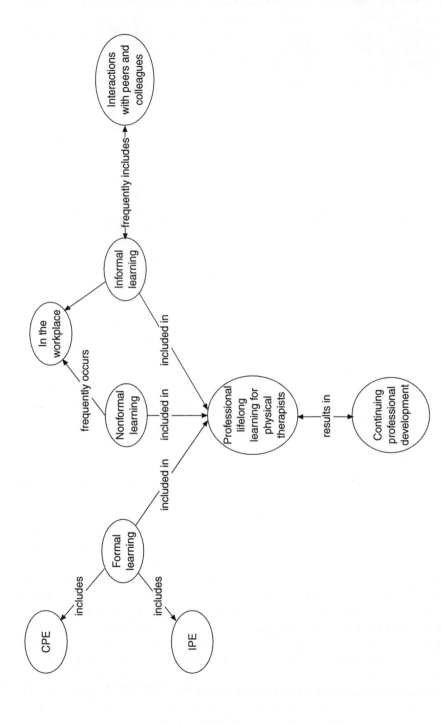

Figure 13.1 Conceptual framework.

How do physical therapists describe their CPD activities?

According to the results of the survey, physical therapists prefer to participate in formal CPE courses. There is a relationship between CPD activities
and job position, association with a physical therapy program, and APTA
membership. However, mandatory CPE does not appear to have any impact
on the CPD strategies pursued by clinicians. Potential reasons might
include the types of CPD strategies that are accepted as meeting the requirements of physical therapy state practice acts. Even though some states give
credit for a variety of learning activities (i.e. participation in journal club,
publishing an article, or providing CPE courses), many accept only formal
courses approved by the state department that regulates professional practice. There is evidence to suggest that mandatory CPE does not alter practice (Ottoson and Patterson 2000; Thomson-O'Brien *et al.* 2001), and
perhaps clinicians are influenced more by an internal, professional desire to
remain current than by any mandate that they must attend courses and document their efforts.

Physical therapists reported that influential formal learning activities
began with their IPE and continued with participation in CPE. Through
interviews, ACCEs/DCEs described experiences during their IPE that had
influenced the direction of their work as physical therapists. Two participants had attended one of the first entry-level post-baccalaureate education
programs and were working in education programs that had developed
unique curricular models. Both believed that they were willing to create
innovative curricula because of their interactions with faculty members who
were able to put into action their vision for the future of physical therapy
education.

Many of the influential experiences from the ACCEs'/DCEs' IPE involved
interactions with specific individuals. One participant reported that her
direction as a physical therapist was changed because her ACCE/DCE placed
her with the Indian Health Service for a clinical education experience.
Another participant reported that she learned about the profession of physical therapy and the availability of post-baccalaureate education programs
from one of her undergraduate professors. During physical therapy school,
she chose clinical education placements across the United States so that she
could travel to places where she had not been. In addition to seeing new
cities during her placements, she met several leaders in the profession who
had profoundly influenced her career. The stories told by these women left a
strong impression on the young student physical therapist. Another participant spoke of meeting her mentor during her physical therapy education.
Both mentor and protégé later became ACCEs/DCEs at universities in the
same state; their relationship led to new service opportunities for the
protégé.

ACCEs/DCEs also reported ways in which their post-professional education had influenced their professional development. Participants reported

that they were eligible to serve as ACCEs/DCEs because of their studies in education. Studying teaching and learning had raised their interest in clinical learning, especially the ways in which it is different from learning in the classroom. One participant discussed the importance of working with faculty from several disciplines during her doctoral education in educational psychology. Working with a diverse group expanded her view of research techniques, introduced her to scholars and research outside of physical therapy, and showed her the importance of cross-fertilization of ideas among different professional groups.

According to the survey, clinicians prefer to participate in formal CPE courses, a finding that is consistent with a recent report describing how rehabilitation therapists gather, evaluate, and implement new knowledge (Rappolt and Tassone 2002). Formal CPE is commonly cited as physicians' CPD strategy of choice to gain new and expert information when considering making a change in practice (Tipping *et al.* 2001). Attending traditional CPE courses had also influenced the ACCEs'/DCEs' professional development. One ACCE/DCE described ways in which she had utilized information from a CPE course to help solve students' learning problems. Another ACCE/DCE reported that remarks from speakers during CPE courses had influenced her philosophy of teaching and developing effective physical therapists. Participants in the second study described an evolution in their reasons for attending CPE, moving from attending to learn new things, to attending to confirm that they knew and were using current knowledge, to attending for an opportunity to discuss problems with other participants.

Despite preferring formal CPE, survey respondents reported participating in a variety of CPD activities, especially during the workday. Frequently used workday CPD strategies included communicating with peers and attending seminars, grand rounds, and staff meetings. Again, this is consistent with the findings of Rappolt and Tassone (2002), who found that participants sought out consultations with colleagues as the first educational resource. Providing opportunities for learning and development within the workplace has been the topic of increased discussion in the literature. A supportive learning culture in the workplace is considered to be vital for the development of successful LLL in the professional setting (Eraut *et al.* 2004; Sim *et al.* 2003).

All ACCE/DCE participants described informal learning experiences that had influenced their professional development. The most influential experiences included interacting with other people. Participants spoke of key learning experiences involving students, clinical instructors, other faculty members, and supervisors. All participants emphasized the importance of learning through interactions with colleagues and peers.

ACCEs/DCEs described significant learning interactions with colleagues locally and across the country. Interactions with colleagues have resulted in growth as educators, researchers, and new service opportunities. Locally, four participants served as members of a clinical education team in their departments. They spoke of the importance of working with colleagues who challenged them to think in new ways and try new things, and who were able to solve student-related problems creatively and fairly. Participants worked with other ACCEs/DCEs in their states and regions to provide clinical instructor training, a relationship that was beneficial to themselves and to the clinical instructors. Clinical instructors benefitted by gaining different perspectives on clinical education; ACCEs/DCEs benefitted through the discussions of the issues and problems related to clinical education with other ACCEs/DCEs. In addition to learning through interactions with local ACCEs/DCEs, the participants reported learning through interactions with colleagues in their departments and across campus. One participant reported that she had observed other faculty members to learn more about teaching methods when she was a novice ACCE/DCE. Another reported that she enjoyed participating in a campus teaching circle with faculty from other disciplines because she gained different viewpoints on teaching and learning.

Professional meetings can provide both structured and nonstructured learning opportunities. Physical therapist administrators and ACCEs/DCEs were likely to attend professional meetings as a means of CPD. ACCEs/DCEs spoke of the importance of talking with ACCEs/DCEs across the country at national physical therapy meetings to learn about challenges to clinical education occurring in various areas. Three ACCEs/DCEs admitted that they attend meetings for the networking opportunities rather than for the scheduled programming.

According to the survey, administrators are more likely to attend professional meetings than clinicians. This finding is not unexpected because administrators tend to have more ability to change their work schedule to accommodate activities that fall outside of the work environment. In addition, administrative job descriptions frequently include expectations regarding keeping current with trends within the profession. Regional and national meetings are an efficient way to meet this work expectation. Staff physical therapists may be deterred from attending regional and national meetings by administrative constraints related to time away from patient care and cost of attendance. Additionally, the challenge of balancing personal and family time with professional development needs may keep clinicians from choosing to attend professional meetings or preparing and giving presentations.

Again, according to the survey, physical therapist clinicians with some association with a physical therapist academic program or who are members of the APTA were likely to participate in professional LLL activities outside of work, read professional journals, use electronic information systems, attend regional/state/national professional meetings, network with colleagues or serve on professional committees. Academic physical therapists, such as ACCEs/DCEs, are expected to participate in these activities. Role modeling and supportive learning environments are important throughout the IPE/CPD learning continuum (Sim *et al.* 2003). For clinicians, association with the physical therapist academic program probably reinforces the benefits of participating in professional meetings and membership in the APTA provides convenience of access to professional journals and electronic resources. Membership dues include home delivery of the professional journal and access to electronic databases. Attendance at professional meetings increases the opportunities for networking.

In the survey of physical therapist clinicians, informal and non-formal learning methods, often involving discussions or conversations with colleagues, were frequently used even though CPE was the preferred CPD strategy. ACCEs/DCEs also emphasized the importance of learning through interactions with colleagues and peers. The results of both studies support the important role that talking about problems plays in the professional development of physical therapists.

How can HRD practitioners and CPE providers work together to provide professional learning opportunities for physical therapists?

The findings from the physical therapist survey (Hall 2005), as well as that of Rappolt and Tassone (2002), found that formal CPE courses are the preferred strategy for CPD. However, since formal courses have limited availability and are not designed to answer questions as they arise in practice, clinicians rely on consultations with peers as their first educational resource. HRD practitioners and CPE providers can work together to support development of the learning experiences utilized frequently by physical therapists.

According to the survey of physical therapists (Hall 2005), formal CPE is the preferred strategy for CPD. Physical therapists may prefer CPE because of the high value placed on formal development methods by licensing or accrediting bodies, or because CPE courses replicate the familiar teaching/learning methods used in IPE. However, even though they are privileged by HRD and policy-makers over other forms of CPD, formal courses that will meet the professional development needs of the individual are not readily available in some areas. Barriers to access of formal methods, or recognizing and encouraging only CPE, may limit the learning opportunities available to clinicians. Several years ago, Karp (1992a) reported that barriers to physical therapists' attendance at CPE included cost of the courses and the need to take time away from family responsibilities and travel a long distance to attend. Additionally, even though physical therapists prefer lectures as the method to deliver education, that format has been found to produce the lowest level of behavior change in practice (Bennett *et al.* 2000; Davis *et al.* 1999). If formal methods are not consistently effective in improving practice and non-formal and informal learning methods are utilized frequently, then it follows that all CPD methods should be considered as important CPD tools by policy-makers, HRD departments, and providers of CPE.

In lieu of formal courses, practitioners rely on consultations with peers as their first educational resource (Rappolt and Tassone 2002). Both physical therapy clinicians (Hall 2005) and physical therapist academicians (Salzman 2003) use peer consultation and networking with colleagues as alternatives to formal courses. Indeed, ACCEs/DCEs and clinicians are most likely to utilize professional development strategies other than formal CPE. Other investigators have found that much of what health professionals learn in professional practice occurs via non-formal and informal methods (Alheit and Dausien 2002; Brownhill 2001; Cheetham and Chivers 2001). Unfortunately, only formal CPE is accepted for credit by most licensing or accrediting bodies. By requiring evidence of participation in formal CPE for renewal of licensure, policy-makers may be inadvertently restricting the professional development of healthcare professionals. It is also reasonable to consider that workplace environments where participation in a wide range of CPD activities is modeled and continued learning is supported will stimulate the clinician to engage in continuing learning practices (Eraut *et al.* 2004; Sim *et al.* 2003).

Professional associations, educators, HRD practitioners, and clinical practitioners should pressure policy makers to recognize professional LLL strategies other than formal CPE courses as valid methods of CPD. In the United States, the APTA is influential in formulating policy and can be a strong advocate for change. For example, the Illinois Physical Therapy Association and IPE school directors in the state of Illinois helped draft the guidelines for mandatory CPE in the state and have been influential in further modification. Physical therapists in Illinois can receive continuing education credit for serving as a clinical instructor, attending a journal club at their workplace, or for being an officer in the professional association. Because of the parties involved in the creation of the guidelines, it is not coincidental that Illinois accepts some non-formal CPD methods as valid indicators of continued competence (Joint Committee on Administrative Rules 2001). In Canada, the College of Physical Therapists of Alberta collaborated with the provincial government to create a continuing competence program for physical therapists in the province. The portfolio program they created requires members to identify areas of their practice that need development, devise a plan to improve practice that can include a range of formal and non-formal learning activities, and maintain a log of activities. This plan acknowledges that continued learning is required to practice effectively, and allows physical therapists in a largely rural province to utilize a wide range of activities to maintain their professional competence (College of Physical Therapists of Alberta 2005).

Continuing education providers and HRD practitioners can work together to develop effective CPD opportunities for physical therapists. Changing the workplace culture to value experienced-based learning methods and encouraging licensing and accrediting bodies to provide credit for learning occurring through a variety of learning strategies may also foster practitioners' professional development. CPE providers can use the information that clinicians participate in non-formal activities within the context of their workday and provide packages that can be delivered as in-services and discussed among colleagues, or by creating online courses that encourage networking. These methods could allow for learning opportunities that are drawn from the needs of the practice environment, increasing the relevance and practical application of the new knowledge. HRD practitioners can facilitate CPD in physical therapists by creating a workplace environment that encourages and rewards continued learning. It is reasonable to consider that clinicians will be stimulated to engage in LLL practices in a workplace environment that encourages and provides a wide range of CPD opportunities (Eraut *et al.* 2004; Sim *et al.* 2003).

Summary and conclusions

The studies described in this chapter illustrate that the CPD of physical therapists begins during their IPE. After licensure, physical therapists prefer to utilize CPE for CPD, however, they also value other learning methods, especially discussions and consultations with colleagues and peers. Discussions that contribute to CPD can occur in the workplace or during formal CPE courses. To facilitate CPD of physical therapists, we encourage HRD and CPE providers to support policy changes that provide credit toward licensure renewal for a variety of learning methods. HRD practitioners can create workplace environments that facilitate and encourage continued learning through discussions with colleagues. By supporting CPD among physical therapists, CPE and HRD practitioners will help to improve the quality of services provided to patients and clients.

Key learning points

- The professional development of physical therapists begins during IPE.
- Physical therapists prefer formal CPE, however, they also value other learning methods, especially conversations/consults with colleagues and peers
- Non-structured learning occurs in the context of practice and during CPE.
- HRD can facilitate the professional development of physical therapists by creating an environment that encourages and supports continued learning.
- HRD can facilitate the professional development of physical therapists by advocating policy changes that provide credit for learning through methods other than formal CPE.

References

Alheit, P. and Dausien, B. (2002) 'The "double face" of lifelong learning: two analytical perspectives on a "silent revolution",' *Studies in the Education of Adults* 34(1): 3–22.

American Physical Therapy Association (2005a) *Doctor of Physical Therapy (DPT) Degree: Frequently Asked Questions*. Online, available at www.apta.org/ rt.cfm/education/dpt/dpt_faq? (accessed 15 February 2005).

American Physical Therapy Association (2005b) *Number of Physical Therapy Programs*. Online, available at www.apta.org/Education/educatorinfo/program_numbers (accessed 18 February 2005).

Beissner, K.L., Jonassen, D.H. and Grabowski, B.L. (1994) 'Using and selecting graphic techniques to acquire structural knowledge,' *Performance Improvement Quarterly* 7(4): 20–38.

Benner, P. (1983) 'Uncovering the knowledge embedded in clinical practice,' *Image* 5(2): 36–41.

Bennett, N., Davis, D., Easterling, W., Friedmann, P., Green, J. and Koeppen, B. (2000) 'Continuing medical education: a new vision of the professional development of physicians,' *Academic Medicine* 75(12): 1167–1172.

Brownhill, B. (2001) 'Lifelong learning,' in P. Jarvis (ed.) *The Age of Learning: Education and the Knowledge Society*, London: Kogan Page.

Case-Smith, J. (1999) 'Developing a research career: advice from occupational researchers,' *American Journal of Occupational Therapy* 53(1): 44–50.

Cervero, R.M. (1988) *Effective Continuing Education for Professionals*, San Francisco: Jossey-Bass.

Cervero, R.M. (1990) 'The importance of practical knowledge and implications for continuing education,' *Journal of Continuing Education in the Health Professions* 10: 85–94.

Cervero, R.M. (1992) 'Professional practice, learning, and continuing education: an integrated perspective,' *International Journal of Lifelong Education* 11(2): 91–101.

Cervero, R. (2000) 'Trends and issues in continuing professional education,' in V. Mott and B. Daley (eds) *Charting a Course for Continuing Professional Education: Reframing Professional Practice*, San Francisco: Jossey-Bass.

Chartered Society of Physiotherapy (1994) 'Continuing professional development: what is it and what does it mean?' *Physiotherapy* 80(9): 623–624.

Cheetham, G. and Chivers, G. (2001) 'How professionals learn in practice: an investigation of informal learning amongst people working in professions,' *Journal of European Industrial Training* 25(3): 248–292.

College of Physical Therapists of Alberta (2005) *Continuing Competence Online*, available at www.cpta.ab.ca/member/competence_main.shtml (accessed 14 April 2005).

Creswell, J.W. (1998) *Qualitative Inquiry and Research Design: Choosing among Five Traditions*, Thousand Oaks, CA: Sage.

Daley, B. (1997) 'Creating mosaics: the interrelationships of knowledge and context,' *The Journal of Continuing Education in Nursing* 28(3): 102–114.

Daley, B.J. (1999) 'Novice to expert: an exploration of how professionals learn,' *Adult Education Quarterly* 49: 133–147.

Daley, B.J. (2000) 'Learning in professional practice,' in V.W. Mott and B.J. Daley (eds) *Charting a Course for Continuing Professional Education: Reframing Professional Practice*, San Francisco: Jossey-Bass.

Daley, B.J. (2001) 'Learning and professional practice: a study of four professions,' *Adult Education Quarterly* 52: 39–54.

Davis, D., Thomson O'Brien, M.A., Freemantle, N., Wolf, F.M., Mazmanian, P. and Taylor-Vaisey, A. (1999) 'Impact of formal continuing medical education: do conferences, workshops, rounds, and other traditional continuing education activities change physician behavior or health care outcomes?' *Journal of American Medical Association* 282(9): 867–874.

Dirkx, J.M., Gilley, J.W. and Gilley, A.M. (2004) 'Changing theory in CPE and HRD: toward a holistic view of learning and work,' *Advances in Developing Human Resources* 6(1): 35–51.

Ellinger, A.D. (2004) 'The concept of self-directed learning and its implications for human resource development,' *Advances in Developing Human Resources* 6(2): 158–177.

Eraut, M. (1994) *Developing Professional Knowledge and Competence*, London: Falmer Press.

Eraut, M. (2000) 'Nonformal learning and tacit knowledge in professional work,' *British Journal of Educational Psychology* 70: 113–136.

Eraut, M. (2001) 'Learning challenges for knowledge-based organizations,' Unpublished manuscript.

Eraut, M., Steadman, S., Furner, J., Maillardet, F., Miller, C., Ali, A. and Blackman, C. (2004) 'Learning in the professional workplace: relationships between learning factors and contextual factors,' paper presented at the American Educational Research Association, San Diego, CA.

Federation of State Boards of Physical Therapy (2002) *2002 Jurisdiction Licensure Reference Guide*, Alexandria, VA: Federation of State Boards of Physical Therapy.

Ford, P.J. (1990) 'The nature of graduate professional education: some implications for raising entry level,' *Journal of Physical Therapy Education* 4(1): 3–6.

Glaser, B.G. and Strauss, A.L. (1967) *The Discovery of Grounded Theory: Strategies for Qualitative Research*, Chicago: Aldine.

Guccione, A. (1999) 'A closer look: what is a physical therapist?,' *PT – Magazine of Physical Therapy* 7(10): 12–13, 72.

Hall, K.D. (2005) 'Lifelong learning in physical therapy: characteristics and facilitation of initial and continuing professional education,' unpublished doctoral dissertation, Northern Illinois University.

Hansman, C.A. (2001) 'Mentoring as continuing professional education,' *Adult Learning* 12(1): 7–8.

Houle, C.O. (1980) *'Continuing Education in the Professions,'* San Francisco: Jossey-Bass.

Illinois State Medical Society (2004) The medical liability litigation crisis. Online, available at www.isms.org/legislative/init_profiles/liability/position_paper.pdf (accessed 24 June 2004).

Japsen, B. (2004) Illinois nursing homes lag in Medicaid pay, *Chicago Tribune*, June 24. Online, available at www.chicagotribune.com/business/chi-040620231june24,1,4720587,story (accessed 24 June 2004).

Jensen, G.M., Gwyer, J., Hack, L.M. and Shepard, K.F. (1999) *Expertise in Physical Therapy Practice*, Boston: Butterworth-Heinemann.

Jeris, L. and Daley, B.J. (2004) 'Orienteering for boundary spanning: reflections on the journey to date and suggestions for moving forward,' *Advances in Developing Human Resources* 6(1): 101–115.

Joint Committee on Administrative Rules (2001) Title 68: Professions and occupations, chapter VII: Department of financial and professional regulation. Online, available at: www.ilga.gov/comission/jcar/admincode/068/06801340000061.html (accessed 25 March 2005).

Kaiser, R. (2004) 5 more suits on non-profit hospitals. *Chicago Tribune*, June 23. Online, available at: www.chicagotribune.com/business/chi-0406230184 june23,1,6948816.story (accessed 24 June 2004).

Karp, N.V. (1992a) 'Physical therapy continuing education. Part I: Perceived barriers and preferences,' *Journal of Continuing Education in the Health Professions* 12: 111–120.

Karp, N.V. (1992b) 'Physical therapy continuing education. Part II: Motivating factors,' *Journal of Continuing Education in the Health Professions* 12: 171–179.

Knox, A. (1993) *Strengthening Adult and Continuing Education: A Global Perspective on Synergistic Leadership*, San Francisco: Jossey-Bass.

Knox, A. (2000) 'The continuum of professional education and practice,' in V. Mott and B. Daley (eds) *Charting a Course for Continuing Professional Education: Reframing Professional Practice*, San Francisco: Jossey-Bass.

Maggs, C. (1996) 'Toward a philosophy of continuing professional education in nursing, midwifery, and health visiting,' *Nurse Education Today* 16: 98–102.

Marsick, V.J. and Watkins, K.E. (2001) 'Informal and incidental learning,' in S.B. Merriam (ed.) *The New Update on Adult Learning Theory*, San Francisco: Jossey-Bass.

Mott, V. (2000) 'Development of professional expertise in the workplace,' in V. Mott and B. Daley (eds) *Charting a Course for Continuing Professional Education: Reframing Professional Practice*, San Francisco: Jossey-Bass.

Ottoson, J. and Patterson, I. (2000) 'Contextual influences on learning application in practice. An extended role for process evaluation,' *Evaluation and the Health Professions* 23(2): 194–211.

Pinkston, D. (1989) 'Evolution of the practice of physical therapy in the United States,' in M. Scully and M.R. Barnes (eds) *Physical Therapy*, New York: J.B. Lippincott.

Polyani, M. (1958) *Personal Knowledge*, Chicago: University of Chicago Press.

Polyani, M. (1966) *The Tacit Dimension*, Garden City, NY: Doubleday.

Queeney, D.S. (2000) 'Continuing professional education,' in A.L. Wilson and E.R. Hayes (eds) *Handbook of Adult and Continuing Education*, San Francisco: Jossey-Bass.

Rappolt, S. and Tassone, M. (2002) 'How rehabilitation therapists gather, evaluate, and implement new knowledge,' *The Journal of Continuing Education in the Health Professions* 22: 170–180.

Rice, R.E. and Richlin, L. (1993) 'Broadening the concept of scholarship in the professions,' in L. Curry, J.F. Wergin and Associates (eds) *Educating Professionals: Responding to New Expectations for Competence and Accountability*, San Francisco: Jossey-Bass.

Salzman, A.J. (2003) 'Professional development of academic coordinators/directors of clinical education in physical therapy: portraits of persistence,' *Dissertation Abstracts International*, 64-05, 1495.

Schön, D.A. (1983) *The Reflective Practitioner*, New York: Basic Books.

Schön, D.A. (1987) *Educating the Reflective Practitioner*, San Francisco: Jossey-Bass.

Shepard, K.F. and Jensen, G.M. (1990) 'Physical therapist curricula for the 1990s: educating the reflective practitioner,' *Physical Therapy* 70: 566–577.

Sim, J., Zadnik, M. and Radloff, A. (2003) 'University and workplace cultures: their impact on the development of lifelong learners,' *Radiography* 9: 99–107.

Slotnick, H.B. (1999) 'How doctors learn: physicians' self-directed learning episodes,' *Academic Medicine* 74: 1106–1117.

Strickler, E.M. (1990) 'The role of the academic coordinator of clinical education: a dilemma in academe,' *Journal of Allied Health* 19: 95–101.

Strickler, E.M. (1991) 'The academic coordinator of clinical education: current status, questions, and challenges for the 1990s and beyond,' *Journal of Physical Therapy Education* 5: 3–9.

Thomson-O'Brien, M., Freemantle, N., Oxman, A., Wolf, D. and Herrin, J. (2001) Continuing education meetings and workshops: effects on professional practice and health care outcomes, *Cochrane Review* 3. Online, available at: gateway1.ovid.com:80/ovidweb.cgi> (accessed 24 October 2001).

Tipping, J., Donahue, J, and Hannah, E. (2001) 'Value of unstructured time (breaks) during formal continuing medical education events,' *The Journal of Continuing Education in the Health Professions* 21: 90–96.

Part IV

Evaluating learning

14 The limitations of in-service training in social services

Nicholas Clarke

Aims

This chapter explores some of the critical factors influencing the effectiveness of in-service training within Social Services Departments and provides an illustration of how an evaluation was undertaken to determine the impact of an in-service training programme in needs assessment for care managers. Specifically, the chapter aims to:

1 Examine the importance of undertaking training evaluation within social services and identify what evaluation research tells us about the impact of training within these work environments.
2 Present an approach to training evaluation that might be used as basis for undertaking other training evaluations within social services
3 Present and discuss findings from the evaluation of training that point to a range of problems in securing the actual transfer of training back on the job and identifying particular problems that are often associated with this work environment
4 Consider other alternatives for staff development that might overcome some of the problems to training transfer encountered in this evaluation.

Introduction

For human service organizations such as social service agencies, where people rather than technology are arguably the more critical determinants of success, it is not surprising that training has been heralded as key to organizational effectiveness (Cohen and Austin 1994; Peryer and Goodenough 1992; Scally and Beyer 1992; Williams and Lloyd 1992). Within this context, in-service training in particular is identified as contributing to this endeavour. Wright and Fraser (1987) have suggested that such training within social services has three major functions: (1) to provide staff with knowledge and skills to serve the agency's consumer, (2) to reiterate agency goals and communicate needs up and down the line, and (3) to provide remedial training for the under-performing worker. Similarly, Lindsey *et al.*

(1987) emphasize the importance of in-service training to achieving service aims, arguing that agencies such as social services:

> rely increasingly on short term training to equip staff with the skills and knowledge needed to resolve complex practice problems.
>
> (Lindsey 1987: 623)

Specifically in relation to Social Services in the UK, a number of publications have echoed similar sentiments, hailing the necessity of in-service training for the effective operation of social services departments (Horwath and Morrison 1999; Peryer 1997; TOPPS 2000), often backed by research findings indicating significant participation by staff in the in-service training opportunities provided. Findings from a survey of 1276 managers, social workers, home care workers and residential workers for example, found that short non-qualifying courses were highly supported by social services staff, with 89 per cent of respondents indicating that such courses had enabled them to gain new skills (Connelly 1996). Another study reported that 93 per cent of managers, 90 per cent of social workers, 62 per cent of residential workers and 40 per cent of home care workers surveyed had all received training that was not related to obtaining a qualification during the previous 12 months, much of which would have been in-service training (Balloch *et al.* 1995).

Expectations thus persist that in-service training contributes to achieving agency goals, and not infrequently it has been almost an incumbent belief within departments that the clients or consumers of social services are the ultimate beneficiaries of the investment made in staff training (Doueck and Austin 1986; Schmid and Nirel 1995). However, we begin to face difficulties when we look beyond the rhetoric of training and simple training activity indices for evidence of a more substantive nature concerning the actual impact of training in these work settings. In this respect two key problems arise.

The first relates to the relatively lowly status training evaluation has traditionally been afforded within these work organizations. The training literature is replete with evidence suggesting the absence of a systematic approach to training evaluation, and the largely atheoretical nature of training practice in organizations (Ford *et al.* 1997; Latham 1988; Sogunro 1997; Tannenbaum and Yukl 1992; Wexley 1984). In particular, there is the oft-cited limitation of training evaluations to proceed barely beyond assessing the extent to which trainees have been satisfied with the training they had received, commonly referred to as participant reactions to training (Bell and Kerr 1987; Phillips 1997; Saari *et al.* 1988; The Industrial Society 1994; Training 1999). The Training Agency (1989) found that barely 10 per cent of the organizations they surveyed evaluated training by using pre- and post-training comparisons of trainee behaviour, compared with 90 per cent who utilized reaction feedback. A further survey of training professionals in the UK showed that regular testing of the knowledge learned on a training course was conducted by less than half of the organizations surveyed, with less than 10 per cent stating that they evaluated training programmes in terms of their business impact (Training 1999). A particular problem would seem to be that most evaluation is undertaken for the primary purpose of improving instruction, rather than demonstrating actual outcomes in terms of individual performance (Brandenburg and Smith 1986). Accounts of training evaluation undertaken specifically within the public sector, similarly paint a picture of weak evaluation methodologies and a poor application of knowledge concerning training effectiveness (Datta 1990; Guneskera 1989; Sims 1993). Sims (1993: 591) for example comments that the,

> lack of training program evaluation is even more evident in the public sector, and is possibly the least developed aspect of the training process in public agencies. Yet it is arguably the most important.

Evidence of training evaluation practice within social services agencies in both the US (Snow 1982) and the UK (Rai 1994) would suggest this conclusion is well justified, with authors highlighting a depressing failure of evaluation to determine whether training in any way achieves the changes of which it is expected. Given that investment in staff training is predicated on the basis of its capacity to affect staff performance, the seemingly insurmountable problem we are faced with as a result of this continuing trend in most training evaluation practice, is simply its limited capacity to provide robust and valid information as to whether training actually secures any demonstrable changes in staff performance (Saari *et al.* 1988).

The second problem, however, raises far more worrying concerns. In this respect, of far greater importance have been consistent findings from research showing that although training programmes often can be found to produce positive results in terms of trainees' reactions to training and trainee learning, the capacity of training to produce demonstrable changes in trainee behaviours on the job is far more equivocal (Campion and Campion 1987; Ford *et al.* 1997; Quinones and Ehrenstein 1997). Significantly, such findings have also been found to be consistent in relation to the impact of in-service training in social services.

Empirical context

Clarke (2001) for example, conducted a literature review to examine the results of evaluation studies of social service in-service training published between 1974 to 1997. The criteria for studies to be included in the review were that:

1   Studies should specifically focus on, and provide results from, an empirical evaluation of a training programme and not merely describe training and suggest possible evaluation strategies.

2   Training programmes evaluated must be specifically in-service training, defined as training and development programmes provided specifically for staff in-house by their employing agency.
3   The agency providing the in-service training should be a public sector agency delivering social services.

As a result, only 20 studies were found to have been published in the literature. Of these studies, four concerned training for task-centred casework (Reid and Beard 1980; Rooney 1985; Rooney 1988; Shapiro *et al.* 1980), three studies each reported evaluations of interpersonal/interviewing skills training programmes (Gebhardt-Taylor 1982; Lindsey *et al.* 1987; Stevenson *et al.* 1992), and two studies reported evaluations of supervisory skills training programmes (Austin and Pecora 1985; Rodway 1992). The remaining ten evaluation studies concerned training in the following: Social work values (Ammons 1979); The impact of addiction on child welfare practice (Gregoire 1994); The delivery of home-based services (Pecora *et al.* 1985); Nutrition for the home-bound elderly (Glanz and Scharfe 1985); Evaluating social services effectiveness (Doueck and Bondanza 1990); Functional family therapy (Wright and Fraser 1987); Child protection training (Delewski *et al.* 1986); Case management skills in child protection (Cheung *et al.* 1991); Training the trainer (DePoy *et al.* 1992); Permanency planning in child care (Jones and Biesecker 1980); and Evaluating staff development programmes/parent training (Schinke *et al.* 1981). A chief observation from the review was the variation in methodologies employed in order to evaluate the impact of the training. This meant that in a significant number of instances, only tentative conclusions could be drawn regarding its effectiveness (despite the claims often made by the study's author(s)). For the most part, this centred on limitations associated with the research designs adopted, the extent to which appropriate evaluative criteria were used, the types of measures collected, and generally the consistent absence of longer term follow up of the outcomes of training.

Theoretical context

The need to establish multiple criteria which correspond with the objectives that have been set for the training programme is essential if the programme's effectiveness is to be determined (Goldstein 1993; Phillips 1997; Tannenbaum and Woods 1992), but equally as important is the need to include appropriate behavioural criterion. In this respect there are a number of models within the literature in order to guide training evaluations (Alvarez *et al.* 2004; Kirkpatrick 1987; Swanson and Holton 1999). Kirkpatrick's model in particular has received widespread support within the training practitioner literature and continues to be the most pervasive evaluation typology known to training practitioners (Goldstein 1993; Tannenbaum and Yukl 1992; Wexley 1984). Guidance for social services departments on training evaluation has similarly advocated the use of Kirk-patrick's training evaluation framework (Bramley and Pahl 1996). The model identifies four components of training evaluation and specifically delineates the need to assess the impact of training at the levels of reaction (trainees' reactions to the training process and programme content), learning (knowledge, skills or attitudes gained), behaviour (behavioural changes) and results (overall organizational improvements such as increased productivity or reduction in turnover). However, there was considerable variation in the extent to which these evaluation criteria can be found within the training evaluation studies reviewed. So for example, four studies did not include evaluation criterion beyond the levels of either reaction or learning (Ammons 1979; Glanz and Scharf 1985; Pecora *et al.* 1985; Schinke *et al.* 1981). In this respect these four studies, although distinguished by varying degrees of rigour associated with their research designs, would appear to reflect much of contemporary training evaluation practice within social services agencies in one important regard. Both positive responses from trainees to the training they have received and trainee gains in knowledge, are used to justify claims regarding the effectiveness of training beyond these lower level criteria. Although the remaining studies did attempt to assess behavioural change as a result of the training, here too there were also limitations as a result of the behavioural criterion adopted in the evaluations. Eight studies for example only relied upon self report data as a measure of behaviour change with the limitations this entails (e.g. Doueck and Bondanza 1990; Gebhardt-Taylor 1982; Rodway 1992).

Perhaps of far more importance however, was the extent to which a number of the evaluation studies, which did incorporate more objective behavioural indicators in their research designs, found either limited or no effects of the training on behaviour (e.g. Cheung *et al.* 1991; Jones and Biesecker 1980; Lindsey *et al.* 1987; Reid and Beard 1980; Rooney 1985, 1988; Stevenson *et al.* 1992). Stevenson *et al.* (1992) for example evaluated the interviewing skills component of a ten-day training course in child sexual abuse for child protective service workers, videotaping participants demonstrating particular skills taught on the training programme. Taped interviews were then rated by judges on a Likert-type scale ranging from zero to four using a skill evaluation tool developed by one of the authors. However, measures taken immediately before and immediately following training did not demonstrate any significant changes in the performance of participants. Similarly Cheung *et al.* (1991) evaluated the effects of a 6-hour training programme focusing on the case management skills in child sexual abuse intervention for 18 child protective service workers. Evaluation of trainees' responses was then based on ratings of four conceptual areas, including the trainees' understanding of the problems presented in the vignette, clarity of communication and the inclusion of appropriate information. However, despite finding significant overall improvement following training, the authors highlighted that some targeted behaviour demonstrated no significant change following the training. In addition, after analysis of the size of some of the skill gains obtained, the authors, similar to many other studies referred to above, draw attention to the uncertainty surrounding the practical significance of these results. They suggest that whereas immediate post-testing may act as a baseline for ongoing training and supervision, longitudinal testing is essential to determine whether training has made a lasting and significant impact on worker performance. In terms of its capacity to affect behaviour change and impact on performance, these findings suggest that in-service training in social services clearly gives some cause for concern. Indeed, it requires us to consider at least the extent to which many training programmes actually achieve the aims and objectives that are often claimed by the organizers and sponsors of such training. What seems clear is that we need to know far more about how actually effective is the range of in-service training that is provided to social service workers, and seek to understand better why its impact on behaviour may be so difficult to achieve.

Methodology

Given this context, this study aims to enhance our understanding of how to improve employee development within social service organizations, by reporting the findings of an evaluation study that was undertaken to determine the impact of a training programme designed to improve the needs assessment skills of care managers in a UK social services department. Through undertaking a comprehensive evaluation of the training that combined both quantitative and qualitative methodologies, the impact of the training on actual behaviour change is reported. Importantly, the factors that appeared to impede the effectiveness of such training are identified, and they suggested significant limitations associated with in-service training to achieve discernible changes in behaviour in the workplace. These findings should help inform decisions within social service settings as to how best to support staff development activities and programmes.

The training programme

The main goal of the training programme was stated as to equip care managers to undertake a 'holistic' assessment of social care for adults. The training programme consisted of two days, facilitated by two trainers from the training team responsible for community care and adult services, and was delivered in a centrally located social services training venue. Attendance on the training programme was voluntary, and participants completed an application form to attend. Twenty-two care managers attended the training programme and personal details were obtained from 21 of these. Of these, 90 per cent (19) were women and 10 per cent (2) male; 90 per cent (19) were white and 5 per cent (1) Afro-Caribbean. Thirty-eight per cent (8) were aged between 51–60, followed by 28 per cent (6) aged between 31–40, 24 per cent (5) were aged between 41–50, 5 per cent (1) were aged between 21–30, and finally 5 per cent (1) were aged over 60. Thirty-one per cent (6) of participants had a social work or social care qualification while 42 per cent (8) stated they possessed an alternative professional certificate or diploma. Twenty-two per cent (4) either did not possess any higher qualifications or did not indicate. Fifty per cent (11) stated that they had briefly discussed the course with their supervisor before attending, although all of these indicated that this predominantly involved merely asking their supervisor to sign an authorization form to attend. Approximately 45 per cent (10) of trainees indicated that they had no discussion at all with their supervisor before attending the training course and 5 per cent (1) did not indicate. The mean number of years spent with the organization was 8.5 years ranging from three to 12 years. The mean number of years participants had occupied their current post was three years.

The evaluation methodology

A repeated-measures, pre- post-test design was utilized in the study (Campbell and Stanley 1963). Although the evaluation design should ideally have included a comparison group, both administrative arrangements and resource limitations precluded this. Only behavioural criteria were included in the study as the dependent variables of interest, since from the literature this would appear to be the level at which training often has least impact. In this respect there were three key behavioural indicators: (1) skill acquisition and maintenance was assessed using scores obtained on a behavioural analogue test referred to as the case vignette from data collected (a) pre-course, (b) immediately post-course and then again (c) three months following training; (2) the generalization (transfer) of training to the workplace was measured using supervisors' ratings of trainees' performance in needs assessment both before training, and then again three months following trainees' return to the workplace; and (3) a final indicator of training transfer was assessed by obtaining trainee self-report data (qualitative data) six months following attendance on the training programme. Rossi (1979) has suggested that case vignettes provide a mechanism to evaluate trainees' understanding of complicated issues and the unique characteristics of service users that require analytical judgements. In this instance a case vignette was developed detailing a novel needs assessment situation which was then used to assess specific behavioural dimensions of the needs assessment process. In order to maximize data collection, the case vignette was given to participants to complete immediately before the training programme began on the first day of the actual training course. It was then subsequently administered again at the end of the training course on the second day, with 45 minutes allocated to complete the exercise at both time points. Participants were asked to write up their own needs assessment in a free response format, using their own headings where appropriate. The case vignette was again sent to participants at their workplace three months post-course, with a covering letter asking for their cooperation in completing the case vignette and asking that they only spend 45 minutes on the exercise. The same case vignette was used at all three time points.

(1) Rating trainees' written needs assessments

Participants' skills in undertaking comprehensive needs-led assessments was measured by assessing the written needs assessments prepared by trainees in response to the information contained within the case vignette. Six measures of skill acquisition were obtained: five measures each corresponding to five separate behavioural domains associated with undertaking needs assessments, and one overall measure of skill acquisition, which was a sum total of the five identified key areas. This is referred to as the overall needs assessment skill score. Four qualified care managers in the organization who had completed a university accredited diploma in care management were invited to take part in the evaluation and act as judges for rating case vignettes. The use of multiple raters has been advocated for increased control over rater biases (Murphy 1982). Although the judges were aware a training course was being evaluated, they were unaware of whether case vignettes were pre- or post-course. To further minimize threats to validity, all participants' hand-written needs assessments were typed and randomly coded to eradicate the risk of raters matching participants' pre- and post-test hand-written responses.

The case vignette and rating schedule

The case vignette was a 12-page document based on an actual case concerning an elderly woman of 82 years of age, living alone and isolated, having been admitted to hospital following a fall, with a range of physical and mental health needs. Instructions accompanying the case vignette asked trainees to write up a comprehensive needs assessment in order to facilitate discharge from hospital.

A schedule for rating participants' needs assessments was developed by the researcher with criteria for determining effective performance in undertaking a holistic needs assessment drawn from two key sources: (1) the content of the training programme and (2) the available literature relating to good practice in needs-led assessment, which had also been used to underpin the training programme. Five specific skill domains were distinguished:

Domain 1: Ability to synthesize the assessments of different agencies and individuals into a coherent whole;
Domain 2: Distinguishing between facts and interpretations;
Domain 3: Identifying service users' needs;

Domain 4: Maximizing Independence;
Domain 5: Setting appropriate objectives.

Attached to each of the above skill domains was either a four-point or five-point Likert-type scale against which judges rated all cases. The maximum score possible for each written needs assessment was therefore 24, and the minimum 5. Scores on each domain, as well as the overall need assessment skill score were based on the pooled average scores of raters.

Maximizing inter-rater reliability

Two key strategies were employed in order to maximize inter-rater reliability: the development and use of behaviourally anchored rating scales (BARS), and the provision of rater training. Previous authors have suggested that through carefully defining scale dimensions and providing specific behavioural examples, raters are provided with a standard frame of reference with which to undertake assessments (Fay and Latham 1982; Landy and Farr 1980). A range of effectiveness levels corresponding to each of the five needs assessment domains were anchored to each of the points on the scales. Each effectiveness level was therefore anchored to a description of skills in a particular area associated with undertaking a holistic needs-led assessment. Each of the specific behavioural indicators and their associated effectiveness levels had been identified with the judges during rater training so that it was clear what the service user's needs were as a result of analysing the case study material. The primary measures of reliability of ratings was inter-rater agreement in relation to overall case vignette measures. Overall inter-rater agreement was 0.45. This score suggests that judges had difficulty precisely locating needs assessment behaviours close to the locus of the effectiveness level. It is interesting to note however that of those scores where judges disagreed, approximately 90 per cent were within one scale point of each other. Although not ideal, this level of consistency was considered acceptable for raters to discriminate between differences in written needs assessments.

(2) Supervisor ratings of care managers' performance in needs assessment

As part of the evaluation strategy, supervisors of those taking part in the training undertook ratings of the performance of their supervisees in relation to their needs assessment practice in the workplace. A questionnaire was sent to supervisors to rate the performance of their supervisees two weeks before participants attended the training programme, and then again three months after the programme had taken place. Given that needs assessment comprises a central component of a care manager's job, it was considered reasonable that course participants would have had sufficient time during the three months following the course to utilize any new skills gained.

Ratings were requested on a number of performance dimensions relating to needs assessment, and supervisors were asked to code each questionnaire in order to match responses over time.

Supervisors' ratings

The supervisor questionnaire consisted of a 15-item measure of their supervisee's performance in undertaking needs assessments. The measure was comprised of five subscales, each corresponding to one of the five skill domains developed for rating trainees' written needs assessments. Supervisors were asked to rate the extent to which their supervisees demonstrated specific needs assessment skills, and all items were rated on a five-point Likert-type scale anchored to the following: $5 =$ excellent, $4 =$ satisfactorily, $3 =$ poorly, $2 =$ very poorly and $1 =$ not at all. The maximum and minimum scores possible were therefore 75 and 15 respectively.

(3) Trainee self-report data

Following recommendations made in other social service training evaluation studies (Gebhardt-Taylor 1982), qualitative data were also collected both to supplement and as a means to triangulate findings from the quantitative data. Due to time and resource constraints qualitative data were obtained through the use of free response questionnaires sent to course participants six months after the training course had been completed. Information was particularly requested regarding participants' experience of using the training on the job as well as any difficulties they had encountered. Sample questions included 'What factors helped or have impeded you from implementing what was taught on the course?' and 'What factors do you think would have made (or have made) it more likely that you implement the training you received in your practice?.'

Results

The impact of the training programme on trainee skill acquisition

The findings reported here in relation to needs assessment skill acquisition are based on mean ratings of both individual needs assessment behavioural domains and the overall needs assessment skill score. In order to determine the impact of the training programme on skill acquisition a series of statistical tests were undertaken. Univariate F-tests were performed as a first stage of data analysis. These statistical tests help us to see whether there are any differences between the scores that were obtained at the two different time points that could be attributed to more than just chance alone, and permit us to examine a number of variables all at the same time. Results of these tests are presented in Table 14.1.

Table 14.1 Training-related changes on dependent measures, univariate F-tests with (2,45) df

Variable	Sum of Squares (SS)	Error (SS)	Mean Squares (MS)	Error (MS)	F ratio	Significance of F
Domain 1	13.48	55.18	6.74	1.23	5.50	0.007**
Domain 2	7.96	30.24	3.98	0.671	5.92	0.005**
Domain 3	12.63	46.99	6.31	1.04	6.05	0.005**
Domain 4	4.04	22.93	2.02	0.510	3.97	0.026*
Domain 5	2.19	29.72	1.10	0.66	1.66	0.201
Overall needs assessment score	172.13	683.67	86.07	15.19	5.66	0.006**

Notes
$*p < 0.05, **p < 0.01$.

With the exception of domain 5, [$F(2,45) = 1.66$, $p < $ ns (non-significant)] the results indicate significant improvement on all dependent measures: Domain 1, [$F(2,45) = 5.50, p < 0.01$]; Domain 2, [$F(2,45) = 5.92, p < 0.01$]; Domain 3, [$F(2,45) = 6.05, p < 0.01$]; Domain 4, [$F(2,45) = 3.97, p < 0.05$]. However, the significant F values only indicate that particular group means are unequal. In order to determine which means were significantly different from each other, multiple post-hoc comparison procedures were used (Bonferroni F-test). This enables us to see which scores had changed at which of the different time points. Follow up univariate F-tests results are presented in Table 14.2. The results demonstrate that significant changes occurred between time 1 and time 2 for domain 1, [$F(1,39) = 10.23, p < 0.01$], domain 2, [$F(1,39) = 10.12, p < 0.01$], domain 3, [$F(1,39) = 12.81, p < 0.001$], domain 4, [$F(1,39) = 5.48, p < 0.05$], and the overall needs assessment skill score, [$F(1,39) = 9.99, p < 0.01$]. Changes between time 2 and time 3 for all dependent measures were not statistically significant. An inspection of the group means in Table 14.2, indicate that in relation to domains one, two, three, four and the overall needs assessment skill score, participants' needs assessment skills remained fairly constant subsequent to the first post test, suggesting that skills acquisition had been maintained three months following attendance on training. These results demonstrate that with the exception of domain five, the training programme had been successful in trainees gaining improved skills in needs assessment in four of the five skill domains examined.

Use of skills on the job

Although all supervisors eventually returned their pre-course ratings of trainees performance in conducting needs assessments, workload pressures

Table 14.2 Means and standard deviations and analyses of variance of dependent measures across the three time points

Measure	Pre course Time 1 M (SD)	Post course Time 2 M (SD)	Post course Time 3 M (SD)	F Ratio Time 1 – Time 2	F Ratio Time 2 – Time 3
Domain 1: Ability to synthesize the assessments of different agencies and individuals into a coherent whole	1.84 (1.08)	2.92 (1.07)	2.86 (1.28)	10.23**	0.016 ns
Domain 2: Distinguishing between facts and interpretations	1.59 (0.77)	2.37 (0.80)	2.50 (1.04)	10.12**	0.119 ns
Domain 3: Identifying users' needs	2.00 (0.95)	3.08 (0.98)	2.86 (1.35)	12.81***	0.216 ns
Domain 4: Maximizing independence	2.34 (0.66)	2.84 (0.71)	3.07 (0.89)	5.48*	0.470 ns
Domain 5: Setting appropriate objectives	1.86 (0.79)	2.08 (0.80)	2.50 (0.91)	0.746	1.31 ns
Overall needs assessment Sk.ll score	9.64 (3.59)	13.29 (3.80)	13.79 (5.04)	9.99**	0.073 ns

Nctes
*$p < 0.05$, **$p < 0.01$, ***$p < 0.001$.

and other commitments meant that only nine supervisor ratings of trainees were returned before trainees actually participated in the training programme. As a result, only nine complete data sets were used in the evaluation. The results of t-tests for all five performance domains and the overall needs assessment performance score are presented in Table 14.3. These results were far more disappointing and show that no significant changes occurred as a result of the training programme in relation to the transfer of skills back to the workplace (Domain 1: $t(6) = 0.66$; Domain 2, $t(8) = 0.32$; Domain 3, $t(6) = 1.57$; Domain 4, $t(7) = 2.16$; Domain 5, $t(6) = 1.87$ and Overall needs assessment skill score, $t(8) = -2.16$. In all cases $p <$ ns).

Trainee self report data

Questionnaires were used to ascertain participants' views of the success of the training and the extent to which training had been transferred to practice. All trainees identified some factors that they considered to have influenced their learning on the course. In each case these related specifically to the design of the training programme. Programme design factors considered to facilitate learning included the trainers' expertise in relation to the topic, the relevance of the material for actual care management practice, and the use of case studies as a learning method. Factors identified as impeding learning were the lack of illustrations/cases appropriate to specific client groups, too much information included within the training sessions and an over-reliance on the use of a lecture format. A number of trainees' comments illustrate some of these points:

> Proactive training by listening, then good practice on how to implement this by using examples. What was difficult to absorb and take on board as there was so much delivered so fast and for a longish time without a break. More courses needed which reflect the high quality input this one had. Perhaps it was because most speakers were hands on practitioners with a good theoretical/research knowledge as well.

> The methods used on training course were very relevant – it is one of the best courses I have been on for many years. Contents of course were very relevant and up to date. Trainers know what they were talking about. As I have previously mentioned I felt that this course was one of the best I had been on for a very long time. The contents were very relevant for today's type of work, i.e. continuing care criteria, joint working with primary health care teams. Trainers were very good, as taken from the workplace.

> Useful doing the case study. Direct talks not so helpful. I enjoyed the training and felt involved. I liked having a file prepared. I keep this close to me at work and use it. I would say that all care managers should have similar training especially if not experienced. I have had years of

Table 14.3 Mean scores, standard deviations and t-tests for pre- and post-course supervisor ratings of performance

Measure	Pre course time 1 M (SD)	Post course time 2 M (SD)	t-value (df)	Sig.
Domain 1: Ability to synthesize the assessments of different agencies and individuals into a coherent whole	11.86 (1.07)	11.43 (2.15)	0.66 (6)	0.534
Domain 2: Distinguishing between facts and interpretations	3.78 (0.67)	3.67 (0.87)	0.32 (8)	0.760
Domain 3: Identifying users' needs	20.43 (2.37)	18.57 (3.91)	1.57 (6)	0.168
Domain 4: Maximizing independence	12.50 (1.41)	11.50 (2.0)	2.16 (7)	0.068
Domain 5: Setting appropriate objectives	10.71 (1.60)	9.86 (2.12)	1.87 (6)	0.111
Needs assessment Behaviours score	51.67 (11.08)	57.56 (7.40)	−2.16 (8)	0.063

experience as a hospital social worker and some management but I found it useful and informative. Relevant to day-to-day work.

It was aimed at care managers working with older people, e.g. from hospital setting. This was not as relevant to client group that I work with, i.e. people with learning disabilities.'

I think if the 2 days had been split into four morning sessions only and spaced out at fortnightly intervals for example, I think I may have digested more facts than I did.

Trainees were also asked whether there were any specific features associated with the workplace which impeded their use of the training on the job. Most comments in this area by far referred to excessive workloads and time constraints:

Number of clients and time to spend on each client is a problem in locality teams as caseloads are very high.

The large workload and constant demands from on high such as 'we need this information by yesterday' without their real understanding of what this actually means in workload, e.g. transfer of clients to new care agency when the Elderly Services lost contract home care hours.

Heavy workload and demands from management for additional statistics as soon as possible. Need for crisis response.

Due to pressure – workload. It is more difficult to implement changes – its very easy to follow old habits as change takes time and effort.

Workload management and team/duty responsibilities. Non-cooperation from certain GPs who withhold information at times and who can be reluctant to refer elderly people for appropriate consultant assessment are all impediments.

Sometimes there isn't time to prepare for an assessment, especially with elderly clients due to emergencies, sudden changes that need immediate action. Not ideal but I'm trying to use the training. I am trying to manage time better.

Non-availability of enough time, e.g. pressure to arrange discharges and transfers to other wards before all assessments taken to completion (my ward is an assessment ward). I Endeavour to use the training points but circumstances just don't always allow for that type of thoroughness, as patients don't stay on ward for full stay and time pressures.

Time, The understanding and attitude of others – plus time constraints felt by them.

A number of trainees also referred to the lack of supports or mechanisms available in the workplace to facilitate the transfer and maintenance of skills they had gained on the training course. Where support was identified, by far the major source was through team supervisors. Supervisory support appeared to vary across a spectrum ranging from merely being available to provide support should the care manager request it, to some discussion regarding the benefits of the course once the trainees returned to the workplace. Importantly there seemed to be no concerted effort to provide ongoing reinforcement by supervisors of any skills gained on the course. Indeed, organizational mechanisms to support the transfer of training were notably absent. Trainees' comments included:

There is a lack of consistency in the way that individual care managers complete their assessments. It is therefore more difficult to get positive reinforcement of what was taught. Care managers do not seem to discuss/share the way in which they complete assessment in any great detail.

No [support] other than supervision from line manager when required.

Some support through discussion with the assistant team manager about the course and discussion with colleagues of the benefit of the course, the latter being to encourage others to undertake it.

I received encouragement by my assistant team manager to complete summaries.

I work on my own at a community hospital so am disciplined in a professional way. My manager, is based elsewhere, supports the necessity to complete the care managers' assessment summary when applying for funding for a package of care.

Supervision that included appraisal of my assessment methods would have helped, smaller caseload, higher profile of models of assessment within the locality. It doesn't often appear to be an issue.

Future training courses to enhance skills/knowledge would help. Because of time lapse since the training I have found it hard to recall specifics of the training. A refresher half day would be very useful.

Discussion

The results of the evaluation clearly demonstrate that the training had an impact in improving the needs assessment skills and knowledge of these care managers, and these improvements were shown to be maintained up to three months following attendance on the training programme. Specifically, statistically significant improvements were found on four of the five skill domains considered necessary for undertaking holistic needs assessments. Nevertheless, despite trainees' gains in skill, additional findings suggest that the training programme failed actually to penetrate beyond skill acquisition into the actual working practices of trainees, mirroring similar findings reported in other training evaluation studies (Russell 1984; Russell *et al.* 1984), and within social service agencies more specifically (Reid and Beard 1980). The results from the supervisor ratings failed to identify any statistically significant changes in terms of the impact of training on trainee performance back in the workplace. Furthermore, self-report data from a number of trainees six months after their attendance on the programme, would appear to provide additional support for the lack of penetration of training into actual work practice. Trainee self-report data indicated that trainees had found the programme useful, felt they had gained increased confidence in undertaking needs assessment, and importantly indicated that the course had provided them with an opportunity to reflect on their current practice. However, in terms of any tangible impact on practice, trainees' comments indicated that this was confined predominantly to changes in the way they both completed and recorded information on particular care management assessment forms. In very few instances were specific changes identified in the way trainees conducted needs assessments or performance changes, such as, for example, in terms of how they interacted with users or carers during the course of assessments or worked with other professionals.

One might expect that in order to implement these skills in practice, trainees are likely to need to devote far more time and effort to the needs assessment process. However, self-report data from trainees overwhelmingly identified workload pressures and time constraints as major factors impeding their use of training, and presumably influencing the choices they make in how best to obtain needs assessments. Under such circumstances, where enormous pressures are brought to bear on care managers in terms of managing high caseloads, and having both to obtain needs assessments and to arrange appropriate care plans fairly rapidly, the working environment would seem to militate against training transfer. Indeed, within such a working environment, considerable energies are often instead directed to ensuring that the necessary paperwork is satisfactorily completed to comply with procedural regulations, rather than channelled into implementing more labour-intensive work practices. In this respect, it is interesting that the most tangible impact on practice identified by most trainees was the improved use of assessment forms. This work environment, a culture seemingly characterized by a dominant concern for procedural accountability (Harris 1987; Lewis and Glennerster 1996) places severe constraints on innovation, particularly as regards the implementation of new work practices. This is likely to be exacerbated by the limited support identified within the work environment for actually implementing any of the trained skills initially acquired. Evidence elsewhere has accumulated identifying the importance of reinforcement strategies, such as feedback and praise to support desired behaviours within the workplace, especially as a result of training (Alavosius and Sulzer-Azaroff 1986; Komaki 1986; Langeland *et al.* 1998; Williams and Luthans 1992). In this instance however, minimal reinforcement from supervisors could be found, with little evidence of support to implement the training they had received on the job. Where trainees did indicate support from supervisors, this tended to be in the form of general comments regarding how useful trainees found the training, rather than any explicit focus on supporting the transfer of skills. Given the constraints within the workplace identified by many trainees, the results would seem to suggest that behavioural reinforcements within the work environment generally support retaining most features of previous practice, rather than adopting new approaches. Information provided by trainees that they valued attendance on the training programme, because of the opportunity it provided them to reflect on their practice deserves some comment. It is possible that this may reflect care managers' ambiguity within the agency in relation to the actual skills, or perhaps more specifically the standards of practice, required in relation to needs assessment. If this is the case, it is possible that the training programme offered an opportunity for trainees to confirm/disconfirm perceptions they held about levels of skill and standards required, especially in the absence of information from other sources provided by the agency. In particular, the suggestion that there is minimal feedback from supervisors on performance, would appear to indicate that very few opportunities exist within the agency for care managers to receive clear information regarding both their role and competence in relation to conducting needs assessments. Without clear signals or messages within the agency regarding both expectations of practice and associated standards, significant variations in practice both within and across care management teams are likely to emerge. Under these circumstances, it would again be difficult to conceive how trained skills are to be reinforced and maintained within this particular work environment, particularly given that trainees' peers within their specific teams are likely to be pursuing different styles and approaches in needs assessment practice.

To date, social support within the workplace has generally received the most empirical support as a mediating factor in the transfer of training (Rouillier and Goldstein 1993; Tracey *et al.* 1995), and findings obtained here would appear similarly to suggest that social support, in particular from supervisors, plays a significant role in influencing the penetration of training into the workplace. The identification that time constraints and workloads were major workplace factors overwhelmingly impeding training transfer is of major significance. A number of previous writers have similarly identified these specific factors as influencing the use of training on the job (Huczynski and Lewis 1980) and especially too within social service agencies (Austin *et al.* 1984; Clarke 2002a,b; Gregoire 1994; Rooney 1985; Vinokur-Kaplan 1986). Findings here, then, would appear to confirm that despite acquiring knowledge and skills through training, these factors in the work-place simply militate against their actual use in practice. Increasingly, the environment within social services agencies, incorporating elements such as organizational climate, structure and agency policies, is being recognized as mediating the effectiveness of training (Austin *et al.* 1984; Marks and Hixon 1986). In particular, the role of the supervisor has been identified as occupy-ing a significant role in maximizing the transfer of training as well as the alignment of training with organizational procedures and policies (Clarke 2002a,b). Gebhardt-Taylor (1982) has previously suggested that factors such as negative attitudes towards the training by supervisors and administrators, the fact that training was mandatory, and the characteristics of the social and political milieu of the agency where training was taken place, were all significant impediments to learning on training programmes. Gregoire (1994) also, described a number of barriers cited by course participants as impeding them implementing practice goals they set following training. Significantly, a lack of time and resources, the daily demands of child welfare practice, and the refusal by supervisors to endorse proposed practice changes, were all cited as major work-related impediments. Conversely, particular characteristics of the work environment were also suggested as significantly facilitating the transfer of training. Manipulating the work environment was suggested by Wright and Fraser (1987) to have resulted in the positive training effects they demonstrated. Social services workers who attended training in family therapy, identified the increased availability of their supervisor for case conferences and changes in agency policies regard-ing case management, as the most significant factors assisting the transfer of training they had received. In particular, supervision practices were adapted to facilitate the implementation of the newly acquired skills, reinforcing the transfer of training through feedback and guidance. However, despite a recognition of the role of the supervisor as an important aspect of the work environment influencing the transfer of training, research in social services suggests a more prominent role for supervisors in social services in this respect may be somewhat difficult to achieve in practice. Clarke (2002a), for example, has previously found that supervisors in social services took a minimal role in encouraging or supporting the use of risk assessment train-ing attended by trainees. In relation to other continuous professional devel-opment, Cooper and Rixon (2001), also found that only 50 per cent (9) of social workers they surveyed who had completed a post-qualifying training programme discussed their progress in supervision. Clarke (2002b) sug-gested that one of the most significant factors influencing the use of risk assessment skills training in social services was the workload of supervisors. He argued that the size of the work unit will influence how much time the supervisor may have available to support the reinforcement of training. Given the way in which social services departments in the UK are currently organized and the intense staffing pressures that exist, the requirement for supervisors to undertake a pivotal role in facilitating training transfer may be far from realistic.

Although the qualitative findings appear to offer some convincing explanations to explain the failure of the training to transfer, limitations associated with both the study's research design and methodology suggest some caution may need to be exercised in interpreting the results. A pre/post-test design does not suitably control for hawthorne or maturational effects as possible explanations accounting for the positive changes in skill acquisition identified. Similarly, the small sample sizes involved place restrictions on the generalization of the study's findings. Elsewhere, studies seeking to determine the effects of in-service training within social services on trainees' practice have highlighted the problems in selecting or developing valid and reliable instruments for assessing practice skills (Stevenson *et al.* 1992), and similar difficulties have been encountered here. In particular, a number of challenges to validity in relation to the dependent measures used may have introduced some error into the results. In relation to the needs assessment rating schedule, there is some indication that the behavioural anchors associated with each of the skill domain effectiveness levels, were not sufficiently precise to facilitate the most accurate discrimination of skill utilization by judges. Although high levels of reliability were found for judges' ratings during rater training, inter-rater agreement was subsequently fairly modest at 0.45. Elsewhere Ostroff (1991) has suggested that behaviour or performance rating scales may simply not be sensitive enough to detect training effects, which may have accounted for the failure to demonstrate positive findings in some training evaluations (e.g. Noe 1986; Russell *et al.* 1984; Sorcher and Spence 1982). Despite rater training being undertaken as a safeguard to minimize rater error, it is likely that psychometric errors and the time lapse between rater training and actually undertaking the ratings will have influenced the resulting scores to some degree. As a result, the validity of the scores obtained here may be in question.

The findings from the study also highlight particularly the limitations associated with using the case vignette as a means to best equip these care managers with transferable skills for use in the workplace. Although such behavioural analogue tests may be useful teaching tools, they may suffer considerably when trainees are faced with the requirement to carry out needs assessments within a real-life context. Instead here they are influenced by the myriad of environmental contingencies that impact on their professional practice while on the job. Indeed, many of the trainees' comments regarding the problems associated with actually carrying out needs assessment on the job, draw into sharp view the extent to which the learning they use on the job is considerably influenced by the specific social and cultural context surrounding them. This being the case, we are forced to consider how effective such in-service training interventions are and whether other approaches to employee development might be more favourable, especially within these work settings.

Conclusions

This study has highlighted the potential for knowledge and skills to be gained through training. However it is at the level of transfer that major difficulties seem to arise. Despite the limitations associated with this research the findings here do seem to correspond with much of the previous research discussed earlier regarding problems in relation to training transfer in social services agencies, and as a result suggest a number of key learning points.

Key learning points

- Over recent years, much research has examined how training such as this requires additional strategies in order to increase the likelihood of skill transfer (Marx 1982). Drawing upon much of the research into training transfer (Baldwin and Ford 1988; Alvarez *et al.* 2004) these strategies have tended to look at ways in which trainees' motivation can be increased, the design of training can better mirror the real life situation, and additional support and reinforcement can be provided in the workplace once trainees return on the job.
- Although these strategies have certainly met with increasing signs of success, transfer is still considered very difficult to achieve in practice. This becomes even more difficult the more complex the skills required. This has led many writers and researchers to examine whether other learning methods might be more appropriate than training such as this, to ensure the greater use of learning on the job such as workplace learning methods and approaches.
- Over the past ten years in particular, there has been a growing realization that perhaps on- the-job learning methods, often referred to as workplace learning, might be far more effective at equipping workers with the knowledge and skills that they require for effective practice. This includes a range of learning activities such as mentoring, coaching, team and peer learning events, job rotation and secondments as well as undertaking special assignments or projects on the job. Compared to the extent of research that has been undertaken in relation to the effectiveness of training, effectiveness research in the area of workplace learning is very much in its infancy. However, a number of studies from a variety of settings have begun to show promising results with such approaches, particularly in relation to their increased potential for securing a greater use of learning on the job (e.g. Larsen 2004; McDowall-Long 2004).

The findings from this study suggest that such approaches may possibly overcome some of the factors contributing to the ineffectiveness of this training programme.

• Previous research has identified time and workload pressures as undermining the effectiveness of in-service training so that it has been seen as less effective than experience gained on the job, especially through undertaking special projects (Crosbie *et al.* 1988). However, in relation to both training and workplace learning, it is difficult to escape the fundamental role that the work environment plays; in particular, the relationship between supervisor and supervisee in terms of implementing new learning. In this respect, given the economic constraints affecting public services, social service departments may need to consider far more systemic and cultural changes in their approach to staff development if greater gains from staff development are to be made.

References

Alavosius, M.P. and Sulzer-Azaroff, B. (1986) 'The effects of performance feedback on the safety of client lifting and transfer,' *Journal of Applied Behavior Analysis* 19(3): 261–267.

Alvarez, K., Salas, E. and Garofano, C.M. (2004) 'An integrated model of training evaluation and effectiveness,' *Human Resource Development Review* 3(4): 385–416.

Ammons, P. (1979) 'Inservice training in social work values,' *Child Welfare* 58(10): 659–665.

Austin, M. and Pecora, P. (1985) 'Evaluating supervisory training: the participant action plan approach,' *Journal of Continuing Social Work Education* 3(3): 8–13.

Austin, M.J., Brannon, D. and Pecora, P.J. (1984) *Managing Staff Development Programs in Human service Agencies*, Chicago, IL: Nelson-Hall, pp. 149–188.

Baldwin, T.T. and Ford, J.K. (1988) 'Transfer of training: a review and directions for future research,' *Personnel Psychology* 41: 63–105.

Balloch, S., Andrew, T., Ginn, J., McLean, J., Pahl, J. and Williams, J. (1995) *Working in the Social Services*, London: NISW Research Unit.

Bell, J.D. and Kerr, D.L. (1987) 'Measuring training results: key to managerial commitment,' *Training and Development Journal* 41(1): 70–73.

Bramley, P. and Pahl, J. (1996) *The Evaluation of Training in the Social Services*, NISW Research Unit: London.

Brandenburg, D. and Smith, M. (1986) *Evaluation of Corporate Training Programs*, ERIC monograph, TME Report 91. Princeton, NJ: Educational Testing Service.

Campbell, D.T. and Stanley, J.C. (1963) *Experimental and Quasi-experimental Designs for Research*, Chicago: Rand McNally College Publishing.

Campion, M.A. and Campion, J.E. (1987) 'Evaluation of an interview skills training program in a natural field setting,' *Personnel Psychology* 40: 675–691.

Cheung, K.M., Stevenson, K.M. and Leung, P. (1991) 'Competency-based evaluation of case management skills in child sexual abuse intervention,' *Child Welfare* 70(4): 425–435.

Clarke, N. (2001) 'The impact of inservice training in social services,' *British Journal of Social Work* 31(5): 757–774.

Clarke, N.R. (2002a) 'Job/work environment factors influencing training effectiveness within a human service agency: some indicative support for Baldwin & Fords' transfer climate construct,' *International Journal of Training and Development* 6(3): 146–162.

Clarke, N. (2002b) 'Training care managers in risk assessment: outcomes of an in-service training programme,' *Social Work Education* 21(1): 461–476.

Cohen, B.J. and Austin, M.J. (1994) 'Organizational learning and change in a public welfare agency,' *Administration in Social Work* 18(1): 1–19.

Connelly, N. (1996) *Training Social Services Staff: Evidence From New Research*, London: NISW.

Cooper, B. and Rixon, A. (2001) 'Integrating post-qualification study into the workplace: the candidates' experience,' *Social Work Education* 20(6): 701–717.

Crosbie, D., Vickery, A. and Sinclair, I. (1988) 'Schemes and social workers: issues of time pressures and training,' *Social Work Education* 7(3): 30–34.

Datta, R.C. (1990) 'Evaluation of training in an economic framework,' *Indian Journal of Social Work* 51(2): 261–271.

Delewski, C.H., Pecora, P.J., Smith, G. and Smith, V. (1986) 'Evaluating child protective services training: the participant action plan approach,' *Child Welfare* 65(6): 579–591.

DePoy, E., Bunce, J.P. and Sherwen, L. (1992) 'Training trainers: evaluating services provided to children with HIV and their families,' *Research on Social Work Practice* 2(1): 39–55.

Doueck, H.J. and Austin, M.J. (1986) 'Improving agency functioning through staff development,' *Administration in Social Work* 10(2): 27–37.

Doueck, H. and Bondanza, A. (1990) 'Training social work staff to evaluate practice: a pre/post/then comparison,' *Administration in Social Work* 14(1): 119–133.

Fay, C.H. and Latham, G.P. (1982) 'Effects of training and rating scales on rating errors,' *Personnel Psychology* 35: 105–117.

Ford, J.E., Kozlowski, W.J., Kraiger, K., Salas, E. and Teachout, M. (eds) (1997) *Improving Training Effectiveness in Work Organisations*, Mahway, NJ: Lawrence Erlbaum.

Gebhardt-Taylor, M. (1982) 'Educational training programs for social service workers: a quantitative and qualitative evaluation,' *Journal of Social Service Research* 5(¾): 85–93.

Glanz, K. and Scharf, M. (1985) 'A nutrition training program for social workers serving the homebound elderly,' *Gerontologist* 25(5): 455–459.

Goldstein, I.L. (ed.) (1993) *Training in Organizations: Needs Assessment, Development and Evaluation*, 3rd edn, California: Brooks/Cole.

Gregoire, T.K. (1994) 'Assessing the benefits and increasing the utility of addiction training for public child welfare workers: a pilot study,' *Child Welfare* 73(1): 69–81.

Gunesekera, R. (1989) 'Evaluation's serendipity: a new approach in evaluating training impact,' *Public Administration and Development* 9: 505–511.

Harris, N. (1987) 'Defensive social work,' *British Journal of Social Work* 17: 61–69.

Horwath, J. and Morrison, T. (1999) *Effective Staff Training in Social Care*, London: Routledge.

Huczynski, A.A. and Lewis, J.W. (1980) 'An empirical study into the learning transfer process in management training,' *Journal of Management Studies* 17: 227–240.

338   *Nicholas Clarke*

Jones, M and Biesecker, J. (1980) 'Training in permanency planning: using what is known,' *Child Welfare* 59(8): 481–489.

Kirkpatrick, D.L. (1987) 'Training evaluation,' in R.L. Craig (ed.) *Training and Development Handbook: A Guide to Human Resource Development*, New York: McGraw-Hill.

Komaki, J.L. (1986) 'Toward effective supervision: an operant analysis and comparison of managers at work,' *Journal of Applied Psychology* 71: 270–279.

Landy, F.J. and Farr, J.L. (1980) 'Performance rating,' *Psychological Bulletin* 87(1): 72–107.

Langeland, K.L., Johnson, C., Merle, C. and Mahwinney, T.C. (1998) 'Improving staff performance in a community mental health setting: job analysis, training, goal setting, feedback and years of data,' *Journal of Organizational Behaviour Management* 18(1): 21–43.

Larsen, H.H. (2004) 'Experiential learning as management development: theoretical perspectives and empirical illustrations,' *Advances in Developing Human Resources* 6(4): 486–503.

Latham, G.P. (1988) 'Human resource training and development,' *Annual Review of Psychology* 39: 545–582.

Lewis, J. and Glennerster, H. (1996) *Implementing the New Community Care*, Buckingham: Open University Press.

Lindsey, E.W., Yarborough, D.B. and Morton, T.D. (1987) 'Evaluating interpersonal skills training for public welfare staff,' *Social Service Review* 623–635.

Marks, J. and Hixon, D. (1986) 'Training agency staff through peer group supervision,' *Social Casework* 67(7): 418–423.

Marx, R.D. (1982) 'Relapse prevention for managerial training: a model for maintenance of behavioural change,' *Academy of Management Review* 7: 433–441.

McDowall-Long, K. (2004) 'Mentoring relationships: implications for practitioners and suggestions for future research,' *Human Resource Development International* 7(4): 519–534.

Murphy, K.R. (1982) 'Difficulties in the statistical control of halo,' *Journal of Applied Psychology* 67: 161–164.

Noe, R.A. (1986) 'Trainees' attributes and attitudes: neglected influences on training effectiveness,' *Academy of Management Review* 11(4): 736–749.

Ostroff, C. (1991) 'Training effectiveness measures and scoring schemes: a comparison,' *Personnel Psychology* 44(2): 353–374.

Pecora, P., Delewski, C., Booth, C., Haapala, D. and Kinney, J. (1985) 'Home-based, family-centred services: the impact of training on worker attitudes,' *Child Welfare* LXIV(5): 529–540.

Peryer, D. (1997) *Human Resources for Personal Social Services*, The Local Government Management Board.

Peryer, D. and Goodenough, A. (1992) *Workforce and Training in the Personal Social Services: A Programme for Action*, Association of County Councils.

Phillips, J.J. (1997) 'A rational approach to evaluating training programmes including calculating ROI,' *Journal of Lending and Credit Risk Management* 79(11): 43–50.

Quinones, M.A. and Ehrenstein, A. (eds) (1997) *Training for a Rapidly Changing Workplace: Applications of Psychological Research*, Washington, DC: American Psychological Association.

Rai, D.K. (1994) *Developments in Training in Social Services*, London: NISW.

Reid, W.J. and Beard, C. (1980) 'An evaluation of in-service training in a public welfare setting,' *Administration in Social Work* 4(1): 71–85.

Rodway, M.R. (1992) 'Motivation and team building of supervisors in a multi-service setting,' *The Clinical Supervisor* 9(2): 161–169.

Rooney, R. (1988) 'Measuring task-centred training effects on practice: results of an audiotape study in a public agency,' *Journal of Continuing Social Work Education* 4(4): 2–7.

Rooney, R.H. (1985) 'Does inservice training make a difference? Results of a pilot study of task centred dissemination in a public social service setting,' *Journal of Social Service.*

Rossi, P.H. (1979) 'Vignette analysis: uncovering the normative structure of complex judgements,' in R.K. Merton, J.S. Coleman and P.H. Rossi (eds) *Qualitative and Quantitative Social Research*, New York: Free Press, pp. 176–186.

Rouillier, J.Z. and Goldstein, I.L. (1993) 'The relationship between organizational transfer climate and positive transfer of training,' *Human Resource Development Quarterly* 4: 377–390.

Russell, J.S. (1984) 'A review of fair employment cases in the field of training,' *Personnel Psychology* 37: 261–276.

Russell, J.S., Wexley, K.N. and Hunter, J.E. (1984) 'Questioning the effectiveness of behaviour modelling training in an industrial setting,' *Personnel Psychology* 37: 465–481.

Saari, L.M., Johnson, T.R., McLaughlin, S.D. and Zimmerle, D.M. (1988) 'A survey of management training and education practices in U.S. companies,' *Personnel Psychology* 41: 731–743.

Scally, M. and Beyer, S. (1992) *Using Training to Improve Services, Social Care Research Findings*, York: Joseph Rowntree Foundation.

Schinke, S.P., Smith, T.E., Gilchrist, L.D. and Wong, S.E. (1981) 'Measuring the impact of continuing education,' *Journal of Education for Social Work* 17(Winter): 59–64.

Schmid, H. and Nirel, R. (1995) 'Relationships between organizational properties and service effectiveness in home care organisations,' *Journal of Social Service Research* 20(3/4): 81–92.

Shapiro, C.H., Mueller-Lazar, B.J. and Witkin, S.L (1980) 'Performance based evaluation: a diagnostic tool for educators,' *Social Service Review* 54(2): 262–272.

Sims, R.R. (1993) 'Evaluating public sector training programs,' *Public Personnel Management* 22(4).

Snow, C.W. (1982) 'In-service day care training programs: a review and analysis,' *Child Care Quarterly* 11(2): 108–121.

Sogunro, O.A. (1997) 'Impact of training on leadership development: lessons from a leadership training program,' *Evaluation Review* 21(6): 713–737.

Sorcher, M. and Spence, R. (1982) 'The Interface project: behaviour modeling and social technology in South Africa,' *Personnel Psychology* 35(3): 557–582.

Stevenson, K.M., Leung, P. and Cheung, K.M. (1992) 'Competency-based evaluation of interviewing skills in child sexual abuse cases,' *Social Work Research and Abstracts* 28(3): 11–16.

Swanson, R.A. and Holton, E.F. (1999) *Results: How to Assess Performance, Learning and Perceptions in Organizations*, San Francisco: Berrett-Koehler.

Tannenbaum, S.I. and Woods, S.B. (1992) 'Determining a strategy for evaluating training,' *Human Resource Planning Journal* 15: 63–81.

Tannenbaum, S.I. and Yukl, G. (1992) 'Training and development in work organisations,' *Annual Review of Psychology* 43: 399–441.

The Industrial Society (1994) *Managing Best Practice – Training Evaluation*, London: The Industrial Society.

Tracey, J., Tannenbaum, S. and Kavagnah, M.K. (1995) 'Applying trained skills on the job: the importance of the work environment,' *Journal of Applied Psychology* 80(2): 239–252.

Training (1999) 'A professional agenda for the millennium,' *Training*, July: 8–10.

Training Agency (1989) *Training in Britain: A Study of Funding, Activity and Attitudes*, London: HMSO.

Training Organisation for the Personal Social Services (TOPSS) (2000) *Modernising the Social Care Workforce – the First National Training Strategy for England.* Leeds: TOPSS England.

Vinokur-Kaplan, D. (1986) 'National evaluation of inservice training by child welfare practitioners,' *Social Work Research and Abstracts* 22(4) (Winter): 13–18.

Wexley, K.N. (1984) 'Personnel training,' *Annual Review of Psychology* 35: 519–551.

Williams, S. and Luthans, F. (1992) 'The impact of choice of rewards and feedback on task performance,' *Journal of Organizational Behaviour* 13(7): 653–666.

Williams, W.L. and Lloyd, M.B. (1992) 'The necessity of managerial arrangements for the regular implementation of behaviour analysis skills by supervisors and front-line staff,' *Developmental Disabilities Bulletin* 20(1): 37–61.

Wright, W.S. and Fraser, M. (1987) 'Staff development: a challenge of privatization,' *Journal of Sociology and Social Welfare* 14(4): 137–160.

15 Evaluating a health education/promotion programme in Romania

Anne Squire

Introduction

This chapter explores the implementation and evaluation of a health education/promotion programme for older people in Romania. It is useful to provide first a very brief overview of the context in which this research was conducted. HelpAge International has been working in partnership with Eastern and Central Europe for many years. The collapse of communism in Eastern and Central Europe, and the subsequent declared intention to transfer to market economies, encouraged optimism both in the East and the West. According to Atkinson and Micklewright (1992), for a brief period there was a widely-shared belief that lives would improve, standards of living would increase, democracy would flourish and that liberation from the polices of the past 40 years would benefit everyone. It soon became patently clear that this hope was not to be fulfilled. HelpAge International became increasingly aware that older people in Eastern and Central Europe were suffering in particular ways from the effects of this transition. A growing proportion of the populations of these countries in this region were becoming older, yet their needs were being ignored.

In 1992, HelpAge International was commissioned by the Directorate General 1 of the European Commission to undertake a study on the needs of the older people in Romania. The study brief outlined the research goal as: 'Learn about the conditions of the older people in Romania so as to assess their more pressing needs and to suggest ways in which they can be helped during the political transition from communism' (HelpAge International Report 1992). Almost all the older people interviewed, regardless of income, identified health care and the promotion of health as a problem.

One recommendation of the HelpAge International research survey was that the Inter-Ministerial Commission should begin to work out a training/education strategy for the care of older people and to commission the development of training programmes at national and local levels to incorporate the following elements:

- training in health education and health promotion;
- training in gathering of information and analysis of needs and identification of priorities;
- training in the care of older people and in the management and support of others who are caring from them. This should include training in how to train community level carers in basic care and support of older people;
- training in the monitoring and assessment of services;
- General Practitioners, as the group of professionals probably with most direct and frequent contact with older people, should receive training to enable them to develop their capacity to give advice and information to older people on the availability of social services. They also should receive training in basic management skills in relation to the care of older people.

HelpAge International (1992) identified the educational and training needs throughout the Romanian health and social care system as it dealt with the problems of older people. These training needs involved the following personnel:

- National and local level administrators;
- Health care professionals at all levels;
- Institutional carers;
- Community carers, family carers and social workers.

Specific training in the needs of older people was minimal across all these groups in 1992, and, because of this, HelpAge International asked The British Association for Services to the Elderly (BASE) to develop educational programmes in the care and health promotion of older people in Romania. Four areas of Romania were chosen for education programmes, Bucharest, Galati, Nehoiu, and Timisoara from 1993–2002.

I was appointed as a consultant/trainer (the lead trainer and educator) for BASE, along with two other BASE consultants/trainers. At my initial meeting in February 1993 with the director of BASE and the two BASE consultants, it was decided, because of the HelpAge International 1992 report, which suggested that most of the older people interviewed clearly wanted to stay in their own homes, to plan a community health promotion/education programme. For many of the older people, support from family members, neighbours or friends was crucial to enable them to continue living in their own homes. This educational programme would, we envisaged, empower older people and carers (whether professional, family or lay carers) by using a partnership/stakeholder approach. Most influential in our reasoning behind this was what we had read about the Romanian people, their oppression and their struggle for survival and independence at this time. Stakeholder participation and empowerment refers to the process by which individuals participate with others while gaining increased control over their lives (Bond and Bond 1987; Thomas 1988). This chapter will describe the critical ethnography, empowerment education programme development and empowerment evaluation research that was conducted in Romania from 1993–2002.

The Romanian context

The following section explains the situation in Romania, which influenced the development of the HelpAge International/BASE education programmes drawing on the 1992 HelpAge International Research Report (HelpAge International 1992).

The Population and society

The total population of Romania in 1991 was 23.19 million, of which over 88 per cent were reported by the government as being ethnic Romanian with a large Hungarian minority (some 8 per cent of the population) occupying the Transylvania region (Gillion 1991; HelpAge International 1992). During the Ceausescu regime, the Hungarians were subject to a policy of cultural assimilation, including restrictions on the use of the Hungarian language in schools and Universities. After the revolution, the Hungarian minority was eager to reverse the assimilation policy and a political party, the Hungarian Democratic Union, was formed in 1990.

The other major ethnic minority group in Romania are the Roma (Gypsies) who probably number between one and two million. However, due to official reluctance from the Romanian government to identify Roma separately, such estimates are very approximate. Other minority groups such as Germans, Turks, Ukrainians, Serbs and Jews are officially said to comprise about 2.4 per cent of the population. Persistent migration by the German and Jewish minorities has eroded their numbers (HelpAge International 1992).

The era of transition: political change

The abrupt collapse of the Ceausescu regime in December 1989 ushered in a period of rapid change in all aspects of Romanian life, which is usually characterized as the 'era of transition' (Rose 1992). There was a political volatility, as parties formed and coalesced around policy platforms, and economic upheaval with rapid inflation and unemployment. There was understandable anxiety as Romanians faced a future of uncertainty and both economic and social areas of change.

Economic change

After the 1990 election, the 'democratization' process gathered pace, chiefly in the critical area of economic reform, and the movement towards market economy has been a principal feature of the overall transition process since 1990. Prices of commodities other than very basic supplies have been deregulated, resulting in rising levels of inflation and speculation. The consequent price rise and shortages have led to real hardship for an already impoverished population. Agriculture, the country's economic mainstay, has performed relatively poorly and the country suffers from periodic energy shortages. However, it should not be forgotten that during the latter years of the Ceausescu regime, food and energy shortages were increasingly common and indeed were arguably an important reason why the revolution of 1989 won popular assent. External trade, particularly with former Eastern European trading partners, had fallen abruptly and foreign trade with countries of the developing world has also gone into sharp decline.

Social change

The economic situation exacerbated the social pressures in the transition. Indeed, not all the social changes now taking place in Romania are entirely new or unfamiliar. Since 1939, Romania has undergone a transformation from an overwhelmingly rural society to one in which urban life and experience has become much more important, although remaining a predominantly rural culture with the great majority of those not living in the countryside having relatives who do and retaining close ties to their rural roots.

In this period of change, the traditional family structure has been put under great strain. Opinions from the participants of interviews carried out by the HelpAge International study (1992) varied greatly as to whether the multi-generational 'extended family' was still a significant feature of Romania society. There was a widespread view that the traditional family was effectively destroyed by the cooperatization of agriculture, urbanization and the concentration of populations in public housing. Some Romanians argued that multi-generational families stayed together even under the most difficult conditions, but there appeared to be a lack of consensus about this. HelpAge International (1992) reported that some grandparents, parents and children do retain close links, even when geographically spread. However, three-generation households do not necessarily provide positive or desirable living arrangements and what may appear to be traditional extended family arrangements are often forced on people by circumstances beyond their control – notably, in Romania, the massive inflation in housing costs. Where older people do not have family support, their conditions are particularly difficult, given the lack of state compensatory social assistance provision. There is a predominant view that family values have declined, with the blame being placed variously on the decline in religious faith, a negative view of ageing, said to have grown during the Ceausescu years, and current economic hardship.

The urban–rural contrast

Such issues are highlighted in the strong contrast between urban and rural areas in Romania. It is often in towns and cities that the problems of the vulnerable groups such as older people are manifested at their most severe. The break-up of urban communities by the previous regime's policy of wholesale destruction of housing and relocation in apartment blocks, left many older people isolated in new and unfamiliar neighbourhoods. An equally problematic feature of urban life is when different generations of a family share overcrowded accommodation. HelpAge International (1992) maintains that rural communities seem, despite cooperatization and land confiscations, to have retained a much higher level of community solidarity than in the cities, with even casual social contact far more common. The informal economy of the countryside, producing more for consumption than the market, also seems to work to the benefit of groups such as the older people. However, isolation in rural areas can be just as profound as in the cities. Health care is conspicuous by its absence in remote areas of Romania and, here, social services frequently do not exist at even the minimal levels of urban centres. Housing standards can also be an acute problem for rural older people.

The situation of older people in Romania

The reliability of official Romanian statistics of any kind and particularly population statistics was highly questionable up to 1989, under the communist regime. Thus, population projections and longitudinal population studies are riddled with problems. No detailed information was available for the ethnicity of older people. Given these limitations, only a brief review of population statistics for the over 55 years age group is possible here.

A total of 5.06 million (21.8 per cent) were 55 years or over, according to figures released in 1992 by the National Commission of Statistics (1992). There was a higher percentage of woman aged over 55 (55.2 per cent) as compared with men (44.8 per cent). In terms of geographical distribution of the over 55 year age group, there is a concentration in rural areas. Of the over 55s 59.1 per cent live in rural areas, as compared to 40.9 per cent living in urban areas (National Commission of Statistics 1992). Such differentiation between rural and urban locations is most marked for those between 55 years and 69 years, reducing gradually for older age groups. This overall distribution contrasts with the total population, 54.1 per cent of who live in urban areas and 45.9 per cent in rural areas.

In 1956, 50 per cent of the population of Romania was under 25 years old. By 1989, the median age was approximately 32 years of age. By 2020, according to United Nations (1988) projections, the median age is expected to be 35 years. The average life span in 1992 was 69.56 years.

The structure of health and welfare provision

At the national level, responsibility for provision for the health and welfare of older people in Romania in 1993 was divided between three ministries. The Ministry of Labour and Social Protection (MLSP) was mainly responsible for those receiving state pensions, administering the pension system and resources. The State Secretariat for the Handicapped was a new ministry responsible for (amongst others) older people without pensions, for whom it ran residential homes. The Ministry of Health was responsible for the general health care needs of the population, including older people. These areas of health and welfare responsibility are discussed in turn.

Pensions

In 1991, pensions were paid to some 2.94 million Romanians (National Commission of Statistics 1991). At that time, such pensions were based on the number of years' work registered by the pensioner and his/her salary over the last five years. The vast majority (95.7 per cent) of social insurance pensioners are paid under the category of *state social insurance*. Agricultural pensions are paid to those who work in farm cooperatives but these are much lower than the MLSP pension levels. Both the levels of pensions, and the number of pensioners, have risen sharply over recent years: those not entitled to a pension receive social assistance payments. The MLSP estimated in 1991 that 100,000 people received no pension but could not supply precise figures of what proportions of these did or did not receive social assistance.

Local service provision

At the local level, social provision is mainly social assistance payments through Social Assistance Board offices (local branches of the MLSP) and free meals offered by 79 social canteens. Town mayors had the responsibility for the funding and operating of these canteens. The canteens were concentrated in the towns, as was health provision via medical polyclinics. All provision appeared very patchy with some older people receiving help while others did not. With the exception of pensions, services offered to older people were very dependent on the individual initiative of local officials.

The needs of the older people

Many of the needs of the older people reflect those of the population as a whole. These can be related to Maslow's hierarchy of needs for food and shelter, safety, affection and self-esteem (Maslow 1954). However, for the older people of Romania, these needs have been made more extreme for several reasons. The older people rely for their income on a pension or on state support, immediately disadvantaging them in relation to those earning an income. At times of rapid inflation, as in Romania in 1992, pensions may well not keep up with the rising cost of living. Older people are likely to become less active as age increases and experience more difficulties with their mobility, which can affect access to food, services outside the home and socialization. The most pressing needs of the older people relate to income. Too many older people in Romania have insufficient incomes for their immediate needs of food, heating and medicine. This is the context in which the work described was undertaken.

The theoretical context: critical ethnography, empowerment programme development and empowerment evaluation

In this study, I used a combination of methodological approaches in research: critical ethnography combining elements of critical theory, empowerment programme development and empowerment evaluation of the education programme.

The BASE trainers were becoming increasingly aware of how we would be working between two cultures and that this would mean having to engage with at least two very different sets of ideas of how the education programmes, research evaluation and practice development should be conducted. The methodologies could be different, as well as the cultural, social and academic traditions. At this time, I found Marsden and Oakley's (1990) work on evaluating social development projects helpful for deepening my examination of my role as a consultant trainer/educator going to Romania for the first time while also conducting a critical ethnography, setting up empowerment educational programmes with a empowerment evaluation. Marsden and Oakley provide reminders of the need to acknowledge the potential development of tensions and that one's methods should 'provide a forum where these might be publicly dealt with and which can produce something which is less hierarchical' (Marsden and Oakley 1990: 9). The role of the consultant in developing countries has been much criticized, not least within the context of Eastern Europe (Aubrey 1998; Fleming 2000). At the time, I noted many reasons why the Romanian participants might not necessarily welcome or trust the programme team, such as:

- most obviously, we would be unable to speak their language;
- visiting with the pre-determined aim of developing a training and education programme for older people and carers could be seen as an unequal relationship in defining goals;
- in coming as consultants and as 'experts' in the care of older people and developing carers' organizations, this may also have suggested potential inequalities of contribution;
- we might be seen as trying to impose our knowledge and experience onto the Romanian participants;

- we could be seen as foreigners attempting inappropriately to transfer practices and methods from one cultural situation to another;
- we might lack sensitivity and responsiveness to national and local differences;
- our expectations (or perhaps mutual expectations) that Romanian people should just listen to and learn from us, that we from Western Europe 'knew best' – again promoting a one-sided relationship;
- our potentially not understanding the complexities of the Romanian participants' political, economic and social situation and therefore not having relevant knowledge to contribute or be able to participate meaningfully.

Arnfred and Bentzon (1990: 36), in relation to working in complex social situations, suggest that 'To get things moving in the right direction, development planners, practitioners and researchers alike, have to give up one of the fundamental self established rights – the right to define what is the problem, whose problem is it, how to solve it and why.' I found the principle of not assuming such rights for myself important for making a start in beginning work in Romania.

The two consultants from the BASE and I had frequent meetings to discuss these issues in the UK before our first visit to Romania. Using ethnographic principles for engaging with the context, we therefore read as much as we could about the country's history, politics, economics and health, during and after the Communist regime, to raise our awareness of national and local differences as well as social, economic and political issues. At this time we found that up-to-date materials on the country were scarce. We all learned some of the language to ensure that we at least knew everyday greetings and remarks. However, we assumed, naively, that by using an approach combining critical ethnography, empowerment programme development and an empowerment evaluation, that this would provide some ready-made route to overcoming the problems flagged above. We found that many issues and means of addressing them only became visible as we moved into the field.

We were aware that, in this project, there would be many stakeholders: the older people, the potential volunteer carers for older people; national and local level administrators; medical and nursing staff; health care professionals at all levels; institutional carers; community carers; social workers; Romanian national and local government officials and a HelpAge International fieldworker who was already based in Romania. All these people would have different perceptions about our educational/training programmes and differing expectations. We would need actively to promote dialogue on Freirean principles (that we all have things to learn from each other) to understand how far our and their perceptions and expectations might converge (Freire 1972).

We felt a partnership approach in Romania was especially needed because of their political history and the need for a broad framework for understanding social change. The concept of partnership seemed to us to be essential in effective community support. Community support and integration complement the concept of empowerment with its emphasis on community participation, informal support networks and a psychological sense of community (Adams 1996). I saw the particular relevance of the Ottawa Charter (1986) principle that health promotion works through effective community action in setting priorities, making decisions, planning strategies and implementing them to achieve better health. At the heart of this process is the empowerment of communities and the ownership and control of their own endeavours and destiny (WHO 1986) which we saw as the main aim of the programme. We thought we knew (from reading the press) that people in Romania had had their lives dramatically changed with the fall of communism and we wanted to help older people especially to live in dignity in the community. We wanted to increase older peoples' power, choice and control and give them a voice in their own health and well being, which we believed had not been given to them under a communist regime in Romania. The evidence for this also came from the HelpAge International Report (1992) which suggested that older people were not valued by the Romania community. Helping older people and carers to gain control of their own lives and their health and well being, so as to achieve self-empowerment, requires support. This would call for an identifying, initiating and supporting process, which would enhance the aptitude of both individuals and communities to support health and human growth. To be empowering, such support should be fostered in a manner that does not detract from older individuals' dignity, self-efficacy and self-esteem but which encourages older people and carers to work together in partnership.

Methodology

Whilst addressing how we were going to assess, plan, implement and evaluate the education programmes, it seemed both possible and most useful to progress the programme through an empowerment evaluation. I saw this as an opportunity to gather and to develop new information, knowledge and understanding of the health and well being and the empowerment of older people through the education of professional and lay carers.

My previous experience suggested that it would not be enough to focus only on doing what we, as trainers, thought was the ideal way to improve health and well being. From the very beginning of the consultancy process it would appear that there were unequal relationships. We wanted the participants of the programme to make their own decisions of what the programme should be about, to have personal control of the programme and be involved in the evaluation of it.

Studies have demonstrated that participation and decision making can enhance self-worth (Lindgren and Linton 1991) and that personal control is beneficial for psychological well being and empowerment (Oleson 1990). According to Oleson (1990), empowerment resulting from freedom of choice is a key element in perception of quality of care. However Barnes and Wistow (1994) caution that there are dangers in collaboration and participation. 'Providers should be sensitive to the demands they are placing on people whose lives are already complex and demanding. They should be ready to ensure that people derive some direct benefits from participation, as well as ensuring that participation is justified by the outcomes it achieves' (Barnes and Winstow 1994: 91).

The 1990s have observed the emergence of an approach to evaluation that blends aspects of both reflective practice and empowerment evaluation (Shaw 1999). The underpinning premises of this approach are that all professionals should be reflective, enabling and rigorous evaluators in practice and the qualitative methodology offers the basis of such a methodological practice (Shaw 1996; Shaw and Lishman 1999).

Qualitative research

Qualitative data were collected by observations, semi-structured interviews, narrative interviews and focus groups because they provided an appropriate type of data for answering our research question on the empowerment of the participants. The term 'qualitative research' has been used by sociologists such as Filstead (1970) and Bogdan and Taylor (1975) to refer to a series of research strategies such as participant observation, in-depth, unstructured or semi-structured interviews and documentary evidence. These methods are directed towards providing a richness of contextual information, enabling an understanding of phenomena which cannot be achieved by quantitative methods (Guba and Lincoln 1985). Many sociologists use qualitative methods to elucidate the meaning of social situations by focusing on the diversity of ways in which different people experience, interpret and structure their lives (Burgess 1984).

Qualitative methods can be used to reduce the likelihood of the researcher unknowingly imposing their own subjective concepts and views on the participants, and to allow for a greater depth of exploration of participants' attitudes, perceptions and social situations. This means the researcher being concerned with the in-depth study of human phenomena to gain an understanding of the meanings they have for the people involved (Guba and Lincoln 1985; Hunt 1991; Corner 1991). As qualitative research is less concerned with objective knowing than understanding and meanings, this often involves acknowledging that the researcher's values, attitudes and beliefs play a part in the research process. This notion is reflected by many researchers who identify how qualitative methods recognize the social and behavioural background in which phenomena occur, so increasing the empathy and understanding of the observer, as behaviours are seen in their context and not removed from the social and personal values that make them meaningful to participants. It is therefore integral to most qualitative approaches that the experiences, wishes and rights of the participants must be acknowledged and respected. The importance given to meaning, context and interaction in research are further clarified by Morse (1991) who identifies three features that distinguish qualitative from quantitative research.

- The emic perspective, which allows the researcher to elicit meaning, experience or perception from the participant's point of view.
- The holistic perspective, which means that the qualitative approach allows for the consideration and inclusion of underlying values and the context as part of the phenomena.
- The inductive and interactive process of inquiry.

This literature provided good reasons to conclude that using a qualitative approach would help the research in Romania to focus on the experiences of the participants and would emphasize their uniqueness as individuals. Using qualitative methods would allow me to gather data through the education programme from participants, including the older people, which could include social, cultural and other factors that would influence behaviour and experiences. By using a qualitative approach to help me understand the participant's view of the world, I hoped to be better informed to promote empowerment.

Ethnography

Ethnography is a field-based method concerned with people, their race and/or culture (Guba and Lincoln 1985). Fetterman (1989, 2001) suggests that it is the art and science of describing a group or culture which the ethnographer is interested in understanding, and describing a social and cultural scene from the emic or insider's perspective. Field-based methods involve the researcher entering the field and exploring particular phenomena by using interviews and observation techniques, although documentary data may also be collected. Ethnography is the principal method of anthropology and the earliest distinct tradition of qualitative inquiry (Fetterman 1998; Patton 2002). It is concerned with the study of culture where longitudinal data are collected within specific contexts. The significance of an appreciation of culture, in particular in relation to change efforts of all kinds, is the basis of applied ethnography. Ethnography is also one of the terms used to describe a style of research that relies on an observational approach involving a relationship between the researcher and the participants. These observations search for the participants' views of reality through eclectic approaches, such as semi-structured interviews, focus groups and other methods that may be recorded by camera, videotape and audiotape (Patton 2002). As an alternative to seeking out the unusual, ethnographic studies are holistic, usually focusing on the routine and daily lives of people, allowing for a number of views to be examined at the same time. There is emphasis upon group experience and communally ascribed meanings to experience. It is the context of the shared experiences that provides groups with a mutual reference point. The reason for the research is to acquire and display, in as much detail as possible, the understandings and meanings constructed by people as they undertake daily activities. The main focus is on the descriptions of these activities. By encouraging participants to describe their culture, the ethnographer can build up an overall picture and look for anthropological categories of meaning, such as myths, rituals, language, relationships and the social structure (Hammersley 1992).

Qualitative interviewing has long been linked to ethnographic fieldwork but the primary method of ethnographers is participant observation in the tradition of anthropology. This means intensive fieldwork in which the investigator is engrossed in the culture under study (Goodenough 1971; Spradley and Mann 1975; Spradley 1979; Patton 2002). Fetterman (1989, 1998) suggests that it is more often than not an idealized blueprint or map that helps the ethnographer conceptualize how each step will follow the one before to build knowledge and understanding. Ethnography requires a researcher to be a skilled observer in the field, and careful preparation for entering into fieldwork is essential. Patton (2002) implies that scientific inquiry using observation methods necessitates disciplined training and meticulous preparation. To this end, Patton (2002) provides a useful framework for the skills required to become a skilled observer: this framework includes:

* learning to pay attention, see what there is to see and hear what there is to hear;
* practice in writing descriptively;
* acquiring discipline in recording field notes;
* knowing how to separate detail from trivia to achieve the former without being overwhelmed by the latter;
* using rigorous methods to validate and triangulate observations;
* reporting the strengths and limitations of one's own perspective, which requires both self-knowledge and self-disclosure (Patton 2002).

Empowerment research

As early as the 1970s, Paulo Freire (1972, 1974) wrote about the challenge posed by the need to involve people in groups and communities in collectively identifying their problems, to learn how to deal with them and to visualize and realize a healthy society. Friere (1974) states the conceptual basis for empowering individuals requires reference both to the psychological process and to the structural context within which the interaction or dialogue between worker and the person is located. Freire's (1974) approach suggests that we can help people more if we treat people as subjects of their own health and not as objects to be controlled by a biomedical approach. If the empowerment and the health and well being of older people are to be widely enabled, equity in health (which is the heart of health promotion) needs to be addressed.

Empowerment evaluation

Empowerment evaluation has its roots in community psychology and action anthropology (Tax 1958). Empowerment evaluation has influenced, and been strongly influenced by, action research. Habermas (1984) and Carr and Kemmis (1986) suggest that at the emancipation/empowerment end of the scale, action research is seen as more than just problem solving, it is a search to understand and improve the world by changing it. In empowerment evaluation, it is stakeholders rather than researchers alone who typically control the study and conduct the work. It comprises collective, self-reflective inquiry that participants undertake in social situations, so that they can understand and improve the practices in which they participate. The participants empower themselves in both forms of inquiry and action. The reflective process is seen as being oriented to action, historically influenced, entrenched in social relationships and culturally and politically influenced. Empowerment evaluation is characterized by concrete, timely, targeted, pragmatic orientations toward programme improvement (Carr and Kemmis 1986). A group collaboratively conducts empowerment evaluation, with a holistic focus on an entire programme. Empowerment evaluation is never conducted by a single individual. Empowerment evaluation is internalized as part of the planning and management of a programme (Choudhary and Tandon 1988; Whitmore 1990; Whyte 1990).

Fetterman (1993) promoted empowerment evaluation: his approach, drawing on Freire, is to view empowerment evaluation as fundamentally a democratic process, recognizing that while empowerment evaluation can be applied to individuals, organizations and communities, the focus is usually on programmes. In common with the theory and practice of community development, an entire group of people rather than a single individual is seen to be responsible for conducting the evaluation. Empowerment evaluation is therefore theoretically underpinned by self-determination conceptualized as a sense of being competent, autonomous and appreciated, able to charts one's own course in life (Zimmerman *et al.* 1992; Fetterman 1993). Self-determination skills may be used to realize the group's own political goals through self-assessment (Patton 2002).

Preparation for entering the field

Empowerment evaluation is underpinned by a concept of self-determination in the sense of participants being encouraged to be competent, autonomous and appreciated, able to chart their own course in life (Zimmerman *et al.*

1992; Fetterman 1993). I saw the need to build such self-determination skills as particularly important for setting up the education programmes in the socio-political culture of Romania. Programme goals needed to include helping participants to become more self-sufficient and personally effective. In Romania, the negotiation of empowerment partnerships between evaluators and programme staff would be especially important (Weiss and Green 1992). Fetterman (1993) characterizes core empowerment evaluation values as:

- helping people to help themselves;
- creating an environment that is conducive to empowerment and self-determination;
- truth and honesty;
- participants' involvement;
- helping people to help themselves.

Each of these is discussed in turn in relation to decisions about how to realize these in our work in Romania.

Helping people to help themselves

If people are to be helped to help themselves this suggests that some form of self-evaluation and reflection should be promoted within the evaluation. One way of doing this would be for all programme participants to conduct their own evaluation, with the programme evaluators only acting as facilitators. An evaluator, acting separately, will not empower anyone. Rather, people empower themselves perhaps with assistance and teaching.

Environment

Empowerment evaluation therefore has to create an environment that is conducive to empowerment and self-determination. This process, Fetterman (1993) suggests, is fundamentally democratic in the sense that it invites participation, examining issues of concern to the community in an open forum. Such collective examination and any resulting action will change the context as a result so that it is not one assessment of the programme's value and worth that is seen as the endpoint of the evaluation, as in traditional evaluation. Empowerment evaluation is seen, rather, as part of a process of programme improvement, which will be ongoing.

Truth and honesty

An important starting point is to try to begin to understand a situation from the participants' point of view as accurately and honestly as possible and then to continue to make improvements in that situation by developing goals and strategies seen as significant to participants, and developing documentation of the process which can be seen to be credible.

Participants' role

Empowerment evaluation findings are based on data that should include participants' criticisms of the programme as well as information about its strengths. An important difference from traditional evaluation is that the participants, programme facilitators, funders and other external agencies work to establish their own goals, processes, outcomes and impacts. The programme staff members and participants will therefore conduct self-evaluation usually with training.

Data collection strategies used in the study

The foundation of empowerment research is that research should not be detached from practical activities. Projects should learn from the information produced by research as it becomes apparent and should be incorporated into the process (Fleming 2000). The participants agreed that I could use observational data and that they could see my results. This involved me being in or around the social setting; the purpose of this is to make the qualitative analysis of that setting. Fieldwork, according to Fetterman (1989), is the most characteristic constituent of any ethnographic research design, which is exploratory in nature. This approach shapes the design of all ethnographic study. The activities of the education programme, the people who participated in the programme and the meanings of what was observed from the perspectives of those observed, are essential observational data (Bee 1974; Dorr-Bremme 1985; Fetterman 1986, 2001). The quality of the observational data is moderated by the extent to which that observation permits the researcher to enter into and understand the situation described. The participants and I decided that, because the study was an empowerment educational programme and empowerment evaluation, I needed to be an active participant employing multiple and overlapping data collection strategies. Methods of data collection were discussed with the participants about what information should be collected and why and how it should be presented and to whom. The researcher and the participants agreed on the data collection methods. Field notes, data from personnel, eyewitness observations, semi-structured interviews, semi-structured conversations, review of secondary sources, policy documents and international materials were used. Because of the evolving nature of the project, narratives, focus groups, SWOT analyses and participants' descriptions were also used, the author being fully engaged in experiencing the setting, whilst at the same time, observing and talking with the other participants.

Some interviews were tape recorded with the agreement of the participants. Tape recording interviews helps when the discussion is free flowing and covers many topics, the tapes can also be open to independent scrutiny and inspection from the participant, which can assist in determining the validity of the research. Tape recordings can be translated from Romanian to English; it was for all these reasons that I decided to seek permission to record the interviews. The value of the mixed methods lay in the depth of richness of the qualitative data gathered. This provided the participants and researcher with clear descriptions of problems and, most importantly, opportunities.

Data analysis

The approach to data analysis in ethnography begins from the moment a field worker selects a problem to study and only ends when the ethnographic account has been completed (Fetterman 1998). A hand-written transcription was always completed following each interview and prior to the next, with a preliminary analysis occurring in order to identify key aspects; this was discussed and agreed upon by the participants. Concurrently, extensive field notes were compiled and reviewed to develop key points of analysis. Extracts from field notes and interview data were used in the developed analysis to illustrate these key points. The author and the participants looked for patterns of thought and behaviour which appeared to be repeated in various situations and with various participants – as well as exceptions. The ethnographic approach adopted here meant processing information found meaningful and useful, in order to understand the setting, into themes, categories and concepts, tracing the interwoven strands that help to reveal patterns of thought and behaviour. The naming of concepts, subcategories, categories and the core variable was done in an intuitive process guided by the participants, a combination of previous literature, the researcher's professional experience and a process of trial and error to determine the labels and terms that most accurately describe the phenomenon under investigation. This involved identifying key words and phrases that may have appeared repeatedly in the interviews.

The education programmes

The education programmes were carried out in a variety of venues in Bucharest, Galati, Nehoiu and Timisoara, preparing volunteers, family members and professional people for caring for older people in the community, many older people also attended the sessions. The participants published their first book after the initial training programmes, called *Youth without Oldness* which was written in Romanian, translated into English and published by the Romanian Alzheimer Society. Later education programmes included the training of family members in the care of their relatives, the training of personal assistants and medical assistants. We also helped with the implementation of a permanent training scheme for home carers for older people. This programme developed in two stages, first, training the home carers and then training trainers to train the future home carers. This new role of home care for older people was approved and validated by the Romanian government as paid employment. A network of non-governmental organizations was set up that actively supported older people.

All of the project, including the research activities, was undertaken, planned and evaluated together with the Romanian partners, a HelpAge international project worker and three BASE consultants. The training and education programmes addressed a wide variety of topics chosen by the participants; topics were addressed depending on the individual and group needs in each area of Romania. The programmes had a research element in order to plan and evaluative the programmes and develop a firm information base on the situation of older people living at home in the chosen areas of Romania. The results were critically examined by older people, participants of the education programmes, volunteers, professionals and families so that suitable models of care for older people in their own homes could be developed.

The results of the Romanian partners and the researcher

The approach used was quite new to all the participants who, at first, wanted to be told what to do by the so-called 'UK experts'. The benefits of the empowerment approach for the situation in Romania were realized because all the participants were involved in the training programmes and the evaluation. This widespread ownership of the project, its implementation, findings and solutions promoted unanticipated changes. Although, at first, the participants found it difficult to be fully involved in the planning and interpretation of the programmes, participants later in the project took part in and commented on the research methodology quite freely, and critically discussed how appropriate it was to them as Romanians. Some participants attended all the programmes, many coming when they had worked all night as doctors, nurses and health care assistants.

Evaluations

The evaluations often said that: 'I will from now on respect older people like my grandmother.' 'I thought looking after the elderly was just keeping them clean.' 'I respect older people now.' 'We should not abandon older people.'

At the beginning of the programmes, all the evaluations were very positive with no negative comments in them. Later evaluations gave constructive criticisms about the programmes and the research. 'The methods we have learnt relate theory to practice, but how can we do all this with no money?' 'We will ask older people what they want but what if they ask for something we can't give them?' 'How can we help older people, in the winter time I make a fire only when it is very cold? I cannot afford to buy wood, how can I help them when I cannot help myself?' We became more aware of all the problems the participants had to cope with as the programme progressed. Participants began to enjoy the group work, presentations and focus groups and began to have better self-esteem and self-efficacy. At first they were reluctant to take part in group work and just wanted to take notes, later they organized themselves into groups with no prompting from us and wrote on flip charts some excellent ideas. They began to 'problem solve' and realized that 'as Romanians we must find Romanian answers to Romanian problems.'

Critical analysis

Language

The issue of language was problematic even though we tried to learn the Romanian language and many participants spoke excellent English. Of particular relevance to this study is the issue of language translation and its effects on the reliability and validity of the findings of the study. The use of translation was therefore seriously questioned when considering the rigour of the research process. Twinn (1997) examined this type of issue and demonstrated some important issues when using translation in qualitative research – in particular the complexity of managing data when no equivalent words exist in the target language, and the influence of the grammatical style on the analysis. In this study, the reliability of the interview questions, transcriptions and translations, as well as the data analysis was checked by the participants who reviewed the English and Romanian translations.

Our first interpreter did not interpret what we had said during out first educational session. It was only when a Romanian medical student informed us that the interpreter was talking about communism that we were aware of the problem. The participants' knowledge and views relating to the concept of empowerment was a difficult issue at the early stages of the study. Before asking the participants to describe situations in which they had felt empowered or they had empowered an older person, the researcher first ascertained their understanding of the term by asking them to define empowerment. For many of the participants this proved extremely difficult, others however defined empowerment as 'being in control of your health' 'having choices and things' and 'having the choice to do what you want.' One has to question whether these definitions were the original thoughts of the participants, as the wording in these definitions is similar in parts to explanations given to the participants by the researcher. The concept of power was often seen to be related to the government by many participants. Definitions of control also were a problem, because language is more than just the meaning of the word. There were deeper differences and complex sets of meanings that may not be understood even with fluency in Romanian. The words 'empowerment' and 'control' were new to many Romanians. There is no word for 'evaluation' in Romanian language and the English word 'assessing' was chosen by the participants. The word 'volunteering' caused many problems with some participants associating the word with 'telling on your neighbour,' 'spying on them.' These small but important matters often held back progress.

Partnership

Very quickly, the participants and the community saw the relevance of the programme and we were inundated with people wanting to come on the programme, which was difficult at times when we had agreed to 20 participants and 50 people turned up! Many people saw the benefits of international partnership and recognized the values we were trying to implement. On occasions the project got very political with local dignitaries trying to take over the project and wanting the funding. The television network appeared one day without telling us and filmed a 'teaching' session.

Research methodology

Participants were, at first, wary of the empowerment methodology but soon commented on its appropriateness for their situations. Lots of fun was had collecting and analysing the data, the programmes and research often going in different ways then they had anticipated. 'I never thought I could be part of an education programme and that I could help to plan it' 'This is the way all research should be done, all of us taking part.'

Cultural awareness

It was a culture shock for the participants and the BASE trainers. We realized that we had not got enough knowledge of the Romanian way of life but, because this was a longitudinal study, we did manage to address this later. The lack of facilities – such as services we take for granted – for example, shortage of water, lack of food and fuel, lack of money, people working but not getting paid, lack of education and training, was difficult for us to come to terms with at first. Winter was an especially difficult time for older people with the temperatures dropping to as low as $-20°C$. The Romanian participants had a rosy view of the UK and thought we had no problems in the health and social care field and that we were all very rich. All this was relative and it took many discussions for us to understand each other and our countries. We sometimes felt that the Romanian officials lacked commitment to the project and to be involved in financing it. At all stages of the project the government officials in health and social care changed frequently so that it was difficult to get continuity. The empowerment programme needed a 'bottom up' approach but we were continually pressurized to let officials take over from the participants often because they wanted the finance. Inflation levels reached a high of 400 per cent when we there in the early years, this led to price increases disproportionate to increases in income. For older people that meant a drastic reduction in the purchasing power of their pensions.

Conclusions and future progress

Our Romanian partners have made enormous progress during the education programmes and the study. The Societatea Romania Alzheimer has to be congratulated, especially on all the work it has carried out for older people since joining in with the education programmes.

Meals on Wheels or Foot, Day Centres, Social and Medical Assistance Centres have been started in Bucharest, Galati, Nehoiu, and Timisoara. Information and health promotion for older people has been published in newspapers, radio and television programmes. Booklets on health promotion and care of older people has been published and a Help Line for older people and their families has been developed. Home visiting to older people is now implemented in some areas. Trained carers and trainers of carers now exist in all the programmes areas. Training materials have been developed for these training sessions by the participants of our education programmes. There are still many things to be learnt about empowerment research and pro-grammed development and about working in partnership with other people from a different country. We have learnt so much from one another and have been impressed with the commitment of the Romanian participants of the programmes, such as coming during their lunch time and after working all night to join in the programmes. We still keep in touch with many participants who now have email and feel optimistic when they tell us about all the work that they are doing with older people. The empowerment study as a whole was not easy to do but as a participant said, 'I have learnt so much and now feel a new person ready to help older people,' which made it all worthwhile.

Key learning points

- This chapter presents an innovative case study of empowering research and practice in Eastern Europe.
- It describes and analyses the value of an international partnership approach.
- One of the key outcomes of such international research is the need for cultural awareness.
- Similarly, and perhaps more obviously, researchers and practitioners need language awareness, particularly in view of the potential to misin-terpret, whether deliberately or not.

References

Adams, R. (1996) *Social Work and Empowerment*, London: Macmillan.

Arnfred, S. and Bentzon, A. (1990) 'The language of development studies,' *New Social Science Monographs*, Roskilde: Roskilde University Centre.

Atkinson, A.B. and Micklewright, J. (1992) *Welfare State Programme No 72 Distribution of Income in Eastern Europe*, London: School of Economics.

Aubrey, J. (1998) *A History and Critique of Development Literature and its Application to Eastern Europe*. Unpublished paper.

Barnes, M. and Wistow, G. (1994) 'Involving carers in planning and review,' in A. Connor and S. Black (eds) *Performance, Review and Quality in Social Care*, London: Jessica Kingsley.

Bee, R.L. (1974) *Patterns and Processes: An Introduction to Anthropological Strategies for the Study of Socio-cultural Change*, New York: Free Press.

Bogdan, R. and Taylor, S.J. (1975) *Introduction to Qualitative Research Methods*, New York: John Wiley.

Bond, J. and Bond, S. (1987) 'Developments in the provision of evaluation of long term care for dependent old people,' in P. Fielding (ed.) *Research in the Nursing Care of Elderly People*, London: Wiley.

Burgess, D. (1984) *Qualitative Research Methods*, London: Sage.

Carr, W. and Kemmis, S. (1986) *Becoming Critical: Education, Knowledge and Action Research*, London: The Falmer Press.

Choudhary, A. and Tandon, R. (1988) *Participatory Evaluation*, New Delhi, India: Society for Participatory Research in Asia.

Corner, J. (1991) 'In search of more complete answers to research questions. Quantitative versus qualitative research methods: is there a way forward?' *Journal of Advanced Nursing* 16: 718–727.

Dorr-Bremme, D.W. (1985) 'Ethnographic evaluation: a theory and method,' *Educational Evaluation and Policy Analysis* 7(1): 65–83.

Fleming, J. (2000) 'Action research for the development of children's services in Ukraine,' in H. Kemshall and R. Littlechild (eds) *User Involvement and Participation in Social Care: Research Informing Practice*, London: Jessica Kingsley.

Fetterman, D.M. (1986) 'Beyond the status quo in ethnographic educational evaluation,' in D.M. Fetterman and M.A. Pitman (eds) *Educational Evaluation: Ethnography in Theory, Practice and Politics*, Beverley Hills, CA: Sage.

Fetterman, D.M. (1989) *Ethnography: Step by Step*, Thousand Oaks, CA: Sage.

Fetterman, D.M. (1993) 'Theme for the 1993 annual meeting: empowerment evaluation,' *Evaluation Practice* 14(1): 115–117.

Fetterman, D.M. (1998) 'Empowerment evaluation and the Internet: a synergistic relationship,' *Current Issues in Education* (online), 1(4). Available online at: cie.ed.asu.edu/volume1/number4/index.html.

Fetterman, D.M. (2001) *Foundations of Empowerment Evaluation*, Thousand Oaks, CA: Sage.

Filstead, J. (1970) *Introduction to Research Methods*, London: Routledge.

Freire, P. (1972) *Pedagogy of the Oppressed*, Harmondsworth: Penguin.

Freire, P. (1974) *Education and the Practice of Freedom*, London: Writers and Readers Publishing Co-operative (originally published in Portuguese 1967).

Gillion, C. (1991) 'Aging populations: spreading the costs,' *Journal of European Social Policy* 1(2): 107–128.

Goodenough, W. (1971) *Culture, Language and Society*, Reading, MA: Addison-Wesley.

Guba, E.G. and Lincoln, Y.S. (1985) *Effective Evaluation: Improving the Usefulness of Evaluation*, San Francisco: Jossey Bass.

Habermas, J. (1984) *The Theory of Communication Action*, Vol. 1, Boston, MA: Beacon.

Hammersley, M. (1992) *What's Wrong with Ethnography? Methodological Explorations*, London: Routledge.

HelpAge International (1992) *Study on the Elderly in Romania*, Report Commissioned by the Directorate General 1 of the European Commission, Brussels.

Hunt, M. (1991) 'Qualitative research,' in D.F.S. Cormack (ed.) *The Research Process in Nursing*, Oxford: Blackwell Scientific Publications.

Lindgren, C.L. and Linton, A.D. (1991) 'Problems of nursing home residents: nurse and residents perceptions,' *Applied Nursing Research* 4(3): 113–121.

Marsden, D. and Oakley, P. (1990) *Evaluating Social Development*, Oxford: Oxfam.

Maslow, A.H. (1954) *Motivation and Personality*, New York: Harper and Row.

Morse, J.M, (1991) *Qualitative Nursing Research: a Contemporary Dialogue*, London: Sage Publications.

National Commission of Statistics (1992) 'Average number of pensioners and average monthly pensions in 1991,' *Social Protection Working Papers* No. 1, April.

Oleson, M. (1990) 'Subjectively perceived quality of life,' *Image* 22(3): 187–190.

Patton, M.Q. (1990) *Qualitative Evaluation and Research Methods*, 2nd edn, London: Sage Publications.

Patton, M.Q. (2002) *Qualitative Research and Evaluation Methods*, 3rd edn, Thousand Oaks, London: Sage.

Rose, R. (1992) *Who Needs Social Protection in Eastern Europe? A Constrained Empirical Analysis of Romania*, Centre for the Study of Public Policy, University of Strathclyde, Glasgow.

Shaw, I. (1996) *Evaluation in Practice*, Aldershot: Ashgate.

Shaw, I. (1999) *Qualitative Evaluation*, London: Sage Publications.

Shaw, I. and Lishman, J. (eds) (1999) *Evaluation and Social Work Practice*, London: Sage Publications.

Spradley, J.P. (1979) *The Ethnographic Interview*, New York: Holt, Rinehart and Winston.

Spradley, J.P. and Mann, B.J. (1975) *The Cocktail Waitress: Women's Work in a Man's World*, New York: Wiley.

Tax, S. (1958) 'The fox project,' *Human Organisation* 17: 17–19.

Thomas, N. (1988) ,'Evaluation research and the personal social services,' in J. Lishman (ed.) *Evaluation: Research highlights in Social Work*, (8) 2nd edn, London: Jessica Kingsley.

Twinn, S. (1997) 'An exploratory study examining the influence of translation on the validity and reliability of qualitative data in nursing research,' *Journal of Advanced Nursing* 26: 418–423.

United Nations (1988) *World Demographic Estimates and Projections: 1950–2025*.

Weiss, H.B. and Greene, J.C. (1992) 'An empowerment partnership for family support and education programmes and evaluations,' *Family Science Review* 5 (1, 2, February/May): 145–163.

Whitmore, E. (ed.) (1990) *Understanding and Practicing Participatory Evaluation. New Directions for Evaluation*, Vol. 80, San Francisco: Jossey-Bass.

WHO (1986) *The Ottawa Charter for Health Promotion*, Copenhagen: WHO.

Whyte, W.F. (1990) *Participatory Action Research*, Newbury Park, CA: Sage.

Zimmerman, M.A., Israel, B.A., Schulz, A. and Checkoway, B. (1992) 'Further explorations in empowerment theory: an empirical analysis of psychological empowerment,' *American Journal of Community Psychology* 20(6): 707–727.

16 Creating a profession

Action learning in developing social care in Russia

Kate Gilbert

Introduction

Action Learning is now well-established in the repertoire of management development methods and systems, and has become widely adopted as a method of choice for work-based group and individual learning, using as learning material the real-life, real time context of organizational issues and projects. This chapter presents, through a case study of the introduction of Action Learning to an emergent profession, i.e. social work in Russia, an argument that Action Learning can also be a powerful tool on a wider scale, establishing the parameters of professionalism in the context of massive and systemic change. It provides a 'safe' milieu in which professionals, moving from practice into management professions, can deal with the intellectual and emotional challenges along the way, and resolve the phenomenon of 'splitting' the professional self from negative emotions.

In the early 1990s, following the break-up of the Soviet bloc, Western funders, such as the World Bank and the European Union Tacis[1] programme, sought to contribute to the transformation of the region by concentrating support funding on the fabric of the economy, specifically in the fields of finance, manufacturing and energy (Dyker 1992; Frydman *et al.* 1993). Their approach has been thoroughly critiqued by a number of studies (Holloway and McFaul 1995; Gilbert 1998; Wedel 1998; Zanini 2002), both for their failure to secure the economy, and for the implicit neglect of the social fabric of society in these countries. After the financial collapse of 1997, Europe re-evaluated its interventions in Russia and the neighbouring states, and re-directed much of its aid efforts towards building institutions of regional and local government, and towards developing more sustainable systems and structures of civil society (Tacis 1997; Henderson 2002). One such system was the system of social services in Russia. From 1997 to 2003 the author[2] participated in two major projects, the first funded by the European Union and the second by the British Department for International Development. This chapter is based on those experiences, which formed part of an extensive multiple case study of the activities of Western consultants in Russia. The unit of analysis in this study was the aid project as a whole, including the organizational context as well as the principal actors. The data on which this chapter is based are interview, observation and first person documentary accounts, at the interpersonal level.

Two case studies form the empirical basis of the chapter; the first a European-funded project to develop the system of social services for a range of client groups in Moscow, Penza and Samara,[3] and the second, a British-funded project with similar aims but an exclusive focus on services for the elderly, in Novokuznetsk.[4] From September 1997 to November 2003, I participated in a team of Western and Russian consultants making regular visits to these regions. My role was to develop HRD capability through a combination of 'training the trainers' initiatives and management development. The first case study revealed an unexpected dimension in the learning – that of the strength of the emotional or affective element in the work, both for the social workers and the consultants. The psychoanalytic concept of the 'rational-emotional split' (Winnicott 1947; Clarke 1999; Kilborne 1999; Layton 2000) was found to have explanatory power when applied to this context, and was particularly useful in illuminating issues of conflict and resistance that emerged from the case study. Not only was evidence of this splitting evident in the behaviours of the social workers and their managers, but also in the comportment and words of the western consultants.

In the second case study I, as consultant, made a conscious decision to deal with this dimension by harnessing the power of action learning methodology, following the model set by Revans (1971, 1998) as the main medium for the learning of a group of social work managers, led by a local team of trained facilitators. Analysis of data suggested that not only was this approach seen as a relevant and effective method of training for social workers; it also had the effect of increasing the social workers' confidence in their own professionalism, by resolving some of the conflict and distress caused by the rational-emotional splitting they had experienced previously. In so doing, they were able to use the safe action-learning environment to enhance their emotional intelligence (Goleman 1995; Mayer and Salovey 1997) and thus their professional resilience.

Taking a broadly interpretivist position, the chapter starts with a section giving background contextual information about the situation of social care in Russia, before introducing key theoretical concepts of leadership and emotionality that are expanded in the findings sections. The findings are presented as a narrative, in which, in the tradition of interpretivist research, the findings and analytical interpretation are interwoven.

The empirical context – social care in Russia

It is estimated that about 40 per cent of the population of Russia is living below the poverty line (Kolenikov and Shorrocks 2005; Takeda 2004). Social tensions are unavoidable in such circumstances, and the system of social protection for vulnerable people plays a very important role, not only in compensating for the decline in living standards of individuals and families, but also in preventing serious breaches in the fragile fabric of public and social order (Templeman 2004). In the UK, the social worker is a professional who works on behalf of the state to ameliorate some of the human problems on the margins of an established and stable social order. In Russia the role of the social worker is relatively undeveloped and little understood. The profession did not exist before 1991. In Russia, the institutions for protection of the most vulnerable groups in the population, and the legislative frameworks for these institutions (the social safety net) are being radically redrawn in efforts to forestall the direst social consequences of a rapid shift to the market. The challenges are immense: as well as providing care for those sectors of society traditionally falling within the remit of social care, such as people with disabilities and the elderly, towns and cities have had to cope with alcohol and drug abuse, and the consequent plight of the abandoned children of addicts. The privatization of housing resulted in thousands of children and old people being thrown onto the streets. Only 45 per cent of newborn children are considered healthy at birth. The complexity of social and health problems arising from the cataclysmic and rapid changes of the last 15 years can hardly be underestimated (Swett 1992; Tregoubova 2000; Rusinova and Brown 2003).

Perhaps the task would not be so daunting if the country were not starting from such a low base of provision, compared with what is generally taken for granted in 'developed' countries.[5] Western projects and consultants have been importing knowledge based on the assumption that the 'welfare mix' (Anttonen and Sipila 1996) will be spreading the burden and the strain.

The welfare mix

The welfare mix, in stable developed countries, consists of a combination of:

- state provision met through general taxation;
- the voluntary or independent sector, ranging from self-help groups and unpaid volunteers to large non-profit organizations;
- the commercial sector where care services are provided for profit, which is distributed to members or owners;
- the informal sector of family, friends and neighbours.

The UK has seen a shift in recent years from a heavily State-supported system towards a liberal market system, in which the mass of the population meet their needs for domiciliary or residential care through the operation of market-oriented organizations and financial institutions. The State picks up responsibility for residual means-tested provision for the most vulnerable. It could in fact be argued that the heyday of the Welfare State in Britain was, in fact, an aberration, and that we have now reverted to a more 'normal' pattern consistent with UK culture. The liberal model contrasts, on the one hand, with the universalistic social democratic model of Scandinavia, and on the other hand with the family care model of Mediterranean countries such as Spain. Germanic countries display a subsidiarity model, the family having the primary responsibility, supported by a strong voluntary sector and relatively limited services from the state (Anttonen and Sipila 1996).

The very phrase 'welfare mix' carries connotations of variety and plenty, and so may distort our perceptions. In Russia, a shrinking cake might be a better image. The state sector, or the cake, is still regarded as the first port of call. Although paralysed by debt and inadequate legislation, the federal government can take some credit for spearheading the development of social provision and the social services, continuing a process that began during the *perestroika* period (Wiktorow 1992; Shipitsina 1998; Lane 1999). While it cannot be said to be flourishing yet, there are developments in the voluntary sector. The burgeoning of voluntary organizations seen in Hungary post-1989 (Munday and Lane 1998) has not yet been experienced in Russia, and may even have suffered some setbacks during the Putin era, although some self-help and self-advocacy groups are established. These have tended to operate as lobbying groups at federal and regional level, rather than being service providers themselves. The religious revival, generating philanthropic organizations, sometimes linked to western evangelical movements, has had a marginal impact in some large cities.

Beyond the provision of primary healthcare, there is very little evidence of a commercial social care system (Burger *et al.* 1998; Rusinova and Brown 2003). Unlike the United States, for example, where the social worker is an independent licensed practitioner who may advertise his or her services in the Yellow Pages, Russia has adopted the European model of the social worker as employee of a government agency, managing a centre or caseload on its behalf. It is unlikely that the economy could support a robust commercial sector in the foreseeable future, except for small niche operators for the wealthy. The long-term prospects for commercial social care, such as nursing homes for the frail elderly, will depend on where Russia eventually falls on the liberal–social care continuum and on the development of a reasonably affluent middle class.

Much has been written about Russian communitarianism as a long-term cultural dimension (Berdyayev 1990; Vlachoutsicos and Lawrence 1990; Holden *et al.* 1997), but current demographic and economic factors are clearly putting great strain on families, who are struggling for survival in the medium term. The stress of unwelcome change and hardship has taken its toll on families, who can be expected to focus their energies on taking care of themselves and their immediate kin, rather than looking outside for an outlet for their altruism or community spirit.

Perspectives on the clients of social services

People with disabilities

It is arguable that the extent of a civil society can be measured by the degree to which people with special needs can integrate into mainstream life. In Russia people with disabilities have traditionally been treated with a medical approach; their physical impairments are seen as a medical rather than a social issue. The Russian term for a disabled person is 'invalid.' The environment – urban and rural – remains largely unadapted to the access needs of people with mobility or sensory impairments, and, until recently, people with learning disabilities had rarely been seen in public places. People with disabilities have generally been segregated from the mainstream, either housebound or institutionalized. Classification of disability, including registration, has traditionally been made on medical grounds without reference to the preference of the individual. Once made, the decision is not usually reviewed. People with a minimal level of disability typically live in long-term institutions, despite not requiring a high level of care. Russian people with disabilities have not enjoyed the legislative assistance of equal opportunities policies at either federal or local level. All this is set to change, as there is some evidence that self-advocacy organizations are developing among key groups, particularly the young. Those few who have found ways to develop IT skills have become Internet-savvy and have learned on the Web about international approaches to working with people with disabilities.

The elderly

The plight of the elderly has been one of the more pitiful aspects of the demise of the Soviet Union. The problem with pensions is well-known. Less well-documented is the psychological effect of having the past wiped out. Many old people are eking out their final years in despair and isolation, unable to afford adequate food or medicine. There are many stories of elderly parents being kicked out of their apartment to make space for other members of the family. For many, the best option is admission to an institution, because of homelessness or hunger. Thus, there are many in long-term care who don't need to be there because of physical or mental incapacity. The system of social care for the elderly also faces a psychological issue. The Soviet attitude towards older people was that a man or woman would toil all their working life in relatively poor conditions, with the promise of a reward when they reached pension age – this reward was in the form of free social and leisure facilities, free medicine and care, and free holidays. War veterans would benefit most of all. For the Soviet citizen, old age began at the age of 60. Today, social care providers are facing a major challenge in persuading older but fit adults that they have no entitlement to free care and facilities as of right.

Children and families

The abuse of children did not officially exist as a social problem in the Soviet Union (Wiktorow 1992). The discovery of the existence of physical, mental and sexual abuse and neglect, coupled with a massive increase in child poverty and homelessness, the phenomenon of the 'social orphan' (Join-Lambert 1999), has been a major shock at the public and private levels. Vast numbers of children are classified as vulnerable or at risk, and because the predominant model of crisis intervention has been institutionalization rather than prevention, short-term models of child care such as fostering are relatively poorly developed.

The place of social work

The role of social work management is to broker severely limited resources between these groups, to try to make resources go further through coordination, and to prevent the system from collapsing under the weight of demand. In some countries the concept of social services embraces *both* social care, i.e. the provision of specific services and activities for people with special needs, e.g. people with disabilities, vulnerable children, the homeless etc, *and* social security – a system of compensatory payments for people on low incomes, such as pensioners. In the United Kingdom these two functions are separated. They are not so clearly separated in Russia, where social security is the responsibility of local government. At the service delivery level, calculations of entitlements to means-tested benefits are the responsibility of social workers. This places a double burden on social work managers, who are simultaneously charged with distributing material benefits (which also entails rationing and refusing), and providing services to individuals and families in a situation of socio-economic near collapse. In Penza, one of the regions chosen for Tacis support in the 1990s, over 50 per cent of the population were living on benefits. However, ironically, in that cash-strapped region, the basic old age pension was higher than a social worker's salary.

Andrei Panov, Deputy Minister of Social Protection, stated in 1999 that what was needed in Russia was no less than a change in social consciousness in order to develop the possibility of independent living for vulnerable people, particularly people with disabilities.[6] Until then, social work in Russia today, to a large degree, represents an extension of women's traditional caring role inside the home to the external community, that caring role being exercised in a partial vacuum created by the collapse of the former system, and the parlous state of the economy.

The theoretical context

Patterns of leadership

Russian local administration managers have to be strong leaders, behaviourally, intellectually, and by disposition. In the social sphere they face immense resource difficulties in the face of rising demands, and depend heavily on personal power bases to maintain a level of service. In structural terms, the position of managers has changed little since Soviet days. The workings of hierarchy and, consequently, notions of accountability and team management, reveal fundamental differences in approach between Russia and the west.

Differences between Western and Soviet conceptions of hierarchy are illuminated by the metaphor of the *matrioshka*, the traditional set of Russian nesting dolls in which each doll snugly holds another smaller one, down to the very tiniest (Vlachoutsicos and Lawrence 1990; Lawrence and Vlachoutsicos 1992). This metaphor, as well as being culturally very neat, carries explanatory power, demonstrating how the Soviet system of task units or brigades differed from the commonly accepted Western model of hierarchy. In the Western model, a manager at one level in a hierarchy is responsible to the manager above, and responsible for the activities, outputs, etc of the next layer down in the hierarchical chain. Beyond that, further responsibilities are delegated to the next level down. In the Soviet system, every manager was responsible for everything in the hierarchy underneath him, and thus even the top manager had to concern himself or herself with basic operational issues. Lawrence and Vlachoutsicos (1992) in their groundbreaking comparative study of life in US and Soviet manufacturing factories, emphasize the punishing long hours worked by the Soviet manager, and the amount of time put in by top managers to walking round the plant, dealing with routine operational matters, which in a Western factory would be left to the foreman or junior managerial level. These findings reinforce the observations made by Manoukovsky (1993) about the prevailing Russian management style being at once autocratic and open.

In social services, we observed a distinct matriarchal variant of this management style. In the regions, we found leaders of exceptional vision and ability, who inspired passionate loyalty in 'their' people. Senior managers in the social sphere nevertheless work under extreme pressure, exacerbated by rising expectations on the one hand and diminishing resources on the other. Service heads were accustomed, not only to being open to personal representations from their staff, with whom they enjoyed fiercely close working relationships; but also to receiving at their headquarters successive waves of the aged, infirm and otherwise distressed with personal pleas for help. Many people with problems would travel long distances and sit in the corridor for hours on end, looking as though they were prepared to wait for days if necessary.

Departments operated rather in the manner of a royal court, each leader having an entourage of secretaries, personal assistants, even dressers and cooks. In return for long hours, total commitment and unstinting loyalty, members of the team would be rewarded with the devotion of the leader and an element of reflected glory and influence. These leaders (mostly women) and their teams operated at a high emotional level. Driven by the excitement of innovation and adaptation to the challenges facing them, they were also easily moved to tears and under visible strain. A strategy for coping was to find solace and strength through bringing religious or spiritualist practices into the workplace. For example one top manager had a special room in her suite of offices containing an icon; another professed himself an 'extrasense' or clairvoyant, and made no secret of his use of New Age contraptions to make his work environment more positive. Such eccentricities would tend to be dismissed in the West: in the Russian context they seemed to provide, in the absence of a coherent ideological framework for society, a much-needed personal defence mechanism against anxiety and despair.

The role of the social worker

The social worker tends to view herself or himself as there to solve people's problems, the last refuge between unfortunate people and the abyss. This would be a severe mental and emotional burden at the best of times, triggering acute anxieties. The Russian social worker, typically a female ex-engineer or scientist who lost her job when the command economy collapsed, is hardly well-prepared or well-equipped to cope with her own and others' expectations that she will solve problems for people, especially in the absence of other social structures and systems to complement her role. Russian social care organizations make extensive use of specialists. For example, social workers were excluded from making assessments of clients – all assessments of clients were carried out by qualified psychologists. This meant that social workers were frequently unclear about their own role vis-à-vis the health professionals alongside whom they are working, and felt like poor cousins.

In social care situations, a key difference between Western and Russian experience is that Russian managers, unlike their British counterparts (Hearn *et al.* 1992) are unlikely to have been social workers themselves (Iarskaia-Smirnova and Romanov 2002).

The rational/emotional split

Winnicott (1947), in his work on the 'good enough' mother, recognized the resentment and self-denigration experienced by mothers of demanding and utterly dependent babies. Several writers (e.g. Menzies 1960; Obholzer and Roberts 1994; Albrow 1997) have identified similar responses in members of the helping professions. Obholzer and Roberts (1994) extended the concept from the individual to the organizational level, suggesting that individual distress may be mirrored and manifested at the organizational level. Where such negative feelings are perceived as unacceptable, or unprofessional, they may lead to a splitting off of the negative emotion, which may be projected onto other groups in the form of blame.

In contemporary Russia, many problems are insoluble, and the social worker can do little more than listen and absorb the fear and resentment of clients. This becomes internalized as stress and anxiety, and feelings of failure. Workers worry about how to communicate with clients, about how to manage the contradiction between professional objectivity and human sympathy, about how to say no to people in desperate need. They suffer from guilt at how little they can do, and some feel ambivalence about losing their former professions and material security. Into this situation comes the Western consultant.

The research project – approach and methods

In September 1997 my colleagues and I, from the UK, Belgium and Germany, in the Tacis project 'Developing a system of social services for vulnerable groups in the Russian Federation,' arrived at last in the two regional experimental sites. The lead-in time had been long and the inception period protracted. The previous spring, in Moscow, we had found Ministry staff to be suffering from extremely low morale, due to lack of funding for staff, lack of federal resources to develop and deliver services, and disappointment at statements coming from Ministers. Deputy Ministers responsible for formulating policy felt inadequate to the task and ill prepared. No support or education appeared to be available to them. A salary increase for staff, produced by decree, remained unpaid.

This was one of the most ambitious and widely-scoped of the Tacis social welfare projects in Russia; there being four working teams, on services for the elderly, for children and families, and for people with disabilities, plus our team focusing on professional and management development. In the training team I had two strings to my bow; trainer training and management development. Each team was to work in the experimental sites developing innovative practice. In addition, some experts would also work at a Federal level with the Ministry of Labour and Social Development, giving advice on developing service standards and on drafting legislation. Expectations of the project and its consultants were immense as, in just over a year, it was to produce a list of outputs ranging from development of model service delivery centres, through introduction of 'optimal monitoring systems,' to overhaul of the curriculum for university preparation of the new generation of social workers. This overloading of expectations on the project can be interpreted as mirroring and projecting, through pressure from the Ministry and regions, the overloading of expectations on social workers and social services at the operational level.

This project, and the follow-up project in Novokuznetsk, offered a unique opportunity to gather longitudinal data on the development of social care systems in a transitional environment. The first case study, using data collected from Penza and Samara, adopted a classic case study approach as expounded by Yin (2003), in which tentative theoretical propositions are explored through the gathering and comparative analysis of multiple sources of data. In this case, data sources included internal project documents, participant observation, diaries, artefacts (such as flipchart sheets from training seminars), and interviews. Data were collected both in English and Russian, and interviews were conducted either in English or Russian, or occasionally, a mixture of the two. The data gathering included interviews with interpreters, a group of interlocutors often neglected in cross-cultural research.

The second case study adopted a slightly different approach. Although data collection methods were virtually identical, in this case the subjects of the research – i.e. social workers, their trainers and their managers, and the western consultants – were brought into the process as collaborators in the enquiry, more in accordance with the philosophy and procedures of action research. There were two overriding reasons for this. The first case study, once the data were analysed, revealed a psychological and emotional dimension of the project that had not been recognized or acknowledged elsewhere. Once this dimension emerged, it became impossible for me, the researcher, to continue to work in the rather detached way prescribed by the multiple case study method. To do so would have seemed exploitative. There was clearly a degree of distress manifesting itself, which challenged us as consultants and researchers to abandon the distance between ourselves and our 'client' groups. In the second case study, therefore, we jettisoned plans to use a similar programme of seminars and short courses, and developed instead an infrastructure to initiate and support Action Learning Sets for social care managers.

This entailed developing local capability to organize, facilitate and evaluate action learning interventions. As there was no experience or understanding of the concept of action learning, I had to locate a group of people who could quickly be brought 'up to speed' on action learning.

Findings

First case study – the seminar programme

We were to make several visits to Samara and to Penza, the second experimental region, with a Russian partner from the Excellence in Qualifications Institute in Moscow. At first, our Russian partners expected that our knowledge and expertise would be imparted solely through the medium of lectures and seminars. That first three-week visit, dubbed 'consultancy,' comprised 15 days solid of presentations and seminars, punctuated by overnight train journeys. Possibly we were being worked like circus horses to show that Tacis would be getting value for money. Approximately half of the sessions were designed as management development and delivered to mixed groups of senior regional officials and service providers.

As time went on, it became possible to work in a more process-oriented way with workers in the regions. While this was welcome, gradually the focus of the consultancy changed, at first almost imperceptibly, but finally substantially, away from management development to an almost exclusive emphasis on professional development for social workers and trainer training. Why was this? Initial seminars on management of social services had been well attended and enthusiastically received, particularly in the regions.

Subsequent analysis and reflection revealed that, while the managerialist subject matter was, on the surface, uncontentious and unproblematic, there were strong emotional undercurrents within the situation which were being channelled away from the 'formal' consultancy arena of seminars and meetings, to be expressed elsewhere, particularly in the relationships in the consultant team and between the consultants and other parts of the project. Conflicts surfaced in several critical incidents. These focused, for example, on the quality of accommodation, boundaries between work time and time for relaxation and privacy for consultants outside work time, as well as more technical issues such as giving one another feedback on how things had gone at the end of the day.

The first seminar in the Ministry took place the day after the Western consultants met their Russian counterparts.

> 20 people attended the morning session. We had agreed, on the insistence of Russian colleagues, that the seminar should run with only a short break at lunchtime and an early finish, so as not to 'lose' the audience. However, when lunchtime came everybody left the room and went off to the canteen anyway. We continued with 12 after lunch, which *we* considered reasonably successful. . . .[7]

The context of the text reveals anxiety and conflict on a number of levels. The issue of lunch had been a major point of contention the previous day. The Westerners insisted that seminar attendees should have a proper lunch break: the Russian experts said no, if you let them go to the canteen you will never get them back. They will go back to their desks in the Ministry for the rest of the day. While we would have given participants the benefit of the doubt, and felt in some way that our credentials as training providers were at stake, we reached a compromise position, and light refreshments were brought into the room. But all the participants took the cue and disappeared for their usual substantial meal in the canteen. Given the dire warnings from our Russian colleagues, and what we knew about morale, we chose to view the return of more than half of them as a measure of success. After all, we were just starting our work on the project and needed to maintain our confidence. Nevertheless, a struggle was engaged. From now on, there would be an uneasy truce between us as to which 'side,' Russian or Western, had the most consistently reliable perspectives on what was happening and how we should respond.

Blurring of the boundaries between roles, characteristic of the Russian organization, and fuzzy lines of accountability and reporting, can prove a challenge to a Westerner, however experienced and culturally sensitive he or she may be. Work pressure and isolation raise anxieties and insecurities, and consultants are not immune. However, little of this experience is communicated, and the pressure to maintain a neutral professional tone leads to a rational/emotional splitting (Obholzer and Roberts 1994), in which the emotional element is depressed or cauterized. As this happens, language also tends to become more vague and generalized, as evidenced by this report extract, written after field visits to an orphanage:

> We are not at all optimistic about the possibility of reforming the Children's Houses and orphanages and we believe that the current emphasis on developing community support services is the right approach. We recognized that social care systems in Sweden and the UK have found it difficult to change the pattern of work of their large residential units.[8]

In contrast, the same impressions were relayed to fellow consultants in the following terms:

> We were deeply disturbed by our experience . . . [T]he level of emotional and psychological distress was marked. We saw children who were in tears, other showing clear signs of deep depression and a general state of emotional blankness in many of the children . . . This behaviour was either ignored by the senior staff or explained away.[9]

Later, field notes allude to the distress felt by workers who were forced to send children from broken families to orphanages:

> Our job is to do everything we can to stop children going to the Children's House because it is not a family.

These extracts relate to the phenomenon of institutionalization in staff, although only the second communicates the attendant despair, embarrassment, and denial. While justifiably avoiding any connotations of blame or judgement (note the implied message 'we have the same problems as you'), the tendency to split off the emotional experience from what is communicated in formal documents may lead to habits of vague expression which, as well as avoiding emotion, also avoid commitment to specific forms of action. Here is an example from the project Inception Report:

> Most of the care provision currently available in Russia is based on institutional care . . . An expensive method of social protection [that] can

often not target and assist the most vulnerable. We are recommending a shift towards a more community-based care system and one where people are treated as individuals with individual needs.

A comment from the Ministry in Moscow complained that the project's Inception Report was superficial – 'reflected too little of the policy conversations in Moscow and did not describe in sufficient detail what the remedies for change might be.' But the consultant would be unlikely to frame firm recommendations to the Ministry under such circumstances, preferring to play safe with appeals to general principles and 'artfully vague language.' One of the consultants expressed his frustration thus, 'There was a lot of unsureness. Nothing is structured well . . . We are running the same way as the Russians, having ideas but without content, or context,' Frustration was channelled into arguments over project administration, falling short of modelling ideal management for our Russian colleagues. In turn, these conflicts generated a good deal of heartache and anxiety, as the team continued to cling to the process consultancy ideal (Schein 1988) in the belief that one of the most powerful sources of transfer of meaning (Jankowicz 1994) is through *how* you communicate what you know through how you behave.

On one occasion, I was presenting the topic of team management. I was working through an interpreter, which is never ideal, and energy in the room was low. A Russian colleague interrupted and suggested that the concept of team was problematic because there are several Russian words that denote 'team,' and the choice of the correct one to communicate *my* meaning was rather crucial. As we opened up the discussion to investigate the semantic possibilities (were we aiming for connotations of a brigade, or a group, or a sports team, for example?) I began to be acutely aware of the complications. By referring to 'team management' was I communicating, through the interpreter, the concept of management *through* a team, *by* a team, or management *of* a team? (For a debate on the particular problems posed by transfer of terminology in the context of management knowledge transfer see, for example, Jankowicz 1994; Holden 1995; Gilbert 1998).

I wanted to be able to clarify the message and eliminate the confusion, but found myself in a dilemma – the deeper we got into the discussion about what do we mean by team, the more I would be exposing the vagueness and non-specificity of our common management terminology in English. It had been a long and very trying day. Time was short and I had not bargained for this linguistic diversion. Eventually my frustration broke through. I had had enough, I was near to tears, and I wanted to go home.

I stopped pretending to be cool, calm and collected, and dropped my 'expert' veneer, it was obvious to everyone that my patience was spent. Immediately, I was congratulated. 'We didn't know what you were talking about until you got angry. Before, it was just words. Then, suddenly we could see that your idea of management *meant* something.' The emotional outburst was a key incident in the development of mutual understanding. It was a salutary lesson to me that the breakthrough occurred only when I let my professional persona drop, along with its customary splitting off of negative emotion from reason, and my 'real' integrated self showed through.

Second case study – the action learning approach

Having worked with Action Learning for many years in the UK, I had long considered that Action Learning could be a powerful tool in Russia to unlock the situated learning of local managers and professionals, and also a powerful antidote to the prevailing philosophy that Western consultants were the fount of all knowledge, theoretical and practical. But two factors prevented its introduction. First, the need for the facilitator to be able to work directly with a group without the intermediation of an interpreter.[10] Also, Action Learning is a relatively facilitator-intensive form of learning in the early stages when the group is dependent on the facilitator to model and monitor the process, and experienced facilitators were nowhere to be found.

In Novokuznetsk the answer to the problem presented itself in the form of a voluntary organization set up to provide telephone counselling to children at risk of abuse or actual victims of abuse. The service had been set up by a local psychologist using ChildLine as a model, although she had had no direct contact with the UK-based charity and only had literature to go on. The service had expanded from one person to a dozen trained counsellors, most of whom were professionally qualified psychologists. They were looking for ways of extending their network of contacts with the statutory services, and were extremely excited by the possibility of acting as facilitators in a new form of 'training technology' as they put it. A one-day seminar was held for them giving the historical and theoretical background to Action Learning, modelling the process of an Action Learning Set (ALS), and discussing the role and capabilities of the set facilitator.

Subsequently, six Action Learning Sets met for three hour sessions once a month for six months, involving a total of 28 social workers and six facilitators, all of whom were qualified psychologists and trained counsellors, although none of them had worked with Action Learning before. They had a one-day training seminar on facilitation. The theme of the groups was 'tackling professional problems.' As a way of communicating the essence of the Action Learning methodology within the set, and emphasizing the difference from a 'normal' group discussion situation, it was described as a process consulting analogy. During the time when they were presenting their issue, the individual was in the role of a client, and the other members of the set were to be in the role of consultant. In other words, they were there for the client and focusing on the client's needs and reality, rather than their own.

The groups spent a portion of their first meetings setting ground rules, which, while thoroughly in tune with standard ALS practice, also reflect the psychotherapeutic leanings of the facilitators. These included:

- staying in the here and now;
- confidentiality – nobody should be identifiable in the reports of the groups;
- acting as a critical friend;
- everybody speaking only for herself;
- not criticizing.

Each presenter (termed a client within the group) would have 30 minutes of airtime in which to present her issue and receive questions from the rest of the group. The facilitators made sure that within each three-hour session, at least four people would be able to present.

Several of the social workers involved in the Action Learning Sets worked inside institutions, such as hospitals and residential homes for the elderly and infirm. They felt their lack of influence with other professionals, particularly medical professionals, for example, in trying to get physiotherapy for a client. ALS participants found it difficult at first to accept that they could find any answers to their problems from within their own group. Accustomed to having to refer to clinicians for information and licence to act, they had a tendency at first to plead lack of authority or expertise: 'What can we do? We're not psychologists.'

However, after a while, as the facilitators modelled questioning techniques aimed at helping the presenter to surface the true nature of the problem, participants began to appreciate that they were the experts on their own problems, and that the combined focused attention and constructive questioning of their peers was in many cases sufficient for them to find a way forward. They began to understand that no-one but themselves had genuine insight into their daily working lives, there being no parallels with other professionals and, crucially, no local (Russian or Siberian) tradition of social work praxis on which to draw. Action Learning provided a unique opportunity to explore the nature of their problems without having to expose their lack of knowledge (as they perceived it) and lack of experience.

Several of the more senior staff, with operational managerial responsibilities for centres or service areas, had experienced a certain loss of identity as a consequence of the 'upgrading' of their work roles (this term 'upgrading' corresponding to promotion). They reported a sense of displacement, having lost their previously intense and emotionally rewarding relationships with clients; furthermore, they had little sense at first of how to discover a sense of identity and belonging as managers. They had to discover new forms of satisfaction in their work, new forms of emotional reward, and much of this emerged through facilitating the development of more junior staff.

Typical issues the groups worked with included:

- Working in a multidisciplinary team – winning the respect and support of other professionals, particularly medical professionals.
- Dealing with conflicts. Conflict was a constant in the lives of these man-

agers, as they were simultaneously required to assess clients' needs and be providers. Often clients would be confused and aggressive, sometimes physically so, and there were frequent attacks on staff.

• Sharing information when information management systems are incomplete and imperfect,

• Dealing with resource disputes and disputes about status and boundaries.

In one instance, a social work centre manager, responsible for a service providing home care for elderly clients, brought to the group a problem that had been tormenting her for many months, but that she had been ashamed to voice in any other forum. A trained chemist, she had lost her position in the metallurgy plant and had become a social worker as a second career. She cared deeply about the plight of the people she came into contact with on a daily basis, and also cared very much about her staff. The problem was that she found herself appalled, to the point of revulsion, by many of the old people. She was shocked by their living conditions and depressed by the thought that she was not too far away from being old herself. The prospect frightened her. At the same time, she felt that she must be a bad person for having these negative thoughts about the old, and would have to leave her job, because she was not a fit person to be a social worker. She was oppressed by the image of the social worker as a loving, caring, self-sacrificing person.

Under the skilful and patient tutelage of the ALS facilitator, the group was able to explore, with this individual, the question of boundaries between the personal self and the professional self, between personal reaction and appropriate professional response. Thus, they were able to identify for themselves the essence of good practice in dealing with challenging clients on the one hand, and personal feelings on the other. Western borrowings had been unhelpful. It transpired that there had been considerable pressure created by taking the concept of 'unconditional positive regard' for clients out of context, this having been translated as 'approve of your client whatever he or she does.' In turn, this had become jumbled up with a misappropriation of the marketing slogan 'the customer is always right' – an idea that was being used by clients to bully workers, particularly managers who had to apportion resources. The ensuing Action Learning process enabled the manager to find a resolution between her feelings of revulsion and her positive work ethic, resolving the 'splitting,' and she was able to move forward with more confidence. At the same time, the general issue had been noted, and the ALS as a whole felt able to initiate a wider debate within the workforce about the parameters of 'caring' in the professional context.

In another instance, the manager of a domiciliary service was troubled by a seemingly intractable problem of resources. She was responsible for a team of social workers charged with delivering food to housebound elderly people as part of their daily duties. This entailed going to the depot and loading up with two bags weighing up to 12 kilos each and then delivering them to the clients' homes. But in this local version of 'meals on wheels,' the wheels were those of the bus service. Workers were wasting hours and exhausting themselves. The manager was torn between her determination to make the service work and her suppressed anger that social workers were being used as packhorses. The ALS process enabled this manager, and her peers, by surfacing her anger, to challenge the idea that this was an appropriate part of a social worker's workload. This led to a revised system of food distribution, and within six months, a re-structuring of the service to relieve scarce professional workers of the more menial and heavy aspects of the domiciliary service.

Cultural challenges to Action Learning

The learning described above was not gained painlessly. There were aspects of the Action Learning style of discourse that were quite alien to the Russian managers. First, their tendency, from years of soviet-style 'storming,'[11] was to go straight to a solution, the first that presented itself, rather than ask questions to elucidate more of the nature of the problem.

Having been introduced to the concept of learning styles and Kolb's learning cycle model (Kolb 1984), the facilitators were initially preoccupied about the learning styles of group members, wondering whether training and learning opportunities should be chosen to match learning styles or to challenge them, in the belief or hope that this would get people out of their comfort zones and then accelerate learning. It was recognized that getting out of the comfort zone might induce some people to set up barriers to learning, and it was also suggested that people were outside their comfort zone in much of their daily life, so did not need to be challenged too much in a training situation. Facilitators needed to be reassured that the participants in the Action Learning Sets would themselves be responsible for their own learning and that the onus was on them to create and model the conditions for that to happen, rather than to exercise control.

According to the learning styles instrument (Honey and Mumford 1992) employed in the project, a large proportion of this cohort of social workers scored highly as 'Reflectors.' This may represent a learned aspect of learning style, as the Russian educational system is highly theoretical and tends to adopt an approach to learning converse to the Anglo-Saxon model. In the UK, the learning situation is often predicated on the principle of having the experience first, reflecting on it, and then theorizing. UK managers, in particular, constantly demand that training should be 'practical' and not 'theoretical.' In Russia, managers expect to be taught the theory first, before being required to put anything into practice. In fact, in an evaluation discussion, the social workers did admit to being used to waiting for someone to tell them what to do. To an extent, Action Learning methodology might be said to emphasize the Activist and Pragmatist styles, seeing as the participant is expected to carry out action 'in the real world' of work, and report back to the group, and the emphasis is on making a difference. However, Action Learning provides a balanced learning experience in that the reflective mode is emphasized during set sessions.

There was a problem of nomenclature, as 'Action Learning' does not translate well into Russian. The link between the group sessions and individual action was not always grasped, and sponsors, and eventually the groups themselves, adopted the phrase 'self-training groups.' This introduces the risk that, as it becomes generalized through the service, the technique of Action Learning will become diluted and obscured, and it is difficult to know how this could be controlled.

Conclusions

Russia is one example of many countries and settings where the current focus locally is on developing practice rather than developing managerial capability. In Russia and other countries of the former Soviet bloc, Western management concepts delivered through group training programmes are not yet fully relevant. Workers in an emerging profession need to be supported to develop their own practice and ethos, rather than having Anglo-Saxon models foisted upon them.

Formal management development may have to follow later, when modes of working have become established and service structures are sufficiently developed to require concentration on specific management techniques of integration and coordination. An interim approach is to offer supervision and mentoring to managers on an individual basis, and Action Learning on a group basis. As the experiment showed, Action Learning has a multiplier effect. In generating solutions it develops the capacity to confront new problems. It develops the consultancy skills of facilitators and participants. Action Learning can support professionalism. It challenges the image of the foreign consultant as an expert who is importing knowledge, thus reducing dependency on practice developed elsewhere for different circumstances.

As the 'foreign expert' I had to stand back, having done what I could to prepare the facilitators, and let the process take its course. This was nerve-racking, especially as no-one else in the project was convinced that it was going to work, and failure would have meant loss of face for me and a severe censuring from the funders. Thus, the experiment took me out of my comfort zone too, and exposed me to a set of anxieties different from the normal 'stagefright' nerves of presenting a series of seminars. But the process at least had the security of authenticity, and the conviction of the facilitators, who went on to offer their new 'learning technology' to other agencies.

Finally, the high level of emotional openness and risk-taking in the Russian Action Learning Sets is a reminder of the place of the affective dimension for those who work in caring professions, and those who seek to facilitate their learning. None of us are, or should be, immune from stress or fear. Recognizing the endemic projected anxiety in our own social and helping organizations may mean that we discover that something can be learned from Russian leaders of social services. The big question for management development is how to confront and reconcile the split between the rational and the emotional in management.

Key learning points

- In Russia, as in many parts of the former soviet bloc, social work with the most vulnerable and dependent groups in the population is being invented, virtually from scratch, as a new profession. This development is occurring in a context of massive social and economic upheaval, in which the divide between the winners in the changes, and the disadvantaged has grown ever wider.
- As a new profession, it has its own patterns of organization, training and development, principles of good practice, styles of leadership etc, that are specific to that context and culture. Thus, it is inappropriate for trainers and consultants to seek to 'import' and apply at face value concepts developed elsewhere.
- Professionals in health and social care, whatever their level of qualification and experience, have a tendency towards the 'rational–emotional split,' splitting off their emotional selves from their professional selves.
- This is also a tendency among trainers and developers, particularly when evaluating or communicating their work to outside sponsors and funders. While it acts as a form of defence mechanism, the rational–emotional split can get in the way of effective communication and learning, especially in a cross-cultural context.
- Action Learning presents an effective alternative, or supplement, to traditional forms of HRD in such situations (i.e. cross-cultural, bilingual, in settings of systemic change, where language and culture would often create barriers to learning) because it challenges the assumption that knowledge is the domain of the trainer.
- Action Learning has the added power to enable participants, acting individually and collectively, to set for themselves the parameters of professionalism within their own meaning and context, and so is a general catalyst to the development of professional ethics, principles and practices.

Acknowledgement

I would like to acknowledge the help and support of the following people: Olga Krasnova, Antonina Dashkina, Tony Widmer, Olga Gutak, Natalya Sosnovskaya, Sveltlana Stefanishin, and all members of the staff of the Centre for Psychological Support, Novokuznets.

Notes

1 Tacis originally was an acronym, standing for Technical Assistance to the Commonwealth of Independent States.
2 From here on the chapter is written in the first person.
3 The Penza region lies in the heart of southwestern Russia south of Moscow, and Samara is in the Volga basin.
4 Novokuznetsk is a steel town in the Kuzbass area of Central Siberia.
5 This phrase is not intended to indicate a view that the Soviet Union was not a developed country. In terms of industrial capacity it certainly ranked among developed countries. However, the networks and institutions of what we generally call civil society were not developed; nor was quality of life of the mass of the population.
6 Presentation to the project team, 1999.
7 Extract from research diary.
8 From a formal project report – written by a consultant from Sweden.
9 From an internal briefing note, written by the Swedish consultant.
10 I had good expressive and receptive Russian, but was not sufficiently fluent in naturalistic conversation.
11 Term describing the common process of getting 'all hands to the wheel' to complete the quarterly plan in double-quick time, after months of waiting for essential supplies to come through.

References

Albrow, M. (1997) *Do Organizations Have Feelings?* London: Routledge.
Anttonen, A. and Sipila, J. (1996) 'European social care services: is it possible to identify models?' *Journal of European Social Policy* 6(2): 87–100.
Berdyayev, N. (1990) *Sudba Rossii: opyty po psikhologii voiny I natsionalnosti*, Moscow: Izdateltsvo MGU.
Burger, E.J., Field, M.G. and Twigg, J.L. (1998) 'From assurance to insurance in Russian health care: the problematic transition,' *American Journal of Public Health* 88(5): 755–758.
Clarke, S. (1999) 'Splitting difference: psychoanalysis, hatred and exclusion,' *Journal for the Theory of Social Behaviour* 29(1). 21–36.
Dyker, D.A. (1992) *Restructuring the Soviet Economy*, London: Routledge.
Frydman, A.T., Rapaczynski, A. and Earle, J.S. (eds) (1993) *The Privatization Process in Russia, Ukraine and the Baltic States*, London: Central European University Press.
Gilbert, K. (1998) 'Consultancy fatigue: epidemiology, symptoms and prevention,' *Leadership and Organizational Development Journal* 19(6): 340–346.
Goleman, D. (1995) *Emotional Intelligence: Why it Matters more than IQ*, New York: Bantam Books.
Hearn, B., Darvill, G. and Morris, B. (1992) *On Becoming a Manager in Social Work*, London: Longman.
Henderson, S. (2002) 'Selling civil society: western aid and the nongovernmental organization sector in Russia,' *Comparative Political Studies* 35(2): 139.
Holden, N.J. (1995) *Management Education in Russia: Issues in Course Design, Development and Evaluation*, Manchester: Brooke Publications Ltd.
Holden, N.J., Cooper, C. and Carr, J. (1997) *Dealing with the New Russia*, London: Wiley.
Holloway, D. and McFaul, M. (1995) 'Aid to Russia: what difference can western

policy make?' in G.W. Lapidus (ed.) *The New Russia: Troubled Transformation*, Oxford: Westview.

Honey, P. and Mumford, A. (1992) *The Manual of Learning Styles*, Maidenhead: Peter Honey.

Iarskaia-Smirnova, E. and Romanov, P. (2002) ' "A salary is not important here": the professionalization of social work in contemporary Russia,' *Social Policy and Administration* 36(2): 123–141.

Jankowicz, A.D. (1994) 'The new journey to Jerusalem: mission and meaning in the managerial crusade to Eastern Europe,' *Organization Studies* 15(4): 497–507.

Join-Lambert, H. (1999) 'The evolution of the system of care for social orphans in Russia. The Soviet inheritance and the current trends in Saint Petersburg,' *International Journal of Child and Family Welfare* 4(2): 149–163.

Kilborne, P. (1999) 'When trauma strikes the soul: shame, splitting and psychic pain,' *American Journal of Psychoanalysis* 59(4): 385–402.

Kolb, D.A. (1984) *Experiential Learning: Experience as the Source of Learning and Development*, London: Prentice-Hall.

Kolenikov, S. and Shorrocks, A. (2005) 'A decomposition analysis of regional poverty in Russia,' *Review Of Development Economics* 9(1): 25–46.

Lane, G. (1999) 'Russia: the forgotten ideal,' *Social Work in Europe* 6(2): 56–58.

Lawrence, P. and Vlachoutsicos, C. (1992) *Behind the Factory Walls: Decision Making in Soviet and US Enterprises*, Boston, MA: Harvard Business School Press.

Layton, L. (2000) 'Cultural hierarchies, splitting, and the dynamic unconscious,' *Journal for the Psychoanalysis of Culture and Society* 5(1): 65–71.

Manoukovsky, O. (1993) 'Russian Management: how far from the West?' *EFMD Forum* 93(2): 28–32.

Mayer, J.D. and Salovey, P. (1997) 'What is emotional intelligence?' in P. Salovey and D. Sluyter (eds) *Emotional Development and Emotional Intelligence: Educational Implications*, New York: Basic Books, pp. 3–31.

Menzies, I.E.P. (1960) 'Social systems as a defence against anxiety: an empirical study of the nursing service of a general hospital,' in E. Trist and H. Murray (eds) *The Social Engagement of Social Science; Vol. 1: the Socio-psychological Perspective*, London: Free Association Press.

Munday, B. and Lane, G. (1998) *The Old and the New: Changes in Social Care in Central and Eastern Europe*, Canterbury: European Institute of Social Services.

Obholzer, A. and Roberts, V.Z. (1994) *The Unconscious at Work: Individual and Organizational Stress in the Human Services*, London: Routledge.

Revans, R. (1971) *Developing Effective Managers: a New Approach to Business Education*, Harlow: Longman.

Revans, R. (1998) *ABC of Action Learning*, Bromley: Chartwell-Brett.

Rusinova, N.L. and Brown, J.V. (2003) 'Social inequality and strategies for getting medical care in post-Soviet Russia,' *Health* 7(1): 51–72.

Schein, E. (1988) *Process Consultation, Vol. 1*, New York: Addison Wesley.

Shipitsina, L. (1998) 'Russia,' in B. Munday and G. Lane (eds) *The Old and the New: Changes in Social Care in Central and Eastern Europe*, Canterbury: European Institute of Social Services.

Swett, E. (1992) 'The health care crisis in Russia,' *Caring* 9(10): 46.

Tacis (1997) *Tacis Interim Evaluation Report*, Brussels: European Commission.

Takeda, Y. (2004) 'Poverty dynamics in Russia during the 1990s,' *Slavic Studies* 51: 241–272.

Templeman, S.B. (2004) 'Social work in the new Russia at the start of the millennium,' *International Social Work* 47(1): 95–108.

Tregoubova, T. (2000) 'Challenges for modern social work in Russia: problems and prospects,' *Professional Development, the International Journal of Social Work Education*, www.temple.edu/professionaldevelopment. Accessed July 2005.

Vlachoutsicos, C. and Lawrence, P. (1990) 'What we don't know about Soviet management,' *Harvard Business Review* 68(6): 50–54.

Wedel, J.R. (1998) *Collision and Collusion: The Strange Case of Western Aid to Eastern Europe 1989–1998*, Basingstoke: Macmillan.

Wiktorow, A. (1992) 'Soviet Union,' in J. Dixon and D. Macarov (eds) *Social Welfare in Socialist Countries*, London: Routledge, pp. 184–207.

Winnicott, D.W. (1947) 'Hate in the countertransference,' in D.W. Winnicott (1958) *Collected Papers: through Paediatrics to Psychoanalysis*, London: Hogarth Press and the Institute of Psychoanalysis.

Yin, R. (2003) *Applications of Case Study Research*, London: Sage.

Zanini, G. (2002) *Assisting Russia's Transformation: an Unprecedented Challenge*, Washington, DC: World Bank.

17 Making an impact through integrating learning methodologies

A large-scale, collaborative, systems-based learning network in the British National Health Service

Jane Keep

Introduction

This chapter asks 'how can HRD practitioners combine learning methods to produce an effective national HRD programme?' Adopting an action research/learning and reflective practice perspective, it describes the development of an evolving learning network that has been independently evaluated. It suggests that using a combination of learning methodologies is powerful and can change local practice.

Rationale

Attempts have been made at large-scale learning, cascading learning, and sharing practice, across the British National Health Service (NHS), but these attempts have often been undertaken in 'silos,' as isolated, or as one-off, flavour-of-the-month initiatives (such as various quality improvement type or large-scale learning initiatives), and, some have had little or no reported impact outside the pioneering sites. Indeed, many NHS employees and human resource development specialists have long forgotten some of the national and local learning programmes and interventions undertaken in the NHS in the last decade, and in some of the learning institutions such as the NHSTD (NHS Training Directorate) and some of the early iterations of the NHS Leadership Centre. Perhaps as a consequence of this and the lack of reported success of large scale learning interventions, there is little published research or evidence to assist decision-makers and HRD specialists alike to guide them when making large-scale learning intervention and implementation decisions.

The Engaging Communities Learning Network (ECLN) outlined in this chapter, was developed in response to this paucity by a small team of HRD facilitators/specialists, academics and NHS colleagues who had all too often experienced the (often unmemorable!) singular, isolated programmes, and were searching for a more integrated and effective approach to HRD as a national learning and capacity building approach. This Learning Network was an HRD Programme, which was able to work in the complex operating context, and responded to the need to deliver rapid and effective change, being an intervention that could evolve in the prevailing context. It added value to day to day tasks being tackled by busy healthcare practitioners, and created 'space' for thinking 'out of the box' collaboratively, and in a more joined-up way by connecting participants to each other, and connecting a number of approaches to learning. This chapter outlines this 'tried and tested' approach to HRD, which combined a number of well recognized learning methods: systems thinking; learning networks; action learning; action research; knowledge management, reflective practice and story telling; to produce a dynamic national HRD programme.

The theoretical context

In 2000/2001 there seemed to be little theoretical or empirical material concerning the complex processes of learning and development in, amongst or around healthcare organizations, although there was recognition that managing learning and development in the NHS is a complex process (Burchill and Casey 1996). Throughout the last decade, learning and development in the NHS had faced many challenges to 'deliver' in adding value and making a real difference. It moved from a myriad of bulk-bought 'off-the-shelf' approaches to development – such as supervisory and management development programmes, health and safety training, or IT training – to bespoke interventions that were far more context- and learner-specific, such as locally developed team building, locally implemented appraisal training, or local, organizational-specific induction programmes. However, bespoke learning interventions in many ways created more heterogeneity and took place often with little evidence of successful application within the NHS context, and even with the knowledge of the need for a more bespoke approach to HRD, NHS HRD practitioners 'blindly' followed trends, fads or fashions in whatever the 'latest' learning concept there was at the time. For example, in the 1990s, the Learning Company (Pedlar *et al.* 1991), business process re-engineering (BPR) (Hammer and Champey 1995), were all 'implemented' partially into NHS organizations, without either connecting them to other learning initiatives, or ascertaining the 'value addedness' of them, let alone consideration of sustainability or mainstreaming of them. There was also often a view that 'one size fits all' in that if an intervention worked in one part of the country, it would naturally work in another part requiring no local adaptation or translation. In addition, various attempts at implementing TQM (total quality management) and CQI (continuous quality improvement) have not produced results. Blumenthal and Kilo (1998) could not 'identify a healthcare organization that has fundamentally improved its performance through CQI (or any other means). There are simply no organi-zation-wide success stories out there – no shining castles on the hill to serve as inspirations for a struggling industry.' This finding underlines that the emphasis on TQM as 'an organization-wide approach and philosophy' (Ovretveit 2000) poses a formidable, if not insurmountable, challenge to implementation in healthcare settings (Mcleod 2005). On an NHS-wide scale, previous attempts at large-scale HRD include the NHS Beacon Pro-gramme (NHS Beacon Services 2000) which was part of a then 'NHS learn-ing network' with little impact or lasting memory and a seeming lack of research or empirical study surrounding this work.

In addition to a lack of reported success of long-term large-scale HRD programmes up until recently, there was a lack of published research or eval-uations of effective combined learning methods across large scale complex public sector organizations.

There have however, since the development and delivery of the ECLN in the past four years, been a number of research evaluations, and critical analy-ses, as well as papers written about some of the more recent attempts and approaches to large-scale HRD programmes in the NHS. These include service improvement with the NHS 'service improvement' initiative which has achieved 'much progress' (Maher and Penny 2005) and, in 2004 is reported to have achieved 'extensive activity in every part of the NHS; thou-sands of staff trained in service improvement techniques; strong evidence with outstanding improvements in access and quality and improvement at the heart of the NHS Plan and established as a world leader in the field' (Fillingham 2004), as well as the breakthrough series (BTS) collaborative model (Mcleod 2005), NHS Collaboratives (Mcleod 2005) and social move-ment (Bate *et al.* 2004), but these weren't readily available at the initial design stage of the ECLN HRD programme.

During the design and early development time of the ECLN (2001–02) there was much theory and practice sharing around the role, utilization and impact of singular methodologies often, in other contexts, particularly whilst the ECLN facilitators searched for a 'model' or framework from which to develop the pilot 'learning network.' Following lengthy delibera-tions amongst the ECLN facilitators, it was felt that, if a number of singu-lar methodologies were developed as an interconnected 'cluster' this seemed to offer a more holistic solution to provide a national learning network. The singular methodologies and ideas were based on the follow-ing definitions.

Systems theory

> in any organization, the multitude of parts and processes are so inter-related and so interdependent that a small change in one part necessit-ates changes and adaptations in other parts.
>
> (Wilson and Rosenfeld 1990)

Systems thinking managers know that simple solutions are bound to fail when pitched against complex problem situations. They are willing to struggle with more complicated ideas that, at first acquaintance, may be more difficult to understand. They hope to emerge from this engagement with systems thinking better equipped to cope with complexity, change and diversity. This hope is based on the fact that systems thinking is holistic rather than reductionist and, at least in the form of critical systems thinking, does everything possible to encourage creativity.

(Jackson 2003)

Action learning

way of learning from actions and what happens to us and around us by taking time to question, understand and reflect, to gain insights, and consider how to act in the future. 'Involves group of people working together on their doing and their learning. And requires regular rigorous meetings to allow space and time for questioning, reflecting, understanding.'

(e.g. Weinstein 1999)

Learning networks

(e.g. the Inter-Organizational Networking (ION) Research Project by George Tsekouras, John Bessant, CENTRIM, Brighton.)

One feature of the emerging business environment is the need for more extensive networking between organizations, and CENTRIM has explored good practice in learning networks, where they cite 'a reasonably new form of learning. An increasing number of firms worldwide are attracted to the idea of enhancing an organization's knowledge by collective learning; both SMEs and large companies find this approach suitable to their needs, as it gives them opportunities to share expense and, more significantly, experience with other organizations including universities, suppliers, customers and even other competitors.'

Action research

(Lewin 1946) described action research as 'a spiral of steps, each of which is composed for a circle of planning, action, and fact-finding about the result of the action'. 'Action research underlies most current OD approaches for studying and simultaneously changing social systems.'

(French *et al.* 2004)

Knowledge management

has taken a soft systems approach as a theory (Keep 2005). Collinson and Parcell (2001) suggest KM 'is not about creating an encyclopedia that captures everything that anybody ever knew. Rather it is about keeping track of those who know the recipe, and nurturing the culture and the technology that will get them talking,' shifting the emphasis from knowledge libraries to placing more value on thinking and ideas and finding ways to increase mobility of knowledge and understanding. (Keep 2005)

Reflective practice

process of learning and developing through examining our own practice and opening this to wider scrutiny by others and studying texts from other spheres (Bolton 2001). Reflection *in action* – during practice, attentive practitioner, observes, interacts, and adjusts – and approaches through thinking in a focused way whilst working. Reflection *on action* – occurs after action when details are recalled and analysed through careful unpicking of all aspects of the situation.

Story

narration of a chain of events told or written/report or statement on a matter or event. Stories – an attempt to create order out of a chaotic world ... but for our experiences to develop us, socially, psychologically, spiritually – our world must be made to appear strange, we must be encouraged to examine our story making processes critically.

(Bolton 2001)

Experiential learning

Learning relating to or derived from experience, based on the work of Kolb (1984) and discussed in McGill and Beaty (1993). The experiential learning cycle works through the stages of experience, reflection, generalization and testing.

Process consultation

(Schein 1969, also discussed in French and Bell 1990) 'Process consultation consists of many different interventions, it is not one single thing the consultant does' (French and Bell 1990). 'The job of the process consultant is to help the organization to solve its own problems making it *aware of organizational process*, of the consequences of these processes, and of the mechanisms by which they can be changed. The ultimate concern of the process consultant is the organization's capacity to do for itself what he has done for it. Where the standard consultant is more concerned about passing on his knowledge, the process consultant is concerned about passing on his skills and values.

(Schein 1969)

The empirical context

Since 2000, the National Health Service's operating context has become increasingly more complex, timescales for change, and then re-adapting those 'changes' (in structure, policy, or legislation for instance) are swifter with some new structures or initiatives even being 'restructured' more than once within a 12 month period. This includes national learning institutions such as the already transforming NHSU (NHS university), and the various iterations of the NHS Leadership centre. With over 1 million staff employed in the NHS, and the need to be continually learning, adapting, and innovating to ensure the provision of professional and high quality services, HRD plays a key role. Whilst health and social care organizations are large and important sectors of the British and global economy, there had been an ongoing unease among HRD professionals and learning specialists particularly around large-scale HRD. Training, education and development had remained a heterogeneous area *within* the various iterations of national HRD organizations, as well as *amongst* these organizations and NHS organizations themselves, and no obvious interdependencies had been developed or sustained. One of the consequences of the constant restructuring and various iterations is that the organizational 'learning memory' had been destroyed and with little or no 'archiving' of learning or knowledge materials, which often led to a sense of déja vu when the next national 'HRD programme' or organization was introduced. One of the other counter 'forces' to a more whole systems focus to learning in the NHS is the 'silo' approach to National policy and change, whereby one part of say, one national NHS policy team may instigate a new initiative or policy lever, and another national NHS policy team – or one of the 'arms-length' bodies within the NHS umbrella – may well initiate another policy lever, without the obvious connections made between them, thus creating an implementation gap and incongruity locally. All of these can create a sense of 'pushing' uphill for HRD practitioners to implement learning and change, calling for a need for a more dynamic 'whole systems' and sustainable approach to national NHS policy and practice implementation, including HR and HRD initiatives.

One further contextual aspect to highlight here is the underlying cultural and behavioural operating context of the NHS. 'Modernization' and innovation have been at the forefront of change in the NHS. However, a 'micro'-performance managed drive in recent years, as a way quickly to achieve a multitude of standards and initiatives, has impacted on the openness and willingness to learn by NHS employees, or on the time made legitimately for learning by managers for their employees, often with a sense of feeling unable to participate in learning because of pressures to meet 'tick box' initiatives. If learning seemed 'faddy' or only partially thought through or disconnected from many previously disconnected approaches to learning, this also created an apathy to become involved in HRD initiatives by NHS employees, and worse still, in a centralized policy and performance context, it also created an expectation of needing to be 'spoon fed' with learning and development and a learning 'laziness' or dependency. Equally, nervousness around being 'counter-cultural,' and that it may 'waste time' (e.g. thinking or learning differently in a centralist day-to-day operating context) even in a learning environment, had also created barriers to HRD initiatives.

There have been (and still are) various NHS policies – life long learning, national HR strategies such as Working together, learning together (DoH 2001); HR in the NHS Plan (DoH 2002); The NHS Knowledge and Skills Framework (NHS KSF) and the Development Review Process (DoH 2004) – which have provided some local and national baselines for HRD in the NHS. These, may have added value, however there was, during ECLN, no real evidence or experience to base this on as to their impact as wide scale, national HRD policies and programmes.

What was the impetus for the learning network?

One way organizational development can be understood is as 'Consciously adopting procedures whereby an organization's or network's overall effectiveness is improved and the capacity to make future changes is enhanced' (adapted from various definitions of French *et al.* 2005). Between 2002–05, NatPaCT (the National Primary and Care Trust development programme, part of the NHS Modernization Agency) developed a national organizational development programme of learning to support and enable Primary Care Trusts (PCTs) in the NHS to emerge and deliver their key objectives. It offered PCTs a huge amount of learning and development support. Its website, with its learning resources and policy updates, regularly reported its success in 'connecting' these 302 disparate PCT organizations.

During the same time-frame, new legislation and policy drivers emerged, to support patient and public involvement in health, to enable healthcare organizations to involve patients and the public in the pre-design stages of planning and service change in the NHS, and to ensure a clear overview and scrutiny framework for the engagement and involvement of patients and the public (Health and Social Care Act 2001, Sections 7 and 11; Strengthening Accountability, DoH 2003).

During 2002–05, as part of an aim to support PCTs to build their skills, knowledge and confidence in meeting the needs of the new legislation and policy, in engaging communities and patient and public involvement in health, the Engaging Communities Learning Network (ECLN) was commissioned (by NatPaCT), and designed and delivered, by two independent 'facilitators' who both had complementary and diverse skills sets (e.g. of engaging communities, or engaging staff), and who had similar skill sets around small and large-scale learning methods and processes in complex operating environments.

As the NHS operating context had become more complex, working lives busier and more intense, and the pressure to deliver was constant, local and sometimes isolated, bouts of sharing and networking had played an important role in learning and in delivering change. It was the independent facilitators' view that building capacity required an approach that didn't create a dependency, but instead, created a 'network-ability' and a 'learning-ability' built on available assets and resources (e.g. individuals' experience) to enable confidence and courage to stimulate change through a whole systems approach. Networking and networks had emerged during recent years as a learning methodology to support capacity building, particularly where large-scale learning was required (Tsekouras and Bessant (ongoing)). However, during the early stages (2002–04) of the ECLN, to the facilitators' knowledge there had not been any other learning network in the NHS which was to have been as large as the ECLN, nor combined a wider number of learning methods and processes; in addition, to their knowledge, no large scale learning network had been developed that role-modelled the very values and methodologies that it was 'tasked' to build capacity about (e.g. whole systems thinking locally amongst communities, and participatory working cultures).

What was the Engaging Communities Learning Network (ECLN)?

More specifically, the ECLN was a national HRD programme – a learning network for Primary Care Trusts in the NHS with a purpose to enable PCT and other colleagues in and around the NHS to build their capacity to engage with their local communities through experiential and action learning, and networking to share and support. At the beginning it had 12 PCTs who were members and the pilot/anchor sites that were the test bed for the co-design of the methods and processes to be adopted in the network. By the end it had over 280 PCT members/sites and a database of these PCTs, and Strategic Health Authorities (SHA), other NHS organizations, wider agencies including from the voluntary sector, national NHS and local policy makers and various 'experts' in many related fields, including participatory cultures, patient and public involvement, OD and change, reconfiguration and restructuring, critical incident analysis, dialoguing, action learning, evaluation and many more, to total over 2000 network 'members' nationally across England, located anywhere from Sunderland to Southampton, and Shropshire to South Gloucestershire.

This learning network was created as an integrated approach to HRD, and combined a number of well-recognized learning methods outlined earlier in this chapter. It took an organizational development approach that utilized and interconnected the well-recognized, often independently employed, learning methodologies and brought together personal, management, leadership, and organizational development into one framework. In fact, as the network emerged, it was harder to separate these interrelated elements than to connect them. The ECLN success criteria evolved continually, being based around an overall aim to create a deeper 'networkability' of and amongst Primary Care Trusts in the NHS who were able, whilst working on key policy themes, to network with one another to solve engaging communities problems, share learning and solutions, raise their engaging communities capability and thus achieve some of their priorities. And to achieve this through PCT's engaging actively with the network, through an infectious sense of curiosity and passion around the topic of engaging communities and patient and public involvement in health, and around using networking and learning to build their own and each other's capability. Following the co-development of success criteria, through an open dialogue with PCT colleagues, co-facilitators and other non-PCT associates, a number of values were created (which enabled some glue of 'togetherness'). This was found to be important, particularly as the network was a combination of being face-to-face and virtual in its methods and approaches. Role-modelling the work that the learning network was attempting to build capacity about (participatory and inclusive work environments) with key values such as inclusivity; using easy-to-understand language (and 'jargon busting') and acting with integrity, were developed and at all times role-modelled by the ECLN facilitators. In addition, from a learning perspective, values emerged around basing all learning activities on real 'in-tray' issues; celebrating success; enabling equity and fairness amongst anyone who wished to be involved; and brokering and creating interdependencies; also, attempting to balance concept and practice became enacted as the underpinning behaviours of ECLN.

The ECLN methodologies

In essence, the two independent facilitators, through their roles as design facilitators, worked with the grain of local experience and of new policy priorities to enable the development of substantive tasks (of the network members, and national policy makers) and, concurrently, increasingly developed and implemented the effective use of the learning network itself. They weaved the various methodological components together by working through a deliberative, conscious action learning/action research (values based) approach in an emergent way. This was done with quarterly reflection and synthesis 'time out' by the lead facilitators to 'weave' and review progress. Part of this journey was independently evaluated by Williams and Burgoyne (2004) and there were also regular process review and reflective meetings and evaluations with the core team of ECLN.

The Engaging Communities Learning Network's 'Knowledge Management' infrastructure is outlined in Figure 17.1. This was co-developed by the core ECLN facilitation team. This, in itself was iterated as the network membership increased. Understanding how this looked 'pictorially' enabled the core ECLN team of facilitators and the Hub to understand their roles more readily.

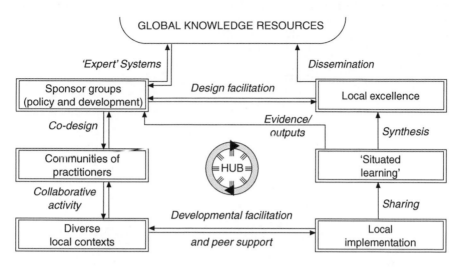

Figure 17.1 Network 'knowledging' architecture.

The ECLN facilitators developed three interconnected 'systems,' which became much clearer as the ECLN evolved. These were the social (and learning) system, the technological system and the task system which, by working in a whole-systems way, allowed these systems to evolve and enabled the ECLN facilitators to understand and develop the interconnectivity of these. The 'technological system' (Figure 17.2) included the 'team, infrastructure and the practical support, and ECLN experience (Tsekouras and Bessant (ongoing) and Williams and Burgoyne 2004) has shown that networks do not continue for long without a friendly hub fulfilling a brokering/linking function – a conduit for basic information and continuous feedback (not a 'call centre'). Good governance, support and accountability are critical. This itself was a brokering function that regularly ensured interconnectivity and a relationship with and between policy and practice, and with the growing knowledge resources (papers, notes, tools, techniques), developed through the ECLN learning activities with network members, and archived by the ECLN team

The 'hub' function included a Programme Manager who coordinated events, maintained the database (with the support of a specialist IT consultant who built the database and hub technology tailored to exact requirements) and acted as the relationship, marketing and finance manager, and 'steward' of good governance.

Weaving the learning methods to be used led to what emerged as the social and learning system. The process interventions and learning methods thus formed the 'social system' (Figure 17.3) in the learning network/knowledge management infrastructure: This was constantly reviewed and regularly

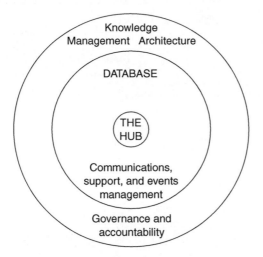

Figure 17.2 The technological system.

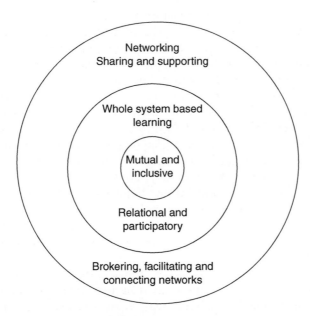

Figure 17.3 The social system.

'weaved' by the facilitators to achieve the 'blended' effect and ensure no disconnections occurred.

With this, a range of learning processes (which role-modelled participatory approaches to involving and engaging people) evolved. This included basing learning on practice using stories, real 'in-tray' tasks; solving wicked problems amongst the participants, strengthening the 'habit' of critical co-buddying and critical friendships across localities, continuous collaborative reflective evaluation; creating forums for intellectual challenge and 'safe' time-out for reflection; and testing evidence and theory and re-creating knowledge through practice in developing an ongoing evidence base to all that was done. The learning activity used was developed in reflection and 'on-the-spot' during learning network forums and meetings, in dialogue with members of the learning network themselves, and, so as to build capacity in more than one way, the facilitators also shared how they were undertaking each of the learning processes 'live' with process reviews, even down to sharing difficult and successful moments that the facilitators of the event or forum might have had so as to enable learning through the process, about the process, and during the process (of the content and process itself!). The types of roles the lead independent facilitators and other facilitators played included: connecting often disparate national policy initiatives, in the NHS and wider public or voluntary sectors; watching and enabling positive group dynamics including 'holding the space' for safe and often challenging discussions and debates amongst participants; enabling buddying amongst participants through their Needs and Offers (like a problems-based 'dating agency'); connecting with the hub to enable continuity within both a virtual learning network and an ever-changing operating context (the NHS); brokering any relational or political issues that arose that may have challenged the learning, any events, or the network itself, and thus acting as whole system brokers and buffers (and 'master weavers'!). The Engaging Communities Learning Network facilitators also enabled local PCT facilitators (members of the ECLN who asked for extra 'learning and development' to become 'Development Facilitators to work locally to support implementation of new learning in the specific local context').

In a busy operating context, in order to 'value-add' every learning intervention requires substance, with real task themes from the 'in-trays' of those participants (or learning network members) undertaking the learning. Thus, the 'task system' emerged through synthesis and interrelating national policy initiatives. Learning in a busy operating context can no longer be unrelated to workplace issues and tasks faced by learning participants, hence the underpinning principles of this learning network were around action learning, reflective practice, and real 'stories.' One of the keys to this was spotting (often before they have become mainstream policy initiatives in the NHS) key policy areas linked to the substance of the learning network. From the beginning of the ECLN, due to the extensive networks in and around the NHS of the two lead independent facilitators, a loose 'network'

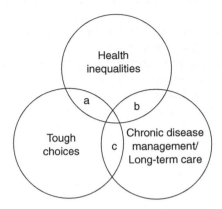

Figure 17.4 The interrelated policy/tasks undertaken by ECLN in 2004–05.

of associates (policy, expert, facilitators) was formed, on whom PCTs could draw on in order to develop their learning and local practice. In addition to this, the policy makers were able to come along to learning interventions to gauge views and ideas from PCTs about new and developing policy before it was 'in tablets of stone,' thus giving the policy makers a chance to test out ideas and assumptions. This two-way relationship also enabled the ECLN to be at the 'leading edge' of these policy areas. An example of how the task system worked, during the final year of the ECLN programme is outlined Figure 17.4.

The findings

During the ECLN programme, there were many challenges, including understanding of the complexity of the learning network itself within a disparate and fast-paced NHS operating context. The rapid expansion of the network from 12 PCT members to nearly 280+ (and then a database that grew to 2000+ or so in a short space of time) was challenging as the small initial network learning events rapidly expanded to sometimes having 100+ learning participants (all with individual 'in tray' tasks they wished to solve during the day!). Other challenges included: constant pressure from local and national politics (e.g. tokenism/rhetoric), exhaustion and frustration of rapid knowledge synthesis, and fairly large learning events. These were at times the enemy of innovation and creativity. In addition, there was pressure from some key players within and around the ECLN to play 'the numbers game' with targets as an objective in terms of membership number as opposed to looking at the quality of work being undertaken by the network; limited and finite resources were initially challenging, although in later years the network was able to work in collaboration with non-NHS agencies bringing more resource to the overall 'pot' as joint learning objectives were agreed; there were pressures to conform in other ways, e.g. use tables at events or lecture theatre style seating for large groups (e.g. over 80) when it was found that, for instance, the dialogue runs better in horseshoe-shaped seating or small circles of chairs (cabaret without the tables!); there were overly elongated NHS annual procurement processes, stalling the ongoing work at the early part of each year; and there were pressures in keeping in touch as a small virtual team, logistically sometimes working miles apart. As this was an innovatory approach to learning, bearing in mind the challenges above, there was a need to have 'contingency' plans about the risks (for instance if there were database problems, or equipment failure – were there any back ups). The evaluation processes highlighted other challenges more latterly, such as avoiding getting drawn into the politics and too emotionally involved in things that ECLN could not control (e.g. NHS national and local delivery pressures); the need to find further ways of enabling Chief Executives and NHS leaders to really understand and endorse the value of learning and the network, thus legitimizing learning network participants to be involved in the ECLN regularly; and to start where people are, not where you think they are often requiring a 'straw poll' at the beginning of any learning event to ensure the event 'hit the spot.' All of these challenges were overcome, and learning about the experiences of overcoming these by the ECLN facilitators helped to add to the sophistication of the programme.

The things that were given highly positive levels of feedback from the ECLN members (either in the external evaluation, via direct feedback, or our own internal evaluation) were:

- A human welcome from the hub and an e-newsletter;
- Deliberate alignment of network activities with key service priorities in the NHS;
- Trust between those in the network and the hub/core team. ('Trust is the glue') meant lasting and meaningful relationships developed;
- 'Loose and tight' involvement with the network for participants with no expectations about how actively or passively involved people 'should' be, which was in contrast to the plethora of 'must-dos' and has nurtured goodwill and genuine enthusiasm and enjoyment when network members have engaged;
- Role-modelling participation and involvement in the approach to co-designing and organizing events. By facilitating people in the network to work together to do this has led to courage and a sense of empowerment. The outcomes have been impressive and within the pressurized context of PCTs, and this was testament to this approach;
- Consideration of language (e.g. plain English) for different audiences. Not easy and time consuming, but essential as busy NHS managers and practitioners sometimes did not have time to decipher, for instance, complex philosophical papers;
- Risk, and building it into events, making it okay during events by

contracting jointly with participants, at the outset of each intervention. Careful listening and attention to the dynamics in the room was key to this at all times;

- Discussing the undiscussable and taking the lid off taboo topics, allowing diverse perspectives to flow and not forcing a sense of consensus where one did not exist;
- Storytelling has captured imaginations and made it easier to make sense of complexity;
- Simple closure mechanisms, e.g. solving and sharing Needs and Offers for personal 'in-trays' and enabling, buddying up amongst network members, to ensure everyone could answer 'so what?' when they left an event.

One of the things that the lead facilitators also observed was that, about midway through the three-year ECLN project, many practitioners in the NHS, for example in local facilitation of patient and public involvement, had spent a lot of time implementing the 'breadth' of initiatives or tasks (quantity) and less time (if any) on deepening their implementation of their local change management projects (e.g. to tackle deep-seated cultural issues around developing participatory cultures, rather than to continue to add lots of new processes and communication channels to already growing lists of engaging and involving processes). Thus, one learning task was to enable opportunities for practitioners to tackle breadth *and depth* of the tasks they were facing.

The ECLN 'End Results' as taken from the evaluations (Williams and Burgoyne 2004; Hardacre 2005) included:

- Genuine local culture change – practical real examples, plus transferability of ideas;
- Developed 'box of tricks, and tactics' – locally used and practically benchmarked amongst ECLN network members virtually through the internet, or face-to-face;
- Policy/legislation had been influenced in the making and by network members in dialogue with policy makers;
- Involvement is now a priority for PCTs and understanding the nature of participatory cultures has grown more sophisticated;
- Learning networks have truly been created amongst PCTs and individuals (locally and nationally);
- A knowledge that this model (learning network) is a tried and tested model enabling wide scale/national change and development.

Interpretations, conclusions, critical analysis

It is possible to have an integrated approach to large-scale HRD in the NHS by weaving a number of well-known learning methods and theories – a robust model was developed and viewed as a successful learning intervention (Williams and Burgoyne 2004).

Factors contributing to success of the project included having experienced facilitators (in learning processes as well as content/substance, in addition to understanding the nuances of the NHS); the development of administrative systems and databases and effective personal communications; and acknowledging that information-giving does not by itself promote behaviour change. There was the need to create a sense of 'belonging' and an engagement because of the practical-outcomes focus of the learning network. Ongoing formative evaluation was also a factor in providing evidenced feedback to the team and contributing to the project's success. Feedback has consistently been that the specially-tailored database is well designed and user friendly, and it had the potential for more extensive use across other parts of the NHS.

From the work over the three years of the ECLN, a 'generic' Organizational Development Checklist for large-scale HRD programmes, such as a national learning network, was developed. Each component requires careful and ongoing consideration when designing and implementing a large-scale HRD programme such as this.

Checklist for large-scale HRD programmes

- Ensuring an organizational development or learning reference point/framework/evidence base for example, references from other similar work, or theories to help underpin the following:
- Co-developing shared purpose and goals and aims;
- Having clear operating principles/values;
- Having an understanding, and analysis of relationship and social capital strategies, structures, networks, boundaries, interfaces, interdependencies, stakeholders, power, politics, commitment plans;
- A change plan itself – and framework/project or programme plans and management – critical pathways, flow charts and good programme management techniques;
- Consideration of involvement, co-design, co-creation from the start and how the intervention is fully participatory during the design and implementation stages by those facilitating *and* those participating as learners;
- Being clear about the must dos/givens/quick wins (not fixes) in the context;
- Resource planning (e.g. knowing how long any task or intervention takes to develop, how much each will cost);
- A development plan to support (e.g. management and personal development for all the core team where necessary – in the ECLN all of the facilitators were learning all of the time – this included peer learning and critical friendships);
- Having clear governance, risk, contingency, stewardship plans;

- Ensuring clear monitoring, review, adding value mechanisms, and evaluation processes;
- Ensuring open reflection, sharing, recognition and dissemination of everything that is undertaken (in bite-sized chunks so as not to over-whelm people!).

Key learning points with some points for key stakeholders of the ECLN

At the end of the Engaging Communities Learning Network programme the following questions were still being deliberated upon.

- *Governance.* In a large-scale learning network (HRD programme) how can you sustain the productive syntheses between central support and facilitation, and increasing ownership and participation by network members and associates locally?
- *'Knowledging'.* How can you, in any learning network, both sustain the active sharing of learning and support, and the energy and relationships on which the learning network is based, whilst also contributing to the wider NHS reform/policy agenda – which is changing all the time?
- *Infrastructure.* Will organizations like the British NHS in the future invest in the powerful synthesis of 'customer care'/relationship communications and database management skills needed to ensure that the net-working works?
- *Levels of engagement and sustainability.* How can you ensure that learning networks or other large-scale HRD programmes can become self-sustaining when the original, start-up project/programme is wound up?

Key messages for various stakeholders to bear in mind if wishing to replicate work such as the ECLN are as follows:

HRD specialists (training managers), practitioners

- More sophisticated large scale HRD programmes are required to build capacity and change and to enable sustainability;
- There are many regularly utilized learning methods and approaches that when combined create more impact;
- Ample time for 'back-stage' working to synthesize and weave the complex relationships between learning methods can create a powerful combined approach of a range of learning methods;
- Learning in fast-paced working contexts benefits when directly related to the achievement of in-tray tasks;
- Underlying values are the 'glue' to large-scale complex learning approaches;
- Action research and action learning (including ongoing evaluation)

provide the opportunity for any HRD programme to evolve towards a higher level of sophistication and impact;
- Building on the 'resource' of the learners (e.g. their experience and stories) is crucial to building confidence, and 'networkability' amongst learners;
- Lead facilitators need to broker, buffer and weave within the operating context, the policy context, and the social and learning context;
- Technological, social and task systems underpin large-scale HRD programmes such as learning networks.

Educationalists

- The role of HRD professionals is complex, and requires detailed knowledge of the design of learning interventions, and the ability to facilitate the development itself;
- Critical appraisal, and knowledge and theory synthesis skills will enable HRD professionals to increase their intellectual abilities – and the ability to deal with complexity in learning;
- Self-awareness, and reflective practice, as well as the ability to work as critical friends with co-facilitators enables a dynamic and developmental approach to HRD;
- Understanding the dynamics within any live learning intervention – and of the learning intervention 'infrastructure' – helps when working in a political minefield, and with learners who won't always be comfortable to 'bare all' or 'take the lid off the box.'

Researchers

- Further work to understand sustainability and mainstreaming large-scale HRD programmes is required. Particularly if learning is 'counter-cultural' to the prevailing operating context of delivery against large numbers of task targets.

Policy makers and budget holders

- Learning does increase the speed of implementing complex change initiatives;
- Legitimizing 'time out' for learning enables a better learning process once participants are at any event or forum;
- Complex large-scale national HRD programmes do not cost a huge amount and can reach large numbers of participants regularly, both face to face and virtually via e-based mechanisms;
- Investing in some resource to evaluate all large-scale HRD programmes enables a more robust outcome;
- Public Sector procurement processes are necessary but need streamlining

so that the timescales, particularly mid-way in the delivery of programmes, are not prolonged;
- National Learning institutions, and national policy initiatives need
  interrelationships between the substance (e.g. of the policies) and the
  social processes (of the institutions);
- Some form of ongoing 'archive' of learning for public sector organizations is required to stop the loss of organizational memory and create
  stability around learning and innovation.

A NatPaCT paper written in early 2005 (Callaghan 2005) demonstrates the
potential contribution of consolidating NatPaCT's networking capability
into a performance improvement framework. These are key requirements
that resonate with the findings in the research by George Tsekouras and
John Bessant (Centrim)

- Networks are grounded in active problem-solving related to current
  priorities: central and local;
- Relationships matter ('Trust in the glue') and there is no substitute for
  participation at a number of levels: from large events, to 'buddying' and
  coaching;
- Provision of a 'hub' – administration, coordination, communications,
  events management and 'customer care' – is central to any networking
  capability;
- An accessible interactive website, with confidential domains, adds considerable value: especially when it enables feedback, shared learning,
  and evidence for improvement.

Clearly, collaborative learning network HRD programmes have a key part to
play at the interface between policy implementation and performance management in the British NHS, particularly at a time when recent policy
developments had required PCTs to lead a fundamental shift in the nature of
NHS business and in the ways in which the NHS conducted its business. In
addition, the ECLN's 'hub' model is transferable to other settings.

Acknowledgement

With thanks to the ECLN team, Jane Keep, Bob Sang (Lead Facilitators);
Chris Dabbs, Bec Hanley and Jeanne Hardacre, (Associate Facilitators);
Kathie Andrews (Programme Manager) Janine Zdziebczok (Administrator),
David Common, (Associate Director, NatPaCT), Tom Hain (Manager, of
the ECLN's hub 'Host' organization – Centre for Health Information
Quality (CHIQ)), Claire-Louise Noonan (Database and IS/IT system devel-
oper and support), Andy Cowper, Freelance Journalist, Sadie Williams and
John Burgoyne, Henley Management College, Andrew Donald, Alison
Straughan + NatPaCT colleagues, the many associates from a variety of

policy, facilitation and expert backgrounds, and most of all a huge thanks and recognition for the PCT and SHA colleagues who supported the work, allowed us to try and test methods and processes live, joined in with the dialogue, and contributed not only to the development of policy and practice, but to the ongoing development of action learning, and learning networks.

References

Bate, P., Roberts, G. and Bevan, H. (2004) 'The next phase of Healthcare Improvement: what can we learn from social movements?' *Quality and Safety in Healthcare* 13(1): 62–66.

Blumenthal, D. and Kilo, C. (1998) 'A report card on continuous quality improvement,' *Milbank Quarterly* 76(4): 625–648.

Bolton, G. (2001) *Reflective Practice: Writing and Professional Development*, Paul Chapman Publishing, pp. 2–4.

Burchill, F. and Casey, A. (1996) *Human Resource Management*, Mcmillan Business, p. 124.

Callaghan, J. (2005) 'Networking the networks,' paper for NatPaCT.

Collinson, C. and Parcell, G. (2001) *Learning to Fly: Practical Lessons from one of the World's Leading Knowledge Companies*, Capstone Publishing.

Department of Health (2001) *Working Together, Learning Together. The Framework for Lifelong Learning for the NHS*, Department of Health.

Department of Health (2002) 'HR in the NHS plan: more staff working differently,' 01/07.

Department of Health (2003) 'Strengthening Accountability and Health and Social Care Act 2001. Sections 7 and 11.'

Department of Health (2004) 'The NHS knowledge and skills framework (NHS KSF) and the development review process,' (October).

Fillingham, D. (2004) 'The future development of NHS modernisation,' Presentation to Modernisation Leaders Conference, 1 April, London (in Maher, L. and Penny, J. 'Service improvement,' Chapter 5, in *Organisational Development in Healthcare, Approaches, Innovations, Achievements* Radcliff Publishing).

French, W.L. and Bell, C.H. Jr (1990) *Organization Development: Behavioural Science Interventions for Organization Improvement*, 4th edn, Prentice Hall International Editions, p. 152.

French, W.L., Bell, C.H. Jr and Zawacki, R.A. (2005) *Organization Development and Transformation: Managing Effective Change*, 6th edn, McGraw-Hill Irwin.

Hammer, M. and Champey, J. (1995) *Re-engineering the Corporation: a Manifesto for a Business Revolution*, London: Nicholas Brealey.

Hardacre, J. (2005) 'Evaluation report for ECLN,' NatPaCT March.

Jackson, M. (2003) *Systems Thinking: Creative Holism for Managers*, London: Wiley.

Keep, J. (2005) 'Systems theories and their applications,' in E. Peck (ed.) *Organizational Development in Healthcare*, Radcliff Publishing, p. 135.

Kolb, D. (1984) *Experiential Learning*, Englewood Cliffs, NJ: Prentice Hall.

Lewin, K. (1946) 'Action research and minority problems,' *Journal of Social Issues* 2: 34–46.

Maher, L. and Penny, J. (2005) 'Service improvement,' in E. Peck (ed.)

Organizational Development in Healthcare: Approaches, Innovations, Achievements, Radcliffe Publishing, p. 97.

Mcleod, H. (2005) 'A review of evidence on OD in healthcare,' in E. Peck (ed.) *Organizational Development in Healthcare: Approaches, Innovations, Achievements*, Radcliffe Publishing. pp. 252, 260–266.

McGill, I. and Beaty, L. (1993) *Action Learning: a Practitioners Guide*, Kogan Page.

National Primary and Care Trust Development Programme, NatPaCT OD programme www.natpact.nhs.uk.

NHS Executive, NHS Beacon Services (2000) HSC Health Service Circular, Feb. 1999 034.

Ovretveit, J. (2000) 'Total quality management in European healthcare,' *International Journal of Healthcare Quality Assurance* 13(2): 74–79.

Pedlar, M., Burgoyne, J. and Boydell, T. (1991) *The Learning Company*, Maidenhead: McGraw Hill.

Schein, E. (1969) *Process Consultation: it's Role in Organisational Development*, Reading, Mass: Addison-Wesley, p. 135.

Tsekouras, G. and Bessant, J. (ongoing) The Inter-Organisational Networking (ION) Research Project CENTRIM, Brighton.

Weinstein, K. (1999) *Action Learning: a Practical Guide* 2nd edn, Gower Publishing, p. 3.

Williams, S. and Burgoyne, J. (2004) 'Report on the external evaluation of the ECLN,' Henley Management College.

Wilson, D. and Rosenfeld, R. (1990) *Managing Organizations: Texts, Readings and Cases*, London: McGraw Hill, p. 315.

Contact websites for the Engaging Communities Learning network.

www.networks.nhs.uk/

or Jk1@janekeep.co.uk for further details.

Part V

Conclusions and challenges

18 HRD in health and social care

The emerging challenges

Jim Stewart and Sally Sambrook

Introduction

The chapters in this book will have suggested that the health and social care sectors are facing major challenges arising in part from connected and linked economic and technological developments within the wider environment. This in itself creates challenges for HRD theory and practice but that practice is itself affected by similar developments; e.g. use of information and communication technology may create new and innovative approaches to design and delivery of HRD interventions but these inevitably alter the economics of HRD practice and usually require significant front end investment. Therefore, HRD in these sectors faces the general challenges of practice experienced more widely in the profession and also the specific and particular challenges facing all those responsible for managing in health and social care organizations. One of these specific particularities is the simple one of size and scope. The history of the British NHS is one of responding to the impossible task of managing or limiting the demand for health and social care. We feel almost as overwhelmed by the size of our task in this final chapter as those responsible for the British NHS must sometimes feel when contemplating the size of their task. The preceding chapters have examined HRD practice in a multitude of different national contexts, different organizational contexts and have focused on a great variety of HRD practices and methods as well as adopting various and varying perspectives in their individual studies. Our purpose in this final chapter is to attempt to make some overarching sense of this polymath of contributions in order to facilitate an increased value from the book. We do this though with the caveat of our attempt being just one possibility within what is probably an infinite number of potential interpretations of key themes and issues arising from the chapters. It seems to us though, that the main themes which provide the organizing principles of the book's sections, with a few additions, are as useful a device as any to identify the main messages of the book. The additions include that of internationalization since it appears safe to say, based on the chapters in this book, that there is much in common across the world and that those commonalities are as significant as the equally clear and significant national differences. Therefore, we attempt in this chapter to identify emerging challenges for HRD in the health and social care sectors by examining the following major themes.

- HRD as discourse;
- Management development;
- HRD as workplace learning;
- Evaluating HRD practice and interventions;
- International factors.

HRD as discourse

A generally accepted and established view of HRD is that it is a straight-forward technical activity that supports the achievement of organizational objectives through developing the knowledge, skills and competence of employees. This is perhaps a simple caricature of the 'performance' view of HRD and also perhaps is one that associates HRD most closely with train-ing and development. Much recent work though has demonstrated that HRD goes beyond training and development and is bound up with a range of additional and alternative concepts, such as organizational learning, knowledge management, politics, power and ethics (see for example the col-lection edited by Woodall *et al.* 2004). This shift in focus is associated in part with the growing interest in critical perspectives applied to organi-zation and management studies more widely. A major focus in critical man-agement studies is questioning the purpose of work organizations and their contribution to improving the human condition, and similar questions are necessarily and perhaps rightly directed at HRD as an area of academic enquiry and organizational practice. One influential theoretical construct that is helpful in posing and attempting to answer such questions is that of discourse analysis. This construct does not necessarily lead to a sterile decon-struction of language and its use in social practices, although we acknow-ledge that can indeed be the case. It can, in contrast, lead to much richer understanding of the social and material interests of those involved in HRD practice and, in so doing, raise relevant questions of purpose, costs and bene-fits and ethical decision making (Stewart, in press).

Critical approaches and the use of discourse analysis are becoming an established perspective in HRD research and theorizing (Stewart *et al.* 2004; Elliott and Turnbull 2005; Rigg *et al.* in press). A number of chapters in this book demonstrate the value of this perspective to not only theorizing HRD but also its value to informing practice. The chapters by Sally Sam-brook and by Nadine Bristow in particular show most clearly that this is the case but other chapters such as those by Rona Beattie and by Anne Squire utilize an arguably related approach of ethnography to achieve comparable purposes. It seems to us that the health and social care sectors are particu-larly appropriate for such studies because of the human-centred nature of both the work and services provided and of the professions involved in that work. The challenge is to ensure utility and value as well as validity in adopting this perspective so that practical as well as theory-related outcomes are achieved. That may be a false distinction, and probably is, but it is one that is commonly applied. The chapter by Bob Hamlin and David Cooper in this volume, while not in the critical perspective, argues the case for evidence-based practice in HRD as well as clinical practice and we endorse that argument. We agree therefore that HRD practitioners, whether working in organizational or policy contexts need to ensure their practice is informed by sound research and evidence. Given the complexity of the sector though, we also believe that studies adopting critical perspectives, which also pay attention to specific contexts, will be of most utility and value in informing practice. The challenge is to achieve that praxis of theory and practice.

Management development

Given the complexity of the sectors and the current challenges being faced by organizations operating in them, it is probably axiomatic that the role of managers at all levels is crucial in ensuring appropriate and effective responses. That might be said about any and all managers but there is, we believe, something particular about the sectors examined in this book. The case for this is present throughout the book but is particularly evident in the chapters by Clair Roberts and Sally Sambrook and by Ken Bartlett. Neither of these chapters addresses management development directly but they do usefully deal with the complexity in which management practices occur and, in Bartlett in particular, the international and cross-national nature of that complexity. The message is reinforced by those chapters that do directly address management development (MD). However, an examination of the content and relevance of management development to the sectors is not limited to those chapters in that section of the book. Action learning, for example, is a well-established method in management development and so too is application of the concept of competence. Both of these provide a focus for chapters in other parts of the book and the content there will have application in the context of MD. In addition, the role of informal and work-based learning is a well-established focus for and site of research and writing on MD and is seen by some to be more critical than formal and planned programmes (Mumford and Gold 2004). The chapters in the book on that topic therefore are also transferable to a consideration of MD.

It seems to us that a number of assertions are at least tenable from the evidence and arguments presented in this book. First, that the management capability of organizations in the sectors is more critical now than perhaps it was in the past. It certainly seems to be the case that the role, purpose and outcomes of managerial processes receive greater attention compared to the professions than used to be the case. Second, that the historical and established importance attached to professional education and development is now also being recognized as equally significant for non-clinical staff and, especially, that of managers. As this becomes more widespread so too does the level of resources, both in absolute and proportional measures, allocated to MD increase. Third, there is a variety of approaches and methods available to apply in conducting MD. Examples of these are not limited to those considered in Part II but are also apparent in many of the other chapters. Fourth, there is much more to be known and understood about the processes of both managing and learning to manage in the sectors. The chapter by Bob Hamlin and David Cooper shows very clearly that the question of management processes and associated skills is still open in all sectors. That work provides support for the view that managerial effectiveness is less context specific than is argued by others but even so it is yet to be established in any definitive sense and in any case the work of Hamlin and Cooper itself suggests that a component of some size will always be dependent on context specific factors. Some of these are likely to be related to a particular and given organization but some will be connected to the sector and others to various and varying characteristics of the individuals concerned. In any case, there is a need to expand the research base of management competencies and skills and, in particular, processes of learning to manage. The chapter by Nadine Bristow is an example of the kind of research that is needed.

Finally, there is a connection with the previous major theme. Previous work has shown that managerial discourse is immanent in understandings of organization culture (Rigg and Trehan 2004). It seems to us that the power and role of discourse in organizations will be an important component of the content and process of MD. This is particularly important in the sectors examined here since it is clear that the competing intra and inter discourses of the professions and managers is of great significance in building coherent organization cultures. The challenge though is clear and that is to incorporate MD into the professional development culture of the sectors in ways which reflect the particular and specific context and challenges of health and social care organizations.

HRD as workplace learning

The role and contribution of HRD, and the aspirations of HRD practitioners, have evolved in recent years from provider of planned and formal development opportunities to a greater focus on supporting and facilitating learning at individual, team and organizational levels (Tjepkema *et al.* 2002). Research commissioned by the Chartered Institute of Personnel and Development in the UK indicates that there has been a noticeable shift in focus from 'training' to 'learning' for HRD professionals and that this is associated, as also argued by Tjepkema *et al.*, with a closer connection of HRD with organization strategy. This is one reason for greater attention being placed on what is referred to as workplace – or work related – learning. This term can have a variety of meanings, as will be evident from the

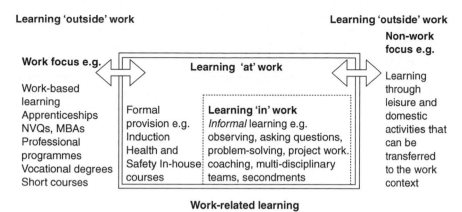

Figure 18.1 Defining work-related learning – learning at and in work (Sambrook 2005).

chapters in that section of the book. While not claiming the last word, a framework developed by Sambrook (2005) is useful for making sense of the variety of views and debates on this subject. The framework is provided in Figure 18.1.

The terms of the debate are set out in the chapters in Part III of the book. An examination of those chapters reveals different conceptions of what the term can mean; e.g. the on-the-job training examined by Rob Poell *et al.* The chapter by Alice Salzman and Kathy Hall suggests a connection too with continuing professional development. Comparing and contrasting these various conceptualizations through the framework in Figure 18.1 provides some validation of the framework and demonstrates its utility. What is also interesting is the variety of contexts within the sectors where workplace learning is becoming recognized as an influential and significant approach to HRD. This is apparent both in terms of organization and service provided as well as the particular professionals involved.

In some ways the chapters in this book might suggest that the sectors are leading the way in workplace learning. An alternative view could be that this is because of, or at least related to, under-investment in more resource-intensive approaches, such as formalized and planned interventions. However, the framework offered here and the chapters for example by Rob Poell and his colleagues suggest that this is a false dichotomy. Workplace learning can be both formal and planned and may in fact be both more efficient and more effective for being so. That said, it nevertheless seems to be the case that workplace learning can be more accidental and opportunistic than alternatives. It can also be more relevant and acceptable to many employees. What is clear in our view is that the workplace and indeed work itself is a legitimate and important site for learning and so for employee and professional development. That has certainly been established in relation to managers and management development. From that premise it seems logical to say that the workplace is therefore a legitimate and important site for HRD practice and that associated methods, both formal and informal, need to be deployed by HRD professionals. The research reported in the chapters in Part III is of value to meeting that imperative since it sets out some of the factors influencing the success or otherwise of workplace learning. If it is accepted that in the generality HRD practice is potentially less resource intensive and more relevant when focused on such learning then, given the challenges facing the sectors, that practice is likely to become more important in the future than in the past. The ability of HRD professionals to facilitate workplace learning will, in consequence, also be more important and a significant challenge.

Evaluating HRD

The problems of evaluating HRD are well established (Stewart 1999) and they are not particular to the sectors examined here. What seem to be particular to the sectors are some innovative and novel responses to the problems. The chapters in this section of the book describe a range of different approaches that appear to have value in assessing and establishing the case for HRD. This is very important, even in a time when resources allocated to and for development are perhaps greater than previously, but, given that the total resource remains under pressure, being able to demonstrate benefits is still of critical importance.

What is particularly striking about the chapters in this volume is first the range of levels that are examined and second the range of methods applied. The first of these does not refer to the well-known 'levels of evaluation' but rather the level of the intervention, which ranges from Jane Keep's whole system analysis to the specific and single training programme that provides the focus for the chapter by Nicholas Clarke. What we draw from this is a view that evaluation is both necessary and achievable at all levels of HRD practice, from national policy level to the smallest intervention. Evaluation effort at these varying levels does need to be linked in some way. The chapters by Anne Squire and by Kate Gilbert demonstrate the case for this. It is clearly important in developing societies and economies that are in the process of establishing new national frameworks that experience and lessons learned at local levels inform national policy and initiatives. However, in our view this is just as important in more well-established contexts such as the UK NHS. It is obviously neither possible nor desirable that every piece of HRD evaluation carried out connects with national frameworks. It is though possible and desirable that links exist and that mechanisms for sharing the results of evaluation are available and are used. The possibility at least is shown in Jane Keep's chapter.

Jane Keep's chapter also illustrates the novel approaches that are being developed in the sectors. So too do the other chapters in this section. The use of Action Learning as both a development and evaluative tool is, in our experience, innovative and is something with potential for much wider application. Nicholas Clarke's chapter shows the use of more traditional evaluation methods. However, a novel feature is the combination of methods, and the work reported there suggests some ways in which the well-established problems of evaluation can be coped with if not finally overcome. It is promising that clear assessments and judgements could be reached on the value or otherwise of the intervention. This point is significant and important because the health and social care sectors are staffed by many different professions and, as indicated above, they are also sectors where management development is critical. Development for professional and managerial roles are two examples where evaluation is commonly said to be most difficult, and that may be the case. However, the chapters here show that it is possible. Even so, evaluating and demonstrating the value of HRD will remain a constant challenge for both researchers and practitioners. One important response to this indicated by some of the chapters here is to shift attention and focus away from purely economic or financial criteria and measures of 'value.' That is perhaps the key challenge for evaluation. The chapters in the evaluation section of the book also illustrate our international focus, with Russia and Romania for example providing some of the research sites and focus. We will now move on to that final major theme.

International factors

The content and focus of this book is international in a number of ways. Our contributors include some who live and work in a number of countries outside the UK and some who live and work in the UK but who report the work they have done in other countries. The fact that we could produce such a collection suggests that provision of health and social care is of international concern in the sense that it is of high priority in many different countries. The fact that some UK academics are doing work in other countries reinforces this point. Our guess is that this is related to the common experience of health and social care being of growing political importance across the world. This in turn can probably, in part at least, be attributed to the general phenomenon known as globalization and the growth of what is termed the knowledge economy (see Stewart and Tansley 2002). These general processes are also subject to particular influences in health and social care, for example by the role of global pharmaceutical companies (Healy 2004). It seems too that attention and concern with HRD within the sectors is international in scope and focus and that this is true of many aspects of HRD with non-UK settings, if not with contributors in every section of the book. So, we can say with some confidence that HRD in the sectors is of international interest.

This general interest has much in common in different national contexts. HRD professionals in the health and social care sectors seem to be facing similar challenges. For example, according to the chapters in this book, workplace learning is being researched and developed in the USA and Holland as well as the UK, and Action Learning is being utilized for both management development and evaluation in a number of different countries. The use of Action Learning in the sectors and in countries outside the UK is of course not new, as it has a long history of application within healthcare services (Revans 1976). What does seem to be new though is the transfer of established ideas to new national and organizational settings. There is much debate about the relevance and transferability of HRD practices to different cultural contexts, although not perhaps as much as there needs to be and not as much as in relation to HRM, for example. Nevertheless, what emerges from the work here is clear evidence that 'western' ideas and practices do have potential value in 'non-western' countries such as Russia and Malaysia. That said, a further lesson from this book is that the transfer of ideas needs careful consideration of the host culture, both national and organizational. We cannot assume or take for granted that what 'works' in the UK or USA, for example, will necessarily be appropriate in the same form in different cultural contexts.

A final observation on this theme is that it is encouraging that the chapters in this book, and indeed the Routledge HRD Series as a whole, suggest growing contact and cooperation within the academic and professional HRD communities across the world. This will help to address the relative weakness and current challenge in international and comparative research in HRD mentioned in the previous paragraph. It will also support mutual learning from academic research and professional experience. We hope and intend that the small community brought together by this project will develop and enhance new international networks as a contribution to the larger need to foster international cooperation in HRD in the health and social care sectors.

Concluding remarks

We have attempted to identify some significant themes that emerge from the book but we do reiterate that many others can be found and that our views on those included in this chapter are by no means definitive. We hope readers will make their own attempt at this, either alone or in conjunction with colleagues. Our main and final hope though is that the book informs both teaching and practice and that it becomes a stimulus for more attention being paid to the specific challenges and context of HRD in these very important sectors.

References

Elliott, C. and Turnbull, S. (eds) (2005) *Critical Thinking in Human Resource Development*, London: Routledge.

Healy, D. (2004) 'Psychopharmacology at the interface between the market and the new biology,' in D. Rees and S. Rose (eds) *The New Brain Sciences: Perils and Prospects*, Cambridge: Cambridge University Press, pp. 232–248.

Mumford, A. and Gold, J. (2004) *Management Development: Strategies for Action*, London: Chartered Institute of Personnel and Development.

Revans, R. (1976) *Action Learning in Hospitals: Diagnosis and Therapy*, Maidenhead: McGraw-Hill.

Rigg, C. and Trehan, K. (2004) 'Now you see it now you don't: comparing traditional and discourse readings of HRD in small organisations,' in J. Stewart and G. Beaver (eds) *HRD in Small Organisations: Research and Practice*, London: Routledge, pp. 48–73.

Rigg, C., Stewart, J. and Trehan, K. (eds) (in press) *Critical HRD; Beyond Orthodoxy*, London: Prentice Hall.

Sambrook, S. (2005) 'Factors influencing the context and process of work-related learning: synthesizing findings from two research projects,' *Human Resource Development International* 8(1): 101–119.

Stewart, J. (1999) *Employee Development Practice*, London: FT Prentice Hall.

Stewart, J. (in press) 'The ethics of HRD,' in C. Rigg, J. Stewart and K. Trehan (eds) *Critical HRD; Beyond Orthodoxy*, London: Prentice Hall.

Stewart, J. and Tansley, C. (2002) *Training in the Knowledge Economy*, London: Chartered Institute of Personnel and Development.

Stewart, J., Rigg, C. and Trehan, K. (2004) 'Special edition on critical HRD,' *Journal of European Industrial Training* 28(8–9).

Tjepkema, S., Stewart, J., Sambrook, S., Horst, H., Mulder, M. and Scheerens, J. (eds) (2002) *HRD and Learning Organisations in Europe*, London: Routledge.

Woodall, J., Lee, M. and Stewart, J. (eds) (2004) *New Frontiers in HRD*, London: Routledge.

Index

Page numbers in **bold** indicate tables or figures.